6

THE WORLD IS BURNING

Also by Alex Shoumatoff

Florida Ramble
The Rivers Amazon
Westchester: Portrait of a County
The Capital of Hope
Russian Blood
The Mountain of Names
In Southern Light
African Madness

THE WORLD IS BURNING

Alex Shoumatoff

Little, Brown and Company

Boston   Toronto   London

First Edition

Portions of this book originally appeared in *Vanity Fair*.

The author is grateful for permission to include excerpts from the following:

God and Man in the Green Hell by Clodovis Boff. Copyright © 1980, Editora Vozes Ltda (Frei Clodovis Boff).

"A Death in Brazil" by Tom Wicker (December 27, 1988) and "Brazil Burns the Future" by Tom Wicker (December 28, 1988). Copyright © 1988 by The New York Times Company.

Tropical Rain Forests and the World Atmosphere, edited by Ghillean T. Prance. Published by Westview Press, 1986, Boulder, CO.

"The Farmer and the Cowman" by Richard Rodgers and Oscar Hammerstein II. Copyright 1943 by Williamson Music Co. Copyright Renewed. All rights reserved.

Library of Congress Cataloging-in-Publication Data

Shoumatoff, Alex.
    The world is burning / Alex Shoumatoff.
        p. cm.
    Includes bibliographical references.
    ISBN 0-316-78739-6
    1. Mendes, Chico, d. 1988. 2. Conservationists — Brazil —
Biography. 3. Forest conservation — Brazil. 4. Forest
conservation — Amazon River Region. 5. Deforestation — Brazil.
6. Deforestation — Amazon River Region. 7. Rain forests — Brazil.
8. Rain forests — Amazon River Region. I. Title.
SD411.52.M46S34   1990
333.7′2′092 — dc20
[B]   90-37151

10 9 8 7 6 5 4 3 2 1
MV PA

Published simultaneously in Canada
by Little, Brown & Company (Canada) Limited

Printed in the United States of America

Para o povo brasileiro, for the Brazilian people,
who are among the sweetest and most generous on earth:
May you *chegar lá,* take your place among the great nations,
but remember your wise saying —
"O apressado come cru,"
He who is in a hurry eats raw.

Alas, poor country!
Almost afraid to know itself. It cannot
Be called our mother, but our grave; where nothing,
But who knows nothing, is once seen to smile;
Where sights and groans and shrieks that rend the air
Are made, not marked; where violent sorrow seems
A modern ecstasy; the dead man's knell
Is there scarce asked for who; and good men's lives
Expire before the flowers in their caps,
Dying or ere they sicken.
— *Macbeth,* act 4, scene 3

Do you think we will ever do anything
but confirm the incompetence of Catholic America,
which will always need ridiculous tyrants . . .
While men exercise their rotten powers,
Indians and padres and animals,
negroes and women, and adolescents
make Carnaval.
— Caetano Veloso, "*Podres poderes*"
("Rotten Powers"; translation by the author)

Contents

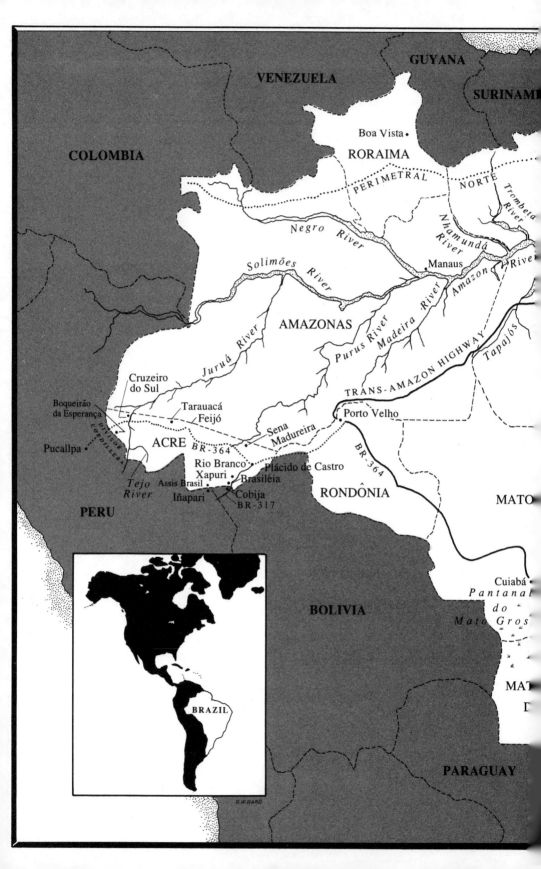

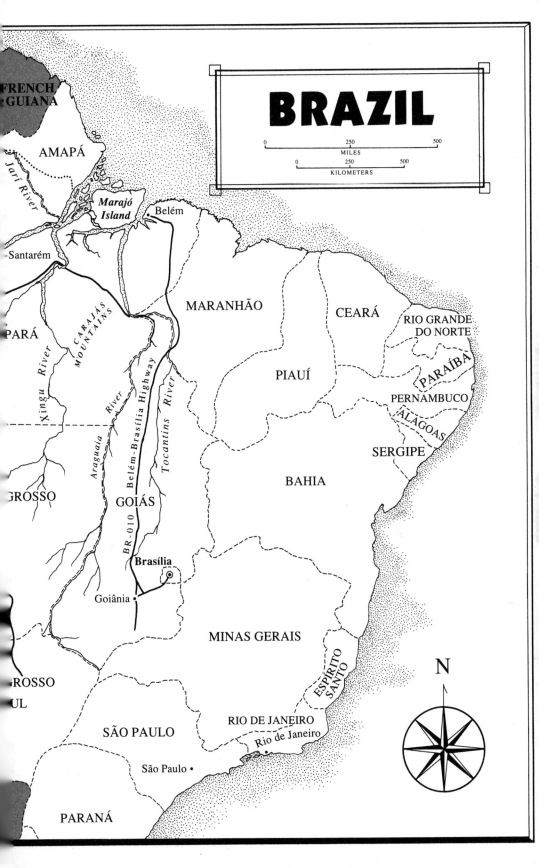

Caveat Emptor

In many ways this is a book of opinion, because the "facts" of this story, which I have diligently and impartially endeavored to set forth, sometimes don't add up. Part of the problem is the general difficulty of obtaining reliable information in the Amazon, which has plagued researchers for centuries and which is discussed in the section "The Amazon Numbers Problem" (it is also a leitmotif of my earlier book *In Southern Light*). Part of it arises from the passionate and conflicting responses that Chico Mendes's work and his murder elicited: depending on whom one talked to, and on that person's class and kinship loyalties, he was either Christ or the Anti-Christ. Most of my sources, including the Brazilian newspapers — which were sometimes the source for important parts of the story — were polarized between these two political positions, and I therefore had to weigh their information very carefully. Wherever possible, I collected as many versions of a given incident from interviews and other sources as I could, and in the end I often had to make a judgment call in deciding which version seemed closest to what happened. Distortion through translation was not a factor, since in the fourteen years I've been writing about Brazil I've become reasonably fluent in the language, but my evaluations of the veracity and the motives of my informants are another matter. In some cases I had to rely on my journalistic instincts. As with everything in history, no one will ever know exactly what happened. But then again, to what extent can you believe in anything? Especially in a place like Brazil, where the general outlook on the passing scene is so fluid, where so many things — cultural attitudes, even the continuously changing currency — conspire against the vision of a stable, fixed reality. It's different down there.

PART ONE

Murder in the Rain Forest

THE ANÚNCIO

In Brazil, when someone calls you up and tells you that you are going to die, it is not so much a threat as a statement of fact. You have been, in the Portuguese term, *anunciado*. This means that you can run to the ends of the earth, you can vanish into Rio de Janeiro or São Paulo, you can surround yourself with all the protection money can buy, but it won't do any good, because you are dead. The *anúncio,* a Brazilian friend explained to me, is a form of torture. You increase the pleasure of killing your victim by first destroying him psychologically.

And so on the night of May 24, 1988, when Chico Mendes was *anunciado* in Xapuri, a small town in the Brazilian Amazon about twenty miles from the Bolivian border, he knew his number was up. Mendes was the leader of a grass-roots movement that had arisen among the several hundred thousand people who make their living by tapping the rubber trees scattered in the rain forest, and he was emerging as a major player in the international struggle to save the Amazon. He had already survived five attempts on his life. The last would-be assassin had slipped on a loose board while climbing up to the roof of the little hall of the Xapuri chapter of the Rural Workers' Union, where Chico was presiding over a meeting.

Chico's life had been in danger since 1980, when the previous leader of the rubber tappers, Wilson Pinheiro, was gunned down on the porch of the union hall in Brasiléia, the next town to the west. The tappers had executed a local rancher, Nilão de Oliveira, in retaliation, believing him to have been one of the *mandantes,* the masterminds of the assassination. Knowing that Nilão's friends would be looking for him, Chico had gone into hiding for ninety days, sleeping each night in the house of a different *companheiro.*

There are no more than 130 ranchers in the state of Acre, a wedge the size of Iowa that straddles the frontier with Bolivia and Peru, yet in the last two decades they have expelled tens of thousands, probably well over a hundred thousand, tappers from the forest with their *pistoleiros,* or hired gunmen. Chico knew that his enemies included not only them, but also the authorities in Acre themselves. He knew that Mauro Sposito, the state superintendent of the Federal Police, had it in for him, having denounced him variously as a police informant and Communist agitator. He also knew that eighty-eight union leaders had been killed in Brazil the year before, and that since 1980 land conflicts had resulted in more than a thousand murders, but in only two cases — the murders of priests — had there been any convictions. He knew that the police in Xapuri were all bought or afraid and that there hadn't been a jury trial in the town in twenty-three years. Dozens of murder cases were sitting in the judge's desk drawer because no one dared prosecute them.

When Chico received the anonymous call informing him that he would not live out the year, it could not have been a surprise. The *anúncio* could only have come from two local ranchers, Darli Alves and his brother Alvarino. One evening the previous March, Chico and six *companheiros* had been walking home from a union meeting when they saw the brothers coming down the street, Alvarino looking like a Wild West bad man with his cowboy hat and his *bandido* mustache — a look he apparently cultivated. The Alves boys were the terrors of the region, semiliterate frontier types with violent pasts, wanted for a string of murders in southern Brazil. They were said to have killed maybe a dozen of the peons working for them and wiped out a whole family of tappers in the process of consolidating their six-thousand-acre spread. They are now under investigation for having been part of a syndicate that smuggled drugs and arms from Bolivia, killed for hire, and overlapped to some degree with the secret death squad in the Acre Department of Public Safety. No one stood up to them, because they were always armed and looking for trouble. When Darli and Alvarino got within firing range they started to take their guns out; Chico's friends surrounded him, forming a protective wall. The brothers passed, laughing.

Several weeks later, while Chico was home asleep with his wife, Ilzamar, and their two children, a voice called, "Help, Chico, help!" from the darkness outside the house. Ilza peered through a crack in the wall and saw a strange man waiting at the door with one hand behind his back.

Darli had recently acquired, probably to provoke a confrontation, dubious title to part of the Seringal Cachoeira, a rubber estate a day's walk from Xapuri where Chico had grown up, and where his people had tapped for generations and still lived. In April, Darli went there to start clearing the forest with a chain-saw crew protected by a squad of off-duty Military Police and was met by a human blockade of rubber tappers and their families, organized by Chico. Not only did Chico succeed in preventing Darli from clearing his land, the state expropriated the land to establish an "extractive reserve" — a new type of park Chico had invented that would save the forest and allow the tappers to keep living there.

This was too much for Darli. From then on, he went around telling people openly that he was going to kill Chico.

Several weeks after Chico was *anunciado,* friends appealed to the governor of Acre to provide him with protection, and the governor authorized two Military Policemen to be with him at all times. But the policemen were young, and their guns were old.

On June 18 Ivair Igino, a promising young member of the tappers' movement who was running for the Xapuri town council on the Workers' Party ticket, was gunned down as he was returning to his house with milk for his children, in a sort of death rehearsal. The shots — twelve shotgun blasts — came from the trees across the street.

So Chico knew it was only a matter of months before *pistoleiros* got him, too. He saw them in his rearview mirror tailing him in Rio Branco, the state capital. He was informed about a meeting of the ranchers in Brasiléia that was called to plan his death, and he provided the police with a list of who was there. He desperately telexed the state superintendent of the Federal Police, the state secretary of Public Safety, the president of the state Tribunal of Justice, the editor of the local newspaper the *Gazeta,* the governor, the federal superintendent of the Federal Police, the minister of justice, and even the president of the republic, telling them he was going to be killed and by whom and begging them to do something, but none of the telexes was answered. Chico had no interest in dying or becoming a martyr. "Public gestures and a well-attended funeral will not save Amazônia," he said in one of his last interviews. "I want to live."

On the evening of December 22, 1988, he was killed by a shotgun blast to the chest as he stepped out into his backyard, headed for the shower.

THE RESONANCES OF THE MURDER

One of the most striking things about the tragedy of Chico's death is its inevitability. Everyone knew that Chico, like the hero of a Greek drama, was going to die. "He was like a steer that had strayed from the herd," one of his friends recalled afterward. "We all knew it would happen around Christmastime. We begged him to stay in Rio or São Paulo through New Year's, but Chico insisted he wanted to spend the holidays in Xapuri with his family, so we felt there was nothing more that we could do. We thought, If it has to be done, then let it be done. We let it happen."

The ranchers even made a kind of oblique *anúncio* in their newspaper, *O Rio Branco*. There was an announcement in its December 5 edition that a "two-hundred-megaton bomb" was soon going to explode in Acre "with national and international repercussions."

But nobody was prepared for the tremendous international outcry over the murder. The crime focused a growing anxiety in the United States and Europe about the fires in the Amazon and the effect all the carbon dioxide they were spewing into the atmosphere might be having on the world's climate. That year a murderously hot summer had parched an area from New Mexico to Pennsylvania and from Idaho to South Carolina. Forty percent of the counties in the United States were declared drought areas. Forest fires collectively the size of Connecticut raged in the American West. Yellowstone National Park went up in smoke. Worldwide, 1988 turned out to be the warmest year on record.

The climate was clearly out of whack, and it was obvious that, as ecologists had been warning for decades, we were poisoning the planet, that ignorance, greed, and overpopulation, aided by modern technology, were beginning to cause the breakdown of major systems. Suddenly a term, "the greenhouse effect," coined in the thirties to describe the buildup of atmospheric carbon dioxide that traps solar energy and heats up the earth's surface, was on everyone's lips.

More than half of the excess carbon dioxide in the atmosphere comes from the burning of fossil fuel by internal-combustion engines, especially those in cars; the rest is from the incineration of "modern biomass" — living plant and animal matter — especially tropical rain forests. The fires in the Amazon account for something like 17 percent of the total.

The single greatest contributor of carbon dioxide to the atmosphere is in fact the United States, but in the curious way such things happen, everyone became very concerned about the rain forest. And Chico Mendes, whose struggle few outside of Acre and the small world of rain forest conservationists had ever heard of, became a symbol of the cause. He put a "human face on the issue," as Thomas Lovejoy, an American conservationist who has been struggling to save the Amazon since the early seventies, put it. "The murder sort of lanced the boil."

But it wasn't just the climate linkage, the connection between the burning of the Amazon and global warming, that accounted for the incredible indignation over the murder that arose spontaneously in country after country. It wasn't just the media bandwagon effect, in which every station and magazine and newspaper has to cover a subject once it is established as important news. It wasn't just that we were projecting our own anguish, our panicky realization that summer that we'd finally gone and done it, wrecked the environment for good. It wasn't just that the rain forest had become an ecovogue.

There was something about the image of this gentle, heroic man being killed in cold blood because he was trying to save the forest that was particularly saddening and outrageous. It wasn't, moreover, just any forest. It was the Amazon forest, the largest, most biologically diverse, and most mysterious wilderness on earth; a place with a special mystique even for those who have never been there, as the source, the mother of us all, the holiest natural sanctuary on the planet. And this sanctuary had been violated; the man who had been guarding it had been cynically assassinated. The murder of Chico Mendes was far more than an ordinary murder. It was as if a high-ranking man of the cloth had been cut down. It was murder in the cathedral.

It was also . . . a great movie.

A VISIT WITH SOME TAPPERS

Two weeks after the murder I was sitting in Chico's house with his thirty-year-old brother-in-law, Raimundo Gadelha; his widow, Raimundo's younger sister Ilzamar; and a detribalized Indian tapper who was guarding the place. The Indian told me he was a Monteiro, from the Rio Iaçu. "*Eu corto seringa,*" he said, with solemn pride — "I cut rubber."

Ilza was a tall, poised, striking woman of twenty-four. She looked Polynesian, like a Gauguin. She modeled the towel, now bloodstained and torn by buckshot, that Chico had thrown over his shoulder just before heading out the kitchen door. It was a relic now. I remembered a photograph I'd seen of a mother in eastern Amazônia — another region of violent land conflict — holding up the blood-soaked shirt of her son, a priest who had championed the landless peasants and been shot by *pistoleiros.* The glorification of bloody martyrdom — such a big part of Latin American Catholicism.

The Mendeses' four-year-old daughter, Elenira, who had been watching television in the front room when her father, mortally wounded, staggered back into the kitchen, showed me the bloodstains on the bedroom floor where he had died. She was named after a famous young female guerrilla who was killed by the military government in the sixties. Her two-year-old brother was named Sandino, as in the Sandinistas. Good names for the cause. Chico had been very attached to his children — he would spend hours sitting on the floor and playing with them — and they to him. Whenever they saw a plane now they would ask their mother, "Is that Father?" She would tell them: "Your father is in the sky. He's coming home, but not now."

Raimundo explained how each tapper rises at the crack of dawn to work one of his *estradas,* or trails, and how each *estrada* links about 180 rubber trees. "I've fed and clothed myself my whole life in three *estradas,*" he said, and I realized that was where I wanted to be, not here, making Chico's family relive the tragedy, but on a *colocação,* one of the homesteads in the forest where a family of tappers or often several related families live.

The Seringal Cachoeira, where Chico had spent most of his first thirty years, was an eight-hour walk. It was the rainy season, and the road there was too muddy for even a four-wheel-drive vehicle. There wasn't much enthusiasm for the trip. "What about something closer?" I asked Raimundo. He said, "I know a family of tappers that lives not far up the river. But we'll have to find a boat."

So we went to the house of a rich man Raimundo knew and asked if we could borrow his skiff for the afternoon. Soon we were heading upstream, below the juke joints and the stores of the Syrians, which extended from the riverbank on pilings.

Xapuri is a local Indian word meaning "the place where there didn't used to be a river." According to legend, one day a crack opened in the earth, and water soon found its way along it. The town of Xapuri grew up where the Xapuri River runs into the river Acre. Neither river at this point is more than seventy-five feet wide. Raimundo's friends lived up the Xapuri.

So much of the immediate area around the town had been cleared that we had to travel fifty minutes in the briskly moving outboard-powered skiff to reach the nearest patch of forest. "We are leaving behind the world of lies and dirty dealing," Raimundo said as we passed under the socklike nests of a colony of crested oropendolas dripping from the branches of a silk-cotton tree. Occasionally a brightly painted shack would appear on the bank, framed by the splayed leaves of cecropia trees. A pair of green parrots with yellow wings flew overhead, followed by a pair of green parrots with red wings. We waved to a boy in a dugout who was pulling in a trapline of thrashing silver fish — probably *piranambú,* larger, less toothy relatives of the piranha. Raimundo reeled off the names of several delicious catfish that swim in the river. I asked if there were any *candiru.* He laughed and said, "Sure. Loads of them." The *candiru* is a small catfish the size of a toothpick that wriggles into mammalian orifices and then throws out an excruciatingly painful set of retrorse spines. It can only be removed surgically.

Soon after passing a stand of twenty-foot-tall plumed reeds, we put ashore and made our way up a steep, slippery bank through a small blizzard of cabbage butterflies to where three men were waiting with their dogs. "*Opa,*" Raimundo said, and we shook hands with Antônio, Francisco, and João Rocco do Nascimento, brothers who had known Chico Mendes all their life. They were working the same *estradas* their father and grandfather had. We entered their house, which stood in a neatly swept clearing, on stilts to keep out insects and vermin. The walls and floors were slats of *jariná* and *aricuri* palm. Next to the house was a tree sagging with huge green gourds, which were halved and used as bowls.

The brothers' mother, an old woman who was working in the kitchen, noticed that I had a cough, a bad one I'd been unable to shake for a week. She picked some leaves of *jambu,* an herb she had planted on the edge of the clearing, and brewed a tea from them. The tea stopped my cough in its tracks for the rest of the day. I recalled the statistics: 25 percent of the medicine on drugstore shelves contains rain forest products, but only 1 percent of the plants in the rain forests have been analyzed for their medicinal potential. What about the cure for cancer or AIDS? It might be over in that vine.

Francisco picked up a special tool for scoring the rubber trees, and we headed for the forest, passing a homemade press for squeezing the prussic acid out of manioc roots, which are grated and roasted into *farinha* — an Amazonian staple. We stopped at the smoking shed. "We heat the milk from the rubber trees in this metal basin and keep stirring it with a paddle and pouring it on this slowly turning stick," Antônio explained. Eventually a ball of rubber, known as a *prancha,* weighing usually 30 to 50 kilos — the distillation of maybe five days of tapping — builds up. It's a nasty job: carbonic acid from the fumes gets to your eyes.

João picked up an old biscuit of rubber, squeezed in a press, that bore the stamp of the former owner of the Seringal Floresta, as the place was called. "We never knew who the owner was. We never met him, only his 'representative,' the *seringalista* [rubber boss] José Ademir, who dominated us and a hundred and eighty other tappers. We had to give José Ademir a hundred and twenty kilos a year as 'rent,' which he said was for the owner, and we had to buy his merchandise at outrageous prices. Twenty years ago we realized there was no owner, and José Ademir left."

We continued through fields of corn reaching far above our head, of manioc and dry rice, through a nettle-infested thicket, and finally into the forest itself. The brothers had four *estradas* from which they said they tapped 1,000 kilos of rubber during an average year, up to 25 kilos a day when the milk was flowing. They set out before daylight, lighting their way through the forest with helmets, known as *parongas,* that have a wick dipped in kerosene placed in front of a reflective disk.

We stopped at the first rubber tree, which was scored with chevrons of incisions like upside-down sergeant's hash marks, except that one wing of each vee was longer than the other — a pattern known as the flag cut. Other tappers prefer the continuous spiral cut. Francisco cut a new wavy line just under and parallel to the last vee. The milk immediately began to seep down along it, and where the wings converged, at the apex, he placed an empty tin can. Then he went on to the next tree, maybe thirty yards down the trail. "It's like making love to the same woman every day," he said.

Are there any dangers? I asked.

"Plenty," he said. "The *pica de jaca* [the snake known as the bushmaster]: it's black and yellow and gets to be twelve palms. The *jararaca* [fer-de-lance]. Its bite affects people differently. Some go blind in ten minutes. Some just swell up. The *tocandeira* [a solitary black ant, an inch and a half long, very common on the forest floor, whose sting can put you into anaphylactic shock]. Falling branches. We call them monkeys, *macacos*."

Where I come from, they're known as widow makers, I said.

"Some trees have been bled so much you have to go up a ladder to get to where the milk will come out, and there's the danger of falling," Francisco went on.

"Two hours later we come back to collect the milk," Antônio explained. "We're back for lunch by eleven. Then, in the afternoon, we do the smoking and take care of our crops. Then the next day, the same thing again." But at this time of year daily deluges made tapping impracticable. "It would take you five days to collect two days' worth of rubber," he said. So the brothers were gathering Brazil nuts, their next most important cash crop. The rubber sold for 1,000 cruzados — currently 50 cents — a kilo, bringing in maybe $500 or $600 a year: enough cash, with the income from the Brazil nuts, for their families' needs, since they grew, hunted, gathered, and fished almost all of their food.

João picked up a wooden globe the size of a softball from the forest floor — the fruit of a Brazil nut tree, known to botanists as a *pixidium* and locally as a *cengo* — and split it open with his machete. Inside were a dozen seeds, the Brazil nuts of commerce. The Brazil nut tree, *Bertholletia excelsa,* is one of the monarchs of the forest and grows up to two hundred feet high. You get beaned by one of these *cengos,* and it's all over.

Where the trail looped back and converged with another *estrada,* I sat on the trunk of a prostrate tree and looked up in the dappled light. High in the canopy a rainbow-billed toucan was gobbling *paxiúba* palm nuts.

What about Curupira? I asked — the Amazonian Bigfoot whose feet are said to point backward to throw off trackers. "No, we haven't seen him," Antônio said. "Here we have the Caboclinho da Mata, the Little Man of the Forest. He spirits off your dogs if you shoot more than one deer a week. And there's the Mother of the Waters, who tips your canoe over if you catch more fish than you need."

And what about the *bôto?* "Sure, he's around," said João. The *bôto* is the red freshwater porpoise, widely believed to be able to change into a man and come ashore, where he seduces women — a useful mechanism for explaining embarrassing pregnancies and social diseases.

The brothers showed me the green pods of wild *cacau* — chocolate — sprouted right from the trunk, and the fresh tracks of an armadillo. The trunk of this laurel is good to make dugouts from, they explained. The root of this bamboo, steeped in water, reduces swelling. The berries of this big *imbiriba* make a delicious wine . . .

They showed me where João had met a black panther head-on just last week. They showed me the *copaíba* tree, whose high-octane sap you can supposedly pour into your gas tank and drive off with, and dozens of other marvelous things. We stood and listened to the liquid improvisations of the *uirapuru,* the gray-flanked musician wren. "He is the poet of the forest," Antônio explained. "When he sings, the other birds fall silent. You hear the *uirapuru* and you say to yourself, I'm going to come out here tomorrow and cut another *estrada.*" He emphasized how important it was not to tap the trees too often, to let them rest for several days, or the milk would turn to water. "You fall on a forest like this, *senhor,* and it gives you everything."

CYCLES OF GREED

"There is no sin south of the Equator."
— a saying of the early Portuguese navigators
who mapped the coast of
South America

The history of Brazil, like that of most tropical countries, is made up of one wave of exploitation — of raw materials and of people — after another.

The sixteenth century was the century of brazilwood, for which the country was named. The tree yields a rich red dye that was in great demand in Europe for cardinals' robes, among other things. Brazil was divided into twelve captaincies, each of which was a private fiefdom ruled by a concessionaire who had the power of life and death over his subjects. The native "Indians" were a ready source of labor but didn't adapt well to slavery. They ran away, they pined, they stabbed their masters in the back at the first opportunity, they died like flies from flu, measles, and smallpox. Black slaves, proving more malleable, were brought over from West Africa. The slave trade peaked in the seventeenth century, the century of sugarcane. The Dutch established a thriving cane colony on Brazil's northeastern bulge, in the region of Pernambuco, but were expelled by the Portuguese with the help of conscripted natives.

In the next century gold and diamonds were discovered in the mountains of Minas Gerais (General Mines), north of Rio. The mines were financed by the British, who kept the Portuguese elite in fine food and feathers, china and tea, and controlled the Brazilian economy. The gold and diamonds flowed through Portugal to England, where they helped capitalize the Industrial Revolution. Some see the present century, with the riches of Brazil flowing north through a small elite controlled by foreign — particularly American — and multinational interests, as a reprise of the eighteenth. The things gold makes you do produced a devious cultural type known as the *mineiro,* the native of Minas Gerais. Darli and Alvarino Alves, the brothers who have been indicted as the masterminds of Chico Mendes's murder, are *mineiros.*

In the nineteenth century, coffee, introduced from Abyssinia and planted mainly in the south of the country, was Brazil's big contribution to the world, and it remained so until the crash of the American stock market in 1929 drove down the price and bankrupted the coffee aristocracy. A similar plantation system existed in Bahia, based on the native cocoa. The planters were known as colonels and had private armies of *pistoleiros* to keep the laborers in line. Their feudal baronies collapsed in the thirties, but colonels still control much of the northeastern backlands.

Amazônia, the impenetrable, forested northern half of the country, was a world apart. It was so remote that there was no way for the rest of the country to profit from it. From Manaus, the dissipated backwater that had sprung up a thousand miles up the river, at the mouth of the

Rio Negro, it was easier to get to Lisbon than to Rio. So the profits were local. The trade was in various types of gold. The Indian slave trade — "red gold" — quickly wiped out the vast chiefdoms along the river. The native population of the valley fell from an estimated six million at the time of contact with Europeans to the hundred thousand or so remaining today. Actual gold was also a magnet from the beginning. Large expeditions set off in search of the legendary El Dorado, whose kingdom was always over the next rise. In 1595 Sir Walter Raleigh made a fruitless search for it up the Orinoco River, in Venezuela, and returned raving about "a country that hath yet her maidenhead, never sacked, turned, or wrought," with a charming description of the equally elusive Amazons that he obtained from a local chief: "They doe accompany with men but once in a yere . . . and after the queenes have chosen, the rest cast lots for their Valentines."

Today one in five Brazilians, having no hope to make a life for himself where he is, heads for the Amazon. Many hope to strike it rich. For the past decade tens of thousands of muddy bodies, nicknamed *formigas* — ants — have been digging for gold at a huge crater at the Serra Pelada, in the state of Pará, swarming over ladders with sacks of dirt on their backs, in a phantasmagorical scene resembling the paintings of Hieronymus Bosch. Forty-five thousand prospectors have overrun the state of Roraima, on the frontier of Venezuela, invading the lands of the Yanomamo, one of the last large neolithic groups in the world — a cultural collision even more devastating than that of the tappers and the ranchers in Acre. In the state of Rondônia, which borders Acre, tens of thousands of colonists lured in the eighties from the South by government reports of rich soil, and by offers of generous terms to whoever was willing to give it a go, have abandoned their homesteads after the second planting, when nothing came up. Turning to prospecting, they are poisoning rivers and creeks with mercury used to separate gold from its matrix. The local Indians and the *caboclos* — the highly independent and largely self-sufficient families of mestizos scattered along the rivers — depend on fish for protein. But the fish are contaminated with mercury, and mercury produces birth defects in the children of people who metabolize it. This second, concomitant tragedy — the poisoning of the Amazon's waters and of its people — is even more out of control than the burning of the forest.

THE AMAZON RUBBER TRADE

A number of plants around the world yield rubber. The Mesoamerican civilizations played a semireligious game in pits with a ball made from the latex of the desert shrub guayule. The discovery in the Congo of several huge lactiferous vines in the genus *Landolphia* led to the enslavement and barbaric treatment of the natives there by the Belgians during the reign of Leopold II, in the late nineteenth century. Workers who returned from the forest without the required quota of rubber had their hands cut off, giving rise to a belief that persists in Zaire to this day, that whites are cannibals — why else, the natives reasoned, would they have wanted our hands? India rubber comes from a fig tree native to India and Malaysia: gutta-percha is still the nonpareil for golf balls.

But the best rubber in the world comes from ten species of trees in the genus *Hevea,* in the spurge family — the same family to which the poinsettia, which also has an acrid, milky juice, belongs. What advantage the latex gives the tree itself is unknown; perhaps it helps the tree to heal wounds. Ninety-five percent of the world's rubber comes from *Hevea* trees. An estimated three hundred million wild trees are scattered in the Amazon and Orinoco River basins. The most productive species is *Hevea brasiliensis,* which can grow to be a hundred feet high, two hundred years old, and ten feet in circumference. Roll a dab of its milk in your fingers and it will soon coagulate into a spongy little ball.

The Indians were of course aware of the possibilities of the milk. The Omagua, one of the great prehistoric chiefdoms of the middle Amazon, made rubber pouches, booties, and syringes for injecting enemas of medicinal herbs. Commercial interest in rubber began to take off in 1823, when a Scotsman named Charles Macintosh took out a patent for cloth coated with rubber, which made it waterproof. In the following decade Charles Goodyear discovered that sulfur could be added to rubber so it wouldn't soften with heat and would retain a hard consistency, and in 1844 he took out a patent for this process, which he called vulcanization. In 1888 John Boyd Dunlop patented his discovery, that ''a hollow tyre,'' a rubber wheel inflated with air, reduced vibration and gave a much smoother ride than metal hoops. The tires were put on carriages, bicycles, and, by the turn of the century, Henry Ford's wonderful new invention — the motor car. The rubber dealers in Manaus discovered they had a virtual monopoly on the substance. They were sitting on a gold mine, a "black gold" mine. By 1913 rubber accounted for half of Brazil's foreign exchange. A small class of fat cats, the rubber barons — the Amazonian counterparts of the North American robber barons who were making fortunes in steel, coke, and coal — made over Manaus with palatial mansions and even put in a sewage system. They sent their laundry to Paris, where it was piled with dirty shirts from gold prospectors who had struck it rich in Irkutsk, Siberia. Slab by slab, a magnificent domed marble opera house (where Enrico Caruso never sang and Sarah Bernhardt never performed, though legend says they did) was shipped from Carrara, Italy.

While the barons in Manaus were lighting cigars with bills of large denomination, Indians were being marched out of the forest at gunpoint and forced to work in rubber gangs. Some of the most appalling atrocities in the record of human depravity were committed between 1903 and 1916 on the Putumayo River by a Peruvian rubber company called J. C. Arana Hermanos. The Putumayo describes almost the entire border of Peru and Colombia, and the docile, friendly Bora, Huitoto, Andoke, and Ocaira Indians lived along its banks. At first mistaking the white men for gods, the Indians were incredibly hospitable and submissive, even sharing their women; after they had been induced to tap rubber for Arana, they would lie down for lashes without a word when informed that they had failed to bring in their quota. The men were flogged at whim, and left in stocks without food or water until they were reduced to eating the maggots swarming over their wounds. They were dismembered, crucified upside down, and set on fire for the entertainment their agony provided. Their women were raped before their eyes and added to the harems of the Barbadian gang captains; their children's brains were dashed against trees.

THE FLAGELADOS

The main labor force during the rubber boom, and during subsequent periods of intensive rubber tapping, wasn't Indians, however, but *nordestinos,* dirt-poor refugees from the drought-stricken Northeast of

Brazil, particularly the state of Ceará. At one time the Amazon rain forest extended far to the east, smothering the better part of the Brazilian bulge, but climate changes and clearing pushed it back, turning most of the region into a parched, scorching semidesert — a good approximation of what the remaining forest will turn into if the clearing and burning continues. This transformation has already occurred in much of the state of Pará, in eastern Amazônia, where some of the largest fires in history were set in the 1970s.

The people who lived in the *sertão* — the searing, dusty backlands of the Northeast — were for the most part cowboys, ranch hands, small-time cattle herders. They belonged to the Brazilian cowboy culture. They wore leather helmets, and their skin was like cracked brown cowhide. It's ironic that the victims of the ranchers in Acre were once ranchers themselves. But such are the twists of history.

To understand the *nordestino* heritage of the rubber tappers of Acre, listen to the records of Luis Gonzaga, the Johnny Cash of Brazil. He was the king of *baião,* the mournful country music of the Northeast. His famous song *"Asa Branca,"* "White Wing," tells the story of the *nordestinos'* wanderings.

> What a furnace, what a brazier,
> Not a plant standing in my fields.
> For lack of water
> I lost my herd,
> My horse died of thirst.
>
> Today, many leagues away,
> In the saddest loneliness,
> I wait for the rain to fall again
> To return to my beloved backlands.
>
> When I see the green of your eyes
> Spread over my fields,
> I promise you, don't cry, my heart,
> I'll come back, believe me.

Gonzaga lapsed into terminal illness soon after Chico Mendes was killed and died during my second visit. The country went into mourning for one of its greatest cultural heroes. His death seemed to mark the end of the Brazilian rural tradition, which is being overwhelmed by television and progress, and to underscore the particular violence of this transition in Acre. On his last record Gonzaga had a tribute to Chico.

The *nordestinos,* of which the Mendes family was typical, are sweet, meek, patient, dignified, long-suffering, generally short, with wavy hair over a characteristic flat head. Many have quick, penetrative minds. They have their own syndromes of violence, stemming mainly from liquor, jealousy, and slighted honor. A lot of innocent men are blown away on suspicion of fooling around with someone's woman. One *nordestina* recalls that when she was twelve and already a lush, desirable woman, she went to a *forró,* a local shindig. A man came up and asked her to dance. She refused. He whipped out his sheath knife — all the men at the *forró* were wearing them — and, plunging it into the table where she was sitting, he proclaimed, "Well, then nobody else is going to dance with you, either."

The *sertão* is also one of the world's most feud-prone regions. A feud between the Alencar and the Sampaio-Saraiva families, who come from the remote farming community of Exu (where Luis Gonzaga was born and laid to rest), has been going on since 1949. The trouble started when the unhappy wife of an Alencar moved out and shacked up with one of the Sampaios. The couple tried to kill the husband with strychnine but failed. He sent her divorce papers, which her lover made his lawyer eat and then wash down with his own urine. A few days later the first Alencar was gunned down in the main plaza, and since then there have been dozens of deaths. Remote cousins who left Exu years before the feud broke out have been hunted down and shot dead in the streets of Rio de Janeiro.

Every so often the Northeast is hit with a particularly bad drought. The cattle grow weak and more emaciated and finally drop in the empty creekbeds, and long, downcast processions of *flagelados,* as the refugees are called, head, like Okies leaving the Dust Bowl, for São Paulo or Rio, the Marvelous City, whose granite domes are honeycombed with slums of former *nordestinos.* The largest of Rio's slums, Rocinha, has four hundred thousand people, the population of all of Acre. A *flagelado* is someone who has been scourged by nature. In 1989 terrible floods unleashed another wave of refugees, who were also known as *flagelados.* The last figure I have for the number of *nordestinos* without a permanent roof over their head, even in the best of times, is thirty million, but this figure is ten years old. There are probably closer to forty million now — a huge and growing pool of perpetually famished people for whom there are no chances, no room in the Brazilian dream, and who represent an easily exploitable source of cheap labor. As Harry Truman put it, "We depend on misfortune to build up our supply of migrant workers."

Another favorite destination for the *flagelados* of the Northeast is Amazônia. During the rubber boom, recruiters from the rubber companies would gather crowds in the dusty little towns of the *sertão* and promise free passage to the prime rubber forests of the Upper Juruá and Purus valleys — God's country, where you could make enough cutting the rubber trees in Acre in just one year to set yourself up for life, to come back and live like a king. But it didn't turn out that way. Few made it back. The passage was debited to your account, so by the time you ever set foot on Acrean soil you were already a couple of hundred bucks in the hole, and you just got deeper in debt working for the *patrão seringalista,* the rubber boss. He had you coming and going; he bought your rubber for half of what it was worth and sold you goods for twice what he paid for them, which was already outrageously high, since they had passed through a succession of middlemen on their way up from Manaus, each of whom had to make a profit. But you couldn't do anything about it, because if you tried to sell to or buy from somebody else, or to leave, he'd have his *pistoleiros* on you in a minute. It was a terminal, no-win situation. Its formal name was *aviamento* — the truck system, or debt peonage, in English. Kentucky coal miners called it owing your soul to the company store.

This is how most of the fruit and vegetables in the American South and Southwest are still harvested, by captive work forces of chicanos, blacks, Jamaicans, and down-and-out white drifters known as fruit tramps. The latest technique of thralldom is addicting the workers to drugs, paying them in marijuana or crack instead of cash. Refinements of the *aviamento* system still practiced on the Upper Juruá include debiting the tappers for downriver taxes and transportation costs, deducting a fixed percentage of their credit to compensate for weight loss as the rubber dries, and charging "rent" for the *estradas,* the paths that lead to the rubber trees.

The migrant *nordestino* tappers were known as *arigós.* Fever carried most of them off within a couple of years. The ones who survived lowered their sights. They dreamed of making just enough so they could pay off their account at the company store and go home. But few of them saw home again. Most of them were illiterate, unable to detect the boss's legerdemain with the books. According to stories told by the old *seringueiros*, or tappers, there were so few women on the Upper Purus that when a tapper found a female footprint on one of the forest paths, he would cover it with brush so he could come back and worship it. One enterprising rubber boss got the idea of importing wives for the tappers. It took six years to pay one off — one of the better deals.

First-cousin marriage was common in the *colocações*, or tappers' homesteads, deep in the forest, and so was incest. The third prosecutor in the Chico Mendes case in seven months (it wasn't a job the civil servants in Acre were fighting over) told me about an incest case involving a family of tappers on the Upper Juruá that he'd been working on before being transferred to Xapuri. "One night one of the daughters was rocking in her hammock. She kept nudging the foot of her father, who was lying on a nearby bed. He told her to cut it out, but she kept doing it, so at last he got up and fucked her. Sometime later he got drunk and beat up his wife, and she went to the police and told them that he had committed incest with their daughter. But it was natural, she explained. She provoked him."

Acre, as the nineteenth-century engineer and journalist Euclides da Cunha put it, was yanked from the womb of Amazônia by the *nordestinos*.

A horrendous *seca*, or drought, in the Northeast in 1888 sent boatloads of *arigós* steaming up the Purus and the Juruá — enough Brazilians for a revolution. Acre was then theoretically part of Bolivia. In 1900 an expedition of Brazilian poets, writers, and journalists, fired up with the same sort of Manifest Destiny jingoism with which American colonists fifty years earlier "liberated" Texas from Mexico, tried to take Acre by force but was beaten back by the Bolivians with the help of a British-American rubber syndicate based in New York. Two years later came the Grand Revolution. Again the Indians of the Bolivian *altiplano* came down the backside of the Andes, but they suffered terribly in the hot, humid jungle and were routed by an army of jungle-wise *seringueiros* under José Plácido de Castro, who, standing in the main plaza of Xapuri, declared Acre an independent state. The following year a penniless Spaniard named Luis Galvez Rodrigues de Arias proclaimed himself the emperor of Acre, and, telegraphing the news of his accession in French to all the important countries, he began erecting public works. In 1904 Acre was turned over to Brazil. Two years later, while riding through his rubber forest, Plácido de Castro was gunned down by unknown *pistoleiros* hidden in the trees, thus becoming one of the first of Acre's many victims of ambush. His last words were "So many glorious occasions to die and these *cavalheiros* shoot me in the back."

THE END OF THE RUBBER BOOM

The seeds of collapse were already sown in 1876, when seventy thousand *Hevea* seeds were shipped out of the Amazon to Kew Gardens, in London, by Henry Wickham, one of a number of free-lance British plant collectors combing the globe for species with commercial potential. The story that he smuggled the seeds out was furthered by Sir Henry himself (he talked his patriotic act of derring-do into a knighthood), perhaps to gain backing for future projects. In fact, it was perfectly legal to export plants from Brazil in those days, although as a result of this rip-off of the national patrimony the laws today are much stricter. Wickham even threw a party for the customs officials in Belém to expedite the shipment.

As it was, only two thousand of the seeds survived to germinate. These became the source of millions of acres of *Hevea* trees in Malaya. Far from their insect and fungal predators, which oblige *Hevea* trees in their native habitat to be spaced dozens of yards apart from each other, hidden among hundreds of other similar-looking trees, the Malayan transplants could be grown in rows and easily tapped, their latex coagulated by a large, willing work force. By World War I the Malayan plantations were producing rubber at a fraction of the extortionate prices the rubber barons in Manaus had been getting. In 1910 a pound of rubber peaked on the world market, at 13 shillings. By 1921 it was down to 1 shilling.

The boom ended very quickly. Bankruptcy spread upriver from Manaus, from the mansions of the rubber barons to the various middlemen and finally to the *seringalistas,* who had no choice but to release their peons. Freed of their masters but with no market for their product, the tappers reverted to the wild. They went off the cash economy (to the extent that they had ever seen any real money) and became more like the Indians: the forest "internalized the Indian culture," as one of them described it to me. They hunted, fished, planted a few crops, gathered Brazil nuts and the numerous other edible fruits in the forest. They had no schools, no medicine except the forest plants the Indians showed them. They lived in the Fourth World, or perhaps the Fifth, close to nature, out of touch with national society, in a sort of posttribal limbo. Amazônia stagnated, gaining no population between 1920 and 1940, while the population of Brazil as a whole rose 35 percent. Acre actually lost people during that period and ended with 79,768, down from 92,379.

In 1913 a mulatto tapper in Xapuri named Irineu Santos, who had learned from the Indians the use of the hallucinogenic brew of the *Banisteriopsis* vine and the *Psychotria* shrub, founded a cult whose followers came to regard him as a reincarnation of Christ. Today several hundred thousand members of several splinter groups, most of them tappers or marginalized urban descendants of tappers in Acre (although the cult has spread to Rio and even to Boston and Southern California), drink *daime,* as Irineu called the brew (the name means "give me"; i.e., give me light, give me force; the most common Indian names are *yagé* and *ayahuasca*). *Daime* is supposed to bring you into synch with a pantheon of Afro-Catholic spirits similar to the ones worshiped by the adherents of the popular Brazilian spiritist cults, *macumba* and *candomblé.*

The tappers interbred with Indian women, were often part or completely Indian themselves; but they also exterminated and overran the Indians. They were not gentle, passive extractivists any more than the Indians were noble savages. There were massacres until very recently. The plane home from my most recent trip to Acre stopped in Porto Velho, the capital of Rondônia, where the most devastating fires of the eighties were concentrated. A man in his thirties who looked and talked like Bob Dylan (but in Portuguese) took the empty seat beside me. His hair was shoulder-length, and his wrists were wound with bracelets of black *tucum* palm — Indian work, the real thing, not tourist stuff. Must be an anthropologist, I thought, and hazarded aloud, indicating the bracelets, Nambiquara? "Right," he said. His name was Mauro Leonel, and he turned out to have been a friend of Chico's. "I saw Chico often at conferences to decide the fate of the people of the forest," he told me. "He had a magnetic presence and a real way with words. I think it was the isolation of the tapper's life that made him such a great conversationalist." Leonel worked with a tribe called the Urueuwauwau, some of whose villages are still uncontacted, although most have been decimated by the recent colonization project in Rondônia. He told me about a massacre in 1963 by tappers on the Rio Pacas Novas, led by a *seringalista*, in which thirty-one Urueuwauwau were killed and twenty-eight taken captive — women and children whom he distributed to his tappers. He later killed seven of them in a *queima de arquivo*, a burning of the archive, so they wouldn't talk. "Only one Indian tapper, Calixi, who participated in the attack and married one of the victims, survived to give deposition to the judge of Guajaramirim," Leonel went on. "As usual, the case is still sitting in the judge's drawer. The *seringalista* is still there, the local king of the forest, with a harem of three or four of the abducted *índias*."

In 1943 there was another big *seca* in the Northeast. The Allies were cut off from the plantations in Malaya, which by now were producing 95 percent of the world's rubber. The price shot up to forty dollars a kilo, and there was a desperate new demand for Amazonian product. The call went out for tappers. It's your patriotic duty to take the next boat to Acre, the recruiters told the crowds of *flagelados*. Fifty thousand *soldados da borracha*, soldiers of rubber, as they came to be known, responded.

One evening in the municipal market of Xapuri I got talking with a spry, radiant old woman named Vicenza Bezerra. Alone now, she was making ends meet by running a little restaurant, just a couple of tables. She cooked and served. "I came in 'forty-three with Father," she told me. "He was a *soldado da borracha*. I lived for thirty-four years in the forest. The life there is a thousand times better. If I had my husband I'd still live there. Joaquim tried the city life [by which she meant Xapuri, three thousand souls] but didn't like it." She took out a creased, old snapshot from her purse. Joaquim looked like a typical *nordestino* — honest, humble. "I married him at sixteen. He was forty. He had credit at the company store. He was rich. I thought it was a miracle. He was a good man. He never put a cup to his lips.

"There were eleven in our family," she went on. "One time I almost died of malaria. My mother gave me liver of the *macaco prego*, the capuchin monkey. When there was no kerosene we burned candles of *cernambi* [coagulated latex peeled from incisions in the trees]. It was thus that we overcame.''

The next evening when I dined at her restaurant Dona Vicenza had brought a plastic bag full of yellowed fifty-year-old receipts from the company store to show me. They were impressive documents. She showed me the stamps on each one. Joaquim had brought in *peles de borracha,* biscuits of rubber, and deer hides, and had traded them for salt, sugar, kerosene, coffee, condensed milk, cooking oil, matches, cartridges, a sewing machine, and pills.

Then she recalled the journey to Acre. "We were *flagelados.* Lord, how we suffered,'' she told me. "It took us five months to get here from the port of Fortaleza. It was during the government of Getúlio Vargas. The organization was called the Centra. The Americans gave us blue uniforms and put us on the boat. The first time we applied, Father, who had just had an operation, was rejected from the line. We went out in the middle of the sea, praying we wouldn't be sunk by U-boats. On the seventh of September we reached Belém, at the mouth of the Amazon. We slept on deck in hammocks, and there was nothing to eat but rancid reheated rice and *pirarucu* [salted, sun-dried slabs of the huge, primitive Amazonian fish, *Arapaima gigas*].''

Dona Vicenza began to sing the long, rousing martial song "they taught us,'' and tears ran down her weathered, wrinkled cheeks as the words came back.

"Courageous soldiers of rubber,
Of this humble, manly army,
Involved in the forest and the species,
Don't forget to do your duty in defense of Brazil.
The country at this point needs the dedicated love of its children.
Long live the Brazilian soldier!
Your product will serve the whole world.''

I asked if she had known Chico Mendes, and she replied, "He was sitting right at this table, consoling the mother of a boy who had nearly been killed by a bus. An hour later he was dead.''

THE AMAZON NUMBERS PROBLEM

As I have written elsewhere, numbers are a temperate-zone precision trip. In the tropics they are flourishes thrown out for effect — the figures are figurative. I bring this problem up now, because it will help explain the accretive structure of this narrative and why it is very possible, even probable, that some information that may turn out to be incorrect will be passed on in the course of it.

The problem of getting hard figures, or solid data of any kind, in Brazil is daunting. You would think that the monthly inflation rate, for instance, was a number that could be readily quantified and agreed on, but no. The Ministry of Finance has one figure, the Treasury another, and the prestigious think tank in Rio de Janeiro, the Getúlio Vargas Foundation, a third. The numbers problem is particularly grave in Amazônia, due to its vastness and the widespread unfamiliarity with arithmetic. The best maps, the aeronautical charts, have large blank sections labeled ''Relief Data Unreliable.'' The Kayapó Indians of eastern Amazônia have names for twenty-six species of bee, which they can identify on the wing, but their word for ''ten,'' which until recently they almost never had any use for, is incredibly unwieldy.

People will tell you something happened ''fifteen days ago'' or that they shot ''forty wild pigs.'' It would be a mistake to take these numbers literally. There are a dozen reasons that someone in the Amazon might give you bad information, intentionally or not. One of the most common is politeness. If you ask a question that anticipates the affirmative, the *caboclos* and the Indians are so humble that they will automatically tell you yes, because you, the *civilizado* (civilized one), the white *doutor* (doctor), must know best. So you learn, in trying to ascertain a particular piece of information, to ask as many people as you can, even to ask the same person several times. You circle, double back, play dumb: what was that again? You gather layers of versions, weigh them against each other, blend them and work them into a whole, until at last the piece of information begins to acquire a kind of burnished sheen, and the semblance of credibility.

The more research you do in the Amazon, the more you realize that the truth here does not really reside, is not firmly rooted and lodged, in facts and figures the way it is in the First World. You may even decide,

as many cross-cultural students do, as Sir Richard Burton, the great eth-
nologist of the last century, did, that "facts are the idlest of superstitions" or, as the anthropologist Michael Taussig has, that facts outside
of their interpretation, and truth outside of its representation, do not
exist. "My subject is not the truth of being but the social being of truth,"
Taussig writes in *Shamanism, Colonialism, and the Wild Man,* one of
the most interesting books to come out of the Amazon in some time,
"not whether facts are real but what the politics of their interpretation
and representation are."

The flip side of this, of course, is that every statement of fact, anything anyone tells you, is true on some level.

The numbers for all the big questions about the Amazon rain forest —
how many species there are, how much of the forest is gone, how much
the carbon dioxide from the fires is contributing to the greenhouse effect — are blowing in the wind. There are only educated guesses, faiths,
and political positions. How can you begin to quantify the extent of the
destruction, for instance — a highly controversial and complex question
to which careers are devoted — when, as we shall see, there isn't even
agreement on the size of the seven states and territories, and parts of two
others, that constitute legal Amazônia?

There is incredible divergence in even the relatively easy questions,
like how many tappers there are in Amazônia; the estimates range from
75,000 to 500,000. The problem is compounded by the difficulty of
defining who, exactly, is a rubber tapper. Some sixteen latexes, gums,
and resins are extracted in the Amazon basin, as well as a host of fruits,
nuts, fibers, flours, pigments, oils, and essences. About 1.5 million people in the Brazilian Amazon make their living from forest products,
though some of them (such as the charcoal makers) do not do it sustainably — that is, in a way that allows the resource to regenerate contin-
ually. Many *caboclos* tap a few rubber trees, wild or planted, as part of
a portfolio of activities that keeps them going, but they don't consider
themselves *seringueiros.* I met such a man on the Nhamundá River, one
of the Lower Amazon's lesser-known tributaries, in 1984. He took me
out behind his house and showed me his citrus trees. Behind them were
a couple of dozen rubber trees that he had planted, with tin cups jammed
into the apex of their oozing grooves. He tapped rubber, all right, but
he wasn't a *seringueiro.*

CHICO'S CHILDHOOD

Chico's early life was like the do Nascimento brothers', like that of any tapper in Acre. His grandparents, José and Maria Alves Mendes, were *nordestinos*. They left the state of Ceará in 1926. One of their children, Chico's uncle Joaquim Alves Mendes, now seventy-four, recalled, "It was no longer possible for us to live there because of the drought. My father had been a *seringueiro* before for six years during the boom. He came back to Ceará and married. In 'twenty-six the price of rubber had a little surge, but by the time we got here it had gone down again. There was no money to return, so Father worked in the Seringal Santa Fé for twenty years. He left because the boss was too much." Joaquim laughed. "He'd sell you an object and debit you for three. Today the *seringal* is a ranch."

José and Maria had four daughters and two sons. Chico's father, Francisco, was the firstborn, and Chico, born on December 15, 1944, in the Colocação Pote Seco, Dry Pot, in the Seringal Ecuador, only six kilometers from the Bolivian border, was the first of *his* children and was christened Francisco Alves Mendes Filho. The Colocação Pote Seco is a few hours from the Colocação Fazendinho, Little Ranch, on the Seringal Cachoeira, where Joaquim lived with his wife, Cecília, and his halfwit brother, Raimundo Nonato. "The owner of the Seringal Ecuador, who's in Rio Branco now, sold it to a rancher named Dr. Júlio," Joaquim went on, "and it's half-cleared. There's a widow living at Pote Seco, but she's no relation of ours.

"Chico's father liked to fight. He was hot-blooded and easily provoked. Chico had courage, but he hated violence. He was a very special person. He never offended anybody. If he hadn't died, things would be a bit better for us. He worked for the poor. But now nothing's going to change."

There was no school for the tappers. That was how the bosses wanted it. If tappers learned to add, they would discover how badly they were being cheated. There were no health services, either. When the tappers got sick or injured, they had to heal themselves with forest plants. "We were completely marginalized and excluded," Chico recalled in a series of conversations just before his death, with the sociologist Cândido Grzybowski.

The forest was Chico's first teacher. Instead of memorizing multiplication tables, he tagged behind his father in the forest, watching rainbow-billed toucans gobbling *paxiúba* palm nuts and deducing the basic plant-animal relationships. "I became an ecologist long before I had ever heard the word," he would say years later. He started accompanying his father on his rounds of the *estradas* at the age of eight. His father had soon imparted his very limited grasp of the ABC's and the three R's. Chico eagerly devoured whatever schoolwork his father could get for him. He seemed to have a gift, an aptitude, for learning.

In July 1989, seven months after the murder, I tracked down Chico's twenty-seven-year-old brother, Francisco de Assis, the youngest of the brood, in Rio Branco. He was accused of murdering the *pistoleiro* José Cândido de Araújo, also known as Zezão, on January 9, eighteen days after his brother's death, at a bus stop outside Xapuri. Having been relieved of street duties, he was guarding the Military Police health clinic. That evening there were no patients, and we had the place to ourselves. Assis was not at all the brutal, deadened, inured cop. He had the special Brazilian sweetness and the *nordestino*'s infinite patience. There was a lot of his brother in him. Only for a moment, when he tensed a little at the mention of Zezão, did he seem capable of killing anyone.

We started by getting the genealogy out of the way. "There are three brothers and two sisters alive," Assis told me. "Two brothers and two sisters died. Raimundo, the next after Chico, fell off a rickety ladder onto his shotgun while cutting a rubber tree. It went off and killed him. That was the only tragedy of my childhood. The next was Maria do Livramento. She died during delivery in a *seringal* in Bolivia in 'eighty-three. The other sister, Celina, died in 'sixty-four of some sickness. There was no doctor in the *seringal* to specify what."

We went over the genealogy again. It was a good idea, because there were some changes in the order of birth.

Chico Mendes — deceased
Maria do Livramento — deceased
Margarida — lives in Porto Velho
José Alves Mendes Neto, "Zuza" — lives in Xapuri and
  works for the Rural Workers' Union

Raimundo Nonato Mendes — deceased
Cordolino Alves Mendes — lives in Porto Velho
Me (Francisco de Assis Mendes)
Celiza — lives in Xapuri, married to Zacharias
    (I don't know his last name)
Celina — deceased; died in Seringal Ecuador, from some sickness

"My father, Francisco Alves Mendes, died when I was fourteen," Assis continued. "It was a big blow for Chico. As the oldest brother, he became the head of the family. My mother, Iraci Lopes Mendes, had died when I was two. I don't know where her people were from, if they were *nordestinos* or what."

The death of Iraci was a major blow for Francisco senior, and for the whole family operation. How was he going to take care of all those kids? He never married again; the children went their own way as soon as they could.

"I was born on the Seringal Cachoeira, at my uncle Joaquim's," Assis resumed. "I followed my older brothers on the *estradas*. Chico was a good hunter. He shot *nhambu, jacamim* [tasty birds], deer, both types of peccary [collared and white-lipped], *paca* [a rabbit-sized rodent], armadillo."

What was Chico like?

"He always stayed with me when he was in Rio Branco. He never changed, even when he came back from the States. He never got mad at anybody. And he never got a thing for himself. It was always for the *seringueiro*. He was a truly selfless man. He respected everybody, whether old or young."

Do you remember any special moment? A reasonable journalistic question, but Assis couldn't get into it. Ilzamar hadn't been able to, either. He was stumped. At last he said, "I remember Chico came to my house a few days before he died. It was around three o'clock. He was very happy. He'd just been in Sena Madureira, where he'd persuaded four hundred tappers to join the union, and he came back excited. There were two Military Police guards with him. My wife's cousin saw Darli Alves's car with his sons Oloci and Darci pass the house slowly and follow the three of them as they headed for the main plaza.

"The next day Chico told me, 'The situation is ugly. The circle is closing on me.' "

Some more reporter questions: Did you have any sense he would become so famous? Are you proud of your brother?

"The only thing I can think is I'd rather he was alive."

I saved the most sensitive matter — the murder of Zezão — for last.

"Zezão was a *pistoleiro*," Assis said. "A peon, and hired gun of Darli Alves. He was suspected of killing a kid near our brother Zuza's house in the forest [Zuza later moved to Xapuri, fearing for his life] and of killing Ivair [Ivair Igino, who was bushwhacked six months before Chico]. He threatened to kill Zuza after Chico was murdered. He told me to my face" — which now hardened in anger at the memory — "that he wished it had been him who had pulled the trigger. He had many enemies. After Chico was killed there were many who wanted blood.

"On the ninth of January he was found shot on the road to Brasiléia. I was accused because I was on vacation there. I and the *seringueiro* Bacalhau [Codfish] and Oswaldo, who works on a farm near Xapuri. But I was heard by Nilson and Adair [the detective conducting the inquest into Chico's murder, and the judge who will preside over the trial, if there ever is one] and they decided there was no evidence. I was cleared. There was testimony that put me in the Seringal Cachoeira at the time of the murder, and none that put me at the scene."

I wouldn't talk to the detective Nilson de Oliveira until a few days later, and he said that Assis hadn't been cleared at all; there were five eyewitnesses, including one of his own cousins, who saw Assis shoot Zezão over and over, delivering the coup de grace point blank, through the ear.

Not that there weren't people willing to swear he had nothing to do with it. Raimundo de Barros, Chico and Assis's first cousin and the president of the National Council of Rubber Tappers, said he found it strange that Assis was under suspicion, since on the Wednesday of Zezão's murder he was still in Rio Branco. The Chico Mendes Committee, which was formed after Chico's death to end the violence in the backlands, said Zezão's assassination was a *queima de arquivo* — a burning of the archives — by the ranchers to keep him from talking. The committee claimed its source for this information was one of the *pistoleiros* who had lain in wait for Chico. But it didn't reveal the *pistoleiro*'s name.

Assis told me that Chico had said to him, emotionally, "If I die, others must continue the mission.'' Evidently Assis thought, This is what I can do for it. The family duty, the almost moral obligation, to take revenge would have naturally fallen on him. He knew that, being a cop, it was unlikely he'd be brought to trial. Both sides understood the need for blood, and as far as the ranchers were concerned, Assis had done them a favor. Zezão out of the way was one less mouth to worry about.

But not realizing how strong the evidence was against him, I had no reason for doubting his denial. As he was making it, a huge, saucer-sized morpho butterfly sailed through an open window into the anteroom where we sat talking, as if in some strange, synchronicitous gesture of support. Its wings were iridescent metallic blue on the inside and subtle brown on the outside, with ocelli, big false eyes, to fool birds into striking at a part of its body that it could better afford to lose than its head. Assis didn't even notice it.

ZUZA

There are twelve hours of daylight and twelve of night year-round on the Equator, and darkness falls promptly at six o'clock every day of the year. Sunset is not a drawn-out affair. The bloody disk drops into the shock of silhouetted trees, and everything is immediately plunged into pitch-darkness. So although it had been seven months since Chico Mendes had been killed, I couldn't help but feel a little nervous as I made my way down the path to the shack where his brother Zuza — José Alves Mendes Neto — lived. It was only seven o'clock, and I could barely see a thing.

Zuza's spread was just around the corner, no more than seventy-five yards from the shack where Chico had been murdered. It backed up on the same thicket on the river Acre where the killers had camped for days waiting for the opportunity to get Chico. The path ran along a trench of open sewage that emptied into the river and ended at a high slat fence with a padlocked gate. Inside the compound a shack stood on stilts. The windows were tightly shuttered, but I could tell from gaps in the construction that lights were on inside. On the other side of the fence a vicious dog raced back and forth, barking furiously. I clapped my hands — the way visitors announce their arrival in rural Brazil. A crack opened in one of the shutters, and Zuza — shirtless, in shorts and plastic flip-flops — came out to let me in. He was thirty-four, ten years Chico's junior, and had the same full-term potbelly and laid-back friendliness as his brother. He chained the dog and greeted me in a real country drawl.

"Up to six months ago I was cutting rubber, but we were ambushed, so we came here. I had no experience in Chico's struggle, but I went to Rio de Janeiro and denounced the assassins and their impunity. I still don't feel safe here, either. I think they want to kill me because I won't lie. The other day we found a new little trail in the thicket leading to the road and to the river, just like the trail Chico's killers cut. The courts have done nothing. The ranchers have not seen much of a reaction, so they think maybe they should start killing the rest of us."

Zuza and I went up into the shack and sat in the kitchen. There was no TV, and it was very hot and close in the tiny room. Zuza introduced his wife, Deusamar, Ilzamar's younger sister. The brothers had married sisters. Deusa was a handsome woman, but not a head turner like Ilza. We started with Zuza's memories of the Colocação Pote Seco. His tally of the family members was a little different from Assis's. "My mother had eighteen kids, and only five are left. There was no way, if your kid got sick out there, that you could put him on your back and carry him to the hospital in time. Mother died in childbirth when I was nine. Father was very disoriented. He worked tending the crops, and Chico took over the tapping. Chico cut rubber full-time for twenty-eight years. My sisters made the food. Father grew old and died around 'seventy-three.

"In 1975 Chico went to work at the Seringal Ecuador as a *meeiro* [someone who taps someone else's trees and splits the proceeds fifty-fifty with him] for our future father-in-law, old man Gadelha. There he became fully aware of the injustices of the thieving bosses. The 'good' *seringalista* kicked your ass if you didn't produce enough rubber for him. If you sold your balls to someone who paid better, you were beaten and expelled from the *colocação*. If you asked to settle your account and leave, you were killed by his *pistoleiros* so he wouldn't have to pay you, or — this happened a lot — he'd pay you, then he'd have you bushwhacked on the road as you were leaving, and he'd get his money back. Most of the bosses were bastards."

Zuza's uncle Joaquim told me a few days later that he worked for Gaston Mota, the *seringalista* at the nearby Seringal Filipina, for three years. "That was a bad guy. He had a lot of people put in holes in the ground. He killed his bookkeeper Simão because he was slipping it to Simão's wife. He tied a rock to the body and dropped it in the well. A few months later he said, 'People say I killed Simão. That's a lie. I just saw him, and he's really fat.'

"One day he bragged, 'What I have, not even God could take away.' The next day he lost his boat and became a beggar. His brother was a good guy, though. I'd still be with him if he was alive.''

Mota saw the writing on the wall, got out of rubber, and became one of the main brokers in the selling of Acre to the ranchers. He allegedly got into drug and arms smuggling from Bolivia and became a partner of Darli Alves's. He is implicated in a number of murders, including the massacre of a family of tappers on Darli's land in 1978, assassinations by the secret death squad in the State Department of Public Safety, and the death of Chico himself.

Zuza also worked for Mota. "In 1968 we lived for three months in his *seringal*," he recalled. "He had hired us to cut his corn. One day near the crops, under a big *comarueira* tree, Father discovered a skeleton. 'This is a human being,' he told me. 'It must be one Gaston killed.' I was thirteen or fourteen. We returned to the shed where we used to sleep. Father was very apprehensive. Gaston came up and said, 'What about you, Mendes? Are you going to vote for my party in the next election?' His party, ARENA, was the party of the generals, the party of the massacres. Father said, 'No, only a fool would raise a wild animal that will later kill him.' Gaston said to his foreman, 'Mendes will vote for my party or he is going to pay.' The foreman told Father he'd better clear out if he knew what was good for him, so Father asked for his money and we went back home. After the ranchers came, Gaston became the planner of the deaths of the workers, which he is to this day.''

In one incident — recounted to me by several sources — Mota caught a tapper in his *seringal* selling rubber to another *seringalista*. He wrapped the man in *cernambi* (strips of old, hardened latex) and ignited it. The man died a death no less horrible than the atrocities committed on the Putumayo River. Chico Mendes saw a tapper put to death in this manner, but it is unclear whether he was the one killed by Mota. After Chico's murder Mota was picked up for questioning by the Federal Police, but he was released within twenty-four hours for lack of evidence.

JOAQUIM AND CECÍLIA

Now that the roads were dry, I was able to visit Chico's people in the forest. I had invited a young writer from Rio, Julio Cesar Monteiro Martins, one of the founding members of the Brazilian Green Party, to come along. He had never seen the Amazon, and I thought it would be a good idea to have a Brazilian with me. There was danger to me as an American not only from the ranchers and the police (especially if they had read my article about the murder that had come out in the United States several months earlier) but also from the Shiites, as they are called: the militant left-wingers of the tappers' movement who consider the ranchers allies of American interests and who believe the real enemy, the instigator of all the oppression of the Brazilian poor, to be the CIA.

We hired a man with a pickup in Xapuri and were soon barreling down BR-317, the road to Bolivia, kicking up clouds of dust that settled on the trees along the road, purple *itaubinha,* yellow *faveiras,* scarlet *ipês,* and muted the dazzling brilliance of their flowers. We passed gallinules, purple marsh birds, in a culvert pool, and a peon in a leather helmet scuttling along on a mule behind a dozen emaciated humped zebu cattle. "*Ei, 'tá poeira gostosa,*" exclaimed Chiquinho Barbosa, who had come with us — "Ah, what tasty dust." Chiquinho was the brother of Júlio Barbosa, Chico Mendes's successor as president of the Xapuri chapter of the Rural Workers' Union. He was a tiny, mischievous young man in his early twenties, a little elf.

We turned off on a narrow, deeply rutted road that went on for miles through a tangle of remnant forest and unkempt pasture and finally stopped at a fork, where some of the people who had hitched a ride in the back of our pickup were getting out. It was here, Chiquinho explained, that the confrontation of April 1988 had taken place. Three hundred men, women, and children — all from the Seringal Cachoeira — had stood at the fork in the road and prevented the peons who had come with chain saws to clear the *seringal* from proceeding any farther. One of these demonstrators was an old man who had gotten off the truck and was sitting on a log in the shade, gathering strength for the long walk to his *colocação.* I went over to interview him. "We can't take the sun, because we are people of the forest," he told me.

(Just like the pygmies in Zaire, I thought: they won't work in the fields, because they can't stand direct sunlight.)

The old man's speech was almost poetry. "They're going to wipe out the Brazil nut trees, the noble woods, the water, the game, and our life," he said, shaking his head. I asked his name. Raimundo Batista de Oliveira.

It was here, Chiquinho told me, that Chico picked the fight that got him killed eight months later.

The Seringal Cachoeira borders Bolivia and encompasses 24,898 hectares* of mostly still-virgin rain forest. About 420 people, belonging to 67 families of tappers, live on it. Compared with most backwoods people in the Amazon they make a good living from their combined extractive activities — around fifteen hundred dollars a year per family. In 1980, 50 percent of the people in Amazônia made only half a *salário mínimo*, the official minimum wage, adjusted monthly for inflation. Here many of them make two *salários*.

We continued into the *seringal* and reached the end of the road by late morning. Everybody who had stayed on the truck passed their bundles down and got out. One of the passengers was a cripple whose legs were shriveled to nothing and who stood no more than two feet high. He thanked us and set off cheerfully, brachiating with his strong arms down into the gully, across the creek, up into the pasture, and on to his house in the forest, four hours away. We followed, into a square of maybe seventy-five acres that had been hacked out of the forest and planted with grass and crops, with a few houses in it, and walls of trees soaring in the distance — the Colocação Fazendinha. In the main compound there were a school, opened in October; the storage shed of the recently formed cooperative, stacked with smelly *peles* of rubber (here the latex, instead of being smoked and coagulated into balls, was pressed into "biscuits" — the laminate process, a much healthier system); and the home of Chico Mendes's uncle Joaquim and his wife, Cecília, and Joaquim's retarded brother, Raimundo Nonato. Altogether there were eleven people in three families, all of the men still tapping except Joaquim. "Only I'm too old to do it anymore," he told us.

Joaquim and Cecília were a radiant old couple, and they welcomed

---

*One hectare equals 2.47 acres.

us with the spectacular hospitality that is more the rule than the exception in Amazônia. After decades together they'd developed the same laugh — a wonderfully free, hearty, rollicking cackle. They spoke a lot in proverbs, proven nuggets of wisdom distilled from the shared experience of the humble people of Brazil. Julio Cesar and I spent two days with them, mostly sitting at their kitchen table, and talking about everything under the sun. Cecília told us that she was sixty-three and had had nineteen children, four of whom had died, three of measles in the same week. Assis had given me a partial list: Miguel, Duda, Toto (Antônio), Nilson, Sebastião, Zomar. Julio Cesar tallied her grandchildren, and they came out to exactly a hundred. "*Ishi, Maria* (Holy Mother)," she exclaimed. "A hundred little shoots. Hear that, Joaquim?" she called to her husband in the bedroom. "Julio Cesar here says we have a hundred grandchildren!" She cut loose with the family cackle. "I'm very proud to have created a brood like this."

"Well, no one is born from a seed," was Joaquim's response.

Then she said, "Come on, let's eat," and served us a porridge of hard balls made of sweet manioc.

At the memory of her nephew Chico her eyes filled with tears. "A better person than that isn't born," she said. "He didn't deserve it, but then [consoling herself with another proverb], it's never the bad people who die. He would have lasted longer if he'd had a big house downtown, but he never took care of himself. He chose to remain at a low level, fragile, exposed. 'I must have a simple house, so that the *seringueiros* won't be embarrassed to enter,' he told me.

"After the chain-saw crew was blockaded, he came here and said to us, 'You will live in peace, but this will cost blood.' This is where he felt at home. He'd come into the kitchen and kiss me on the cheeks. Big pig." By now the tears were streaming down her cheeks. "I dreamed of him two nights ago. He came in eating onions. It was a happy dream."

She showed me a booklet that had been put together as a posthumous homage to Chico. There were photographs and a rambling reflection he'd jotted down on a paper napkin that turned up after his death:

> Attention, youth of the future.
> The 6th of September of the year 2120,
> the anniversary of the first centennial

of the World Socialist Revolution,
which unified all the people of the planet
in one sole ideal
and in one dream of socialist unity
and of putting an end to all the enemies
of the new society.

Here remains only the memory
of a sad past and of pain,
suffering, and death.

Forgive me.
I was dreaming when I described these events,
which I myself won't see.
But at least I have had the pleasure
of dreaming them.

These were not the words of an Albert Schweitzer (which is how the Environmental Defense Fund, one of the American groups that had been supporting Chico, tried to portray him in one of their fund-raising letters after his death). They were the words of a revolutionary, a warrior. In the United States, I realized, Mendes would have been considered a pinko tree hugger and a radical labor leader. He would have been bugged by the FBI and audited by the IRS.

They were also the words of someone who knew he wasn't going to be around much longer.

CHICO'S POLITICAL GRANDFATHER

One of the first — and the few — people to address the social inequities in Brazil was an army captain named Luis Carlos Prestes. Prestes was soon to be ninety-one and was still lucid, still a warrior, when I visited him at his apartment in Rio de Janeiro.* An old, worn set of the complete works of Lenin in Portuguese took up several shelves in his study, beside *Das Kapital.* The windows looked out on what is left of the spectacular coastal rain forest, which is full of tree ferns, marmosets, and other wondrous forms of life.

*Prestes died eight months later.

Prestes had belonged to a group of idealistic young officers in the Brazilian army, lower middle-class in background, who in the early twenties determined to put an end to the entrenched corruption and patronage of the old republic. On July 5, 1922, they staged an insurrection at the Igrejinha fortress in Copacabana, in the city of Rio. The fortress was surrounded by three thousand troops, and the last ragged eighteen survivors — the first martyrs of the Lieutenants' Movement — were executed on the beach.

"The movement gathered moral force," Prestes told me. "Two years later there was another revolt, in São Paulo — the Revolução Paulista. I was transferred to Rio Grande do Sul. They couldn't prove my involvement. There we continued conspiring. In 'twenty-four we formed the Column [the Coluna Prestes, as it would become known] to dramatize our demands for reform. We began as a thousand enthusiastic young men and picked up more on the way. In two years we marched twenty-five thousand kilometers.* I wouldn't be so strong at my advanced age today if it weren't for all the walking I did more than fifty years ago. The normal stride of a soldier is seventy-five centimeters. Mine grew to eighty-four.

"As we traveled around the country and saw the full extent of the poverty, injustice, disease, and misery, we became progressively radicalized and evolved into a popular guerrilla movement," Prestes continued. "We walked from Rio Grande do Sul to Santa Catarina, and from there went into Paraguay. Then we reentered Brazil in Mato Grosso and marched to Goiás, Maranhão, Piauí, Ceará, Rio Grande do Norte, Paraíba, Pernambuco, Bahia, and Minas Gerais. In each place we burned all the court cases against the peasants, who didn't even understand how badly they were being exploited. In the interior, on many Sundays at Mass the ranchers would force the voters to sign the ballot list, and that was how the election was done. There was no secret vote, no freedom of the press, no justice, except for the rich. And this is still the case. Nothing has changed. The courts are still the most corrupt political power in the interior."

The rebels became acquainted with the practice known as *grilagem*, still very widespread in the interior, whereby title to land is secured by fraud or force, or a combination of the two. "The way *grilagem* works,"

---

*One kilometer equals 0.62 miles.

Prestes explained, "is you buy fifty hectares, then you go to the notary's office and register five hundred. Later you get it changed to five thousand. You keep adding zeros, while eighty percent of the workers in the fields have nothing. This is what I saw in the Column. We saw sharecroppers, more backward than Indians, digging the earth with knives. We saw the misery of prospectors hiding their little bags of gold dust so they wouldn't be killed. We saw the insatiable *fazendeiros* [ranchers] taking all the land for themselves.

"In Mato Grosso we saw the rubber tappers, already deep in debt for their trip and food by the time they arrived from the Northeast. We saw the *fazendeiros* buying their debt and taking them as peons to their ranches. They had to go. We saw peons living like slaves on the maté plantations of Mato Grosso do Sul. We saw the effects of savage capitalism everywhere we went. And nothing has changed.

"We picked up young peasants, some of them only fourteen. The Column grew to fifteen hundred. Our strategy was to keep moving, because we lacked arms. The *fazendeiros* kept getting the government to send troops against us. The troops were trained in French First World War tactics: entrench and defend. In two years eighteen generals were sent against us. They sicked the *cangaceiros* on us." The *cangaceiros* were cossacklike bands of marauders who terrorized the *sertão* of the Northeast; Prestes described them as "anarchic elements."

"For weeks we hacked through the forest with compasses, guiding ourselves by the Southern Cross. Three lengths below the Cross is the Southern Pole, and Orion pointing to the west. We made maps with information from the local people. The army had worthless official maps. That's why they never caught us."

CHICO'S POLITICAL FATHER

I asked Prestes if the name Euclides Fernandes Távora meant anything to him, and he said no. "There was a Juarez Távora who was one of my subordinates in the Column. I knew him well. But Euclides? It doesn't ring a bell."

He would have been Juarez's nephew, I said. His father, Dom Joaquim, was a bishop. Euclides was born in Crato, Ceará. The Távoras were a prominent, influential family, but Euclides took after his revolutionary uncle.

Here the information is contradictory. Some sources claim that Euclides marched with the Column. This is not impossible; Euclides would have been around twenty in 1930, when the Column disbanded. The second version is more likely, that Euclides, a junior officer, took part in a November 1935 revolt of the army, the navy, and civilians at the barracks in Rio and São Paulo that got Prestes sentenced to forty-seven years. Euclides, too, was arrested and packed off to Fernando de Noronha Island, which is way out in the Atlantic, above the Brazilian bulge. But with the help of his family and their connections, he managed to escape, and he fled to Belém. There he was almost recaptured after participating in an unsuccessful revolution under a certain Major Barata, and he barely escaped to Bolivia, where he soon started to organize strikes for the tin miners, perhaps an even more victimized group than the tappers under the *aviamento* system. But his notoriety caught up with him again, and he just made it over the border into the jungles of Acre, which in the early sixties was a practically roadless terra incognita, a good place to hide. Távora was not the first revolutionary to lie low in the interior of Acre, nor would he be the last.

One day in 1961 or 1962, when Chico was seventeen (according to his brother Zuza), Chico met at the company store of the Seringal Ecuador a man of around fifty-five he had not seen before, trading *pranchas* of rubber for goods. The two of them got to talking. The stranger, who expressed himself in a way Chico had never heard before, said he lived alone on the Colocação RI-4 of the Seringal Cachoeira. Chico was fascinated by the words he used. Zuza recalled, "He was not a young man, but his voice was strong and clear. He knew things."

The stranger, who would not reveal his name — Euclides Távora — to Chico until years later, noticed that Chico was intelligent, and he asked if his father liked to talk politics. Chico said he did, and Távora said, "Well, I'll come and see him sometime." Five days later he stopped by. He had brought some newspapers. Chico had never seen a newspaper before, and he was intrigued. Távora noticed his interest. The upshot was that Chico's father allowed him to take off work early on Saturdays and go to Távora's house to learn to read. It was a three-hour walk from where Chico beached his dugout.

Together the two of them would work slowly through the political columns of the papers that Távora received two or three months late, and soon Chico had learned to read. Sometimes he stayed awake all night listening as Távora told the amazing story of his life, or they would both listen to the General Electric radio, "which got the whole world," as Zuza put it. They'd hear the news from the BBC, the Voice of America, and Radio Moscow — such different versions of what was happening, you wouldn't think it was the same planet.

"I never saw anyone so much for coffee," a merchant in Xapuri who befriended Távora recalled. "He even took a thermos with him when he went out on the *estradas*. People nicknamed him Euclides Pranchão, Big Board, because he was tall and barrel-chested. There was some problem because Guilherme Zaire [a Syrian who had the biggest roof-tile and brick business in town] offered Távora many times out of friendship money to go back to Ceará, and he always said he couldn't take it. He was different. More educated and experienced, a man who knew everything and could talk with any person. He knew nothing about tapping rubber, but he learned fast." But he never learned to cook, and he brought a woman named Neuza to cook for him and to relieve the isolation. Eventually they married.

Chico's new literacy was in great demand, and he was kept busy writing love letters for his illiterate young *companheiros*. Távora began to indoctrinate him. He explained what a union is, how a man could become the master of his destiny, if he didn't die in the attempt. "You, Chico, are very intelligent. You're the only one in this region to start the movement for the liberation of these people."

In 1964 there was a military revolution in Brazil, and a dark period of persecution ensued for anyone smelling vaguely leftist: artists, intellectuals, university students. Deep in the forest, Távora and Chico would tune in Radio Moscow at 5:00 P.M., listen next to the Voice of America and the BBC, and then discuss which one they believed. Moscow condemned the politics of military repression, saying it was a coup backed by the CIA (which was true) and supported by conservative sectors of the Roman Catholic church. It said the real patriots — the militants — were being imprisoned, tortured, assassinated, driven into exile. The Voice of America, on the other hand, said the revolution was a victory for democracy, "a return to democratic normalcy" (when in fact it had set back democracy twenty years), a victory over anarchy, corruption, terrorism, Communism, and "God knows what else," as Chico would recall of those evenings.

What became of Távora is unclear. His merchant friend believes he died of malaria at the *seringal,* but Chico and Zuza have said that in 1965 he became ill and went to Rio Branco for treatment and was never seen again. "We heard he died on the operating table, but Chico checked at the hospital and there was no record of him," Zuza told me. "I think he was picked up by the Military Police. He seemed to know he wasn't coming back, and he gave his milk cow to his boss to cover his debt."

The last time Chico saw him, Távora told him that he could expect ten, fifteen, twenty more years of the brutal military regime, which was financed by the CIA to demobilize the peasants' struggle for agrarian reform. He told Chico that he could do something for the tappers only if they all joined a union. Alone he would never be able to do anything.

The physical Távora was *desaparecido,* but his ideas lived on. He had transformed Chico into a warrior.

"During the following five years or so I became extremely isolated," Chico recalled. "After he disappeared, I thought to myself, What should I be doing? In this extremely difficult moment of military rule I couldn't do many things because I was likely to be persecuted."

Chico started writing the first of hundreds of futile letters to Brasília describing the deplorable conditions of the tapper's life: to President Castelo Branco, to the minister of justice, to the superintendent of the Federal Police, to everyone he could think of. He described how the tappers were marginalized and excluded from society, how they were being robbed at each weighing — if the *prancha* weighed sixty kilos, the bosses said it weighed fifty — and how they had to buy merchandise at exorbitant prices. Chico was a tireless letter writer. It must have been a frustrating experience.

Chico taught many of his *companheiros* to read and add, so they wouldn't be cheated anymore. In 1968 he tried to interest the tappers in organizing to stand up for their rights, to throw off the yoke of the rubber bosses by challenging their illegal monopolies and contesting their titles (most of which were false or nonexistent), by forming cooperatives and establishing their usufruct, or squatters', rights to the land they had been working for years. But there were no takers. Chico ran up against the passivity and fatalism, the infuriating brainwashed meekness, that the tappers had evolved to cope with a situation they thought they had no hope of changing.

This was dangerous subversion that Chico was getting into. Padre José Maria Carneiro de Lima, the priest of Xapuri, was very conservative, in league with the rubber bosses and later the ranchers. He was an old-time padre who boasted that he had outlasted three popes and studied fourteen languages (seven or so of which he spoke), as well as aeronautics, medicine, mechanics, radio electricity, zoology, ethnology, anthropology, and botany. He was also believed to be an agent of the secret police.

FIRST LOVE

Women found Chico attractive. Many were crazy about him, but he never took sexual advantage of his charm and prestige, unlike many public figures of every persuasion. When he was twenty-five he married Eunice Feitosa. According to Ilzamar, Chico's second wife, the wedding was a religious ceremony only. Eunice claims there was also a civil ceremony. The page of the clerk's register that would have recorded the event has mysteriously been torn out.

Eunice was not a hit with her in-laws. According to Chico's aunt Cecília, whom I took with a grain of salt, she was very mean, vulgar, arrogant. "I kept telling him to beat her. She kicked him. People who visited their house said she didn't sleep with him, she slept under the house. She left his dirty clothes on the edge of the creek, so long that the kids brought them back to the house full of roots. She was a terrible housewife. She left pregnant with their daughter, Ângela Maria [now nineteen].

"Why did he choose such a woman?" Cecília asked. "Because it was his fate. He left a lot of other women for her. There was a smart, beautiful school principal, but he didn't want her."

Chico's brother Zuza: "I followed their life together at the Colocaçâo Lagoa. Father didn't want him to marry her because she was of such a family that she had to give much to her father. But they fell for each other. Chico said, 'Father, I need a woman to clean my clothes.' But he would come home from the forest and there would be no food, no clean clothes. He gave her money, and she used it to buy things for her family. He discovered that she ran up huge bills. He hired a hand to help with the tapping, and one day he found the two of them *enamorando,* and he kicked her out.''

Chico and Eunice lived together from 1969 to 1971. She is now thirty-six and lives three hours by boat from Xapuri, on the Seringal Nova Esperança, Colocação Isaura, with a man named Antônio Cabral da Silva. The Brazilian journalist Zuenir Ventura hunted her down a few months after her former husband's murder. He found her to be ''once beautiful, perhaps.'' He didn't get much out of her, mostly silence and contradiction.

Eunice's memory of her brief marriage to Chico long ago was different from that of her in-laws. ''I didn't give him reason to leave me,'' she told Ventura. ''He did it himself.'' She explained the absence of a marriage certificate by claiming that Chico had taken it to be able to obtain another document, and had never brought it back. ''I was only fifteen,'' she said. How much of a monster can anyone be at fifteen?

Eunice's lawyer, Norival Camargo Valadão, was confident that proof of the marriage would turn up. He had already found in the index of the marriage register that Francisco Alves Mendes Filho and Eunice Feitoso de Meneses had married on February 7, 1969. The reference was to page 159, the one that had been torn out.

The enterprising Ventura also hunted down Padre José, who allegedly married them. Now seventy-eight and retired in Rio Branco, he said he had hung up his cassock after the advent of liberation theology and was senile now. He just couldn't remember, he said. ''I must have married ten thousand people in Acre. How am I supposed to remember? Go look in the book.''

In 1975 Chico began working as a *meeiro* for Gadelha, his future father-in-law. Zuza's memories of the Gadelhas' *seringalista* are not fond. ''Chico documented everything in a book that's been lost. One time Deusa was bitten by a *jararacuçu* [a species of fer-de-lance] and was near death. Her father needed medicine to save her. The *seringalista* wouldn't give him any, so he sold *princípios* [little balls of rubber] to another boss to raise money. The *seringalista* sent the police to take old man Gadelha to jail for violating his contract. Many people tried to get him released. Finally Senhor Enéas, the government inspector, succeeded, and the old man returned to his *colocação.* The *seringalista* wanted to expel him, but Gadelha said, 'The only way I'm leaving this place is in a coffin.'

"Finally, with hatred of the tappers, the *seringalista* sold his holdings to a rancher from the South, Dr. Gilberto. Dr. Gilberto forced all the *seringueiros* at gunpoint into a room where they had to sign a document agreeing to vacate their *colocações*. Only six or seven, including my father-in-law, refused. The others left. Gadelha's still there at what's left of the Seringal Santa Fé."

There were three Gadelha daughters, and Chico taught them all to read. He gave them the first lesson before he went out to cut the trees, and the second before he returned to collect the milk. This went on for two years. "I didn't even know what an *A* was," Ilzamar recalled. At ten she was already enchanted with her professor, and so were her sisters, and when he went away they all cried. He had brought a wonderful light into their lives, just as Euclides Távora had done for him ten years earlier.

RUDE INTRUSION

The prevailing Latin American attitude toward nature has changed little since the conquistadors' time. Other forms of life are inherently hostile; they exist only to be exploited. There is no love lost on dogs, which are kicked and starved and left outside the house. The forest is a green hell and an obstacle to progress. It is claustrophobic, full of danger and biting insects, and has no redeeming qualities. "If nature is against us, we will struggle against nature," said Simón Bolívar, the Liberator.

This attitude was very much alive in the fifties, a period of tremendous optimism and expansion in South America, as in much of the rest of the world. In Venezuela, military dictator Marcos Pérez Jiménez dreamed of "conquering the physical environment," of blasting tunnels through mountains and running gondolas to hotels on their summits, of bridging gorges and stitching the country together with four-lane highways. In Brazil the dictator Getúlio Vargas, much influenced by the positivism of nineteenth-century French philosopher Auguste Comte, had enlarged the steel industry and kept it in Brazilian hands, neutralizing covetous foreign companies like U.S. Steel and Krupp, as well as the Japanese, by entangling them in regulations. But in 1954 the Brazilian people, who had once idolized Vargas, began to blame him for the riotous inflation, the rampant corruption, and the breakdown of government that they were experiencing, and he blew his brains out.

The remarkably dynamic, Kennedy-like Juscelino Kubitschek, a former doctor, won the next presidential election. He set himself the tremendous task of rectifying the imbalance in Brazil's settlement pattern: 90 percent of the people lived on the coast, and the interior was almost empty. The South was temperate, European, while the North was torrid, neolithic.

Kubitschek's first step was to realize the old dream of relocating the capital from Rio, which had been talked about for years; nothing had been done except for a few expeditions sent out to survey the godforsaken savanna in the middle of the country for possible sites. How Kubitschek got Brasília built in only five years is one of the great epics of modern times. The first bricks were airlifted. The first road connecting the new city with the rest of the world ran south, to Belo Horizonte, the capital of Minas Gerais, which was linked to Rio and São Paulo.

But Brasília was only the beginning. The archbishop of São Paulo, Dom Carlos Carmelo de Vasconcelos, predicted that it would be "the magic trampoline for the integration of Amazônia into the national life," and Kubitschek launched a monumental road-building project comparable to the construction of the Alcan Highway or the American transcontinental railroad the century before: a highway 1,900 kilometers long from Brasília to Belém, at the mouth of the Amazon. At that time there were no more than a couple of million people in Amazônia — a density of less than one per square mile, sparser than any of the world's deserts. Most of the people were clustered in two cities, Belém and Manaus. The economy was stagnant. Per capita income was half what it had been at the height of the rubber boom. There were 6,000 kilometers of road, less than 300 of them paved. The only way to travel to the small towns and villages scattered along the Amazon and its eleven hundred tributaries was by riverboat. You brought your own hammock and hung it on one of the decks. The trip took days, weeks, months.

The Belém-Brasília Highway was intended to be the backbone of a highway system from which lateral roads would shoot out and, a government prospectus explained, "recuperate areas asphyxiated by the want of paths of communication." It took three years to build. Its builders had much to contend with: malaria, mud, torrential rain, the deadly fer-de-lance, the unsuspected irregularity of the terrain under the trees, the rock-hardness of many of the trees themselves. Although the Indians never attacked (as they would on future road-building projects in the Amazon), one sensed they were always near at hand, watching. Provisions and equipment, even live cattle, were airlifted to the front line, where feverish slashing extended the road about a half a mile a day — a thin red thread running through the green hell. The workers had the uneasy feeling that they were ravishing a sanctuary and that sooner or later someone would have to pay for it. Only two weeks before the road was to be inaugurated, on January 15, 1959, a tree fell and crushed to death Bernard Sayão, the herculean man Kubitschek had put in charge of the operation. The jungle had its revenge, and in the process it gave Brasília a martyr.

A year later Kubitschek got the idea of having a "Caravan of National Integration," made up of Mercedes trucks, Ford and Volkswagen sedans, and Willys and Unimog jeeps — all manufactured in Brazil by the new multinational automobile industry he had also created from scratch — travel the entire length of the Belém-Brasília Highway. This would demonstrate the strides that were being made on several fronts of national endeavor. The caravan took a week to complete its mission. There were no serious mishaps, though some of the rivers were not yet bridged and the vehicles had to be floated across on oil-drum rafts. With the paving of the highway in 1964, eastern Amazônia's centuries-old isolation was over.

It was the beginning of the end.

By 1964 the golden Kubitschek years seemed only a dream. Inflation was rampant again, thanks largely to the cost of Brasília, the political situation became chaotic, and the military stepped in. Juscelino was exiled, and was not allowed to return until the following decade, and then only to private life. In September 1976 his car was run off a cliff by a passengerless bus on the hairy, congested highway from São Paulo to Rio. The circumstances of the accident have never been fully explained. There is suspicion that the SNI, the secret police, was involved, because the military was worried about a comeback (like the one Getúlio Vargas had staged) by the still immensely popular Juscelino.

The funeral at Oscar Niemeyer's glass cathedral in Brasília drew three million mourners, the largest crowd ever assembled in the capital. "As a doctor," the local paper eulogized, "he cured the great collective disease of the Brazilian nation — the inferiority complex." He was beautiful, very cheerful, admirable, extraordinary, most human, his friends remembered.

No one would emerge on the national scene with Juscelino's moral prestige until Chico Mendes, whose murder hasn't been fully clarified, either. Like Chico, like King and Gandhi, Juscelino was too good, too dynamic.

OPERATION AMAZÔNIA

It took a couple of years for the generals to get the political situation under control, and once they did, more or less, they cast their eyes again to the North, to the vast ocean of trees frothing over 58 percent of the national territory. If there's one thing the military mind doesn't like, it's anarchy. Peru, Venezuela, Colombia, Ecuador, and Bolivia were all making initiatives to occupy their part of the Amazon basin, and it was high time, the generals argued, that Brazil established a presence up there, took possession of its territory, secured its frontiers, got something happening, started tapping the fabulous wealth that had always been assumed to be there since the early quests for El Dorado.

During this period, moreover, planned colonization of the rain forest was seen by many tropical governments as a solution to their land and social problems. Not only had five of the other Amazon basin countries embarked on colonization programs of their own, but Indonesia was relocating massive populations from Java and three other densely populated islands to outlying ones. This Transmigration Program, the most ambitious colonization scheme in the world, was described by President Sukarno in the fifties as "a matter of life and death for the Indonesian nation." It called for Java's population to be reduced from 54 million to 31 million between 1950 and 1985, and for the eventual relocation to the outer islands of a total of 140 million people. It also resulted in some of the most appalling genocide, of the tribal people on the outlying islands, on record. Some have described it as Third World imperialism, the Third World making war on the Fourth and Fifth. Similarly, the great, vast forest of the Amazon was seen by the generals in Brasília as the country's safety valve, a solution for its albatross — the 30 million *nordestinos* living in landless misery. The answer was to turn them loose on the Amazon.

And so, between 1966 and 1967, a series of acts known collectively as Operation Amazônia was initiated. The slogan of the operation was *Integrar Para Não Entregar*, "Integrate It So As Not to Surrender It" — to foreigners. The plan included an elaborate road-building and colonization program; the creation of SUDAM, the Superintendency for the Development of Amazônia; a regional bank, BASA; and the creation of liberal fiscal incentives for large-scale industrial and agricultural development. What should have been the first order of business — an effort to find out what was actually there — was not made until 1971, by a remarkable undertaking called Projeto RADAM. High-altitude photographs, more revealing than satellite photographs because they were able to penetrate the clouds, were taken with the help of the U.S. Air Force. Blowups of the photographs were pieced together to give an aerial picture of the entire valley. Lots of interesting things turned up, including a new four-hundred-mile-long river in western Amazônia, completely hidden by the trees, whose existence hadn't even been suspected. Teams of geologists, agronomists, forest engineers, geographers, and geomorphologists were sent up unexplored rivers, and dropped deep in the forest by helicopters. Fifty men died in river rapids and in helicopter crashes. They found the long-sought El Dorado, an incredible trove of natural resources: billions of dollars' worth of timber, mahogany and cedar especially, standing there waiting to be harvested, and under the trees, in the Carajás Mountains, between the Tocantins and Xingu rivers, the richest iron deposits on earth — 8 billion tons, so they say — plus gold, copper, manganese, and nickel. They found 600 million tons of bauxite on the Trombetas River, and, elsewhere, tin, cassiterite, niobium (2.9 billion tons — 78 percent of the world's supply — worth about $28 billion), lignite, potassium, and limestone of orgiastic proportions.

The reports on the soil were extremely encouraging and totally erroneous, founded on little more than the prevailing misconception, the assumption that any soil that can produce such lushness must be incredibly fertile. The soil studies confirmed the Amazon's potential to be the "breadbasket of the world," as was being already claimed by the United Nations Food and Agriculture Organization, which concluded that the planet could sustain as many as 36 billion people if the Amazon were farmed intensively.

The Hudson Institute, a New York think tank, came up with an astonishing scheme in 1967: to dam the Amazon at Santarém, forming a great inland lake in the center of South America, such as had existed in interglacial periods long ago, that would be a gigantic source of hydro-electric power and a boon to Pan-American commercial shipping. Such wild schemes understandably made the Brazilians nervous. The Hudson Institute plan was bitterly denounced in the papers as a smoke screen for establishing an American submarine base and a place of permanent exile for Black Panthers and other undesirables. A wave of xenophobic paranoia swept over the country. A casual suggestion in a speech by Harrison Brown, author of *The Challenge of Man's Future,* that India's problems might be "solved" by moving much of its population to Amazônia, made headlines. Artur César Ferreira Reis's book, *Amazônia and International Covetousness,* had gone through four editions by 1972, the year economist Kenneth Boulding suggested moving 200 million Asians to Amazônia.

There was a sense of urgency, excitement, mission, *Integrar Para Não Entregar.* It was like Manifest Destiny on the American frontier, except with twentieth-century equipment to accelerate the process of taming the wilderness. A thick anchor chain dragged between two bulldozers could level forty hectares of the forest a day. Eight men with chain saws could clear a hectare in six days. Planes were a godsend. You could drop Agent Orange or napalm bombs from them, get rid of recalcitrant backwoods cultures — Indians, tappers, *caboclos* — do what had to be done, sacrifice a couple of thousand scattered backward people for the higher purpose of progress.

The old Indian Protection Service, founded at the turn of the century by Colonel Mariano da Silva Rondon on the principle of respect for the Indians' cultures and land (its motto was "Die If Necessary, Never Kill") was dissolved in 1967 when its administrators were implicated in wholesale slaughter of Indians by dynamite, machine guns, and sugar laced with arsenic. The service was condemned as "a den of corruption and indiscriminate killings" by the Brazilian congress, which was itself reduced by the generals to a powerless advisory body two years later.

A bad drought in the Northeast in 1970 triggered the first step of the National Integration Program, which called for the eventual building of 15,000 kilometers of road. Its backbone, its centerpiece, was the Trans-Amazon Highway, which would begin at Estreita, in the northeastern state of Piauí and cross South America at its widest point. Eventually, after 3,000 kilometers in the Brazilian Amazon, and more than 5,000 from Recife, on the Atlantic coast, it would hook up with the Carretera Marginal de la Selva — which Peru's president Fernando Belaúndc Terry was simultaneously embarking on — and with the Carretera Central to Lima and the Pacific. The first leg of the highway was inaugurated by President Emílio Garastazu Médici, the third military president of the revolution, in a grand gesture of national pride and brotherhood with "our neighbors in Peru." As the Dutch sociologist J.M.G. Kleinpenning observes, "Spectacular and exciting actions of government, such as the active development of the Amazon region and enthusiasm for it among larger sections of the population, can result in political conflicts being felt less severely for a time and in attention being temporarily diverted from such matters as lack of political freedom, torture, and social injustices."

The two-hundred-foot-wide swatch of bare red earth moved slowly west, penetrating the heart of darkness — to Marabá, to Altamira, to Itaituba, to Praínha, to Humaitá. The clearing, grading, and surfacing of the road with compacted earth and pebbles were subcontracted in stretches to private companies, who in turn subcontracted the work to individuals known as *gatos,* cats. The *gatos* rounded up work crews — single men from bars and flophouses in Pará and Maranhão who split up into groups of two or three and were paid per area cleared. This was of course a new opportunity for exploitation and debt peonage in the long Amazonian tradition. Middlemen advanced food, cooking utensils, machetes, ax heads, at outrageous prices. The diet was poor: manioc, rice, sugar, coffee. Honey from stingless bees in the forest was a rare treat. "Malaria was a common ailment," the geographer Nigel Smith reports in his detailed study of the trans-Amazon development scheme, *Rainforest Corridors.* "I saw pallid men shivering under sacks in their hammocks in the mid-day heat, their bodies wracked by alternating fever and chills. I do not know how many men expired in the forest. Grave sites are prohibited along the Trans-Amazon."

By late 1972 the first 1,200-kilometer-long section was open. The plan was initially to resettle 70,000 *nordestino* families along it, 100,000 by 1976, a million by 1980, the most ambitious scheme ever attempted in the humid neotropics.

It all sounded very rational, well planned, and doable. One-hundred-hectare lots were made available for $700, payable over twenty years, and two-room houses for $100. Every 10 kilometers there would be an *agrovila:* a government-built community of forty-four to sixty-six houses, with a health clinic, a primary school, a government-run general store, and an office of the Agricultural Extension Service. Every 100 kilometers there would be an *agrópolis* — with a secondary school, a hospital, light industry, and warehouses — and every 200 kilometers a *rurópolis* with 20,000 inhabitants, a trade school, a bank, a hotel, and an airport.

A massive ad campaign with a catchy come-on — "Land Without People for People Without Land" — was launched in Brazilian magazines. It showed the Trans-Amazon paved with gleaming tin, leading to El Dorado, promised thirty-dollar subsidies to each family for the first six to eight months, and guaranteed crop financing.

Incentive packages were created to lure bigger investors. The plan was to get ranchers from the South and multinational companies to clear the forest and grow beef for the First World. This seemed reasonable. Cattle raising is one of the quickest, cheapest, easiest uses raw land can be put to. The incentives included ten- to fifteen-year holidays from corporate income tax, exemption from import and export duties, and more incentives if your project was in western Amazônia, to compensate for the greater distance to markets and the lack of both infrastructure and a local work force. The biggest incentive was an up to 50 percent tax break if the resulting savings were invested in an industrial, agricultural, ranching, or service project located in Amazônia.

But there was a catch: you had to show productive use of the land before SUDAM would give you title to it, which meant you had to clear half of it within a certain time or it would be reappropriated. The cheapest way to do this was to clear, burn, sow grass seed by plane among the charred, strewn logs, turn a few head of cattle loose, and then wait. Once you had title and the highway was in place, you could sell the land for a lot more than what you had invested in it. The income from your cattle was insignificant. You could only pasture one head per hectare sustainably, because the soil proved to be very poor. Each hamburger, by one calculation, wiped out another six square meters of rain forest.

Cattle ranching in Amazônia is one of the most cynical land scams of all time. The cattle are a smoke screen for land speculation. The forest is not even being converted into hamburgers. Most of it is going up in smoke to augment the holdings of the 1 percent of Brazilians who own most of the country's arable land, the majority of which is not in use. Brazil's food is produced mostly by small farmers, who make up 50 percent of the landholders but occupy only 3 percent of the land. A small and powerful elite represents the political force behind the Amazon's incredibly distorted development policies. It is the beneficiary of more than a billion dollars of fiscal incentives, and naturally it is bitterly opposed to any kind of land reform.

So the *flagelados,* who had nothing to lose, and the big companies, which had been offered terms that made it impossible *not* to make a profit, started coming. The first order of business, whether you were a small-time colonist or a multimillion-dollar multinational, was to clear the forest, and then, after letting the slash dry for a few months, to burn it. This is how one takes possession of land in the tropics. Small, shifting populations of tribal people have been slashing and burning the Amazon forest for millennia. The technique is also known as swidden agriculture. You clear a patch and torch it. The ashes give the soil a quick fix of nutrients, a release of minerals that gives the first crop a shock of growth but in the long run kills microorganisms, so that the second or third planting comes up puny. At best you can get maybe five years out of the land; then you have to let it go, return it to the forest, and start the process again somewhere else.

AN AMAZING DREAM

One night in the fall of 1970, I awoke from a fantastic dream. I had never been to the Amazon, nor could I recall ever having given the place much thought, but that was where the dream took me. I immediately wrote down what I remembered of it in my notebook:

> I am on an expedition up the Amazon, paddling with some Indians in a dugout, off the main current, up a narrow channel in the flooded forest, overhung with branches and vines [an uncannily accurate picture of the Amazon's floodplain forest during the rainy season, as I would discover later in the decade]. The channel leads to a large murky pool, which is the "headwater" of the river. The name of this pool is Ondo Pondo. In the middle of the pond was a pole that marked the lair of the monster of Ondo Pondo, which

looked something like this: [I sketched in the notebook a fishlike creature with two fanglike teeth hanging from its upper jaw.] The monster, which was female, was capable of flying as well as swimming. There was no getting around her, no continuing the expedition until she was dealt with.

We tried stringing poles across the abyss, but she would jump up and knock us off them. Several hair-raising scenes of the pole shaking, with the monster's front teeth wrapped around it, convinced us that the only way we could proceed any farther was to somehow placate her. I seized upon the idea of taking the pole that was significantly sticking up in the middle of Ondo Pondo. I pulled it up. It was about twenty feet long and quite thick. The monster seemed to get excited. It lay on its back and curled up its lower part while hovering in the air, parting its fins to reveal a ready vaginal hole. I thrust the pole inside and in this way the monster was completely tamed. While it was thus distracted the Indians paddled along the edge of the pond to the other side. Using the pole as a pole vault, I vaulted over the pond, dropped into the canoe, and we continued.

I was born to a family of naturalists and spent a lot of my boyhood in the woods — the lush, broad-leafed deciduous forest of northern Westchester County, New York. In 1974, in my late twenties, I wrote a book, about cruising around the interior of Florida in an old white convertible, whose euphoric natural descriptions attracted the notice of the editor of Sierra Club Books. He asked if there was any place in particular that I wanted to go to and write about, and, remembering the dream, I said yes. Definitely.

So in September of 1976 I flew down to Brazil, unwittingly following a tradition of temperate-zone writers with exotic fantasies headed for a fall. The Jewish writer Stefan Zweig, for instance, came to Rio in 1941 and wrote an ecstatic book about Brazil. Its title, like those of many other books in its genre *(New World in the Tropics, Brazil: The Infinite Country, The Giant Stirs),* was full of hope: *Brazil: Land of the Future.* It portrayed the country as a racial paradise free of aggressive European nationalism and intolerance. But within a year Zweig had killed himself. The poet Elizabeth Bishop arrived in Rio in 1951 for what she thought was just a short visit and ended up staying eighteen years. Setting up house with her Brazilian friend Lota in the haunting baroque city of Ouro Preto, she wrote home that she was "enthralled by the Brazilian geography and landscape, by the paradoxical, affectionate, spontaneous Brazilian people, and the complications of a world at once feudal, nineteenth century, and contemporary." In 1969, after Lota had committed suicide, she wrote: "I feel her country really killed her, and is capable of killing anyone who is honest and has high standards and wants to do something good."

That's what some people said about Chico.

When I arrived in Pará that fall for an eight-month tour of the Amazon Valley, a fire as big as Rhode Island was raging out of control on the Volkswagen A.G. Ranch in the southern part of the state. I visited a subsidiary of the King Ranch of Texas where the heat from the tremendous walls of flame was so intense that it created local firestorms, complete with thunder, lightning, and mini-tornados. I saw huge trees that had been blasted into the air and had landed upside down with their root buttresses sticking up like the fins of crashed rocket ships. Much of Pará had become, in only half a decade, a charred, sunbaked wasteland, a burnt-out semidesert, as if the *sertão* of the Northeast had moved west, bringing with it the *vaqueiro,* or cowboy, culture, peons in little leather helmets scuttling along on mules, kicking up dust.

It was no longer possible to see the forest from the Belém-Brasília Highway. There had been a tremendous rush of poor migrants in search of land and employment. The human population of Pará had ballooned during the sixties from 100,000 to 2 million, the cattle population from zero to 5 million.

The clearing and burning of the forest was done typically by independent contractors, who brought in teams of men from Maranhão, the next state to the east, to take down the trees. The town of Paragominas was a completely lawless, Wild West cow town, like Dodge City or Abilene, with lush, heavily painted fourteen-year-old whores and trigger-happy cowboys blowing into town for a good time.

There were several kinds of land conflict: squatters *(posseiros)* fighting "legal" landowners, or squatters or legal landowners being driven off by the *pistoleiros* hired by speculators who were acquiring property to sell to big ranchers. Much of the land along the Belém-Brasília Highway was cleared by small farmers without title, who were subsequently chased out by speculators or by big ranchers themselves. In the municipality of Conceição de Araguaia, in southern Pará, the discontent of the squatters was fomented by guerrillas hiding in the forest, causing an explosive situation that was crushed by the army in 1975.

Four months before my arrival, John Davis, a rancher from Alabama, and his two sons had been gunned down by squatters on his unusually fertile land along the Trans-Amazon Highway, near Marabá. Another American rancher who was trying to make a go of it in Amazônia told me, ''Davis should have compromised with the squatters, allowing the established ones to remain in return for keeping out new arrivals. He was a tough character. He thought he was back in the United States, where the law says that a man owns every inch of his land and the authorities back him up. Here you gotta negotiate with the police, the authorities, with the squatters, with everybody. And if you end up with less land than you expected, you still have enough to make it worthwhile.''

Davis and his sons were bushwhacked by a group of about thirty of the estimated two thousand squatters on his land.

MEANWHILE, IN FAR WESTERN AMAZÔNIA

The same thing happened in Acre. Ranchers from the South began pouring in as early as 1970, after the completion of Highway BR-364, a rough dirt track linking Rio Branco with Porto Velho and Cuiabá, the capital of Mato Grosso. The plan of Governor Wanderley Dantas, who invited the ranchers, was to convert the state's economic base from rubber to cattle. The tappers, who constituted virtually the entire rural population, were just going to have to make way for progress. The methods that were used to move the tappers out were the same ones used in the United States to remove the Indians from 1818 on — fraud and violence — and similar arguments about Manifest Destiny and eminent domain were employed to justify rolling over this defenseless subculture. There was a massive transfer of land from the old rubber elite to the newly arrived ranchers. The only positive part of it was that many tappers were released from peonage. But their freedom was short-lived.

No one except Chico had tried to explain to the tappers that they had rights like other people. To the ranchers they were like Indians, subhuman savages, and most of them simply left the forest as they were told. Twelve thousand families went over to Bolivia, among them some of Chico's relatives, and started tapping there, in the Madre de Dios Valley, the forested backside of the Andes (where the Bolivian government has recently launched a new colonization program and the peasants are pouring in — making the area the next time bomb of social conflict). Others headed for the state capital, Rio Branco, doubling and tripling its population and ringing it with slums. Its hotels and flophouses experienced a tremendous surge in patronage; one year 150,000 transients signed their registers. Periodically, labor subcontractors hired by the ranchers would sweep the hotels for drunken former tappers, pay their bill, and take them out to work off their new debt on chain-saw gangs. This was the final humiliation, to be booted off your land and now forced to return and raze it. It was an even worse form of servitude than working for a rubber boss, because you could be killed by a falling tree or the malaria that spread like wildfire over the deforested areas.

The whole question of land tenure and land ownership in Brazil is very complicated. Often a property will have acquired several owners over the years, a situation known as apartment ownership. The latest owner will arrive on the scene to find that people have been living on his land for years. Under Brazilian law, anyone who occupies and cultivates a piece of land for a year and a day has squatter's rights to it; he becomes an official *posseiro,* or untitled occupant; he is in physical if not legal possession. After five years he can gain clear title if he registers his claim with the town clerk, but few *posseiros* have the two-hundred-dollar fee or the know-how to do so. Theoretically a *posseiro* can't be evicted from his land unless he is compensated for the improvements he has made, but in practice *posseiros* are evicted all the time, all over Brazil, by *pistoleiros* in the employ of new owners or speculators. Once he has been physically evicted, the *posseiro* loses all his rights and has no legal recourse.

By 1976 the ranchers controlled two thirds of Acre. Many had expanded their original government grants by *grilagem,* or land fraud. The Amazon was crawling with *grileiros,* land packagers who had illegally put together titles to large tracts of land and sold them to willing accomplices or unsuspecting buyers, sometimes even to squatters who would one day have to do battle with the real owner. The *grileiros* were expert at falsifying documents, turning 1,500 acres into 15,000 by the skillful addition of a zero or a well-placed bribe at the notary public's. They were the same kind of small-time con men who proliferated on the American frontier. Jim Bowie, for instance, hero of the Alamo and allegedly the inventor of the famous Bowie knife, was a major *grileiro,* deep into shady land deals and title forging, first in Louisiana, then in the province of Texas, where the Mexican government was granting land to American colonists. In many ways, the glorious Texan war of independence was a spectacular feat of *grilagem* in which not only Texas but eventually the whole northern half of Mexico was wrested from its rightful owners.

The ranchers who had invaded Acre hung out at the restaurant of the Rio Branco airport, talking about cattle and women in the same crude terms, and carving up the state among themselves. They were none too popular with the locals, but they didn't care. There were only 130 of them, and they had displaced tens of thousands of native Acreans, contributing to the already horribly skewed pattern of land ownership, one of the most regressive in the world. According to a report by Amnesty International, 1 percent of the population owns 43 percent of the productive land, while roughly ten million peasants are wandering around the country looking for a little plot where they can grow enough to feed their families.

Many of the *latifundiários,* the owners of huge ranches, were gentlemen absentee ranchers. They were rich people playing at ranching. Cattle in Latin America, as in many parts of the world, are symbols of wealth. That is their main importance in Amazônia — ornamental.

The Acreans called the ranchers, pejoratively, *paulistas,* but not all of them were from São Paulo. They came from other states in the South as well — Rio Grande do Sul, Paraná. One of the first ranchers in Acre, Benedito Tavares de Couto, was a legend of machismo. He came originally from São Paulo. He was one of four brothers, and after the inheritance of the family ranch was split into four *minifúndios,* he moved up to the interior of Mato Grosso do Sul, to a little town called Dourados. Soon a range war broke out with the local peasants, who had never established title to their land. The other ranchers were driven away; only Tavares stayed. "He never backed down from a fight," his son-in-law told me. "He slept under his bed to avoid being shot." His wife recalled that on the first night of their honeymoon, in 1960, he left to round up a thousand head of cattle and was gone forty-five days. After ten years in Dourados, culminating in his setting fire to the local church — the padre was one of the main instigators of the *posseiros'* resistance — Tavares finally packed it in and headed up to Acre, the new frontier, where a hectare of land was going for only three cruzeiros — cheaper than your pen, as his son-in-law put it. "No one in Acre knew what a *derrubada,* a large-scale clearing and burning of the forest, was. So Tavares flew in two planeloads of Paraguayans. Most of them had never been on a plane and were dead drunk by the time they touched down in Rio Branco, and as soon as the door was opened they bolted."

"It was a stronger race chipping away at the land, the liberty, and even the existence of a weaker," Robin Furneaux writes of the Indians' suffering during the rubber boom. Now the law of the jungle, or the law of history, had reasserted itself, and it was the tappers who had become the victims.

THE ALVES BOYS

The land in Acre that was going for practically nothing attracted not only big ranchers and multinationals, but also medium and small ones, all kinds of adventurers and frontier types — men who were on the run and were wanted in other states, who, like the gunslingers and bad men of the Wild West, left a trail of dead bodies in each new place they went to. Among them was the Alves da Silva family, three of whose members have been indicted for the murder of Chico Mendes. They were real mean country boys, like the James Gang of Missouri. The American cowboy was a direct offshoot of the Spanish-Mexican *vaquero,* so the modern Brazilian *vaqueiro,* who patterned himself after the cowboy of the *bangue-bangues* (the old American Westerns that are standard fare on Brazilian television), was the old *vaqueiro* come home again: he was a cultural back-cross, as it were. Alvarino Alves, one of Darli's brothers, particularly went in for the John Wesley Hardin look, with his luxuriant mustache, his jeans, cowboy boots, and straw Stetson. Chico described how the Alves boys would blow into Xapuri with their *pistoleiros* and swagger down the main drag, holding up traffic as if they owned the place. "One time we counted twenty-three of them together."

The Alveses were originally from Minas Gerais, and they were typical *mineiros* — devious, belligerent, tight with money. In 1959 they were living in a little place there called Ipanema. Sebastião Alves da Silva, who had twenty-six children by three women and adopted three more, was the head of the family. That year three of his sons, Darli, Alvarino, and David (who was gunned down there sometime afterward), allegedly shot a drover named Nequinha da Doce sixteen times, and his son six. Even Nequinha's horse received a hailstorm of lead. The fight was over a woman both Sebastião and Nequinha wanted.

According to the lurid biographies of the Alveses in the Brazilian press, after committing six other crimes, the family fled south to Paraná, where they settled in a little place called Umuarama. There they blew away one of their neighbors, Dirceu dos Santos, in a dispute over property lines, right in the bus station, and invited another neighbor, Acir Urizzi, who owned a sawmill, to the local red-light district to murder him. Their motive, according to the inquest on Urizzi's death, was "perversity." There are two theories about the murder of Urizzi: either it was a land dispute resolved in the usual manner, or Urizzi had been in favor of changing the name of the district of Umuarama, where they all lived, to Nova Jerusalem. The Alveses wanted to keep the old name, Heritage of the Mineiros. One of Sebastião's lovers said in her deposition that "the Alveses killed because they found it was good to kill."

Once again they found it advisable to relocate, this time to Acre, the half-made new frontier, blazing in more ways than one. In 1974 they bought a small spread outside Xapuri, a couple of thousand acres adjoining the mayor's ranch, and called it the Fazenda Paraná. Darli Alves was as prolific as his father, producing some thirty children. He left one of his women, Elpídia, in Paraná but brought two others, Natalina and Maria Zilde, and picked up two more locally. He installed them in separate houses on the ranch and visited them on alternate nights. Chiquinha, a neighbor's daughter, was sixteen when he seduced her and persuaded her to run away from home and live with him. By the time of his arrest for Chico's murder, she was twenty-two and had borne him three children. Margarete was twenty-three; Darli was thirty years older. The four women didn't get along, but Darli said if he ever caught them fighting he'd kill them. It was a Manson-like menage. Darli had them completely under his spell. All four told a reporter whom the *Gazeta*, one of the Rio Branco papers, sent out to the ranch that he was a fantastic lover. "You can't imagine what it's like with Darli in bed," Natalina raved. "He's like a wild bull, or a boy of fifteen who never had a woman before. Four, five times, one after the other. No woman can stand it. And you should see how he's hung." Natalina attributed his stamina to an aphrodisiac she prepared for him whose complicated recipe — the eggs of a certain tinamou, a game bird, prepared with numerous herbs — the *Gazeta* promised to reveal in its next edition, and did.

Once in Acre, the family continued its violent ways, hardly missing a beat. Darli became thick with Gaston Mota, the sadistic former *seringalista* who was now brokering the transfer of Acre to the ranchers. Mota had a dry goods–Brazil nut store in Brasiléia, and he was running goods to the Seringal Puerto Río, in Bolivia. He was also believed to be the head of the ranchers' "executive committee." He was the guy you went to when you wanted somebody taken care of. In 1977, with the help of Gaston, Darli was said to have massacred an entire family of tappers who refused to vacate his expanding ranch. The director of the Judicial Police came from the capital and arrested twelve of Darli's *pistoleiros* and Darli himself, as he was getting on the bus to Rio Branco. But the ranchers had good lawyers. The prisoners were released, and the crime wasn't even recorded.

The taste for killing was transmitted to the next generation, particularly Darli's sons Darci and Oloci, both now in their early twenties. A lot of the killing took place right on the ranch. The peons lived in fear. One has testified that he saw Darli's sons shoot a peon who was sleeping off the previous night's drunken *festa,* pour gasoline on the body, set it on fire, then chuck the remains into some tall grass.

Once on the ranch, the only way to leave was by running away. If you quit and asked for your pay, Darci and Oloci would ambush you before you got to the road. On October 9, 1988, the bodies of two Bolivian brothers, one a law student, the other a medical student, who are believed to have been running drugs for Darli, were found on the ranch, laid out one on top of the other in the form of a cross. Darci and Oloci were accused of killing them in a *queima de arquivo* as they pleaded for their lives. According to one story, they were sent to the ranch by Gaston to pick up a car and spent several days there. By the time they were finally found, they'd been so badly picked apart by vultures that a detailed postmortem was impossible. There was talk of a clandestine graveyard on the ranch. One peon claimed he was fishing in a pond there when he pulled out a skull.

The stories about the Alveses, most of them unverifiable, are legion. Two tappers went with Darli and were never seen again. Darli set fire to a peon named Walcir who had had the temerity to ask for his daughter's hand in marriage; he made a human *churrasco*, a barbecue, out of him. When Darci saw two people talking on the street in Xapuri, he would go up to them, pull out his revolver, and ask them what they were talking about.

Oloci has been charged with the 1988 killing of José Ribeiro, a colonist with a small farm, who had quarreled with him at a party in Xapuri. Ribeiro was drunk and didn't realize whom he had picked a fight with. Leaving the *festa* with a friend, he stopped to pee; his buddy kept walking. Shots from the bushes caught him in the chest. He tried to get up, but his assailant came out and shot him in the mouth.

Back in 1977 Darli's brother Tonico, who beat his peons and took their women whenever he wanted them, told one that he wanted his wife. The peon prepared an ambush and shot Tonico. The peon who was with Tonico, who tried to get a gun, was also shot, in the head. Then the ambusher turned himself in to the police. On his first day out of prison he was shot three times, and for good measure, his father had his nails torn out and was cut into pieces. Subsequently, relatives of the peon's killed Darli's nephew.

A soldier of the Civil Police killed Zé Campello, one of Darli's *pistoleiros,* in a shootout in 1986. The soldier was wounded, but he recovered and was later ambushed as he was going down the river to Rio Branco. Zé Campello's avengers put his body in a wrecked car to make it look like an accident.

One day when I was sitting on a stoop with Chico's uncle Joaquim watching carpenters put up the union's new cooperative, he said, "You want to know about Darli Alves? Talk to him." And he called over Zé Meireles, a short man in his forties who was wearing homemade rubber booties. "I worked four years for him," Meireles told me. "I was a cold meal [i.e., a hand]. I left 'cause things weren't right. My friends Vandico and Juraci were shotgunned in the plantation because they wanted their pay. The police came and took their bodies into town. I told Darli I wanted to leave. He said, 'All I have is five cruzeiros.' So I took what he owed me in merchandise, and he let me go. He always had a revolver. Whatever happened, you couldn't say anything. After I left, it got worse."

"Our friend Ademir Pipim, who lived here, stole a watch at the Fazenda Paraná," Joaquim told me. "Darli came and beat him up and took him away and we never saw him again. Alvarino had taken Pipim's wife, so he took the watch.''

VIOLENCE IN THE BACKLANDS

The Alves boys got away with so many gruesome murders because there was no prosecutor in Xapuri, or in any of the thirteen other judicial districts in the interior of Acre. And there were no prosecutors because only someone with a death wish would take the job. The judges believed in what the ranchers were doing. They espoused the same model of progress and belonged to the same tiny elite. The police were bought or scared. Indeed, as one local journalist told me, doing a stint with the police was the first step to becoming a rancher. It was an entry-level position in the hierarchy.

Darli and Alvarino's nephew Odilon was the clerk at the Civil Police station in Xapuri. Their brother Luis Garimpeiro was said to be a drug dealer with links to the death squad in the State Department of Public Safety. This squad allegedly had a blacklist of marginals, incorrigible criminals and other menaces to society; their hideously mutilated bodies were found from time to time in vacant lots and ditches on the outskirts of the capital. Chico Mendes was reportedly on the list. There was considerable overlap between the death squad and the ranchers' "executive committee," based in Brasiléia. Gaston Mota had done a stint with the police and retained close links with them. The arms- and drug-smuggling network he was believed to be part of used clandestine airstrips on ranches on both sides of the border and, according to the *Gazeta,* was linked with the Medellín cartel, in Colombia. Other members named by the paper included relatives of Darli's; a rancher in Brasiléia named Luis Assem; State Deputy Waldemar Bezerra, who has a ranch in Bolivia; and Raul Mendes, a colonel in the Bolivian army, who was also involved in car theft and allegedly had a mercenary army. One of the clandestine airstrips, the *Gazeta* claimed, was located on land belonging to a cousin of Darli's, Antônio Paraná, at kilometer 64 of the Cobija–Puerto Río Road, in Bolivia. Alvarino, who has been on the lam since September 1988, may be hiding there under the protection of Raul Mendes.

But the Alves boys were nothing special. The lawlessness in Acre was not an isolated phenomenon. It was nothing compared with what goes on in eastern Amazônia, in Pará, Goiás, Maranhão, where the inequity of the landholding pattern, the greed of the landed for more land, and the hunger of the landless spawn almost constant violence. Here, as José Carlos Castro, a defense attorney in Belém, put it, "death has become an insignificant and common occurrence, like a fruit falling from a tree." Indeed, the most violent place in all of Brazil is the so-called Bico do Papagaio, the Parrot's Beak, where Pará, Maranhão, and Goiás meet. One afternoon there in May 1986 Padre Jósimo Moraes Tavares, thirty-three, an indefatigable defender of the impoverished peasants, was shot on the steps of the building housing the Catholic church's Pastoral Commission for the Land, which monitors rural violence. A *pistoleiro* confessed to having been paid 50,000 cruzeiros for the hit (which, if my recollection is correct, was then around $10,000) and was tried and condemned to eighteen and a half years. This conviction, and that of another *pistoleiro* who also killed a priest, are the only ones that have been obtained in some sixteen hundred killings contracted by landowners since 1964; none of the *mandantes* who hired the killers has ever been sentenced. Victims have included not only poor rural workers and *posseiros* but also lawyers, union leaders, judges, state deputies, and Indians. On March 30, 1988, fourteen Tikuna Indians were shot in their canoes on the Solimões River (as the main channel of the Amazon is called between Manaus and Iquitos, Peru) by *pistoleiros* as they were going to testify about attacks by woodcutters who had invaded their reserve. In June 1986 the Order of Lawyers of Brazil concluded after an investigation that justice was completely lacking in the Bico do Papagaio.

The only unusual thing about Chico's murder, then, is that it attracted so much attention.

A detailed report on flagrant human rights violations in the Brazilian backlands published by Amnesty International a few months before Chico's murder concludes, "The campaign of intimidation and assassination developed by the ranchers is not only ignored but frequently helped by the authorities."

Edmundo Galdeno, a federal deputy from Goiás, who was paralyzed from the waist down by *pistoleiros,* made a study of guns for hire and discovered that there are several agencies in Goiânia, the capital, masquerading as law or real estate offices (and one whose business is "rural vigilance'' and that openly calls itself ''the solution''), where anybody can walk in and strike a deal with the agent. He keeps 60 percent of your fee, studies the routine and habits of the person you want killed, plans the hit, and hires the *pistoleiro.* There is even a table of prices: a union leader costs $500 to $1,200; a town councilman or lawyer, $1,500; a padre, $3,500 to $4,000; a judge, state deputy, mayor, or bishop, $25,000. Most of the clientele are *grileiros,* land speculators, and their targets are often rural workers and their leaders. According to Galdeno, the professional gun for hire is ''a solitary subject who demonstrates a certain equilibrium, is distrustful, cold, and calculating. He is much different from the casual *pistoleiro,* who works on his boss's ranch and is a known figure in the locale where he acts, making the law of the strongest prevail.'' Different from the Alves boys and their crew, though also poor in origin, the hired gun lives high for a while after fulfilling a good contract. He is always moving from the police, looking for work. Sometimes these killers come from abroad, like the Argentine Ricardo G., nicknamed Cadito, age twenty-nine, who lives clandestinely in Rio and prefers to do contracts in the North. ''The work is quick and well paid,'' he explained in a recent interview for the newspaper *O Globo.* ''I don't kill women or children, and I don't kill for hatred or revenge. I do a service.''

It is the *mandante* who orders the murder who has the motivation and desire for revenge. More important targets — a judge, a newspaper editor, a bishop who is really messing things up for the *grileiro* — are often subjected to a sadistic twist: the *anúncio.*

The *anúncio* is found not only in Brazil; it is a Latin practice, apparently of Arab origin. Gabriel García Márquez's *Chronicle of a Death Foretold* tells of a man who has been *anunciado* in a community of Syrian merchants in Colombia. The Sicilians, who acquired many Arab customs during the long Saracen occupation, will stuff a dead canary in the mouth of an assassinated stool pigeon or leave one in the car or mailbox of someone who is thinking of going to the police.

The pattern of violence, intimidation, and impunity in Acre is also pan-Brazilian and pan-Latin. Since 1981 more than two hundred judges, magistrates, and judicial aides in Colombia, for instance, have been killed by employees of the drug cartels. Monica de Grieff, a recent Colombian justice minister who has since taken sanctuary in Florida, was told, ''Remember, you are a mother. We can kill your son.'' This is reminiscent of things Darli Alves reportedly has been saying from prison: "I don't think the authorities are going to do anything to me, because they know they have families"; and, as he reportedly said to a local bishop, trying to make a deal: "Get me out of here, and I'll tell my men not to kill you."

THE MOVEMENT IS BORN

By the end of the 1970s Acre had become, in the words of a reporter from the newspaper *Folha do São Paulo,* "a state in agony." Big banks and holding companies, consortiums of investors, had bought up huge tracts of the forest and were starting to burn them off. The Banco Real, according to his article, picked up 500,000 acres; the Grupo Bradesco, 750,000; and the Grupo Atalla, 1.3 million. One group of Caxinaua Indians was expelled from its traditional homeland after the National Indian Foundation, the agency supposedly in charge of protecting them, issued "negative certificates" saying they weren't there so that the Companhia Novo Oeste could move in with bulldozers and chain saws. Twenty-five thousand acres were being cleared annually in the municipality of Xapuri alone. Three hundred and twenty thousand people — displaced by 130 *paulistas* — were living in the state without the right to land, and there was so much violence that "the smell of gunpowder was in the air."

Chico struggled alone through the early seventies. His options were limited. He had no firepower and was opposed to violent confrontation in any event. But he could persuade the tappers to stop paying rent to the *seringalista,* a very effective ploy that put the ball in the boss's court, in that he had to prove ownership to land to which he usually didn't have clear title in order to continue demanding rent. Another of Chico's techniques was to encourage the tappers to sell en masse rather than singly, and directly to the middleman who supplied the bosses. This was dangerous. People had been set on fire for less. Just as Chico was organizing his legal battle to liberate the tappers, the ranchers came along and bought up the rubber estates. Suddenly the bosses were out of the picture. The tappers were freed, but it was like going from the frying pan into the fire. At least the *seringalista* had some respect for the forest.

The first leader of the tappers' movement was not Chico Mendes, but

Wilson Pinheiro, Chico's second mentor. As with Euclides Távora, the information about Pinheiro is scant, beyond the fact that he was a local tapper from Brasiléia. How he got his political ideas, started thinking about unions and resistance, is not known. The church may have played a role. In response to the growing rural violence, the Catholic church's Pastoral Commission for the Land got CONTAG, the National Confederation of Agricultural Workers, to visit the state. The CONTAG representatives began to identify local leaders like Pinheiro and to inform them of their squatters' rights under the land statute. Pinheiro began to get through to some of the tappers, to get them to see that they didn't have to lose their homes, their way of life, and everything they'd worked for, if they stood up to the ranchers. In 1975 Pinheiro founded the first chapter of the Rural Workers' Union in Acre.

And stand up was literally what the tappers did. Pinheiro devised an obvious but brilliantly effective tactic that became known as the *empate*. An *empate* in chess is a draw, so perhaps in this situation it could be translated as a standoff. But it really was a blockade, a human wall. Chico has been credited with inventing the *empate*, but in fact it was Pinheiro's concept. Pinheiro's *empates* were occasionally confrontational, the demonstrators sometimes armed with machetes and shotguns. Chico's *empates* were more pacific. He decided the *empate* could be done with women and children, too. It was classic passive resistance: Chico took the somnolent passivity of the tappers and turned it around. There is no evidence that either Chico or Pinheiro had heard of Gandhi or Martin Luther King, Jr., sit-ins or nonviolent resistance. The *empate* was something Pinheiro came up with intuitively, entirely on his own.

When Chico heard about a part of the forest that was about to be cleared, he would round up the families of tappers who lived in the vicinity and get them to form a wall on the edge of the land so that the *pistoleiros*, and the police the ranchers had hired to see that everything went smoothly, wouldn't dare to shoot. Meanwhile he would walk the line, gently reassuring his *companheiros*, "Don't be afraid. Nothing's going to happen." In one of his last interviews he reckoned that from 1975 on, "we organized forty-five *empates*. About four hundred of us were arrested and about forty were tortured, and a few were killed, but we succeeded in keeping more than three million hectares of the forest from being destroyed. Thirty of our blockades failed and fifteen worked, but it was worth it."

Francisco de Assis, Chico's brother, remembered the first *empate*, at the Seringal Sante Fé, on the *fazenda* of Jorge Horácio, in 1976. "I was thirteen. There were forty tappers, none of them armed. That night everybody went to talk with the foreman of the *fazenda* to ask him to stop the clearing. The next day, we had the *empate*. Wilson started it. Maybe he learned about it from fugitive revolutionaries in the forest."

By now the tappers were more receptive to the idea of organizing, and Chico threw himself into the movement. The Rural Workers' Union, or STR, welcomed not only tappers, but also poor colonists who lived by a combination of farming, fishing, and husbandry. The padre in Brasiléia was a member of the Albanian wing of the Brazilian Communist Party and very supportive of the workers; but it was a different story in Xapuri, where the polyglot Padre José Maria Carneiro was hobnobbing with the ranchers and reputedly informing for the secret police. Chico learned that there were good priests and bad priests. But despite Padre José's denunciations of him and intimidation by the police, Chico succeeded in setting up not only a local of the STR in Xapuri, but also in being elected town councilman, then president of the Chamber of Deputies. These victories did not ingratiate him with the ranchers. In December 1979 four hooded men bundled him into a car in Rio Branco, beat him nearly senseless, and dumped him on a back road.

By 1977 there were chapters of the STR in Rio Branco and Sena Madureira as well, and three years later 60 percent of the municipalities had them and 20,000 tappers had joined. In 1980 ten thousand tappers and colonists marched on the cathedral in Rio Branco when INCRA, the government agency in charge of agrarian reform, inexplicably reneged on its promise to relocate 5,000 displaced rural families on a 408,000-hectare area that it had appropriated, some seventy kilometers outside the capital, and sold the land instead to timber interests.

Wilson Pinheiro had become a real threat: the law and all the petitions the tappers had signed had not worked, but the *empates* had. That year Pinheiro was gunned down on the porch of the STR union hall in Brasiléia. The two *pistoleiros* were identified, and even the price of the hit was learned, but nothing was done to prosecute the crime. The only policeman who showed any interest in doing so was fired.

The tappers wanted blood for Pinheiro's. Fifteen hundred of them queued up to swear vengeance, placing their hands on his corpse. Chico pleaded against violence — one of his favorite sayings was "I don't believe in bodies'' — but the tappers took matters in their own hands and went out to the ranch of Nilão de Oliveira, whom they believed to have been one of the *mandantes,* tried him, found him guilty, and executed him on the spot with thirty rounds. This time the wheels of justice turned with amazing speed. Hundreds of tappers were imprisoned and tortured. Some had their fingernails yanked out with pliers.

The ranchers tell a different story. ''The death of Wilson Pinheiro,'' one of them told me, ''has never been fully explained, but whoever killed him was a friend of his, for reasons of internal politics in the Rural Workers' Union. The national leaders of the PT, the Workers' Party, said the murder should be paid with blood, and the tappers went to the street to get the first rancher who passed. They got Nilão de Oliveira, a kid of thirty; he didn't even own a ranch. He was caretaker of the Fazenda Promessão, and they killed him with the greatest cruelty, cutting off his penis and stuffing it in his mouth. Osmarino Amâncio Rodrigues [one of the tappers' leaders, who has filled the void left by Chico] was one of the killers.''

The rancher's version of what happened may well be disinformation, to which both sides of the conflict, as I would discover, frequently resorted. The way he tried to gain sympathy by emphasizing the sadistic manner in which Nilão was killed was particularly suspect, in the tradition, perhaps, of attributing cannibalism to the Indians to justify exploiting them.

Pinheiro went down as the first martyr to the tappers' cause. But other than having a foundation for political studies named for him by the PT, he won no fame. No fund was set up for his widow, who lives in misery, cooking at peon camps on ranches between Brasiléia and Xapuri. Her oldest daughter, Edia, has been interned three times for mental disturbances, and another daughter makes her living as a prostitute. In a recent interview Pinheiro's widow said she was considering forbidding further use of his name unless the family got something out of it.

I remember asking Chico Mendes's brother Assis, ''Why did Chico become so famous, and not Wilson Pinheiro?'' Julio Cesar, my young novelist friend, with whom I was discussing the same subject, had a good answer: ''Perhaps Chico was no greater a leader than Wilson, but the greatness of a man is the man himself and his historical moment, which belongs to him and no one else, and can't be taken away.''

CHANGES IN THE CHURCH

In the Brazilian system, the church is the moral check, and the military is the check against chaos. When one force gets out of hand, the opposing force eventually will rally to restore balance. This is what happened in the first, brutally oppressive years of the military revolution, during the mid-1960s: the church asserted itself, and the poor won a new ally. There had always been an element in the church that advocated active participation in the struggle against social injustice. The Jesuits had been particularly active on the natives' behalf. In Paraguay they proselytized the Tupi-Guarani with music, teaching them to make their own instruments and play Vivaldi in chamber ensembles while the jungle teemed over the wall. In Mexico there were several mass executions of padres who got too involved with the problems of the poor. The Mexicans have always had a deep ambivalence about the church, and South America has always been the place where an idealistic young Italian, say, who aspires to the priesthood could find eternal glory doing something truly meaningful.

In 1968 the Peruvian priest and theologian Gustavo Gutiérrez unveiled what he called the theology of liberation, which shook the church as it hadn't been since the Reformation. Another of the new movement's articulators, Francisco Leonardo Boff, was silenced by the Pope for eleven months. Liberation theology was the gospel of earthly salvation. "It's a practical vision," Anna Rosa Fioretta, an Italian volunteer with the Lay Movement of Latin America who is involved in the tappers' and Indians' struggle in Acre, told me. "The living faith must be linked to the reality of man, and the reality of Brazil in both the country and the city is that most of the people are wretchedly deprived and exploited." Padre Luis Ceppi, the current padre of Xapuri and a liberation theologian, cited John, chapter 10, verse 10: "Christ said, 'I have come so that they may have life,' and that means not just alms and charity but support of popular class movements so that the weakest can have a full economic, political, social, and religious life through their own organization."

Those who have a dim view of the church in Latin America argue that its new radicalism arose because it was losing ground to Protestant fundamentalist sects and hence had to start relating more closely to the local people, to get new blood to make the sacrifice of celibacy.

The main organ of the church involved in the fight for agrarian reform was the Pastoral Commission for the Land (CPT), founded in Goiânia in 1975, as the land conflicts in Amazônia intensified, to secure basic rights for the rural peasantry and also to monitor and expose violence. It works closely with the Pastoral Commission for the Indians and the Commission for the Defense of Human Rights. CPT headquarters in Goiânia uses a computer to keep track of land-related killings. The names are listed under three categories: those who have been *anunciados* (received death threats), those who have survived attempts on their life, and those who have been killed. "This list is updated daily. People are constantly being transferred from one category to another — from the escaped list to the dead list, like Chico Mendes," said José do Carmo, one of the eight members of the commission in Goiânia, a week after the murder.

The diocese of Rio Branco, which is responsible for eastern Acre, has twelve or thirteen padres, and it adopted the teachings of liberation theology in the early seventies. Old conservatives like Padre José were replaced by young radicals with Marxist, even Stalinist, ideologies. Dom Moacyr Grechi, originally Italian but raised in the southern Brazilian state of Santa Catarina, became the bishop of Rio Branco in 1972. He was a member of the same order as Leonardo Boff and his brother Clodovis, two of the leading exponents of the new theology. A missionary order, the Servants of Mary of Italy, has been working in Acre since 1920. "In 1973 the violence started to become serious," Dom Moacyr told me. "Investors came and, with the greatest facility, took land by fraud and force. The police were corrupt. There was no union. We favored the union. In 1975 it was founded here in the cathedral with the army surrounding us."

Xapuri had good organization and a dense population of tappers, and the second chapter of the STR, founded by Chico Mendes, grew fast. At one time it had four thousand members. Now it is in decline, with only six hundred paying members. At the end of the seventies there were two padres in Xapuri, Tavio Destro, a Brazilian, and Claudio Valone, an Italian. They were good friends of Chico's. They allowed the church to be used for training sessions, seminars on union organization, rap groups on how far to take the struggle. Officially, of course, the church could not endorse violence.

Dom Moacyr worked closely with Chico. It may be to him that Chico referred when he acknowledged in one interview the "important but hesitant support of the church." "Chico was flexible, not rigid in his positions," the bishop told me. "He was never fanatical. It was a very localized, organized struggle, and it evolved from the struggle for land to the struggle for nature, and brought together the Indian and the tapper, who for more than a century had been irreconcilable enemies. Chico came here a lot. Every time, he said, 'I'm in danger.' I tended not to give much importance to such statements because that's what he'd been saying for ten years. So when he was actually killed, it shook me."

In the mideighties Clodovis Boff began to spend his several months of summer vacation from the Catholic University of Rio de Janeiro with the tappers in Acre. Dom Moacyr gave me a copy of a book called *God and Man in the Green Hell,* which Father Clodovis worked up from his diary for the summer of 1979–80. Father Clodovis was impressed with the depth of the tappers' souls. "They suffer great dramas in a silence more profound than the forest and the rivers familiar to them," he wrote.

> When one travels along the rivers and passes before the house of the *seringueiro* it is not rare to notice on the top of the bank of the river, or under a tree, a little bench. . . . At night when the *seringueiro* comes back from the forest he is accustomed to sit there alone contemplating the river, looking to the sky or the forest before him and letting his thoughts go wherever they want.

Some 800 to 1,000 "groups of evangelation" had already been formed in Acre by then to preach the new theology. Each group had ten to fifteen members and a monitor. Chico Mendes was the monitor of a group in Xapuri. There was a lot of discussion at the meetings of these groups about how to proceed, how to organize a popular front, how to play party politics, about the advisability of armed resistance. Recently, a hundred armed workers had stood up against the ranchers. The confrontation was called Operation Get the Ranchers. It is unclear whether it resulted in any shots being fired or any casualties.

Some were in favor of using arms, some were against. But finally "everyone agreed there was no other way," Father Clodovis wrote.

"This shows that the use of force is always a problem for the conscience, but sometimes it imposes itself. The circumstance produces the wish for it."

Father Clodovis would start one of his classes by drawing a pyramid. At its apex he would write, "Rich: 5 percent," in the middle, "Middle Class: 15 percent," and at the bottom, "Poor: 80 percent." The diagram would elicit reactions from the tappers like "The strength of the rich is their wealth, the strength of the poor is their numbers"; "The poor are at the bottom, sustaining the other classes"; "The middle class is more with the rich than with the poor."

Behind the local big shots, he would explain, were the real oppressors, the real enemy. "The big foreign companies called multinationals, which dominate Brazil, are about a thousand: Ford, Volkswagen, Phillips, Coca-Cola, General Electric, Daniel Ludwig's huge project on the Jarí River."

He would ask the tappers, "How is imperialism, the domination by a strong people of a weak one, presented in the Bible? The imperialisms which Israel suffered are compared to horrible beasts: Babylon was the lion, Medea the bear, Persia, a panther, Greece, a wild beast, Rome, a combination of all of them. And Brazil has suffered three imperialisms: Portugal, England, and now, principally, the United States — like the caiman, the anteater, and the spotted jaguar."

Father Clodovis also preached on the radio:

Happy are those who fight for justice.
Happy are those who unite with the people.
Happy are those who go to the side of the oppressed.
Happy are those who struggle to change the world.
Happy are those who die without seeing the results of their efforts.

There are two central commandments of the oppressed, he told his listeners: "One. Do not conform with the situation of oppression. Two. Do not conform with purely individual promotion and success. Or, in positive terms: struggle, and struggle together."

No wonder the ranchers thought it was the church that was at the bottom of their problems.

"In Xapuri last year," Father Clodovis wrote,

we were having a training session when we had trouble with the "Philistines" of today, and their Goliath. In the convent where we were doing the training half a dozen armed soldiers came in and immobilized us. They said this is subversive, they wanted to know who were the leaders, and the monitors said, all of us. They wanted names and everyone refused. They took the projector and slides and both of the padres to the police station, where for two hours they gave testimony. A few days later Padre Claudio was punched in the face by a candidate of the ARENA party, knocked down right in the plaza. The candidate thinks the padre is campaigning for the opposition. The people revolt and want to "clean the honor of the padre." They come from the depths of the forest with shotguns in their hands because they never heard that such an insult could happen. But the padres calm them down. They give Christ as the model: turn the other cheek.

"It's a lot worse today than it was before," Dom Moacyr declared in 1979, after the arrival of big companies like Bordon Meatpacking Company, which tried to clear a ten-thousand-hectare ranch in Xapuri but met with stiff resistance from Chico and his *empates*. "Precapitalism had a face. The tapper and the colonist knew who the exploiters were, and they had faces. Today the person who is exploited doesn't know whom to go to for hope. It's a savage capitalism without a face, where police and women are the cheapest commodities."

In the Acrean Ministry of Justice more than twenty thousand claims arising from land conflict were awaiting attention, and the offices of CONTAG had received more than ten thousand complaints of oppression, exploitation, and dispossession by the *paulistas*. The ten thousand Indians in Acre, the last remnants of once-powerful nations like the Campa, Apuriná, Culina, Jamamadi, Jaminaua, Nukini, Caxinaua, Marinaua, Yauanaua, Paumari, Canamari, Machineri, and Caxarari, were at the mercy of the local fat cats.

CHICO TAKES OVER THE MOVEMENT

Chico is mentioned briefly a few times in *God and Man in the Green Hell*. Father Clodovis described him as a "popular town councilman" who improvises at a rally of the opposition before the governor's palace in Rio Branco and, later, as president of the Xapuri municipal chamber, raising "the level of the debate . . . speaking of the problems of the nation." He is thirty-five, "still young."

It is "the brave Wilson de Souza Pinheiro" who emerges as the leader of the tappers — "tall, thin, tanned by the sun, toughened by hardship, impressive with his conviction." Pinheiro addresses a training session in Brasiléia at which slides are shown by the church's Commission for the Defense of Human Rights. "For four years we've been fighting in the union at Brasiléia, using *empates* to fight the sale of the land," he says. He tells how in 1973 he went with some men to stand up against the *pistoleiros* at Boca do Acre. "Others were scared to go. They said we'll all be killed. There'll be so many widows it'll be easy to choose. But we went and came back victorious."

Pinheiro describes how he goes day and night to the *colocações* and never tires of telling the tappers that they themselves are responsible for their misery. "But many don't want to hear this, they believe what the ranchers tell them, they don't have faith, they prefer to trust the boss, who fleeces them." I myself was a *seringueiro,* he tells them, and I was expelled from my *colocação*.

Father Clodovis's reaction to the murder of this "prophet": "The people who lose their guides are also the people who will generate others."

After the revenge killing of Nilão de Oliveira, it was open season on the tappers. When Chico emerged from ninety days of hiding, the police were waiting for him. He was jailed and tortured three times with electric shocks. After his release he resumed union activities, which had died down in his absence. As the president of the union in Xapuri, he now had the responsibility of leading the tappers squarely on his shoulders.

The violence continued. *Pistoleiros* killed Jesus Matias, a promising young town councilman for the Workers' Party, and two others in the movement. There were five attempts on Chico's own life. The only lull in the persecution of the tappers occurred after the union published a list of ranchers who would be targets of revenge if another of their *compa-nheiros* was killed.

The best news was that Chico had found love again. On his visits to the Gadelhas he couldn't help noticing what a beautiful young woman his former pupil Ilzamar had become. "It wasn't until 1982, when I was seventeen, that we became lovers,'' Ilza told me as we sat in the house he bought her on the Rua Doutor Batista de Moraes just a few months before the murder. ''Three years later we were married. Come into the kitchen,'' she said to me. ''There's something I want to tell you alone.'' We sat at the kitchen table, and for a moment, looking up at the ceiling and remembering whatever it was she wanted to tell me, she became as happy and excited as a child before Christmas. Then she sighed and apparently thought better of confiding such an intimate thing to a stranger. ''*Ave Maria,* he was such a sweet, decent man, no matter how tired or worried he was. He had no salary, but he always did everything so that we wouldn't lack food or medicine. I will remember most his love of the children.

''Fifteen days after the wedding,'' she went on, ''he left, and after that, in the six years we were married, we never had more than eight days together. So we were always on honeymoon. It never became dull routine. There was always that immense love.''

THE LARGER MOSAIC

Chico and his *companheiros* were unaware that the devastation they were fighting against, the local deforestation in the municipality of Xapuri, was part of a much larger mosaic of destruction. In other parts of the Amazon Valley one effort after another was made to conquer the wilderness or at least to establish a viable modern presence, and each met with disaster.

The first disaster was the colonization project along the Trans-Amazon Highway, which failed because the government proved incapable of carrying it out and because the expected migration from the Northeast didn't materialize. The feedback from those who tried it wasn't positive; the attrition rate among the colonists was tremendous. By December 1974, only 5,717 families of *nordestino* homesteaders, whose average size was six, had shown up; the projected migration had fallen short by a factor of more than ten. Four years later there were only 7,674 households along the road. The highway has yet to reach its destination, Peru and the Pacific. Long sections are impassable in the rainy season, and its denuded fringes are for the most part abandoned wasteland.

There were many health problems for the transplanted *nordestinos.*

Anopheles mosquitoes bred like mad in the backed-up culvert ponds and began to transmit resistant strains of malaria, which didn't respond to any of the usual medications. Dysentery carried off a lot of children, and several mysterious local epidemics broke out, like the hemorrhagic syndrome of Altamira, transmitted by blackflies, which provoked spontaneous nosebleeds and, in two cases, death. The colonists were ravaged with worms: roundworms, whipworms, hookworms. Hookworm larvae enter through the soles of the feet. Children, who ran around barefoot most of the time — their footwear was generally saved for Sundays and special occasions — were particularly vulnerable. Signs emphasizing the importance of wearing shoes were ignored by all but the few who could read.

But the biggest and most traumatic disappointment, the final blow, was the quality of the soil along the highway. No detailed soil maps had been compiled before inviting the migration, and most of the soils proved poor. Everyone had presumed that the soils of Amazônia must be very rich to support such exuberant vegetation. Even the great nineteenth-century British naturalist Henry Walter Bates, who spent eleven years in the Amazon Valley, made this assumption. "The country [of Pará] is covered with forests, and the soil fertile in the extreme, even for a tropical country," he reported in 1876. But in reality the soils of Amazônia, and of tropical countries in general, tend to be thin and poor. The lushness of the rain forest results from a delicate balancing act: the forest exists mainly on water and air, on the frenetic recycling of nutrients and moisture from the leaf litter and decaying wood on the forest floor back up into the trees. Once the trees are taken down, the entire system collapses. The soil soon shrivels up in the sun and blows away, or is washed away by rain. After two or three plantings, nothing comes up. Overgrazed pasture turns into a barren, brick-hard wasteland or is "sandified" into semidesert after five or ten years.

Because the expected hordes did not materialize, the Trans-Amazon Highway remained like a "hairline fracture" in the sea of trees, in the geographer Nigel Smith's description, and the burning was not extensive enough to be alarming. For INCRA, the National Institute of Colonization and Agrarian Reform, which located the settlers, clearing and burning the land was part of the contract, a prerequisite to obtaining a definitive title. Smith observed the process:

As soon as the rainy season ends, settlers begin clearing under-
brush . . . prior to felling trees . . . in July or August. The
slash is left to dry for a couple of months before it is fired in
September or October. During the burning season, smoke taints
the sky with a characteristic whiskey-colored haze. The time of
the burns is always a tense period; early rains can soak the slash
and render a good burn impossible. . . . Poorly burned logs and
branches are stacked and fired again.

Very little of the timber was used. Most of the trees went up in smoke.
There were only eight sawmills on the longest stretch of completed highway, from Marabá to Itaituba. But increasingly, as the colonists failed
to materialize, INCRA sold the land to large corporations, which had
the capital and equipment for inflicting more efficient and extensive devastation.

The real victims of the highway were the Indians in its path. Although
the forest was advertised as a "Land Without People," thousands of
Indians, like the Arara and the Parakanas, had in fact been living there
for centuries. But Indians did not count. They were not people. When
civilized and semicivilized Brazilians talk about the Amazon they often
say, "*Lá é terra de ninguém. Só tem índio.*" — "It's a no-man's-land.
There are only Indians."

According to one investigation, the proposed highways of the National Integration Program had been routed through 96 of the 171 known
tribal locations in the Amazon basin, even though the Indians' lands are
supposed to be inviolate. Of these 96 tribes, at least 45 had little or no
contact with people from the modern world, and 11 had populations of
fewer than a hundred. Where the highways were built, the contact was
sudden and devastating. The Indians succumbed to such diseases as measles, and even the common cold, to which they had no resistance. Cultural trauma was another cause of death. The Indians were so totally
demoralized by the gigantic yellow machinery, the graders and cats and
earth movers, that they simply lost the will to live. The women were
forced into prostitution, and the men soon acquired a hopeless craving
for the oblivion of *cachaça,* the fiery Brazilian rum. Wherever a road
went through, this pattern was repeated.

THE GRAND SCHEME

A few foreign biologists expressed concern about the Trans-Amazon Highway. One, fearing its impact on the extraordinary diversity of life in the forest, labeled it the highway to extinction. The newspaper *Estado de São Paulo* called it in 1979 "the longest, poorest, and most useless highway on the face of the earth." But these were small voices in the wilderness, and the powers that be in Brasília didn't want to hear them (they still don't). Brazil was geared up for the big, glorious push: it was arriving among the superpowers, and it didn't want to hear that its grand plans for Amazônia were folly. Besides, there was a lot of money at stake, and the big companies that were getting great deals in the region exerted considerable political and economic pressure.

The game was speculation, tax dodge, inflation hedge; the cattle were purely cosmetic. The more Brazil's inflation approached hyperinflation, the more valuable tangible things like real estate became. In 1979 alone, cleared pasture in Mato Grosso rose 38 percent in value. The land was a commodity, like gold bullion or a rare stamp, as the ecologist Philip M. Fearnside has put it, and "recent land speculation in Amazonian pasture lands . . . probably could be counted among the most profitable investments on earth."

Between 1967 and 1977 SUDAM, the Superintendency for the Development of Amazônia, approved fiscal incentives for 355 ranches in the North totaling 7.8 million hectares. By 1985 the area approved for development had risen to 8.4 million hectares. The most recent tally has 631 ranches, whose average size is 24,000 hectares, given the go-ahead by SUDAM. The biggest ones were Liquigas (678,000 hectares), Suia-Missu (560,000), Volkswagen A.G. (139,000), and the Armour-Swift/King Ranch (72,000). Most of these were Brazilian subsidiaries of multinational corporations. The income from their Amazonian projects was not repatriated abroad, to foreigners, but went instead to Brazilians in the South. So the part of the destruction that these projects were responsible for was not so much the result of direct neocolonialism as of endo-neocolonialism, not so much of imperialism as of subimperialism. The most amazing fact of all was that each of these vast ranches was expected to give jobs to an average of only forty-eight permanent employees.

As it became clear that the Trans-Amazon Highway, the centerpiece of the National Integration Program, was foundering, other arteries of the road system were stopped halfway through, abandoned in the middle of nowhere for technical or financial reasons. The Transpantaneira, an ambitious attempt to cross the Pantanal do Mato Grosso, the biggest swamp in the world, was given up a short way into it. The Perimetral Norte, which was intended to run the entire northern boundary of the Brazilian Amazon, only got as far as the Yanomamo Indian village of Wakatauteri.

One of the key factors holding Brazil back was that very little oil had yet been discovered within the national territory, so the country was at the mercy of OPEC. This unfortunate situation led to further massive devastation in the Amazon as a frenzied campaign to achieve energy self-sufficiency by alternative means was launched. Early in the eighties I was flown by the governor of Mato Grosso's public relations man to a new city called Sinop that had been hacked out of the still largely undisturbed forest in the northern part of the state. Its raison d'être was to produce ethanol fuel, to which Brazilian cars were being converted. Colonists were being enticed from the South to clear the forest and grow manioc, which was fermented into ethanol in a fantastic, futuristic factory in the middle of the jungle. What became of Sinop I haven't been able to learn. It was far from the markets for the fuel, and with the discovery of oil at the mouth of the Amazon a few years ago the ethanol program is being dismantled. The Amazon has a way of swallowing up even well-thought-out projects, especially such high-tech ones.

Projeto RADAM had concluded that if the Amazon and its tributaries, which pour one fifth of the world's fresh water into the Atlantic — twelve times the usual discharge of the Mississippi — were harnessed, Brazil could become the "Saudi Arabia of hydropower." And so the most elaborate hydroelectric grid in history — with at least a hundred dam sites and a combined potential of at least a hundred megawatts — was drawn up, and construction began on a frenzied schedule. The largest dam was the eight-million-kilowatt Tucuruí Dam, on the Tocantins River, which when completed would be the fourth-largest dam in the world: twelve miles long, with a reservoir into which Grenada, Barbados, and Martinique could fit with room to spare.

The purpose of Tucuruí was not only to produce hydroelectricity for the Northeast, but also to attract industry, to help convert Amazônia from a teeming wilderness to a humming industrial hub. Among other things, it would provide power to a $5 billion railway being built simultaneously from the world's richest iron ore deposit, in the Carajás Mountains, to the seaport of São Luís, in Maranhão. Four Japanese financial groups had agreed to contribute together 10 percent of the railway's cost, American banks 5 percent, and the World Bank and the European Economic Community 7 and 10 percent respectively, in return getting pig iron from the mountains at "favorable prices." The dam would also power a $12.6 billion joint Japanese and Brazilian aluminum smelter and refinery under construction in Belém. Huge oceangoing freighters bringing the bauxite down from Dutch, Canadian, and American mines on the Trombetas River became an incongruous but increasingly common sight against the forested banks of the Lower Amazon.

But there was a big problem with the hydroelectric plan. Most of the Amazon basin is dead flat. Trees, other vegetation, and silt soon clogged the new dams' reservoirs. The water became anoxic and began to stink of hydrogen sulfide. The fish died, the dams' turbines were corroded. The worst disaster was the Balbina Dam, a joint Brazilian-French project expected to supply much of the energy for the fast-growing industrial free-trade zone of Manaus. It flooded an area the same size as Tucuruí but, because of the shallow gradient, provided only 4 percent as much power at more than four times the price. The dams also displaced more Indians. In her book, *In the Rainforest,* Catherine Caufield writes of two groups of Paracana who "reacted to the disruption of their lives in a way which is classic in Indian cultures. They chose to commit collective suicide. They stopped hunting, planting crops, and having babies; they simply waited to die."

The Samuel Dam was built to provide power to Porto Velho, the capital of Rondônia, but giant armadillos chewed through its dike, and the dam burst. (Perhaps opponents of the hydroelectric plan should train a brigade of armadillo ecoterrorists.)

Another grandiose scheme, the Grande Carajás Project, will, if it is ever completed, extend over an area the combined size of France and Great Britain — one sixth of legal Amazônia, displacing twelve thousand Indians. There will be thirty mines, which over the next decade are projected to require ten million tons of wood from the forest for charcoal to produce the pig iron, and ten new cities. The price tag for Grande Carajás is $62 billion.

But the most amazing project of all was Daniel K. Ludwig's, on the river Jarí. The generals sold Ludwig in 1967 a patch of forest the size of Connecticut and Rhode Island combined — 4.03 million acres — for 75 cents an acre and gave him carte blanche as far as what he did there. The reclusive billionaire, an intimate of Nixon and prominent Mafiosi, had started as a bootlegger and casino owner, then built up a fleet of oil tankers registered in Liberia and Panama whose Pakistani crews were paid only room and board. By now he was in his eighties, and he was in a hurry. Jarí became the old man's obsession. He kept changing managers, booking a row of seats in economy class on the New York–Belém flight, and paying surprise visits to the project. When a forester explained that it was a "surprisingly fragile ecosystem," Ludwig didn't want to hear about it. "Hell's bells! I spend five million a year to whack down the wild growth that springs up among our planted trees."

Ludwig's approach was multifaceted, a total rape. Convinced that a shortage of pulpwood would grip the world by the end of the century, he replaced the forest with plantations of the fast-growing Asian tree *Gmelina arborea* and had a seventeen-story pulp mill towed over from Japan. The mill passed through the Panama Canal and after three months at sea finally reached the Amazon. But in 1974 the *Gmelinas* were attacked by unidentified caterpillars and a virulent fungus, so Ludwig had them removed and replaced with Caribbean pine and eucalyptus.

The land contained a windfall: the world's third-richest deposits of kaolin, a rare clay used for glazing porcelain and an ingredient in Kaopectate and high-quality paper. But even so, Jarí continued to go deeper in the red, and Ludwig had to dismantle his empire to keep it going. He sold his desalination plant in Baja California, his orange plantation in Panama, his chain of Prince's Resorts, and part of his fleet of supertankers. In fourteen years — until he was forced to sell Jarí to a consortium of Brazilian companies at a huge loss — he poured a billion dollars into the struggling venture.

Ludwig was characteristically secretive about the project, and by the end of the seventies the Brazilian press, shocked to learn that such a huge area of the country was in American hands, started to wonder what was going on up there. A few journalists penetrated the operation and reported that Jarí had its own police and jails and that the workers were paid in chits redeemable at the company store. They had to sign up for

a year. If they tried to escape before their contract was up, they were
shot. It was the familiar Amazonian system of debt peonage.

BRAZIL BECOMES A DEBT PEON

There is no evidence that the United States or the multilateral lending
institutions it largely controls deliberately loaned Brazil so much money
over the past two decades that it could never pay it back, thus creating
a macroeconomic situation remarkably like the debt peonage of the rubber tapper to the *seringalista* or, as a Latin American scholar once described it to me, "a Monopoly game in which one side has all the
hotels." But there is a widespread feeling in Brazil that the loans were
a conspiracy to keep Brazil down and its resources flowing north at cut-
rate prices. One editorial compared Brazil to an innocent young woman
who had been knocked up.

At the time of the 1964 revolution Brazil's foreign debt was $5 bil-
lion. By 1980 it had gone up to $56 billion, and the service on the debt
alone was $13 billion. By 1983 it was $85 billion, and Brazil was in too
deep, on a treadmill, slipping backward. Currently it is something like
$114 billion — the highest of any Third World country.

When I started coming to Brazil, in the last half of the seventies, the
president was General Ernesto Geisel, and the country was modernizing
on a crash schedule. Each time I returned to Rio or Brasília there had
been a spurt of new construction; the progress was dramatically visible.
These were the golden Geisel years, the years of the Brazilian Miracle.
The economy was growing 8 to 10 percent annually, and American
banks were falling over themselves to lend money to Brazil. (I remember
being offered ten thousand dollars by Chase Manhattan Bank to whip up
a forty-page profile of Brazil to be read on the plane by a group of
prospective investors the bank was flying down.)

An American investment banker who specializes in Third World debt
rescheduling assured me there was no conspiracy to drown Brazil in
debt. "It was just pure greed — on the part of the loan-brokers at the
banks, who got bonuses for each deal they put together — on the part
of the politicians in Brasília, who commonly took ten percent off the top
of every deal they packaged and had no qualms about sending the country down the tubes." In Argentina many of the foreign loans made their

way into Swiss bank accounts or were used to buy arms for the confrontation with the British over the Falklands. In Paraguay they spawned a rash of mansion building around Asunción. The Brazilians, at least, were more honorable and patriotic. They did what they were supposed to do with the money. They applied it to crazy, grandiose schemes that were intended to benefit the country: roads that proved unfeasible and stopped in the middle of nowhere, disastrous hydroelectric projects, ill-advised nuclear power plants.

One of the main lenders was the World Bank, the largest international agency dedicated to the promotion of "development." It was founded after World War II to rebuild Europe and since 1950 has been concentrating on Third World development projects. Most of its staff is American, and its president is a rubber-stamped nominee of the president of the United States, approved by a board of directors weighted toward American interests. By 1988 it had loaned so much to the Third World that the negative resource flow from south to north, the difference between the amount of the new loans the countries received and the amount they had to pay the bank for existing loans, was $50 billion. The World Bank was a major player in the Monopoly game.

THE NEW EL DORADO

The deeper in debt Brazil grew, the grander the development schemes for Amazônia became. The government embraced each new one like a gambler staking everything on a desperate last throw of the dice. But always the élan with which the projects were undertaken dissolved, and the darkness of the military period, the poverty, and the misery were still there.

One of the ways to alleviate the debt was to transform the agriculture in the South, replacing the small coffee farms there with large-scale, capital-intensive agriculture, especially soybeans. The phasing out of coffee was already well under way before the debt crisis. Four hundred million trees on coffee plantations were eradicated between 1961 and 1969. Between 1970 and 1980, more than 109,000 farms in northern Paraná smaller than 50 hectares went under and 450 farms bigger than 1,000 hectares. Two and a half million people left, among them the Alves da Silva family, though for different reasons.

The problem was what to do with all these displaced farmers. Send them to Rondônia, it was decided — a huge, practically virgin chunk of the Amazon east of Acre, as big as Wyoming. And so the government sponsored another misguided run on the region. It was not that the generals were cynically playing with people's lives: everyone wanted desperately to believe that the Polonoroeste Project, as it was called, would work.

It should have been clear from the fiasco of the Trans-Amazon Highway that large numbers of people could not simply be relocated to the Amazon and expected to take it from there. But as if it had learned nothing, the government, with the generous backing of the World Bank, embarked on this even more ambitious colonization scheme. Again there was a seductive television campaign, urging the farmers to make a bold march to the west and beckoning them to the El Dorado of the poor with inflated estimates of the amount of *terra roxa,* a relatively fertile, purplish volcanic soil. Between 1982 and 1986 half a million colonists poured into Rondônia, 25 or 30 percent of them from Paraná. Each family was given between 100 and 250 hectares and set to work diligently cutting and burning. Many of the immigrants had been through a series of tenant-farming situations and for the first time were working land of their own. Even so the rates of attrition were high, 50 to 80 percent. By the second or third planting the corn was so scrawny it no longer bore fruit, and the families had no choice but to abandon their homesteads and become sharecroppers again, for one of the big shots who had snapped up the good land, or to try their luck at prospecting. The forest of Rondônia shrank 3 percent a year during the eighties. By 1988, according to a World Bank estimate, 24 percent of the state had gone up in smoke — one of the greatest environmental holocausts ever perpetrated by man.

Highway BR-364 had been roughed out from Cuiabá to Porto Velho in 1960, and the invasion of Indian lands — Nambiquara, Cinta Larga (Wide Belt), Urueuwauwau, Arara, Gavião, Zoro, Surui — was already out of control. The only thing holding back the complete overrunning of Rondônia was the deplorable condition of the road. During the rainy season you could be stranded on it for weeks. Sometimes buses would be found mired, with prospective colonists decomposing in their seats.

The World Bank was in the business of implanting infrastructure, and paving BR-364 was just the sort of project it went in for. Between 1970 and 1979 it loaned Brazil $629 million for construction and improvement of its highways, and it was one of the main backers of the Trans-Amazon Highway. Currently it is considering handing out another $500 million for more huge dams. It had supported many rain forest colonization projects, even though they had poor success rates. If the finger is to be pointed at anyone for destroying the Amazon, probably the first place it should be aimed is at the World Bank.

In its support of the Polonoroeste Project, the bank had hired consultants — anthropologists, ecologists, and agronomists — who reported that only 10 percent of Rondônia was *terra roxa,* and this small portion had already been occupied by big ranches. Ten thousand Indians in more than sixty groups stood to be decimated by the project, and it was certain to be a disaster. It was impossible to sustainably resettle two and a half million small farmers from the South there. But the consultants' objections were overruled by higher-ups interested in moving the money. The business of the World Bank, like that of every bank, is to lend. And 11.6 percent was good money, regardless of the consequences for Brazil. "The aim of [the] development [supported by the World Bank] is not, and never has been, to improve the standard of living, or encourage social justice in the Third World countries," writes David Price, one of the anthropologists hired as a consultant by the Polonoroeste Project. "The Bank is not a charitable institution; it was founded to promote international trade . . . on terms that are favorable to the industrialized nations."

By 1983, several environmental and Indian-protection groups — Cultural Survival, the Environmental Defense Fund, the National Wildlife Association, the Natural Resources Defense Council, the Sierra Club — known in Washington circles as NGOs, nongovernment institutions — had begun to protest the World Bank's role in what was happening in Rondônia. The bank is politically vulnerable, because it needs annual congressional appropriations. So the lobbyists for the NGOs focused their efforts on the Senate Banking, Housing, and Urban Affairs Committee.

Between 1982 and 1984, a total of 1,456 kilometers of BR-364 was paved, and the tide of colonists that poured in was far greater than the ability of the government to provide infrastructure for it. The Indian lands hadn't even been demarcated, and there were numerous clashes. In 1987, for instance, Padre Ezequiel Ramir, who had been working with the Suruí Indians, was shot fifty times in the head by ranchers. Six months later four hundred Suruí, Gavião, and Cinta Larga Indians stole the clothes of some prospectors and drove them out of the region. They were later killed by *pistoleiros* hired by a group of sixteen ranchers.

But in 1985, thanks to the pressure of the lobbyists, there was a major turnaround at the bank. Disbursements on the Polonoroeste Project were suspended pending a review of the environmental problems and the invasion of Indian lands. The paving stopped. But the holocaust continued, without the bank's help.

THE MAKING OF AN ECOLOGIST

In the late 1970s, a young Brazilian anthropologist from the southern city of Curitiba, Maria Helena (or Mary) Allegretti, came to do a master's thesis on the traditional rubber tappers of the Upper Juruá River. She was so shocked to find them living in semislavery, owing their souls to the *patrão seringalista,* that "I decided to do something about it besides write a thesis," she recalled. She concentrated on education and worked up a little booklet that explained the basics of reading and math for the tappers. In 1984 she interviewed Chico Mendes about his *empates* for the *Varadouro,* an alternate paper in Rio Branco, now extinct, that championed the rights of the tappers. She was so impressed by his struggle and his dedication that she dropped everything. "I was very content leaving the role of anthropologist to accompany someone with a real mission," she told me. She went on long walks to meetings in the forest with him and eventually started nineteen schools for the tappers.

"It was clear that Chico was in grave danger," Allegretti continued. "Our only hope of saving him was to make people aware of his struggle, to make him such an important national and international figure that the ranchers wouldn't dare to touch him." She had the contacts and the know-how to organize, in October of 1985, the first National Conference of the Rubber Tappers, in Brasília. There Chico and 129 *companheiros* from all over Amazônia were able to relate their problems for the first time to a larger audience of sympathetic Brazilian and foreign anthropologists and environmentalists. Among them was Steven Schwartzman, an anthropologist who had been involved with the relocation and rehabilitation of the Kreen-Akrore, an isolated tribe that had barely crossed the threshold of settled agriculture and had held out against contact until a road was pushed through its land. The traumatized Indians subsequently came out of the forest, half-starved, reduced to eating dirt, and quickly fell prey to flu and prostitution. Now Schwartzman was with the Environmental Defense Fund, lobbying in Washington against the destructive programs of the World Bank. His first impression of Chico at the Brazilian conference was that he was "very modest and unassuming, not a real fireball. His charisma was in his convictions. Only after talking with him about the history of the struggle did I realize what an incredibly courageous man he was, and the importance of what he was doing. Here was a real grass-roots leader with an extremely organized local constituency fighting deforestation."

Not only that, but at this meeting Chico, in his typically intuitive, caring way, came up with the solution for saving the Amazon, the model that everyone was looking for. The Brazilian government wasn't about to accept foreign environmentalists telling them they couldn't do anything with half the national territory. Something had to be done, but it had to be rational, sustainable, and minimally destructive. Chico had been thinking, What right do we have to mount our *empates* if we aren't offering an alternative to the ranching? He had noticed how the Indians were better off than the tappers because they had reserves that were, in theory at least, legally protected. Why couldn't the tappers have reserves, too, extractive reserves, where they could do what they had always been doing, which was completely rational and sustainable, and save the forest and their way of life at the same time? What an idea! Chico is usually credited with it, although the term "extractive reserve" sounds a little too academic to have come tripping off Chico's tongue.

A number of other agroforestry experiments were already being conducted in other parts of Amazônia, a number of compromise conservation strategies that struck a balance between utilization and preservation. The village of Tamshiyacu, Peru, for instance, has a thirty-five-year sustained-yield agroforestry system patterned after native practices. After a tract of land has been farmed for two or three years, fruit-bearing trees like Brazil nut or *umarí* (*Poraqueiba sericea*) are planted or allowed to regenerate. After thirty-five years the trees are harvested for timber or conversion into charcoal, and the land is farmed again.

But the beauty of Chico's scheme was that it was already in place. The tappers were already in the forest, and they were Brazilian, as was the author of the plan. The government would like that and would be more likely to support the proposal. So the environmentalists needed Chico to save the forest, and Chico needed the environmentalists to save his *companheiros'* way of life. It was a perfect marriage.

Chico would sell better abroad as an ecologist struggling to save the Amazon than as a radical union leader, the environmentalists realized. The Ford Foundation was committed to saving the rain forest, but it would look askance at Chico's affiliations with the Albanian wing of the Brazilian Communist Party. Chico hadn't thought of the tappers' struggle as an ecological one, but he was open-minded.

There was an immediate problem, of urgent concern to them all. Another multilateral lending institution, the International Development Bank, was considering funding the paving of the next stretch of BR-364 — from Porto Velho to Rio Branco. Steve, Mary, and Chico knew that if this happened, Acre would be overrun by the tidal wave that had already wiped out Rondônia. It would mean the end of the forest and the tappers.

In 1987 Chico was flown up to Miami to testify at the meeting of the board of directors of the IDB, where the final decision was to be made. The American, British, and Scandinavian directors were very receptive to his presentation on extractive reserves, but the Brazilian director didn't want to hear about it. Schwartzman emphasized that "extractive reserves are important precisely because they are not simply another U.S.-style conservation proposal, but an organized initiative directly undertaken by Amazonian grass-roots groups and sympathetic national organizations."

Schwartzman also presented a study he and some other scientists had made whose findings were very interesting, and politically explosive: a family of tappers and Brazil nut gatherers made $1,333 a year, while a family of farmers using the same area made only $800 and a family of ranchers only $710. Extractive use of the forest, moreover, required no state financing (although Amazonian rubber is subsidized by an import tax on Asian rubber, which is cheaper on the open market) and was more profitable per capita and per acre — even in the short run.

This finding was later corroborated independently by Charles M. Peters, of the Missouri Botanical Garden, who studied for three years the returns from harvesting edible fruits, oils, and rubber on two and a half acres in the village of Mishara, Peru. He found that they were nearly double the return on timber or the value of the land if it was converted to pasture. In other words, the forest is worth more standing, even without factoring in all the unresearched genetic information it contains.

Another study, of cattle ranching in Acre, found that after the first five years the yield per acre fell by 75 percent and that by 1983 clearing had deprived the state of nearly $6.5 million in potential revenues from rubber and Brazil nuts.

The problem, Schwartzman and Allegretti explained, was rehabilitating the image of extractivism. Living off the forest and the river, off the fruits of nature, was seen as archaic, unprofitable, and decadent. But in fact it had been the mainstay of the Amazon for centuries, the only way people had survived while experimenting with other, less stable ways of making a living.

From Miami Chico flew to Washington and met informally with members of the Senate Appropriations Committee, which decides whether to release funds to the multilateral banks. With Schwartzman translating for him, Chico went over well, a little like Kit Carson or Davy Crockett, the straight-shooting homespun backwoodsman, coming to the capital and telling what it's like on the frontier. The IDB and the Appropriations Committee came around, and in January 1988 the plans for paving BR-364 to Rio Branco were suspended; $58.8 million was allocated for safeguarding the forest and the Indians along the road. It was a temporary victory.

Around this time the World Bank announced that "the most promising alternative to destructive colonization and cattle-ranching is the extractive reserve." Extractive reserves are now one of the main thrusts of Amazonian conservation. Reserves with a total of 13 million acres have been laid out or are in the works: four in Acre, including the Seringal Cachoeira, and five in Rondônia, which, mirabile dictu, are being funded by the World Bank.

For Chico's work, his efforts to save the Amazon and to promote rational alternatives to the destruction, he received two prestigious awards — one from the United Nations Environmental Programme and one from the Better World Society. The latter is a not-for-profit organization founded by communications king Ted Turner. It specializes in TV programming on "these kinds of issues," its executive director, Thomas Belford, explained. Once a year, at a gala awards ceremony in New York City, it recognizes people who have made outstanding contributions in environmental preservation, population stabilization, peace advocacy, humanitarian service. As an adjunct to the award there is a TV special, and later, as happened with Chico, the recipient may become the subject of a documentary.

The awards ceremony that year — 1987 — was held at the Waldorf-Astoria. Chico was put up in a room whose daily rate would cost a tapper several months' earnings, with a television and gold-plated fixtures in the bathroom. The experience confirmed his preconception of America. He was not impressed by the imperialist splendor. This was definitely enemy territory.

"My first impression of Chico was that he was a very quiet, humble, soft-spoken guy, who did not fit the mold of a charismatic," Belford recalled. "But when he stood up in front of seven hundred people in the Grand Ballroom and got his arms pumping, it was clear that he had the ability to light people up. It was a black-tie event, but he had a suit and a rumpled look about him. Clearly this was a major outing for him. I guess he'd been to the States once before. I think he was sort of wowed by it. There were a lot of TV cameras and lights. I think he felt the award served the purpose of getting exposure for the movement. That year awards were also given to the fellow who runs the UN peacekeeping force, and to Phil Donahue and Vladimir Pozner, the senior Soviet broadcaster, who had done a show together. Chico said the award was helpful on several levels. It rejuvenated his own personal juices and he told Ted Turner that he thought it would also help save his life. He also felt it would make officialdom in Brazil pay more attention."

Chico's work and worthiness for recognition had been brought to the attention of the Better World Society by the British documentary film-maker Adrian Cowell. It was Cowell, more than Allegretti and Schwartz-man, who "discovered" Chico and orchestrated his international rise. Cowell was the kingmaker. In the seventies he had made a superb doc-umentary called *The Tribe That Hides from Man,* about the unsuccessful efforts to contact the Kreen-Akrore, the tribe that was later nearly wiped out by cultural trauma and whose rehabilitation Schwartzman got in-volved in. In the eighties Cowell began to document the destruction of Rondônia and the clash between the colonists and the Indians, in a series of harrowing programs for Britain's Central Television. He picked up on Chico and the importance of what he was doing in 1986, started follow-ing him around with a camera, and became a close, trusted family friend.

When Ilzamar went into labor with twins, one of whom she lost, Cowell paid the hospital bill.

In Cowell's documentary *Banking on Disaster,* the footage of Chico campaigning in 1986 for state deputy on the Workers' Party, or PT, ticket captures him at forty-two: a rather short man with wavy hair, a thick mustache, and a genial, humorous face. At times he even has a slightly daft expression, the special Brazilian *esquisito* type of daftness. He seems, as Cowell described him to me, "a placid and comfortable character." He is wearing, as usual, jeans, flip-flops, and a T-shirt. He is fine-shinned, as his aunt Cecília described him, from walking in the forest all his life, but his potbelly has become enormous, because every time he comes to a tapper's house he is invited for a meal, and he has to eat it if he expects the man's vote. He tells Cowell that he is "campaigning with his stomach."

On the day of the election there is flagrant vote buying in the plaza of Xapuri. A kid runs up and says, "Hey, Chico, buy me a soda and I'll make sure you get my mother's vote." Chico tells him, "You know that's illegal, but stop at the union later and I'll see what we can do." Chico got three times more votes than the other candidates, but the Workers' Party won only 3 percent of the statewide vote, and he lost.

Central Television is funded by the United Nations Environmental Programme, so it wasn't difficult for Cowell to get Chico included among UNEP's annual Global 500, the five hundred people who have made the most outstanding contributions to environmental preservation. Chico was flown to London (which, he lamented, there was no time to see), and was given the award in Birmingham. He was paid an eloquent tribute by the environmental journalist Geoffrey Lean, who described the *empates* and the extreme danger Chico was in. Mendes "holds one of the best answers on how to preserve much of the world's fast vanishing rain-forests, the oldest and most exuberant celebration of life on earth, and crucial governors of the world's climate," Lean wrote. The profession of tapping rubber "remains one of the last occupations to concentrate on co-existing with, rather than conquering, nature."

Cowell also documented a real David and Goliath victory by Chico and the tappers, against the Bordon Meatpacking Company, the Brazilian subsidiary of a large multinational corporation, which had been trying to develop a ten-thousand-acre ranch on the Xapuri River. The land had been cleared of tappers in the usual way: by threats, violence, burning of homes and crops. Chico organized *empates* repeatedly until finally it became too much. The manager of the Bordon ranch asked Chico how many head of cattle he wanted to stop. "I'll throw in a good car to cruise around in." Chico, of course, wasn't interested. In the end Bordon just cut its losses and left the state. So did the famous cattleman Rubico de Carvalho, "the King of the Nelore" (one of the most common breeds of cattle in the Amazon), after an *empate* and demonstration in 1981 in which 180 tappers were jailed. It was getting expensive for the ranchers to hire military police to break up these demonstrations. Even though the police were sent by judicial order, the ranchers had to pay them by the hour.

The techniques of the struggle grew more sophisticated with the help of other outside advisers, like Gumercindo Crovis Rodrigues, who came from Mato Grosso do Sul as an agronomist in 1983 and three years later became involved in the struggle full-time as an adviser to the Rural Workers' Union. "I was always learning from Chico how to relate to the workers," he told me in January 1989. "Always learning" was a phrase he used a lot. It had a good revolutionary ring. "I'm much more volatile than Chico was," he told another interviewer. "I get angry at every little thing. He held me back sometimes." Gumercindo always spoke his mind, and sometimes it got him and others into trouble, but that was all right because he was "always learning." He was only twenty-nine years old. "I'll be thirty on the thirtieth, if they let me." He was a provocateur, one of the Shiites, the real radicals in the movement, and he was said to be a member of the Albanian wing of the Brazilian Communist Party.

"Chico taught me that the workers build the structure, you don't impose it. He had real *populismo,* popular appeal, he never lost his simplicity, even when he went to Rio and was made an honorary citizen of the city. He was a great intelligence. He never wanted to be a star. He talked with everybody, with the governor, he patiently answered the stupid questions of journalists without ever changing, and he won them all over."

It was Gumercindo's idea to get IBDF, the Brazilian Institute for Forestry Development, to enforce provisions of the forestry code that prohibited the cutting of rubber and Brazil nut trees and the deforestation of steep slopes and riverbanks. Ranchers who were found to be doing these things were supposed to be denied licenses for deforestation or have their licenses revoked.

Gumercindo also played a major role in the final showdown with Bordon: The Xapuri union demonstrated and was met by military police, but Gumercindo got the state governor to call off the police and to allow the demonstration to continue. He also persuaded IBDF to review the situation. Most of Bordon's land had already been cleared, but IBDF decreed that there should be no further deforestation. At least a little bit was saved for the tappers.

THE RANCHERS ORGANIZE

When Chico came back from the States in 1987, now an internationally acclaimed ecologist, he was greeted by a smear campaign organized by the ranchers in their paper, *O Rio Branco,* and on their radio station. The campaign ridiculed and denigrated him for being, among other things, illiterate, an enemy of Acre, against progress, a tool of the environmentalists, a man who had left the country to say bad things about Brazil.

The ranchers had become more dangerous since the founding of their own group, the Rural Democratic Union (UDR), in 1984. The UDR started as a radical right-wing lobby group after the generals allowed the first steps toward the redemocratization of the country to be taken, in 1984. As the new Brazilian constitution was going through its many drafts, there was serious talk about agrarian reform, about rectifying the incredibly skewed and regressive pattern of land ownership. The ranchers and farmers became worried about being expropriated. Eventually the UDR evolved into something like the John Birch Society or the Ku Klux Klan.

The union started in the state of Goiás. The ranchers there auctioned their cattle to raise money. Before long there were 230,000 members with two hundred chapters in nineteen states. The UDR marshaled 40,000 farmers to march on Brasília to protest the agrarian reform bill and succeeded in emasculating it. No "productive" land could be expropriated — the only land worth expropriating — and only 5 percent of the land targeted for expropriation actually changed hands before the program ground to a halt. The UDR is run by the rural oligarchy, the 2,000 who own ninety-six million head of cattle, the elite 1 percent who own 45 percent of the arable land in the country and who are the political force behind, and the beneficiary of, the billions of dollars of fiscal incentives for developing the Amazon.

The UDR's president, Ronaldo Caiado, who was a candidate in the recent Brazilian presidential elections, was young, dynamic, and articulate. He declared open season on ecologists during the campaign, describing them as "agents of North American leftist [this was a new one] imperialism." All this environmentalist agitation, he said, is a plot to keep us down. Caiado employed the UDR slogan, "Amazônia Is Ours," and his speeches had a demagogic, hate-mongering, redneck appeal. They connected with the autocratic, macho part of the Brazilian psyche: you are the master of your property, and nobody can tell you what to do. You got yours by your own sweat, and if others don't have as much as you do, it's because they don't deserve it. So why should you share it with lazy, incompetent inferiors? Why should we, who know what to do with the land, hand it over to people who have never farmed or ranched? We are the ones who feed the country, who provide the grain and beef. We are the heroes. The riches of Brazil have always come from people like us, from private initiative.

The proceeds of the Goiás cattle auctions were also used to buy guns. The president of the UDR in Goiânia boasted that the organization had seventy thousand firearms, one for each man in it, men who have been "overlooked by the history of our country." Some of the UDR's arms cache has been traced to the burglary of a submarine docked in Guanabara Bay, in Rio de Janeiro.

Since the UDR was founded there has been a tremendous increase in rural violence, seven hundred killings by the end of 1988 as opposed to nine hundred during the previous twenty-one years of military rule. The killings became not only more numerous, but more open. They reached, according to one editorial, "the level of organized political terrorism." They were the same local rub-outs by farmers and ranchers, but they seemed to have become more centralized.

Each local chapter of the UDR is thought to have an executive committee that overlaps with the death squad in the State Department of

Public Safety. The president of the UDR in Acre was João Branco, a lawyer and coowner of *O Rio Branco*. The president of the executive committee was believed to be Gaston Mota.

The fact that there is no direct proof of UDR involvement in a single killing is probably not so much evidence of the organization's innocence as a product of government corruption, incompetence, and cover-up.

In 1988 the Pastoral Commission for the Land's computer in Goiânia tallied 232 *anunciados,* 799 unsuccessful murder attempts, and 93 deaths. The year before, 88 union leaders were killed. Chico must have known that it was just a question of time before they got him. During his unsuccessful 1986 campaign for state deputy, he said to his aunt Cecília at the Seringal Cachoeira, "If I don't win, my death will be no later than 1988." At the election, Sebastião Alves, the father of Darli and Alvarino, was said to have turned to José Américo Freire. Not realizing that Freire was married to Chico's mother's sister, he asked, "Who are you going to vote for? Better vote for our party, because a vote for the PT of Chico Mendes is a vote for nobody. We have *pistoleiros* — three policemen — waiting to take care of him, who can pick him off at a hundred yards."

As far back as October 6, 1984, Chico made a tape, which he left in the hands of Brazilian conservationist José Lutzenberger, to expose the "climate of horror that the government allows everyone who defends the forest to be exposed to." He said his house had been attacked five times that year, and he accused the ranchers and the police of collusion.

THE CIRCLE CLOSES

In 1988 events accelerated and began to take on a tragic inexorability. The strands all came together in the crazy, anachronic mélange that Acre had become, that is Brazil — with the tappers living in the time of Daniel Boone, the Alves boys living in Tombstone, the leaders of the UDR acting out their *Dallas* fantasies, the government encapsulated in the Golden Fifties, the ecologists in the second wave of modern environmental awareness watching the first wave's dreadful predictions come true, with a couple of ex-Nazis and thousands of dispossessed, until recently Stone Age Indians thrown in.

The event that sealed Chico's fate was the *empate* at the Seringal

Cachoeira. One rancher told me that Dom Moacyr and the Shiites put Chico up to it. They wanted a martyr to draw attention to the cause. "For us he was never a problem. He was an excellent negotiator, good at working out settlements, and we weren't interested in violence and radicalization. Chico died because of his naiveté, and because he was induced to take certain attitudes against Darli, who everybody knew was a violent man. He was forced to pick the fight that caused his death."

Darli allegedly sold most of his cattle to buy the land at the Seringal Cachoeira, and he couldn't afford to be expropriated the way a big outfit like Bordon could. So what Chico did to him was not only a slap in the face, it was also a serious economic blow. As Acre UDR president João Branco put it, "Darli was backed into a corner, like a trapped animal. He had no choice but to kill Chico."

After the *empate* in April, Darli went around telling people he was going to get that troublemaker Mendes.

In its bulletin of May 19, 1988, the National Council of Bishops reported that the governor of Acre had been informed of a meeting of the UDR at which members discussed the immediate elimination of Chico and the launching of a defamation campaign against him in the press.

On May 24, Chico was *anunciado.* Someone called and said, "You will not live out the year." Chico now knew that he was done for. This was the recognition scene. He may have had seven more months to walk the earth, but he was in a sense already dead.

Lucélia Santos — former soap opera star, now political activist for the Workers' and Green parties — "a little hurricane," as my friend Julio Cesar described her — now enters the story. We were heading for lunch at Lucélia's spectacular home in a guarded compound in the Barra de Tijuca district of Rio with a dozen exuberant talents — actors, directors, singers, dancers — of the *boêmia carioca,* the Rio art scene. "Lucélia is like La Pasionaria, the guru of the Spanish Civil War, who organized the anarchists and Communists against Franco," Julio Cesar explained. "She has the same trajectory. Many people believe that if she is allowed to live, she will be very important to Brazilian politics in the next century, perhaps the Eva Perón of Brazil."

Lucélia was thirty-one but looked more like thirteen, resembling with her close-cropped hair a fearless, hyper Joan of Arc. Rising from humble origins in São Paulo, she acted for thirteen years in the *telenovelas*. Her most famous role, with which she was still identified, came in 1976. In *The Slave Izaura* she played a white slave, the daughter of a mulatto slave and the white administrator of a ranch in the interior of Minas Gerais, who becomes a leader of the abolition movement. The *novela* was shown in fifty-two countries, and it radicalized her. "It's a story about love and suffering, like Dickens or Hugo," she told me. "Izaura's lover was her owner. I was a typical uninformed member of the post– A 1-5 generation [proclamation A 1-5, in 1968, closed Brazil's congress and imposed press censorship]. But I had friends in prison or exile and they were responsible for my ideological awakening."

One of her friends was Fernando Gabeira, the Abbie Hoffman of Brazil. Lucélia arranged for the three of us to meet sometime later at a Japanese restaurant in the Centro, the business district. Gabeira was natty, elegant, chic, with a foulard. He and Lucélia had just come from a march commemorating the bombing of Hiroshima. His candidacy for vice president on the Workers' Party ticket had recently been rejected by the Albanian wing of the Brazilian Communist Party because he wasn't considered sufficiently hard-line. He was forty-eight, "and for almost thirty of them I've been engaged in subversive activities against the dictatorship," he said. A student leader in the sixties, he participated in the 1969 kidnapping of American ambassador C. Burke Elbrick, in Rio. "We jumped out in front of his car with machine guns and took him to my house. After four days and many interesting discussions, he was exchanged for fifteen *companheiros* in the armed resistance movement." Because of his part in this incident, Gabeira can't get a visa to the United States.

In 1970 Gabeira was shot in a gun battle with soldiers, imprisoned for six months, and exchanged for the German ambassador, who had been kidnapped by other *companheiros*. He went into exile: Algeria, Cuba, East Germany, Red China, Sweden. In 1979 he was given amnesty and allowed to come home.

"I realized that the new struggle is ecological. The classic Marxist struggle is not the only important one. There is the struggle of the women against machismo, of the Negro for cultural autonomy, the struggle of the Indians, the struggle against nuclear arms, the struggle for the urban quality of life. There is a complex of struggles, much more complex than the one between the workers and the bourgeoisie.

"I realized that progress does not go on forever," he continued between nibbles of California maki. "The problem is to get Brazilians to see that at this moment it is not possible for Brazil to join the First World. The model of progress must be changed from the big ranch on the soap operas. We can't keep consuming more indefinitely."

"Fernando is the only one in Brazil thinking about the planet in the third millennium," said Lucélia.

He mentioned some of his innovative solutions: generating power with windmills — "our coast has strong winds" — and, instead of paving BR-364 and continuing it to Peru, which would destroy western Amazônia, meeting local transportation needs with zeppelins.

"The tappers still see the struggle in classic terms," Gabeira continued. "Chico's great singularity was that he had a broader vision."

In 1986 Gabeira, Lucélia, Julio Cesar, and a number of others had founded the Brazilian Green Party. "I was concerned that ecology not be a flag of the right," Gabeira told me, "the more civilized right, whose concern for the environment might inhibit social justice, so I made a strategic alliance between the Green Party and the Workers' Party. Many left because of this [including Julio Cesar, who was drummed out for "ideological incompatibility"; Julio Cesar claims the real reason was that he had better rapport than Gabeira with the young Greens].

"In 'eighty-seven," he went on, "I became involved in the problems of Amazônia and met Chico. We sent someone to examine his work, and after we realized how important it was, we started to create support for him in the cities. We got him the key to Rio de Janeiro."

In May 1988 — the month Chico was *anunciado* — Lucélia went to Acre. A beloved celebrity and a moving impromptu speaker, she was a powerful ally for the tappers. *O Rio Branco* greeted her with a smear campaign. Adalberto Aragão, the mayor of Rio Branco, and his good friend Gaston Mota accused her of bringing AIDS to the state. The reasoning behind the accusation was that Lucélia had recently joined one of the *daime* cults, which was sweeping the *boêmia* of Rio. "I had not succeeded in having a vision until I went to the União Vegetal, one of the *daime* centers outside Rio Branco, and there I found out the level of my blindness. I experienced satori and had a sudden revelation that this society was history. The only way to save it is with a cultural transformation through the youth."

Lucélia's visit to the União Vegetal was noted. Incurable *aidéticos*,

AIDS victims, were also coming from Rio to the *daime* centers in Acre in a last-ditch attempt to stave off the inevitable a little longer. Even the hottest rock star of the moment, Cazuzo, who admitted in one of his songs to being a "screaming queer," had come for treatment with forest herbs, and to get his head straight with the wine of the vine.

Thus the connection in Aragão's and Mota's minds.

"I first met Chico at a national conference in 'eighty-six," Lucélia recalled. "He gave a brilliant exposition on extractive reserves, and talked about the *empates*. It was very moving. I saw that his work was the most important in Brazil." She was the first prominent Brazilian to pick up on it. "In May I went to spend a week in Acre, to help with his reelection [he was running again for state deputy], to write some articles for the *Folha do São Paulo,* and also because Chico had already been *anunciado* and he needed somebody from the South always there [the presence of an outsider who could "blow the whistle" would supposedly deter Chico's enemies from taking action]. I wanted to see, too, what I could do for the women in the *seringais*.* The women there have nothing. Some came from fifteen hours away to meet us. They told me how they give birth out in the crop fields. If the baby is in the wrong position they induce labor by swallowing chicken feathers and palm oil, which brings on strong contractions. Three hundred women came. They complained how often they don't want to have sex after working all day long in the plantation, but the men make them."

Chico took her to the Seringal Cachoeira. "He captivated me. He was so easy to like. He was a very strong illumination. Everything he got he put into the movement. His capacity for work and his intellect were incredible."

As Lucélia walked behind him on the *estradas,* "he seemed a being of the forest — short, potbellied, completely integrated with it. He would talk to the trees, jingling their cups to ask them which would give the most milk, and they would answer by shaking their leaves. It was my first time in the forest. I felt a force of life. I started hearing sounds, this incredible intensity, all these invisible connections, as if the trees themselves were . . . I don't know — almost like people."

Lucélia and Chico went to the governor of Acre, Flaviano Melo, to tell him about the *anúncio* and to ask for protection for Chico. The

---

*Plural of *seringal.*

governor authorized two Military Policemen to be with him at all times. "But the police were inexperienced and poorly armed," Lucélia told me, "and the situation there is so wide open that they were probably friends of the ranchers."

When Lucélia and Chico were walking together in the main plaza of Rio Branco, Chico noticed Darci Alves drinking a beer at an outside table, and he said, "That *pistoleiro* is waiting to kill me." Lucélia asked her photographer to take a picture of Darci, and he did. The picture was later sold to *Paris Match*.

With Chico under around-the-clock protection, Mary Allegretti and the Pastoral Commission for the Land took a step that further sealed his fate: they hired a lawyer, Genésio Natividade, to look into the pasts of Darli and Alvarino Alves, to dig up some dirt, and see if there was some way to get them out of the picture. Genésio traced them back to Paraná and found out that they were wanted for murder in Umuarama. In September a warrant for their arrest from Umuarama was delivered to Dom Moacyr Grechi. The bishop didn't want to give it to the judge in Xapuri, who was seeing the widow of Nilão de Oliveira and was not to be trusted. So instead he gave it to Mauro Sposito, the state superintendent of the Federal Police.

But there was bad blood between Sposito and Chico that the bishop evidently wasn't aware of. Sposito was not particularly disposed or in any great hurry to see anyone who wanted to eliminate Mendes taken off the streets. The trouble dated to 1980, after the execution of de Oliveira, when Chico was interrogated by Sposito for three days, possibly with electric shocks. Sposito had recently been going around calling Chico "a police informant, a stoolie," to denigrate him to his *companheiros*. At the same time, Sposito accused Chico of being a "Communist agitator." The basis of these allegations was Chico's having told him about a militant, code-named Vitor, who was allied to the Uruguayan left and was trying to start a guerrilla movement among the tappers; Vitor was actually a teacher named Reginaldo de Costela in Mary Allegretti's education project, Projeto Seringueiro. Chico had made it very clear to everybody — the directors of the PT, the church — that he was adamantly opposed to armed confrontation, but Sposito may have tortured the information out of him.

Chico was infuriated by these calumnies. He considered Sposito one of his chief enemies in Acre and denounced him to his superiors in Brasília.

Dom Moacyr delivered the warrant for the Alveses' arrest to Sposito on September 26, but for sixteen days it sat on his desk. Nothing was done. Sposito later claimed it got lost in the shuffle. On the next day, the twenty-seventh, Chico and Genésio Natividade went to see Sposito in Rio Branco. As they were leaving the Federal Police headquarters, they spotted Darli drinking a beer at an outside table in the main plaza, and they rushed to Mary Allegretti's room at the Pinheiro Palace Hotel and called the Federal Police. Another police officer took the message and said that Sposito was not available. "Tell him one of the subjects of the warrant is right in front of the building drinking beer." But nothing was done. This may not have been deliberate: the success rate of three-party communications in Brazil is notoriously poor.

Dom Moacyr believes that it was not because of a betrayal that the warrant was not delivered to the police in Xapuri for sixteen days, but that it was a simple case of *inoperância* — a wonderful word, a key word, "failure to get it together," as much to blame for Chico's death as anything. At any rate, someone tipped off Darli and Alvarino — maybe their cousin in the Federal Police in Rio Branco, maybe their nephew Odilon, the clerk at the Civil Police station in Xapuri, only seventy-five yards from Chico's house. Darli later said that it was from his cousin, a lawyer and pharmacist in Umuarama, that he learned about the warrant even before it reached Acre. It could have been any number of people; the Alves boys had lots of friends among the police.

When the Military Police finally got it together to go out to the Fazenda Paraná to pick up Darli and Alvarino, late in October, they were long gone. The brothers stayed hidden in the forest, near, or possibly even on, their ranches. It was inconvenient and humiliating.

Gumercindo Rodrigues, the young, hotheaded revolutionary, did something typically rash. He stood up in the main plaza so all Xapuri could hear and said, "Darli and Alvarino are wanted for murder. The warrant has arrived from Paraná, and they're going to be put away for good."

When Darci later turned himself in and confessed to Chico's murder, he said it was a matter of honor, that he had not been able to stand by and hear his father being vilified. But if this was the case, why didn't he kill Gumercindo?

As the year progressed there were several warm-up killings. On June 18 union activist Ivair Igino was bushwhacked from the trees across the street from his house. Twenty people have given testimony to the detective investigating the case, but it is still unsolved. Oloci Alves is suspected of involvement. It was definitely Oloci, according to the detective, who gunned down the colonist José Ribeiro as he was taking a leak after a party in Xapuri in September.

A photograph of the wake for Ivair shows Chico, Raimundo de Barros, and several others standing over his corpse. It is a powerful scene. There is shock, grief, and rage in the survivors' eyes. Ivair's eyes are closed, and his nostrils are plugged with cotton. The exact scene would be repeated when Chico was killed, six months later. Ana Rosa Fioretta, the lay volunteer with the church in Rio Branco, was at Ivair's wake, and she told me that one of Darli's sons, she didn't know which, burst in drunk and belligerent.

On October 22 the Rural Workers' Union bought a Toyota truck and two boats with foreign grant money wangled by Mary Allegretti. Chico was delighted. "Now we will dribble around the UDR," he said. But driving around Rio Branco in the new pickup, he saw in his rearview mirror that he was being tailed. Ilzamar told me that several times she found Darci and Oloci parked in front of the house, just sitting in the car, and she screamed, "What are you doing here? Beat it before I call the police."

The tappers had their own informants. Through them Chico heard about another meeting of the ranchers, in Brasiléia, to discuss his elimination. According to the *Gazeta,* he sent the governor and the judge of Xapuri a list of who was in the "ranchers' ring": Gaston Mota, Adalberto Aragão, Wanderlei Viana (the mayor of Xapuri), Luis Assem, a rancher simply known as Alemão (the German), Crispim Reis, Colonel Chicão, Zé Elias, Darli and Alvarino Alves, Mauro Sposito, João Branco, Rubem Branquinho, João Tezza, and Captain Tixotes of the Military Police in Brasiléia. The paper quoted Chico as saying, "These are the people who will kill me." Whatever the accuracy of this list, there was no answer. Nothing was done.

On October 28 Chico sent off an equally futile letter to José Carlos Castelo Branco, the secretary of the State Department of Public Safety: "I can be assassinated, I or one of my *companheiros,* because the plans are laid. Only one detail: you, sir, will be considered one of the responsible ones, and when it happens, many will know. Would you like to be considered an assassin?''

Eva Evangelista de Araújo, the president of the Tribunal of Justice in Xapuri, told the *Gazeta* that she received a letter from Chico on the same day, in which he said, ''My blood is destined to be spilled,'' and informed her that the judge of Brasiléia, Heitor Macedo, had been present at the meeting in which his death was discussed. But since there was no prosecutor in Brasiléia to open an inquest into his allegations, no action was taken.

A month later, on November 29, Chico fired off three urgent telexes, to the governor Flaviano Melo, to Castelo Branco, and to the superintendent of the Federal Police in Brasília, Romeu Tuma, saying that Darli and Alvarino Alves were plotting his death and telling about another meeting of five ranchers for the same purpose. The telexes remain unanswered to this day.

He sent three more telexes on December 5: to Tuma; to the minister of justice in Brasília, Paulo Brossard; and to the president of the republic, José Sarney, with the same message — elements tied to the UDR are plotting the death of the tappers' leader. The same silence.

On that very day César Pontes, the director of the Civil Police in Acre, issued a gun permit to Oloci Alves, although Oloci had been accused in the local papers since the beginning of the year of involvement in crimes against the tappers.

Chico was going to a conference in Piracicaba, São Paulo, that day, and he noticed João Branco at the Rio Branco airport getting off his private plane with two strangers. Maybe these are the hit men who have been hired to kill me, he thought. He penned a moving farewell, to whom it is not clear:

> I don't want flowers on my grave, because I know they'll have been pulled up from the forest. But I'd at least like my murder to serve to put an end to the impunity of the *jagunços* [*pistoleiros*] under the protection of the Federal Police of Acre who, from 1975 to now, have already killed more than fifty people like me, leaders of the rubber tappers who are pledged to defend the Amazon forest and make of it an example that it is possible to progress without destroying. Good-bye, it was a pleasure. I am going to Xapuri to a meeting with death, from which I am certain no one can free

me. I am not a fatalist, just a realist. I have already denounced those who want to kill me and no steps have been taken. The superintendent of the Federal Police in Acre, Mauro Sposito, has been persecuting me for a long time. And I don't have the slightest doubt that the *pistoleiros* will come out winners for one reason: Delegado Sposito ordered my gun permit revoked, alleging my ties with a "foreign communist" entity. This is the Ford Foundation, of the United States, if you can believe it.

In November and December Chico gave a number of interviews. One of them was to the American filmmaker Miranda Smith. The great-granddaughter of a Brazilian, Smith had done a documentary about the cowboys of Florida, whose way of life was being destroyed by development. After seeing the "mess there," she went to the Peruvian Amazon in 1987, and, on the Solimões River, downstream from Iquitos, "I got hooked," she told me. "You understand the whole picture of the globe right there in front of you, you see life and death and interdependency. It all becomes clear in one shot."

Smith decided to do a documentary on the alternatives to the destruction. She filmed a colonist who was a little more ingenious than the others: his method of farming re-created the jungle. It was a mishmash, like the Indians' gardens. "This approach lasts much longer," she told me. "The largest return is on the medicinal plants. Why is it that the World Bank will finance dams and cattle, but won't develop the pharmaceutical potential of the forest? These organizations definitely have the capital. It gets down to an attitude."

Smith went to see Chico in July. "There were no bodyguards," she went on. "We walked in the forest and he was very relaxed. Gumercindo at that time was more under threat. He thought he was going to be the next one to be hit. Chico pointed out some intimidating guys in cowboy hats. Those are *pistoleiros,* he explained. Darli's name was mentioned."

Smith's project solidified, and she returned to Xapuri in November to start filming. By then Chico had changed completely. "He was very nervous, he kept looking over his shoulder, starting every time a truck went by." He was surrounded by bodyguards, plainclothesmen with Uzi submachine guns; she wasn't sure if they were police or tappers.

Smith was also doing a three-and-a-half-minute segment on Chico for Ted Turner's Cable News Network, an update on him as one of the recipients of a Better World Society achievement award. When she got back to New York she showed her videotaped interview — the last that would be made of Chico — to Thomas Belford, the society's executive director. "All of a sudden here is this guy surrounded by machine-gun-wielding bodyguards going about his business," Belford recalled. "Miranda's footage really brought home that this is dangerous work. Nobody had comprehended what the climate of violence is like down there. The next month he was killed."

In November and December a sociologist from Rio, Cândido Grzy-bowski, conducted a series of interviews with Chico for a book about more than twenty social movements, urban and rural, that he was editing. But after Chico was killed, the interviews, which ran to fifty pages, were published in a separate booklet, entitled "The Testament of the Man of the Forest: Chico Mendes in His Own Words." From reading them you get the definite impression that they are a summation, that Chico was laying down his achievement for posterity.

"The first method of the ranchers is to use their economic and political power to suborn the authorities," Chico explained,

> even the agents of IBDF in charge of monitoring deforestation. The second, most efficient method is to send *pistoleiros* to intimidate us. The main leaders, not just me, but also other *companheiros,* this year were quite threatened, including being on the blacklist of the assassin squad supported by the UDR. Who commands this squad are Mr. Darli and Mr. Alvarino Alves, owners of the Fazenda Paraná and other ranches in the vicinity. These two command a group of about thirty people. . . . But now it has changed because we succeeded in getting from the State of Paraná an order of prison, in Umuarama, for the two. But I don't know who, whether it is the Federal Police or who, succeeded in warning them. The fact is that they are now fugitives and are letting it be known that they will only surrender themselves after they see my corpse.

On December 9 Chico flew to Rio to represent the National Council of Rubber Tappers at a round table whose subject was "Amazônia Under the Ax and on Fire." While there he gave a long interview to the *Jornal do Brasil,* in which he predicted his imminent death.

"How is the situation in Acre?" the interviewer asked.

My security lately has been reinforced in Acre by the decision of Governor Flaviano Melo. He knows that a murder is going to complicate the situation in the state. Not that the death of a tapper in Acre would be anything new, but it's that our movement has become known throughout the world, principally in conjunction with the authorities of the World Bank, the International Development Bank, and the American Congress. He knows you don't mess with these entities. Today my life is in the hands of the Military Police. I get along well with my guards.

Who has threatened me most publicly are the two ranchers Darli Alves and Alvarino Alves. They are, moreover, fugitives from justice, with warrants out for their arrest. Since 1973 there have been warrants out for them in Paraná. We had these warrants sent to Acre, but trusted unfortunately in the Superintendent of the Federal Police, Mauro Sposito, who held them for sixteen days. According to the judge of the District of Xapuri, this retention was no accident. . . . We are absolutely convinced from information leaked by the Federal Police itself that these two ranchers are friends of the Superintendent, Mauro Sposito. The brothers have already had more than thirty workers murdered [he goes on to cite some of the crimes: Raimundo Pereira and Manuel Custódio, brutally shot on May 27 while demonstrating in front of the local IBDF office; June 18, Ivair Igino, ambushed by two shots from a twelve-gauge shotgun and eight from a revolver, killed by the group in service of these two ranchers; then in September José Ribeiro].

What are these two ranchers threatening to do?

They say they will only give themselves up over my dead body.

Where is the greatest danger?

At the airport. [Because there the guards were changed and for a moment Chico was exposed. That's how Benigno Aquino was assassinated. Takeoffs and landings are vulnerable moments for public figures in the jet age.]

When you go back to Acre now, will your life still be in danger?

I am aware that many popular leaders — lawyers, padres, pastors, union leaders — have been killed. I don't need to cite examples because they are alive in the memory of all. I hope to remain alive. It's by living that we strengthen our struggle. I know I have nothing to fear from the governor of the state. . . . But on the other hand, I have two powerful enemies: the UDR and the Federal Police. . . . The most excellent Superintendent Sposito . . . would be committing a disservice in burning a painting so well known.

Is Xapuri the most advanced front of the intransigent defense of the forest?

One could say it's the green front of Amazônia. It's the only place in the Amazon where in this year of 1988 the ranchers were only able to take down fifty hectares of forest. The projection was to clear ten thousand hectares.

The extractive reserve — is it a creation of yours?

Not directly. Listen. Until 1984 we were doing *empates* but we didn't have much clarity about what we wanted. We knew that the deforestation was the end of us and all the living beings of the forest. But the thing stopped there. People said, do you want to stop the deforestation to transform Amazônia into a sanctuary? Make it untouchable? There was the impasse. The solution came through the extractive reserve. Let's use the forest rationally without destroying it. The tappers, the Indians, the *ribeirinhos* [people who live along the rivers], have been occupying the forest for more than a hundred years and have never menaced it. The threats are the big agricultural and cattle projects, the big timber companies, the hydroelectric dams with their criminal inundations. In the extractive reserve we will commercialize and industrialize the products that the forest generously yields us. We have in the forest wonderful fruits: the *abacaba*, the *patoá*, the *açai*, the *buriti*, the *pupunha*, the *babaçu*, the *tucumã*, the *copaíba*. . . . The university should come and see the progress of the extractive reserves. It's the only way out, the only way to keep Amazônia from disappearing. And what's more, this reserve will not have owners. It will be for the good of all, and will belong to the state. We will have the usufruct rights, but not the ownership. [It was the *seringal* without the *seringalista*, as one journalist put it — what the tappers had always been doing except that their oppressors had been gotten rid of.]

Who first approved this idea?

Incredibly, it was people abroad. I went up to see the banks who were financing the destruction of Amazônia, to explain our fight. I was interviewed a lot by the international press. Not one Brazilian journalist came to see me. I told them about the rape of Rondônia, the greatest violation of all these development projects. Nothing comparable has been done in the world in terms of destruction in such a short time. Fertile land was transformed into pasture, forest burned, tappers were expelled. It was an apocalypse. . . . Today there is a corridor of smoke from Mato Grosso do Sul to Acre. In the last half century Amazônia has never seen so many fires as in 1988. They are burning everything. Our airports were closed one week in 1987 because of the smoke. This year they were closed one month for the same reason. When you look down from the airplane, Amazônia is nothing but smoke. How it hurts! . . .

If an angel from heaven were to descend and guarantee that my death would strengthen our struggle, it would even be worth it, but experience teaches us the opposite. Thus I want to live. Public gestures and a well-attended funeral will not save Amazônia. I want to live.

On the same day the *Jornal do Brasil* also ran an interview with State Deputy João Carlos Batista, of the Brazilian Socialist Party, who had announced in the Tribunal of the Legislative Assembly of Pará that he had been *anunciado*. Batista was the lawyer representing the *posseiros,* and he was murdered that very night — the sixth on a list of eight who had received the *anúncio.*

The two murders have brutal similarities.

CHICO'S LAST DAYS

To the last, of course, there was uncertainty. Maybe he wasn't going to be killed. But, as one reviews the events leading up to December 22, one is struck again and again by the inevitability of the tragedy. Chico had taken on a huge fight, many people would tell me, a fight there was no way of winning. The denouement came down like a textbook tragedy.

In retrospect everyone thought of things that could have been done.

Why wasn't there a high fence and a vicious dog in the yard, like Chico's brother Zuza had around the corner? A larger question is, What happened to the guys with the Uzis? Apparently the tappers ran out of money for them. A number of people blame Mary Allegretti for "projecting Chico but not protecting him." They think she, with her access to foreign foundation money, having made Chico such a desirable target, should have arranged adequate protection for him. Others blame the PT for inducing Chico to take on the fatal confrontation with Darli. They accuse the PT and other factions in the movement of wanting to make Chico a martyr, for the attention and support it would bring.

Júlio Nicásio, a town councilman for the PT and one of the leaders of the tappers, recalled seven months after the murder that when he and his *companheiros* were unable to persuade Chico to stay away from Xapuri over Christmas, "we felt we could do no more to stop him from buying his fate. He had strayed from the herd. We thought, if it has to be done, then let it be done."

So Chico was killed because of indifference, I said to Julio Cesar, who had conducted the interview with Nicásio. The lamb had to be sacrificed. It was in everybody's interest.

"It wasn't indifference that Júlio Nicásio was talking about," Julio Cesar explained, "but fatalism. It's a trait we got from the Arabs, with the help of the Catholic church. The Arabs have a word, *maktub,* that means 'it is written.' We don't believe in action, but this disbelief in the efficacy of action is different from indifference. We just don't believe we can do anything about it. It's more of a cultural than a moral thing."

Chico's last days were taken up with the usual mediations, meetings, intercessions, union business. "Fifteen days" — a figurative figure, i.e., sometime — before his death, Chico's cousin Raimundo was arrested by the Civil Police for killing a man who had assaulted him in the *seringal.* Raimundo, according to Zuza, asked Chico to intervene for him, and Chico refused. He said, "My friend, you know I don't do that kind of thing. Serve your sentence."

On the fifteenth he celebrated his birthday in Xapuri, something he had never done before. It was his last birthday, the Last Supper. Then he went to Sena Madureira and came back excited, because he had brought four hundred more tappers into the union. But on the next day, the eighteenth, he told his brother Assis, The situation is ugly. The circle is closing.

That day — four days before the murder — a certain dermatologist later testified, Gaston Mota entered the Rio Branco Soccer Club, where there was an illegal gaming table, with two of the mayor's bodyguards. One of the players, a professional gambler known as Zé Arigó, said to the dermatologist, after returning to the table from a confab with Mota, "Four days from now Chico Mendes will die." The doctor said, "You shouldn't make jokes like that." Zé Arigó said, "It isn't a joke. Count four days and see what happens."

On December 5, *O Rio Branco* made in its "Off" [i.e., Off the Record] column the curious announcement about the two-hundred-megaton bomb that was soon going to explode in Acre with national and international repercussions. The rest of the column was devoted to a savage attack on Chico Mendes.

The *pistoleiros* staked out an ambush blind and took up a position in the dense thicket between Chico's house and the river. The blind was maybe fifty yards from the back fence. They cut a track to the road out of town and another one to the river — two exits. Each night, in shifts, they went to the blind and waited. Judging from the advanced decomposition of refuse found at the scene — moldy tin cans, turds, stalks of sugarcane the *pistoleiros* cut in the neighbor's yard and chewed — they must have waited there for several weeks. One night it might be Darci's and his brother-in-law Antônio Pereira's turns. Another night maybe Oloci and one of Antônio's brothers, Sérgio or Amadeus (the three Pereira brothers were part of Darli's entourage; they were short mulattos, and people called them the Mineirinhos, the little ones from Minas Gerais), or maybe Luis Garimpeiro and Zezão, the *pistoleiro* Chico's brother Assis would later be accused of killing. When it rained hard in the middle of the night, they huddled under a plastic sheet. Their main sustenance was occasional handfuls from a bag of *farofa,* manioc flour with eggs and shreds of meat. One of them smoked Charm cigarettes.

A prostitute who lived several houses up the street (one of the investigating officers told me) kept noticing a car pull up after dark to the edge of the thicket, let several passengers out, and drive on. She went to the police and said, "There are these guys every night being let off." The policeman said, "It's probably some of your *xodós,* your johns."

On the day Chico was killed she went back to the policeman and retorted, "Now you see who my *xodós* were."

On December 22, Chico came home from Rio Branco for the holidays. Ilza washed his clothes and hung them in the backyard, which was like raising a flag for the *pistoleiros:* Chico is in residence. The word that Chico was back could have gone out through any number of conduits. Genésio Barbosa, a fifteen-year-old peon from the Fazenda Paraná, had been posted by Darli at the Hotel Veneza, a couple of blocks from Chico's house, and told to keep an eye on who came in and out of town. Darli and Alvarino's nephew Odilon was at the little cement station of the Civil Police, seventy-five yards across the street and up another street from Chico's house. Odilon had been showing up regularly for work for the last "fifteen" days, which he'd never done before. The larger Military Police barracks was maybe a hundred yards down the same street, the Rua Doutor Batista de Moraes. Several soldiers in blue uniforms were washing down a paddywagon parked out front as Chico came back from the market, where he had commiserated with the woman whose son had been hit by a bus.

At five-thirty he started playing dominoes with his two bodyguards in the front yard of the house. The three of them were slapping down the tiles animatedly, saying things like "*Nada disso,* no way! Thought you had me? Well, take this!" Inside, Ilzamar, her kids, her cousin Margarete, and Gumercindo Rodrigues were watching a television soap opera called *Anything Goes,* about the decadence and impunity of the rich in Rio. All Brazil was trying to guess who would kill the main character, unscrupulous Odete Roitmann, in the last episode, which was to run on January 6. The sponsor of the *telenovela* had offered a huge cash prize for the correct answer and had already received a million letters. The murder of Odete Roitmann would get much more attention than the murder of Chico Mendes. There was even speculation that they were killed by the same person. In a country where tens of millions of minds are being suborned, perverted, and zombified by television, even before they attain literacy, the distinction between fact and fiction isn't always clear.

Darkness fell promptly at six. Gumercindo left to take a spin around the town on his motorcycle. Chico finished his game of dominoes and went into the house, passing the group glued to *Anything Goes.* He wasn't much for TV. He grabbed a towel in the bedroom, threw it over his right shoulder, and opened the kitchen door to the backyard. It was pitch-dark. The bulb in the outhouse was out. Chico had been meaning to fix it but hadn't gotten around to it. He couldn't see a thing. He didn't have a chance. He had opened the door two thirds of the way and was starting to step down into the yard when a huge explosion shook the house. Chico, his right chest and shoulder riddled with buckshot, staggered back into the kitchen, slumped on the kitchen table, bloodying plates and food, clutched at the wall, smearing it with red fingerprints, reeled into the bedroom, and collapsed on the floor. Ilza rushed in and found him lying faceup, looking up at her with peaceful, glazing eyes. He said, "Damn, they got me." Then the life went out of his eyes.

As soon as they heard the shot, the guards bolted out the front gate and ran for their lives.

PART TWO

The Second Death of Chico Mendes

THE TERRIBLE SUMMER OF 1988

That summer, while an area of the Amazon the size of Great Britain, according to one estimate, went up in smoke, there had been a blistering heat wave in the United States. Twenty states were declared drought areas. Out west firefighters battled blazes the collective size of Connecticut. Half of Yellowstone National Park burned.

It was a clammy, unnatural heat. Just as they were most needed, the beaches on Long Island, New York, were closed because awful things kept washing up on them: contaminated hospital waste, including used syringes with fluids that tested positive for the AIDS virus. Out in the ocean dolphins were dying of a mysterious disease, possibly AIDS. It was "the year the environment talked back," as George Bush described it during his campaign for the American presidency.

This uneasy sense that the world was deliquescing, that maybe we had brought the Apocalypse on ourselves, was even stronger in the Third World. Island nations like Haiti and Madagascar, denuded of their forests, were self-destructing, washing into the sea. Millions were starving in Africa's drought-stricken Sahel. I'd spent much of the year in Mexico City, which in the last ten years or so had become barely habitable. During the months of the winter inversion the air, trapped by the surrounding mountains, was almost unbreathable. Asphyxiated sparrows fell dead out of the trees in Chapultepec Park. Millions of people defecated in the open on the outskirts of the city, and you could catch hepatitis, amoebic dysentery, and typhoid fever from the fecal storms in the air.

The environmental health of the Old World, especially behind the Iron Curtain, was no better. Europe was still recovering from the nuclear disaster at Chernobyl, two years earlier, which had ruined the milk in northern Italy and contaminated the reindeer in Scandinavia. The Mediterranean was dying. And on top of everything there was this heat you could sense wasn't normal. The winter of 1988–89 in Moscow ended up being seven degrees warmer than any previous. Worldwide, 1988 turned out to be the warmest year on record, warmer even than 1980,

1981, 1983, and 1987, the four previous record breakers since measurements of global surface temperatures began to be kept a century ago.

THE GREENHOUSE EFFECT

What was going on? the public wanted to know. Who is to blame for this? The media, after making inquiries among meteorologists, climatologists, ecologists, and other experts, announced that it had to do with something called the greenhouse effect.

The notion that the atmosphere acts like the glass of a greenhouse, letting in the sun's rays but impeding the radiation of their heat back into outer space, had first been advanced by the French physicist Jean Fourier, in the late eighteenth century. In 1896, the Swedish physicist Svante Arrhenius concluded that it was the absorption of infrared radiation by the water and carbon dioxide molecules in the atmosphere that made the earth's climate warm enough to sustain life. But he was worried about all the coal that the newly industrialized countries were burning. We are "evaporating our coal mines into the air," he warned, and this, he predicted, could double the amount of carbon dioxide in the atmosphere, raising the world's temperature by as much as ten degrees.

Arrhenius was way ahead of his time, and his warnings attracted little notice. It wasn't until 1938 that the British engineer G. D. Callendar further explored the link between increased atmospheric carbon dioxide and global warming and for the first time used the term "greenhouse effect." Callendar, however, thought the rising temperatures were "likely to prove beneficial to mankind in several ways," because they would delay the return of the "deadly glaciers" and would expand "the northern margin of cultivation."

Callendar's work attracted no more attention than Arrhenius's. Occasionally, in the decades that followed, intellectuals would get together and talk about the deleterious effects of Blake's "dark Satanic mills." The poet Allen Ginsberg recalls the greenhouse effect being discussed in the late sixties at a meeting that included Gregory Bateson, the husband of Margaret Mead.

One of the first people to revive the concern about global warming in modern times was the American plant ecologist George M. Woodwell. A few weeks after returning from my second trip to Acre I met Woodwell at a conference on global warming in Sundance, Utah, put together by actor-environmentalist Robert Redford. Woodwell told me he had met Chico Mendes at a conference at the Center for the Study of Nuclear Energy and Agriculture in Piracicaba, São Paulo, a few weeks before he was killed. The conference focused on biogeochemistry and was "reaching out for the political implications of land management." Chico was being guarded but the "guards were slouching around and smoking, and were clearly not trained to guard someone whose life was threatened, or doing their job of surveying the landscape. Mendes had done a spectacular thing, leading the tappers in a series of political steps systematically opposed by commercial interests."

During the early sixties Woodwell began a study of the effect of gamma radiation on an oak-pine forest near the Brookhaven Laboratory, in eastern Long Island, where he was working. The study required measuring the metabolism of the forest, its fixation of carbon from the atmosphere by photosynthesis, and its respiration of carbon dioxide back into the atmosphere. "This required measuring the carbon dioxide in the air, which I did by Keeling's standard technique," he explained. Charles Keeling had been measuring atmospheric carbon dioxide from the top of Mauna Loa, Hawaii, since 1958 with a special tube he had invented for the purpose that had an infrared source at one end. "That put us in the position of thinking how the forest is affected by the atmosphere. We discovered that there is an oscillation in the carbon dioxide levels in the Northern Hemisphere. The levels peak at the end of winter and are lowest at the end of summer. What you see in the atmosphere is the residual of two superimposed, slightly out-of-phase curves of photosynthesis and respiration."

Fascinating, I said.

"I was getting much more oscillation than Keeling, which led me to wonder if the climatologists were wrong in emphasizing, as many of them still do, the contribution of the ocean instead of the forests to the carbon dioxide in the air. If the earth keeps warming the way it has been in the last few decades, this could increase the rates of respiration by as much as thirty percent, with little change in photosynthesis. This is something that no one wants to talk about: the increased respiration from the warming itself.

"Since Keeling's and my work, the anticipated rate of buildup of atmospheric carbon dioxide can actually be observed. For the last century and a half the CO_2 levels have been rising not only because of the use of fossil fuel and because of deforestation but, as I maintain, from increased respiration due to the warming itself. Until the midsixties the contribution of deforestation was greater than that of fossil fuel. Then it became around fifty-fifty, and since then the fossil fuel releases have exceeded those from deforestation.''

Even with all the incredible fires in the Amazon since 1970? I asked.

"Yes," Woodwell said. "The total carbon releases from fossil fuel in the course of the past century and a half, when the human population began to explode, are two hundred to two hundred fifty billion tons. Deforestation is one hundred eighty-five billion tons.''

How can you tell which is which? I wanted to know.

"Fossil fuel emissions have a carbon-13 isotope that burning wood doesn't,'' he explained.

And how much of the CO_2 from deforestation comes from the fires in the Amazon?

"There's no way of accurately measuring it,'' Woodwell replied.

Other scientists do have numbers for the contribution of the fires in Amazônia. The Worldwatch Institute goes with 20 percent. Alberto Setzer, of the Brazilian Institute of Space Research, has an estimate of 17 percent, which is accepted by respected American scientists like Thomas Lovejoy. But other scientists at the institute maintain that it is no more than 5 percent. Obviously the figure is political. Since I collected these figures, astonishingly high levels of CO_2 have been found over Africa during the annual burns of the savanna. It's unclear whether this discovery diminishes the importance of the Amazon fires.

Curiously, compared with all the attention the Amazonian fires and their connection with the greenhouse effect received during the terrible summer of 1988, there was very little media attention to the fact that more than 50 percent of atmospheric carbon dioxide comes from the use of fossil fuels; most of this is generated by the emissions of internal-combustion engines, particularly cars in the United States. It was a lot easier to blame it on the bossa nova than to confront our own egregious role in the problem.

A major factor in the sudden concern about the rain forest that swept the First World that summer was the prominent coverage in the *New York Times*. A lot of the credit for this goes to Marlise Simons, a high-powered, cosmopolitan correspondent married to Alan Riding, the dean of

Latin American journalists. One of the great husband-wife teams in modern journalism, the couple took over the *Times*'s Rio desk in 1984. Alan covered coups and the hard political news, and Marlise took on the Amazon, which had not received much attention in the *Times* since Jonathan Kandell had been the Rio correspondent in the late 1970s. Her superb coverage was very much overdue: it was an idea whose time had come.

Interest in the Amazon had been building steadily since the first flurry of anxiety over the construction of the Trans-Amazon Highway in 1970–71. There were articles in *Time* and *Newsweek* expressing concern about the impact of the highway on the still largely unidentified flora and fauna of the rain forest. The situation sounded dire, but it was a long way away, not in our jurisdiction.

In 1975 two ecologists, Robert J. Goodland and Howard Irwin, brought out a book called *Amazon Jungle: Green Hell to Red Desert?*, which spelled out the impending disaster very clearly and got considerable attention. I remember reading an article in *Penthouse* around that time about a huge machine that was supposed to be moving slowly through the forest, chewing up the trees and spitting out pavement in its wake. The destruction of Amazônia was already capturing the First World's imagination. My book *The Rivers Amazon* came out in 1978. I included a paragraph of Woodwell talking about how the deforestation made a double-barreled contribution to the greenhouse effect by pouring CO_2 into the air and reducing the number of trees that could act as carbon sinks, and about his concern that the warming of the climate could wreak geopolitical havoc, wiping out coastal cities, bringing drought to agricultural areas, and creating millions of environmental refugees. *The Rivers Amazon* generated quite a lot of attention, and the interest intensified with the publication of Brian Kelly and Mark London's *Amazon*, in 1983, Catherine Caufield's *In the Rainforest* a year later, and Roger Stone's *Dreams of Amazonia* a year after that.

THE AMBASSADOR OF THE AMAZON

Another important figure in the story of Amazônia's increasing international exposure is Thomas E. Lovejoy. Lovejoy has been a major player in the battle to save the Amazon since the early seventies and is one of the most eloquent spokesmen for the world's tropical rain forests. An ornithologist turned environmental statesman, he now spends much of his time making television appearances and keynote addresses at scientific conferences, taking movie stars down to his research station in the Amazon, winning new friends for the cause any way he can. Natty, bowtied, patrician, he's a rare bird himself, and a vitally important one to the planetary ecosystem.

The son of an insurance executive, Lovejoy grew up an only child in New York City. "People from my socioeconomic background were sent away to school," he explains, and off he went to a place called Millbrook. There he studied with a remarkable biology teacher who "flipped the switch" and awoke in him a fascination for the "magic of living things." By the time he went on to Yale, in the fall of 1959, his path was already chosen. Between his junior and senior years Lovejoy went to Nubia and collected plants and animals about to be flooded by the Aswān Dam. "All I wanted to be was a happy naturalist going to exotic places and doing exotic things," he recalled. But already, as he saw the waters rising, he had glimmerings that all was not right with the world.

He enrolled in graduate school under the great biologist Evelyn Hutchinson, who more than anyone else is responsible for developing the modern science of ecology. Hutchinson had warned about the greenhouse effect as early as 1954. Lovejoy also worked with the famous ornithologist Roger Tory Peterson to save the ospreys that were being decimated by DDT at the mouth of the Connecticut River.

For his Ph.D. in ornithology Lovejoy spent two years in Belém, at the mouth of the Amazon. By then he was married, and his twin daughters were born while he was there. He built a tower up in the forest canopy outside the city and started to catalogue the birds. There are about a thousand species of birds in the Amazon basin — one eighth of all the species in the world — and Lovejoy caught about three hundred of them in his mist nets. He took blood samples and examined them for arthropod-borne viruses. He did a massive computer analysis of his field observations, which shed new light on patterns of diversity and how bird communities are structured.

Just as he was leaving, the Trans-Amazon Highway was begun. Lovejoy wrote an article called "The Transamazonica: Highway to Extinction?" one of the first to warn about the catastrophic impact that the development of the Amazon would have on the unparalleled richness of life in the valley. Many species in Amazônia have small ranges and small populations, he explained, giving as an example the black-chested pygmy tyrant *(Taeniotriccus andrei),* "of which only six specimens have ever been recorded in Brazil." Such species are particularly vulnerable to extinction "if the forest is broken up by extensive colonization along highway systems."

In 1973, he was hired as an ecologist by the World Wildlife Fund. "The more I learned about the problems, the more alarmed I became. When you look at any one piece of the picture, it's not that alarming, but when you put it all together you've got to be terrified. And every one of the elements plays out in Brazil." Lovejoy now gives the planet ten years before its major systems start breaking down. "I'm convinced that most of the great environmental struggles will be won or lost in the nineties, and that by the next century it will be too late." In other words, the decisions made or not made, and the actions taken or not taken, in the next decade will, he feels, determine how much longer the planet will be hospitable to the human species.

I remember reading a prediction by Lovejoy in *Science* magazine in 1976 that a million species were going to become extinct before they were even identified if the clearing and burning of tropical forests continued at the rate at which it was proceeding. When I got to the Amazon and saw the ocean of trees spreading as far as I could see in every direction, I was taken in by what another scientist has called the illusion of endlessness and was skeptical about Lovejoy's estimate. But the more often I went to Amazônia and had the unsettling experience of finding places that had been pristine a few years earlier suddenly obliterated, the more I realized how fast the forest was going, that the rates of destruction were geometric, and that the numbers were not important; the important thing is that it has to stop. In fact, a million species is a perfectly reasonable projection, even a conservative one — for the Amazon alone.

I spent an afternoon in Lovejoy's office browsing through several file cabinets containing his papers and speeches — an incredible output. When I had finished I could see why he was alarmed. Among the subjects were biotic impoverishment, accelerating rates of extinction, conservation of migratory species, the edge effect in isolated forest fragments, the genetic aspects of dwindling populations, the need to think of conservation as not only the preservation of genes and germ plasm but also of evolution and behavior. In one of his speeches Lovejoy quoted a codicil to Benjamin Franklin's 1789 will: "It has been my opinion, that he who receives an Estate from his ancestors is under some kind of obligation to transmit the same to their posterity."

In 1974 Lovejoy took part in a meeting at the Smithsonian Institution in Washington, to set priorities for the world's remaining tropical forests. He met Paulo Nogueira Neto and Maria Teresa Jorge de Pádua (two visionary Brazilians who were already fighting a losing battle against the Brazilian Miracle); Ghillean Prance, the curator of Amazonian botany at the New York Botanical Garden; and Gary Wetterberg, an American forester. As they compared notes, the "message that the Amazonian rain forest was critically endangered came through loud and clear."

The first step in helping the IBDF, the Brazilian Institute for Forestry Development, develop a conservation plan for Amazônia, they decided, was to identify the areas of greatest diversity, the "centers of endemism." During the warm, dry spells of the Pleistocene epoch, sea level dropped and the Amazon forest shrank to a few isolated islands, or refugia, surrounded by savanna, in which there were tremendous bursts of speciation. The ornithologist Jürgen Haffer identified the centers of bird endemism, Prance those of plants, the herpetologist Paulo Vanzolini those of lizards, and the entomologist Keith Brown those of butterflies. Where the four maps overlapped were the areas of the highest priority. The refugia theory has since been challenged, because much of the seasonally flooded forest along the rivers did not disappear during the Pleistocene, and because the areas with the greatest diversity of primates do not correspond with the refugia mapped out for the other forms.

But this was a place to start. Lovejoy presented the maps to the IBDF as a blueprint for the preservation of Brazilian Amazônia. Eventually — by the time Chico was killed — the government created ten national parks, eleven ecological stations, eight national forests, and four extractive reserves. A total of 2.9 percent of legal Amazônia was protected, at least on paper. The ultimate plan is for 5 percent to be protected. This, added to the Indian reserves, plus the 50 percent of their parts of the forest that any developers are supposed to leave intact, was a beginning.

"The problem still seemed manageable," Lovejoy recalled of the conservation efforts in the seventies, "because so many of the agricultural and colonization projects had failed. The big hydroelectric dams and the Carajás project had not happened yet. There had been no gold strikes. There was every reason for real hope.''

But the conservationists grew frustrated as it became increasingly clear that the Brazilian government was only paying lip service to environmental control — so frustrated that eventually even Nogueira Neto and Jorge de Pádua, among the few Brazilians who cared, quit their government posts in disgust. But Lovejoy, typically, kept his cool. His approach was diplomatic: play ball with the powers that be, don't get emotionally involved, always keep your eye on the ultimate goal of saving as much as you can, struggle to be reasonable even if the other side isn't, even though the forces of destruction are so much greater than the forces for conservation and sustainable use. When construction began on Carajás and the hydroelectric dams, Lovejoy worked with agencies involved to create parks to offset the damage.

In 1977–78 Lovejoy, in conjunction with Brazilian scientists, got another extremely important project off the ground, the Minimum Critical Size of Ecosystems Project. Looking at the future, in which the sea of trees would inevitably be reduced by deforestation to islands of rain forest, Lovejoy now began to wonder how large the islands had to be to maintain their integrity. At what point does the reduction of an area of rain forest lead to ecosystem breakdown, massive extinction, the whole system falling apart? It was clear that the smaller the islands, the faster the rates of ecosystem decay.

Again, typically, Lovejoy used the existing sociopolitical structure to his advantage. Not wanting to clear the forest himself, he approached the ranchers around Manaus, where he proposed to set up the project, and asked them that as long as they were going to have to leave half their land untouched, would they mind clearing certain areas while leaving patches of forest in different sizes — one hectare, 10 hectares, 100 hectares, 1,000 hectares, 10,000 hectares — so he could study them. The idea was to study them over time: before, during, and after clearing and burning around them left them isolated. Lovejoy envisaged a twenty-year project.

One of its benefits was that the ranchers themselves would become involved, thus raising their environmental awareness. That was Lovejoy the statesman: win new friends for the rain forest, have a greater vision than conflict. Another plus was that the project would provide an opportunity to train Brazilian and American scientists in tropical forest biology. There are something like only four thousand tropical biologists in the world — far too few for the urgent task of inventorying the rain forest, half of whose species may be lost in the next century.

"Can the cinnamon-crested spadebill, for instance, survive in a hundred-hectare stand?" Lovejoy mused. "We have already made forty thousand bird captures, but the answers are still years away."

The Minimum Critical Size of Ecosystems Project will also provide insights into the global problem of habitat fragmentation and ecosystem decay. "Even if we had just been sitting around drinking *cachaça*," Lovejoy told me, "the project would have had some real benefit. Its existence has influenced people around the world to think about ecosystem decay and to respond by setting aside bigger areas."

THE ULTIMATE FIRE STORY

The destruction in the Amazon was also brought to the world's attention through the work of Alberto Setzer, who is in charge of the Amazon program at INPE, the Brazilian Institute of Space Research. Marlise Simons met Alberto in the spring of 1987, and he told her that he was going to start a remote sensing project that would pinpoint the fires in Amazônia and give a rough idea of the extent of the destruction.

When I dropped in on Setzer at INPE's headquarters, in São José dos Campos, in the state of São Paulo, he was sitting before the screen of a multispectral image analyzer, studying that day's infrared images from the meteorological satellite NOAA-9. The images are beamed to a station in Mato Grosso and then transferred to tape and trucked down to Setzer within several hours. "NOAA-9 is used for day-to-day fire vigilance," he explained. "Its images are good for fire depiction, but their resolution is too low for analyzing the type of vegetation that is burning or the extent of deforestation. For this another satellite, LANDSAT, is used. One of the problems is that NOAA-9 can't see through thick smoke or clouds, so there is actually more burning than it is able to pick up.

"The fire-monitoring research began in 1985," Setzer went on, "with ABLE 1, a joint experimental project in the Amazon with NASA to understand the interaction of the atmosphere and the forest. We found that the fires had a significant effect on the chemical composition of millions of square kilometers, that all sorts of gases and aerosols were being produced.''

One day in early July 1987, in the third year of the project, Setzer made a routine check of the NOAA-9 tapes over Rondônia. ''I just decided to see what was up,'' he said. ''I never thought I'd find thousands and thousands of fires. All of the international furor results from this spot check, which showed unprecedented, uncontrolled burning. The burning continued through September. Up to 1987 the official estimate for the burning in Amazônia was forty-five fires per year, based on reports from park guards. But the satellite showed on a single day more than seven thousand fires all over the valley. The smoke was spread over a wide portion of the continent. It's something that can't go on. It's a crime against our planet and a crime against the resources of Brazil.''

That year, the peak year, 205,000 square kilometers burned. ''Not all of it was primary rain forest,'' Setzer explained, ''much was recently deforested pasture. Brazilians like to burn their fields almost every year. It's a cultural thing. Most of the people who do it are illiterate and have no idea what they're doing, of the far-reaching impact of their actions, any more than the *campesinos* who grow coca, poppies, and marijuana in Mexico, Peru, Bolivia, and Colombia realize the damage their crops will do to young people's minds in the north.

''But for some reason fire has a stronger effect on people,'' he said. ''It catches the attention.''

It was Setzer's report on the fires in Amazônia in 1987 that turned the international spotlight on the Amazon. Fábio Feldmann, the only federal deputy in the Brazilian congress to be elected on the environmental ticket, recalled that ''when I saw the report — that twenty million hectares, two hundred thousand square kilometers, the size of the entire state of São Paulo, had gone up in smoke, eight thousand fires per day — I thought it was an error in typing. Before there was burning, but not of this magnitude.''

Marlise Simons broke the story on the 1987 fires a year later, on August 12, in the middle of the terrible summer of 1988. Her account, headlined ''VAST AMAZON FIRES, MAN-MADE, LINKED TO GLOBAL WARMING,'' was accompanied by a picture of a NASA photograph of a composite of all the fires over west-central Amazônia between August 1 and September 18, 1987. The rash of glowing dots was concentrated along BR-364 in Rondônia. ''From the flames, tons of fumes and particles are hurled into the sky,'' she wrote, ''and at night, roaring and red, the forest looks to be at war.'' The conflagration was so vast that ''it may account for at least one tenth of the global man-made output of CO_2, which is believed to be causing a warming of the earth through the greenhouse effect.''

The area burned in 1987 was one and a half times the size of New York State, she reported. Smoke clouds from the fires ''often rose to 12,000 feet,'' though the gases and particles were lifted up even higher into jet streams and blown south across the South Atlantic to Antarctica, where some of the gases, methane and nitrous oxides, may have interacted with the ozone shield, further enlarging the hole in it, although there is no proof of this yet. According to Simons's article, the 1987 fires sent up carbon dioxide containing more than 500 million tons of carbon, 44 million tons of carbon monoxide, more than 6 million tons of particles, almost 5 million of methane, 2.5 million of ozone, more than a million tons of nitrous oxides and other substances ''that can circulate globally and influence radiation and climate.'' She quoted Setzer, who compared their collective effect to ''the outburst of a very large volcano.'' On September 9, the worst day, 7,603 fires were burning in the valley. By Setzer's estimate, which he said was conservative, there were more than 170,000 fires larger than one square kilometer in Amazônia that year.

Fire stories are a staple of journalism, and this was the ultimate fire story. It went over like a match tossed on a haystack that summer, when the whole world seemed to be burning. The *Times* didn't let go. Seventeen days later, on August 29, it ran a hard-hitting editorial. ''A calamitous cycle of destruction is unfolding in Rondônia. The tragedy is a lesson to Brazil, and to the international agencies that finance its projects, that needless development can wreak havoc with the global environment, not just Brazil's.''

Marlise told me that she had known of Chico Mendes's work for several years and had been meaning to visit him and the tappers in Acre. ''Finally, in December of 1988, I had a long talk with him in Rio to plan my trip. That afternoon he spoke with such conviction that he was going to die that it shook me up. I was reminded of the days when I lived in Central America, where the people who were involved in their own battles and had a sense of doom kept telling about the threats on their life. When we made an appointment for January seventh, I was sure I would never see him again.''

RAIN FOREST CHIC

Simons's story on the fires in Rondônia and their global importance was picked up by the Brazilian press, which often gives front-page treatment to what the *New York Times* says about Brazil; this in itself is news. The Brazilian papers had been carrying a lot of environmental stories. As the military had begun to loosen its grip and press controls were relaxed, the environment became one of the first subjects it was safe to write about.

The fires also went over big in Europe, whose environmental ills were perhaps even more advanced than the New World's. The Netherlands, much of which is below sea level, was particularly alarmed about the burning. It took ''more than an academic interest in what Brazil does to its rain forest,'' as Reuters reported, because a 3- to 9-inch rise in sea level due to global warming had been predicted by the year 2050, which was already up 6 inches from the century before. The Dutch had budgeted billions of dollars to rebuilding their dikes.

All over the West that summer, the papers and airwaves were full of dire predictions, warning how the great capitals — New York, London, Beijing, Rio — and the Nile, Mississippi, and Ganges deltas would be drowned and millions of environmental refugees would be unleashed on the earth, like *flagelados* from the Northeast; how the midwestern grain belt would be desertified, and Canada and Siberia would become the world's new centers of wheat and corn production. There were going to be all sorts of other monumental geopolitical consequences. It looked as if the Maldives would be wiped out completely. Maumoon Abdul Gayoom, the president of the chain of 1,190-some islands in the Indian Ocean, most of which are less than seven feet high, had already addressed the United Nations the year before: ''It is now a distressing probability that the environmental changes caused by industrial progress may slowly drown this unique paradise in its entirety.''

Ecologist George Woodwell warned that it might no longer be possible for forests to maintain themselves as stable communities, that forests as we know them might no longer be sustainable. By the time the trees matured and set seed, the climate would no longer be hospitable for them. Changes that previously had taken place over ten thousand years were now happening in a couple of decades, and the forests couldn't keep up with them. By the mid-1990s some forests may already have disappeared from the southern edges of their ranges.

Daniel Botkin, of the University of California, Santa Barbara, estimated that for every centigrade degree temperatures rose, the forests would have to move 60 to 100 miles north, but the migratory capacity of trees, whose seeds are dispersed by wild animals and wind, is only 20 miles per century. So, with the temperature change over the next century conservatively estimated at three centigrade degrees, plus the fact that the natural migratory routes for the seeds will become more and more scarce with the loss of continuous forest, the forests, left increasingly high and dry — islands in a rising sea of manipulated landscape — won't have a chance.

The same sort of recriminations and finger pointing that the AIDS pandemic had generated was going back and forth between the First and Third worlds. The Third World blamed the First World's cars and smokestacks and conscienceless multilateral lending agencies and craving for beef, while the First World, loath to confront its own predominant role in the problem, found it easier to blame the crisis on Third World slackness. At hastily called conferences on global warming there was a lot of hot air and gasing, further contributing to the greenhouse effect. At one such conference I heard an American politician complain, ''We're hostage to the aspirations of India and China, which are on crash industrialization schedules and plan to burn tremendous coal reserves, and of Brazil, which is burning its forest in a misguided effort to become one of the superpowers.'' Another, more sympathetic participant countered, ''Who are we to talk? Isn't that just what we did to get where we are? Didn't we clear-cut our forest and strip-mine our coal and pave the continent with roads? How can we ask the people in the Third World to make sacrifices on our behalf when they've been making sacrifices all their lives?''

This was a big story, as big as you could get — the Apocalypse — and the media ate it up. It cut through everything: not just the poor countries but the whole world was about to blow. It touched a nerve of liberal guilt. We 220 million Americans have been consuming 66 percent of the world's resources to maintain our standard of living. We've been living off the dawn-to-dusk, backbreaking work of billions of peasants. We've become the hated upper class, and now there's going to be a revolution, a revolution of the very environment, in which humble tillers of the soil, who were there before the machine age and the advent of science and recorded history, and will be there after them, will rise triumphant.

So the sudden acceleration of concern for the rain forest during the terrible summer of 1988 was partly a creation of the media. But it was also a symptom of the anguish and guilt of the modern world. "People are really antsy," a Hollywood scriptwriter told me. "Suddenly they're becoming aware that it's finite, that it's going to be all over. People like Wendell Berry [farmer, essayist, and back-to-the-land advocate] are telling us it's already too late, it's exponential."

As word went around that hamburgers were made of rain forest beef, the hamburger became a potent symbol of the ambush we were setting for ourselves. Feeding our faces, we were doing in the planet and ourselves. People began to plaster their bumpers with "Stop the Whopper" stickers, especially on the West Coast. In fact, none of the beef that ends up at Burger King, McDonald's, and the other American fast food chains comes from the Amazon; this is a popular misconception. The region is actually a net importer of beef. In 1987 Brazil exported seven million tons of beef, but none of it was fresh, because of the threat of hoof-and-mouth disease. For years Brazilian beef exports have been frozen or processed into corned beef. These exports have come not from Amazônia, but from São Paulo, Mato Grosso do Sul, Goiás — the big beef-producing states. Costa Rica and Argentina are the main exporters of forest beef. The campaign against rain forest beef was effective: Burger King suspended its Costa Rican contracts.

One of the best commentaries I have heard on the hamburger connection is from the environmental activist Jeremy Rifkin, who wrote a provocative book on what he calls entropy economics and has recently penned a sequel, *Entropy into the Greenhouse World*. Rifkin explained his thesis: "Economic activity is only the collective transformation, exchange, and discarding of matter and energy. Dust to dust. Short-term gain is always at the expense of long-term environmental and economic losses. The question is, When do you pay the bill? Efficiency always eclipses the sustainable timetable. The real cost of one hamburger is five hundred pounds of carbon, the carbon dioxide the burned trees release into the atmosphere, the methane the cows emit in their paddies, breath and farts (adding to the global warming), the lost genetic stock and germ plasm (which is the only way food plants are going to be able to adapt to the greenhouse world), the birds that fly down to the tropics for the winter and die because there's no habitat for them and no insects to eat, and the peasants who are uprooted.''

The recent concern over the environment was also part ecovogue: the jungle has sex appeal. Those who had already done world hunger rallied to the cause. Peter Max announced a new line of sportswear that included a "Save the Rain Forest" T-shirt. Sting did a rain forest benefit at the Kennedy Center, and the Grateful Dead performed at Madison Square Garden for the smoldering biome. Imran Khan and the marchioness of Worcester lent their patronage to a magnificent "rain forest ball" at London's Hippodrome ("tropical dress" was recommended), and even Kermit the Frog gave his support. River Phoenix, the new post–Tom Cruise teenage heartthrob, interviewed about his dreams, said, "I'd like to buy parts of the Amazon to save the forest from destruction.'' One morning I turned on CBS Morning News and there was Olivia Newton-John and a bunch of friends with headphones on, the whole "We Are the World" schmear, singing for the rain forest.

A plethora of institutions sprouted up, with names like Rain Forest Action Network, Tropical Ecosystem Research, and Resource Alliance International, in defense of the beleaguered life-realm. There were rain forest town meetings, mixed-media installations, and other happenings. The Polish-born artist Frans Kracjberg, who had fled to Brazil from war-torn Europe and was living in a tree house in the mountains above Rio, had an exhibit called "Amazon Cemetery," which consisted of his sculptures of black, singed, fire-eaten, twisted trees. As a comparative veteran of the rain forest scene, I was deluged with all kinds of records, tapes, T-shirts, invitations to openings, and other promotional material. One day I noticed a photograph of a lush forest with tree ferns in the *New York Times*. It was an advertisement: "If our shoes were disappearing as quickly as the rain forest, we wouldn't need a semi-annual sale.''

I asked Daniel Katz, director of the Rain Forest Alliance, a group that formed before the vogue and is one of the most effective ones, why people were suddenly getting worked up about the rain forest when the problem had been clearly spelled out by scientists like Lovejoy and Woodwell ten years before. He said it was partly due to the world's growing together in the global village; the same media currents were spreading the worldwide democracy movement and the craving for the American standard of living. "There's a new sense now that what you do to the rain forest comes back to you, that it isn't just this jungle home to Tarzan and Jane a million miles away, that we're all in this together."

Jason Clay, the director of Cultural Survival, an outfit that has been dealing with the problems of the Amazon's native people for years, was as baffled by the rain forest–chic phenomenon as I was. He offered the theory that "the fires out west became associated in Americans' minds with the fires in the Amazon, so that the whole world seemed to be on fire. And after the western fires died down the footage of the Brazilian fires continued. Then there was the *Exxon Valdez* oil spill and the terrible footage of the dead sea otters and shorebirds coated with oil, and the problems in the Amazon were kept in the public mind that fall with the threatened arrest for treason of [the Kayapó Indian] Paiakan and the threatened expulsion from Brazil of his supporter [American ethnobotanist] Darrell Posey, who were protesting the planned construction of ten hydroelectric dams on the Xingu River."

One day I got a call from a publicist for the World Rain Forest Movement, a militant new group that was going to be presenting three hundred thousand signatures to the United Nations, asking for a complete halt to deforestation of the temperate and tropical forests, and calling for an emergency session of the Security Council to address the problem. The petition included the thumbprints of six hundred Penan tribesmen, who, led by Cheeyoke Ling Penan, had been blocking logging roads in Sarawak, on the island of Borneo, for two years.

Oh yes, I said, I remembered being invited the year before to the Right Livelihood Awards ceremony for S. Mohamed Idris, the head of Friends of the Earth in Sarawak, who had been organizing nonviolent human blockades, like the tappers' *empates,* against the massive logging operations there. Idris had apparently hit upon the strategy independently and had known nothing about the tappers' resistance movement. But Idris had been placed under house arrest and had been unable to come and get his award. The Malaysian government was cracking down on the resisters. There was a new law: anyone causing the obstruction of logging activities faced a two-year jail sentence and a $2,500 fine.

The situation in Sarawak, which provides 58 percent of the world's tropical logs, was as acute as the one in the Amazon. A statement by a woman named Rosalyn Nyagon related how the timber companies "mowed down our forest and leveled our hills. The sacred graves of our ancestors were desecrated. Our waters and streams are contaminated, our plant life is destroyed, and the forest animals are killed or have run away. The forest is our survival. Without the forest we'll all be dead, and now there's hardly anything left. That's why we'll stay at this struggle until they listen to us. We want them to leave our land."

It was the same situation in India. The Gandhian activist Sunderlal Bahuguna had led a five-thousand-kilometer, trans-Himalayan foot march that resulted in the ban on cutting the Himalayan forests. His Chipko movement had begun back in April 1973, when villagers, determined to save their forest, had put their bodies between the trees and the contractors' axes. These were the earliest *empates* that I'd heard of. The movement's slogan was "Ecology Is Permanent Economy."

I asked the publicist for the World Rain Forest Movement if she could explain the sudden interest in the rain forest. "A lot of people are jumping on the bandwagon," she said. "It's the tribals. There's a lot of New Age interest in this tribal stuff. The word has gotten out about the importance of the rain forest to the climate. It's chic. It may be passing but I hope not. I hope they delve into it and really get into the meat of the issue, which is economics. It's not just doing little changes to your life-style. It's major."

Maybe it wasn't just trendy. Maybe the species really was rallying at the final hour to save itself from going under. Maybe we really were going to mend our ways. The environment was moving to the center of geopolitics. There was a growing vision of the planet as a single ecosystem transcending national interests, which was creating exciting new possibilities for international cooperation. A sense of urgency had been mounting, particularly in post-Chernobyl Europe. The environmentalist parties, especially the Green Party, were winning more and more seats in the national parliaments. The prime minister of Norway, Gro Harlem Brundtland, was a Green. Thirteen percent of the seats in the twelve-nation European Economic Community had just gone to the Greens. All over the world the environment was shaping up as the major issue of the twenty-first century. Mikhail Gorbachev, in a speech before the United Nations, mentioned the environment no less than twenty times, comparing its degradations to such threats as war, hunger, and disease. In the United States, Senators Timothy Wirth and Albert Gore, John Heinz and Robert Kasten, picked up the environmental banner and promised to address the greenhouse effect.

Perhaps even Hollywood's great awakening to the global environmental threat represented something more serious. People like Robert Redford, Jane Fonda, and John Denver had already been using their celebrity for years to try to do good for the planet, and now Barbra Streisand, Norman Lear, and Tom Cruise were also assuming leadership roles. Even hard-bitten agents were beginning to describe themselves as environmentalists. The industry had never expressed such concern about anything. There was a growing realization that the big movies of the nineties were going to be about the environment.

I followed with great interest the debates about the greenhouse effect, the postgame analysis of the murderous summer of 1988. The scientists were unable to agree on how much the world had warmed since the Industrial Revolution, on how fast it had been warming, on how specific countries and regions would be affected, and on whether the effect had already begun. The problem was that even the most sophisticated mathematical climate models were limited when it came to predicting the weather, which, like the stock market, is a nonreplicative "chaotic system," notoriously difficult to monitor, its many variables ensuring constant surprises.

One day the *Times* would run a story that since 1895 U.S. data had failed to show a warming trend. A few days later there would be an account that 1988 had been found to set a record for global warmth. Some argued that the record heat of the eighties was "nothing more than normal climate variation" and that there wasn't really any greenhouse effect to speak of. North America and China had suffered heat waves and drought during the summer of 1988, but Ireland and Western Europe had been unusually chilly and wet, while in the Southern Hemisphere (where the seasonal cycle is the inverse of the Northern Hemisphere's) the Gran Chaco region of Paraguay, Bolivia, and northern Argentina had experienced one of the coldest winters on record.

On August 23, 1988, the atmospheric physicist Jim Hansen, director of the Goddard Institute for Space Studies, gave some very dramatic testimony to the U.S. Senate. He was "ninety-nine percent certain" that the recent warming trend wasn't natural variation. It was "time to stop waffling," he said. "The greenhouse effect is here." From now on the dice would be loaded for hot. The probability that most of the country during the nineties would have hotter-than-normal summers was 55 to 88 percent. The annual rate of accumulation of carbon dioxide in the atmosphere was rising by 0.5 percent. Hanson had become concerned after studying spacecraft data on the atmosphere of Venus, where a runaway greenhouse effect has produced temperatures hot enough to melt lead.

Most of the scientists agreed that the greenhouse effect was indeed having an impact. The debate was mainly about how serious it was, and how quickly we would begin to experience catastrophic warming. One model had the atmospheric CO_2 levels doubling by 2060–70 and a 3- to 9-degree temperature rise as early as 2030. Another claimed that by 2075 the burning of fossil fuel would be two and a half times the present level, resulting in a 5- to 15-degree rise. The worst-case scenario had a fivefold increase, with a 10- to 30-degree rise.

RIO REVISITED

On December 23, the day after Chico's murder, I flicked on the evening news in my cabin in upstate New York and saw a familiar scene: a distraught crowd of mestizo people in T-shirts with the acronyms of political parties and the names of candidates for local office printed on them, and colorful shacks up on pilings in the background. That could only be one place, I realized — Amazônia.

Something terrible had happened. Maybe one of the double-decker riverboats had capsized and hundreds of passengers had drowned, as happens once a year or so. I tuned in to the broadcast: a union leader had been shot. His name, Chico Mendes, meant nothing. I knew about the work on extractive reserves; a friend at the Environmental Defense Fund had sent me papers by Steven Schwartzman, Mary Allegretti, and Susanna Hecht. But I hadn't been to the Amazon in four years. I had spent much of the late eighties in Africa, exploring the equatorial forests of that majestic, heartbreaking continent.

But as it turned out, I was already on my way down to Brazil: the *New York Times* had asked me to do an article about the recent bankruptcy of Rio for its Sunday magazine.

I arrived nine days after Chico's murder, on the last day of 1988. The city looked better than I expected, pretty much the same as it would have if it hadn't gone belly up. It was the poor, as usual, who were the most affected. The staffs of the emergency hospitals were skeletal; there wasn't a Band-Aid to be had. The schools were closed because of a strike by the ill-paid teachers, depriving many children of their only square meal of the day.

The main cause of the city's bankruptcy, besides crippling inflation and the repercussions of the foreign debt, was the "bloated public sector, the cannibalization of public revenues by clientele politics," as one economist explained. The outgoing mayor hadn't been corrupt as much as an easy touch. He handed out thousands of jobs to relatives and friends, as was more or less expected, seventeen thousand in the last six months alone. Twenty percent of the new employees were *fantasmas* who never showed up. Five percent showed up but did nothing.

As usual, I stayed in Copacabana. The beach is oilier than those of Ipanema or Leblon, but the scene is more animated. Copacabana was the Brazilian dream of paradise in the forties. People from all over the country came and retired there, and now it has a deteriorated, Felliniesque, Miami Beach quality. There is an old, nostalgic segment of the population — dowagers who take tea on the Rua Barão de Ipanema, white-haired gentlemen with marvelous mustaches reminiscing in bars. The Avenida Nossa Senhora de Copacabana was lined with street vendors displaying digital watches, electronic devices, and other contraband from Paraguay, laid out on tables. Such "informal" activities were flourishing in the economic crisis. Thirty percent of the Brazilian economy was said to be off the books.

Most of the freaks who had been there two years earlier, on my last trip to Rio, were still around. A legless man with an extraordinarily beautiful and dignified profile (he never looked up at you) wheeled up on a tray in the hopes of a handout. Occasionally a street kid tore through the crowd with someone's wallet. The Incredible Hulk, as I called him, a seven-foot-tall mulatto with dreadlocks, wearing only a jacket and underpants, barefoot, his calves swollen with hideous, festering sores, was still wandering around the Avenida. Painted whores in labia-splitting spandex tights, not all of them female, were coming on to Norwegian roughnecks from offshore oil rigs up the coast. I thought how this crazy, magical, wide-open, wonderful country had incredible power now, the power it always wanted, but in a negative way. If it keeps on deforesting the Amazon, it could destroy the planet, and if it defaults on its debt, it could bring down the whole house of cards.

I thought about the importance of the frontier in America's probably never-to-be-repeated rise to greatness. The frontier meant room — to keep growing, to try over, to experiment with new ideas. And now the Brazilians were being denied their frontier. Beset by triple-digit inflation and the threatened degeneration of their attempt to return to democracy into violent chaos, their bad image abroad as ecological villains and deadbeats feeding their inferiority complex as mixed-race former colonials, they were beginning to lose faith in the future, and their famous buoyant joie de vivre was giving way to deep pessimism.

I recalled what Teddy Roosevelt, the ultimate man of action, the bully positivist, said of Amazônia in his book *Through the Brazilian Wilderness:* "This cannot be permitted to remain idle, to lie as a tenantless wilderness." What would we have done if the Amazon had been our frontier at the turn of the century? We would have attacked it like Roosevelt, who descended the unknown River of Doubt with the famous Colonel Rondon, dispatching the innumerable black caimans along its banks, which are now almost extinct. "They are often dangerous to domestic animals," Roosevelt explained, "and are always destructive to fish, and it is good to shoot them. I killed half a dozen and missed nearly as many more — a throbbing boat does not improve one's aim."

But this was not the moment for heavy reflection. It was New Year's Eve, a joyous catharsis for the Brazilians, a time to purge one's soul of painful memories and mistakes and to begin with a clean slate. A few days earlier the traditional blizzard of superannuated paperwork had drifted down into the streets of the Centro, the business district, as people gaily chucked the business of 1988 — correspondence, printouts, receipts — out their office windows. It was a fresh start for Rio, with a new mayor taking office, pruning the municipal organogram of *fantasmas*. Already emergency crews were filling in the 130,000 potholes and replacing the 40,000 blown streetlights left by the previous administration — an important psychological palliative.

Late in the afternoon hundreds of thousands of people began to drift down to Copacabana beach to bring in the New Year together — one of the great gatherings of the species. By midnight two and a half million celebrants were there, according to estimates published the next day. Evangelical services and rites of African *candomblé* and *umbanda* were going on in marquees pitched in the sand. Kneeling people were being blessed by fat black priestesses in white kerchiefs and voluminous skirts; offertory candles blazed in pits scooped out of the sand. Little boats were being launched into the waves, filled with bottles of champagne and other gifts for Iemanjá, the goddess of the sea. Above the scene, the rich, in black tie, stood in the full-length glass windows of the million-dollar apartments on the Avenida Atlântica.

At 11:55 everyone on the beach began to head down to the spotlit breakers. The waves were unusually big, dangerously big. Several hundred yards beyond them dozens of yachts and cabin cruisers with illuminated rigging bobbed. As midnight struck, much of the crowd stepped into the surf. Strangers hugged, lovers clutched, lone women wept in private pain. Sixty tons of fireworks were sent up from nine separate sites, and the tall tower of the Meridien Hotel was totally enveloped in a tumescent cascade of sparkling yellow streaming down from its roof.

But instead of waking up euphoric and rejuvenated, the city was greeted the next morning by the news of a ghastly tragedy. Ten minutes before midnight, though none of us on the beach had been aware of it, a tourist boat, the *Bateau Mouche IV*, taking 124 revelers out to see the fireworks — far more than it could safely carry — had sunk as it rounded the point to Copacabana, and 53 people had drowned, including the wife of the former minister of planning, the actress Yara Amaral (who a few weeks earlier had had a premonition that she was going to die in an accident at sea), and several Italian tourists. The company that had chartered the boat had jacked up the ticket prices, charging more than $200 apiece. The boat was flat-bottomed and wasn't designed for the open sea, especially that night, when the waves were two meters high due to the aftershock of a tempest far out at sea. The port police had ordered the boat back to the harbor, but a bribe of $125 had taken care of their objections. Another tourist boat had passed the boat as it swamped but hadn't stopped, because its passengers didn't want to miss the fireworks. It was the worst accident on the littoral since 1906, and its resonances weren't lost on Millor Fernandes, the *Jornal do Brasil*'s trenchant cartoonist, whose drawing of the tragedy a few days later was captioned: "No genius of police fiction could ever have conceived such a succinct image of the moral, social, economic, cultural, in sum total deliquescence of Brazil" and was followed by fourteen lines of the reprehensible qualities the disaster exhibited, starting with "cynicism, corruption, incompetence, cowardice, ignorance, lack of foresight, despotism, inhumanity." Not since Brazil was knocked out of soccer's World Cup in 1986 (prompting a handful of suicides) had there been such a shock to the collective morale. The accident provoked uncharacteristic soul-searching and deepened the growing pessimism of the *cariocas,* as the natives of Rio are called. "The foreign debt, the fires in the Amazon, the murder of Chico Mendes, and now this," a friend said gloomily. "What must the world think of us?"

THE LAST HOPE FOR MAN

Meanwhile, a tremendous global outcry was being raised over the murder of Chico Mendes. The impact of the bomb the ranchers had promised to set off was far greater than they expected — so great it blew up in their faces.

Again the *New York Times* played a major role. Marlise Simons sent up a story about the murder on December 24, and the editors put it on the front page. "I had nothing to do with its being put there," she told me later, "and to tell you the truth I was somewhat amazed because it wasn't clear that the editors were that aware of who Mendes had been. Maybe they got calls from concerned people. They didn't even ask me if it was 'frontable,' which they sometimes do." The reporter never suggests to his editor that his story is worthy of the front page, she explained.

The story also ran that day in the *Washington Post,* the *Los Angeles Times,* the *Miami Herald,* and the *Boston Globe. Time* and *Newsweek* followed suit on January 9. *Paris Match* had a big story on January 12. The first four pages were double-page spreads with photographs of the fires. The title was *"Notre Oxygène Part en Fumée,"* "Our Oxygen Is Going Up in Smoke." *Der Stern*'s story appeared in February. Perhaps the greatest reaction was in Europe, where the alarm about the fires was greatest.

The Brazilian press wouldn't have given the story so much play if it hadn't been on the front page of the *New York Times,* but in the weeks and months that followed they allotted it a tremendous amount of space. The violence and impunity in the backlands had gone unexposed for far too long. There was one picture — of Chico leaning in the front window of the house on the Rua Doutor Batista de Moraes with his nearly naked two-year-old son, Sandino, in his arms and a radiantly smiling Ilza beside him — that appeared in story after story, in country after country. It was like an icon: the Martyr, the Madonna, and the Lamb of God.

I began to realize that this was a very big story. I had written a piece about Dian Fossey, who had dedicated her life to saving the mountain gorillas of Rwanda and had been murdered three years earlier, also right around Christmas. A new kind of saint — the ecomartyr — seemed to have arrived on the world scene. There were obvious similarities between the two stories, but also important differences. The gorillas and their rain forest habitat had been saved at the expense of the Banyarwanda peasants — twenty-five thousand new families need land each year — and of the Batwa pygmies, who had hunted in the forest since time immemorial and were now classified as poachers. But in Chico's case the interests of environmental protection and social justice coincided. It seemed to be a clear-cut, black-and-white situation. Dian had been a very complex woman who had made a lot of enemies, even among those who were on the same side, but Chico seemed to be a real, old-fashioned hero. In this age of darkness and emptiness and cynicism there was a hunger for real heroes, for causes one could believe in. The concern about the burning of the Amazon had been building to a critical mass, and Chico's murder had pushed it over the edge.

Chico's preindustrial, precapitalistic, locally sustainable model of the extractive reserve was an example. If we could all be content to live like the tappers, the planet wouldn't be in such trouble.

Chico had become almost instantly a symbol not only of the problems of Amazônia and the rain forest, but of the degradation of the environment everywhere. In an interview with the *Boston Globe* just before his death, he had said, "What we demand is a complete reorientation of Brazil's approach to the Amazon. It is the last hope for the rain forest, which is the last hope for man."

The day after the murder, the National Wildlife Federation issued a press release signed by Barbara Bramble, who had worked closely with Steven Schwartzman and Mary Allegretti in their work to promote the tappers and mitigate the destructive Amazonian programs of the World Bank, and by Schwartzman. The release urged people to send telegrams to President José Sarney, Romeu Tuma, Paulo Brossard (the same people to whom Chico had written over and over), protesting the murder, demanding an immediate inquest by independent criminal investigators, and asking that those responsible for this hideous crime be brought to justice. "Please emphasize that those land speculators and cattle ranchers who allegedly are responsible for the assassination should be tried and jailed, not just the one or two gunmen who actually pulled the trigger," the release read.

Within days the Chico Mendes Committee, dedicated to ending the violence in the backlands, had been formed, with chapters in Rio, São Paulo, and most of the other big Brazilian cities. Letters had begun to pour in to the World Bank and the Inter-American Development Bank demanding that all loans and all funding of development projects be suspended pending an investigation of the murder. On December 27 the *Times* ran an editorial by Tom Wicker, who reported that "the assault to which [Mendes] responded in the far-off jungles of the Amazon . . . resulted . . . from the rising demand in the United States for cheap beef to make the Big Macs and Whoppers on which the new fast-food industry was thriving." This was a compelling image, even if it wasn't true.

"Brazil is by no means the only offender," Wicker went on.

> Every year, throughout the world, about 16 million acres of tropical forests and woodlands are destroyed — mostly to clear land for agriculture to feed growing populations, or to supply exchange-earning exports. At present rates of loss, by the end of the decade 2007–2017, several countries will have destroyed *all* their forests: Nigeria, the Ivory Coast, Sri Lanka, Costa Rica, El Salvador.

Thus the kind of fight that Mr. Mendes waged literally to his death was of concern far beyond the Amazon — as are ozone depletion, acid rain, toxic wastes, desertification, ocean spoilage, diminishing resources, rising population.

As if this weren't enough, the *Times* slammed Brazil with an even more scathing editorial the following day, titled "Brazil Burns the Future":

> If Brazil wants the world's sympathy on matters of debt and democracy, it cannot ignore the international outrage at assaults on the environment and those who defend it. . . . Little has come so far from President José Sarney's public pledge to halt the calamitous burning . . . nor is there much confidence in the Sarney regime's capacity to vigorously prosecute the killing of Francisco Mendes Filho, or adequately protect others who follow in his path.

The editorial called for "respect for the common planetary heritage" and ended, "Mr. Mendes will be mourned not just by Brazilians. In a real sense he was defending the very air the world breathes."

My editor at *Vanity Fair* magazine, for whom I'd done the Dian Fossey story, was also aware that this was a very big story. When she found out I was already in Rio, she became even more excited. "I want you on the next plane to Acre," she said when she reached me by phone.

"You're on," I said. "I've always wanted to go there."

THE FUNERAL

As Chico lay dying on his bedroom floor in a pool of his own blood, his guards, Corporal Roldão Roseno de Souza, twenty-six, and Private Roldão Lucas da Cruz, twenty-seven, bolted down the road. Roseno later offered the excuse, "It was very dark and if we had reacted we would surely have been killed," while Lucas claimed, "We were running for reinforcements." The only weapon they had between them was an old .38 that misfired every other time.

Gumercindo Rodrigues returned from his motorcycle spin around town just as Ilza came running out of the house screaming, "Chico's been shot!" Although there was a platoon of police in the Civil Police station, and the Military Police barracks were full — both were within a hundred yards of the crime — no one moved a muscle. "Not one policeman left either station to pursue the two assailants, who were running down the street past a dozen witnesses, even after I screamed, 'God damn it, why don't you do something?' " Gumercindo told me. The first instinctive reaction in Latin America is inaction, suspicion, *inoperância* — the qualities so beautifully illustrated by the *Bateau Mouche* tragedy. The police cars were sitting there. The Military Police paddy-wagon was being washed, but the police complained they had no gas. It was only after the Rural Workers' Union filled them up that they took off after the assailants, who by then, of course, were nowhere to be found. (This is the usual policy in the Brazilian interior: the party that wants the perpetrators brought to justice has to provide the police with gas to go after them.)

Many of Chico's friends and relatives suspect collusion by the Civil Police in the murder. "There were people there to tell when Chico came back," his brother Zuza said. "We suspect that the big ass-kissers in the Civil Police — Chico Lopes, Ramico, Darli's nephew Odilon Alves da Silva — were supporters of the bandits. The police officer Antônio Ferreira Magalhães had been meeting with the *pistoleiros*. Our cousin Zeca Mendes [Joaquim and Cecília's son José Teixeira], who is a commissar in the Civil Police, knows. He told me the Civil Police knows everything, but he is scared to tell.

"Nine days before Chico died he came to my *colocação*. While his guards were having target practice I asked him, Why don't you have more security? Why don't you buy a .22 or a .38? Why don't you go to Rio and stay there for a while? He said he couldn't because he had to campaign for Gilson Pescador [the former padre of Xapuri, who was running for mayor for the PT]. He left very sad. He had not many days to live. He had bought a big fight."

Zeca Mendes later gave me his account of the murder. "I was home watching TV when it happened, and I didn't hear a thing," he told us. "I'd been off working as a mason to supplement my poor salary. That afternoon, around three or four P.M., a few hours before the crime, a nephew of Darli's, Tilinho, came to where I was working to check that I was there, as I now realize. Around five o'clock I went home. My house is two hundred meters from the Civil Police station. The son of one of the policemen came and said, My father is calling for you to come quick. I got my gun and set out on the run. I passed a neighbor and said, What happened? They just killed Chico Mendes, he said.

"By the time I got there, there were already six policemen at the scene, and a big crowd. Chico had already been taken to the hospital. He was dead when he got there. I felt completely stunned and helpless. Then the Volkswagen beetle of the Military Police came down the street so fast that I wasn't able to get out of the way. It hit me and threw me ten meters.''

Julio Cesar, the novelist, always probing for the underlying psychology of events, said later, "He found a way to get hit by that car.''

"I was scared for myself,'' Zeca continued, "because Darli and his *pistoleiros* always come to the wake. They are accustomed every time they kill someone to come downtown and ask what happened, so as not to raise suspicions. Then they go to the wake.

"I never thought they would kill him in town. Two days earlier my niece came to me on her bike. She studies at night and she'd seen two men behind the mango tree at Joffre's [one of Chico's neighbors] house, and she came to ask for protection. She thought they were potheads. She had also seen them several times sitting in a car. She thought they went there to smoke. I took her home for two nights in a row and we saw nothing. It was completely quiet on the Rua Doutor Batista de Moraes.

"The day of the murder Chico came to the police station and played with the pet bird, then he stopped by the house. My wife said, You better take care of yourself, Potbelly. You don't have two lives, you know.''

Nilson de Oliveira, a detective in the Civil Police's department of larceny and armed robbery in Rio Branco, was put in charge of the case, and he arrived in Xapuri at three-thirty that morning, about nine hours after the shooting. One of his first actions was to deputize Zeca Mendes. "He's a good cop, plus he was Chico's second cousin,'' Oliveira explained to me. "I asked Zeca, Are you ready to help? It may mean going into the jungle, manning roadblocks, even flying to the United States if necessary, and Zeca said he was. He interviewed eight witnesses from the street. They all said they saw two men running from the scene. One was white and was wearing a motorcycle helmet and was carrying a shotgun. The other was short and dark-skinned and had pulled his T-shirt over his head.''

Seven months later a scared old woman finally told Zeca that a small car had parked that night in front of her house. Nilson thinks it could have been the getaway car — Darli's Saveiro — with Oloci Alves at the wheel.

Ilzamar's brother Raimundo Gadelha is one of those who believe Zeca knows about the Civil Police's involvement in the murder. "After it happened, my two brothers and I threw him up against a wall and said, You knew everything and didn't do anything. He said nothing. Right after the murder, Chico Lopes, Ramico, and one other man in the Civil Police said to the crowd, This should have happened long ago. Chico Mendes was asking for it, and he ended up getting it.

"The police in Xapuri only beat up drunks. The wild animals they treat like little sweeties. Two months ago, two women started fighting in the street, pulling each other's hair over a man. Six cops surrounded them with drawn guns."

A very curious and important fact was not noticed in the confusion, and only raised eyebrows when the ranchers' paper, *O Rio Branco*, came out the next day. An hour and a half after the murder, four reporters and a photographer arrived on the scene in a Volkswagen Gol sedan. The photographer took pictures of the buckshot-riddled body of Chico laid out on a table in the hospital, which were later sold to the wire services in São Paulo for three thousand dollars.

In the next morning's paper, the reporters told gloatingly how they had gotten the scoop, arriving from Rio Branco in only an hour and a half, with time to change a tire and stop for a beer to boot. Their story was that someone had called them and told them about the murder right after it happened. (In fact, the sister of one of the leaders of the tappers, Júlio Nicásio, did call both the *Gazeta* and *O Rio Branco*. The woman who answered the phone at *O Rio Branco*, after being told that Chico had been killed, said, "Great, it's about time." The woman was the widow of Nilão de Oliveira, the rancher killed eight years earlier by the tappers in revenge for the assassination of Wilson Pinheiro.) But it wasn't true that *O Rio Branco* got the scoop; the *Gazeta* also had a story on the murder on December 23. The headline was "A SHOT IN THE CHEST LIQUIDATES LEADER CHICO MENDES," and the editorial said, "This corpse will be very expensive. The passivity that followed the murder of Ivair [Igino] by Darli's *pistoleiros* in June will no longer be observed. . . . Enough of so many deaths, we will take revenge in the same measure and intensity."

The account in *O Rio Branco* got people thinking. Nobody could get to Xapuri from the capital in an hour and a half, even in daylight in the dry season, let alone after dark in the rainy season, when the road is so muddy that it's barely passable. Someone in the crowd that gathered after the murder came forth and recalled that he had put his hand on the hood of the reporters' car right after it arrived and discovered that it was cold. Nilson de Oliveira suspects that the reporters must have been waiting at a nearby ranch for the murder to happen. They must have been tipped off. "The reporters did themselves in by boasting in the paper that they had made it from Rio Branco in an hour and a half," Nilson told me. This blunder, plus the previous announcement in the paper about the bomb that was going to explode with international repercussions, are two of the detective's main reasons for believing that it was not just a lone assassin or assassins who killed Chico, not just a family grudge, but that his death was engineered by a broader conspiracy.

About half an hour after the murder the bus from Rio Branco pulled in. On it was Norman Lippman, an American documentary filmmaker connected with the Missouri Botanical Garden, who was coming to interview Chico for a documentary he was filming on tropical rain forest agro-ecosystems. Lucélia Santos gave me his number when I returned to Rio from Acre in January, and I rang him ten months later.

"I had called Gumercindo, and we had set up an interview with Chico that night," Lippman told me. "The bus got into the main plaza at six-thirty, forty-five minutes after the murder. As we entered town, we knew before we even arrived that Chico had been killed. People were running alongside the bus, shouting the news. I thought with as much publicity as Chico was getting that it would have protected him, but Darli didn't read the *New York Times*. That's where they miscalculated. And his work wasn't much publicized in Brazil."

You didn't happen to pass a speeding Saveiro on the way into town, did you? I asked.

"I don't remember seeing it, but of course I wasn't looking for it," Lippman said.

"Did you ever see the movie *Cabra Marcado Para Morrer?*" he asked. "It's about the murder of a union organizer of sugarcane cutters in the Northeast. The film was destroyed, but a negative remained in storage for twenty years. After the *abertura* [when the military stepped down], the director produced it and tried to track down the victim's family. When he finally found them they had changed their name. They were in hiding, still scared to talk. I felt when Chico was killed that nothing had changed.

"It was already dark when we got off at the bus station, which was in the main plaza, fifty yards from the union and the church. My assistant and I unloaded our luggage. There was a big crowd. We had no idea what to expect. All we had was tourist visas, but we had a lot of film equipment. We were taken to Chico's house. Everyone was in shock and very nervous. Gumercindo apologized for not being able to receive us well. He was almost crying. I sensed an element of guilt that Chico had not been protected well.

"No one knew how many killers there were or exactly what had happened. They asked me to go to the hospital and take pictures. Gilson Pescador was there, very solemn. Ilzamar was crying '*Meu Deus,*' really wailing. It was heartrending. Eventually she was led away. I had never photographed a dead person. I didn't want to use flash. It felt too obtrusive.''

Lippman never saw the photographer from *O Rio Branco* at the hospital. He evidently got there first.

"Later there was machine-gun fire — the Military Police, firing into the darkness, to do something. People were more afraid of them than of another assassination attempt. I got back to the house where we were being put up, a few doors up the street from Chico's. My assistant was on the floor under the table. Realizing this was a historic moment, I told him to set up the cameras and start filming.

"By noon the next day the press started to arrive, with serious video cameras and motor-driven Nikons. The first people who seemed foreign in Xapuri, who were dressed in stylish city clothes, showed up: Lucélia Santos from Rio, Mary Allegretti, Fernando Gabeira, Adrian Cowell's cameraman, a Brazilian from Goiás, but not Adrian himself, and Lula'' — Luis Ignácio da Silva, the PT's bearded presidential candidate.

Mary had rushed back from a meeting of the International Tropical Timber Organization in Tokyo. By begging people on booked-up planes to let her have their seats, she had made it to Acre in record time. Lula had rented a Learjet to get to Xapuri, where he was making the same sort of incendiary speeches he had made eight years earlier over the body of Wilson Pinheiro. (Lula had been very involved in the tappers' union movement and had been one of those detained after the murder of Nilão de Oliveira.)

Romeu Tuma, the tough, macho superintendent of the Federal Police in Brasília, arrived to personally oversee the investigation, in response to the international outcry. Tuma told the press that it was "a matter of professional dignity that this crime be punished," especially in light of the possible complicity of the Federal Police's state superintendent, Mauro Sposito. He promised that the same errors that had been made recently during a similar case, a bungled operation in the Bico do Papagaio region, would not be repeated. The same team that had identified, with only a minute possibility of error, the remains of Josef Mengele in 1985 would be doing the forensic work, Tuma said.

The government had snapped to, at least verbally, and was being very responsive. The Ministry of External Affairs, ITAMARATI, announced that it had created a Division of Ecology and Human Rights (to handle all the flak it had been getting in these departments), and secretary-general of ITAMARATI, Paulo Tarso Flexa de Lima, declared, "This heinous crime, which certainly can be used against us, which is repugnant to our civilized conscience, must be punished."

Chico's body went to Rio Branco for an autopsy and initial forensic work and returned embalmed in a coffin with a glass window, through which his face was visible, as if he were an astronaut about to embark on a long journey into interstellar space. As he lay in state in the building next door to the church, the tappers came in, and the leaders of the movement made lengthy political statements all day and through the night.

Ever the militant, Gumercindo said, "Not one more tree will fall in Xapuri. The whole municipality will be a huge extractive reserve. This is the price that the big ranchers will pay for having assassinated Chico Mendes, and even so it's a very small price."

Lula said, "It was an action of barbarians, of cowardice. A crime like this should be sufficient for the resignation of the minister of justice, Paulo Brossard." Although Lula had only a fourth-grade education, he was a master at inflaming a crowd. "Let's elect Chico a symbol of the lack of credibility of the government," he said. He even compared Chico to Christ. "Could it be that these people are so stupid that they don't see that killing Chico won't kill his ideas? Could it be that these rich don't see that they have killed Jesus Christ? But the people won't forget his ideas.''

Fábio Feldmann, the federal deputy and environmental activist, spoke, and the Indian leader Airton Krenak. The new padre in charge of the parishes of Xapuri and Brasiléia, Gilson Pescador's successor, a handsome, young, long-haired Italian and committed liberation theologian named Luis Ceppi, who had arrived a year earlier, kept the crests of emotional energy from getting out of control and demonstrated considerable political and media savvy. All the Brazilian TV stations were there, and the major players in the movement were obviously concerned about lining up airtime and promoting their agendas.

On December 28, Mary Allegretti announced that the creation of the Chico Mendes Foundation (a separate group from the newly formed Chico Mendes Committee) had been approved by the union. Its purpose was to keep alive the flame of the struggle and to train new leaders with the techniques developed by the educator Paulo Freire. The house on the Rua Doutor Batista de Moraes that Chico had bought for Ilza earlier that year, where he had been killed, would now become the seat of the foundation. Its president was Ilzamar. "I feel enthusiastic," Ilza said, "although I don't have the means to do the same things Chico did."

Another purpose of the foundation was to guarantee the future of Chico's children, so that they wouldn't be left destitute like Wilson Pinheiro's family.

After the wake, Chico's body was taken to the cathedral in Rio Branco for the well-attended funeral that he had grimly predicted he would get. Around two thousand mourners turned out, despite a torrential downpour, many with black bands on their arms or foreheads. Bishop Moacyr Grechi conducted the funeral Mass. "Happy are those who are persecuted for the cause of justice, for theirs is the kingdom of heaven," he said. Lucélia Santos spoke stirringly. The service reached an emotional high point when the T-shirts and sandals of Chico and Ivair Igino were placed on the altar. After people had paid their last respects, the coffin was taken out in the pouring rain, followed by Ilza, who had been gazing adoringly through the glass window and was now leaning on Mary in a daze of grief. The procession was led by Padre Luis, who looked, in his long white robes and drenched long hair and beard, like Christ himself. There were heavy overtones of bloody martyrdom. It was as if the very heavens were showing their grief.

The *Jornal do Brasil* reported that Chico was laid to rest in a "climate of tension." The crowd outside the cathedral was bristling with placards that said things like "JUSTICE!" and "DEATH TO THE UDR!" As Chico was laid to rest in the cemetery in Xapuri, a chorus of tappers chanted, "We must take revenge, revenge, revenge!"

MORE ANÚNCIOS

Two hundred members of the Chico Mendes Committee demonstrated in front of the mayor's palace, demanding that Acre's UDR president, João Branco; Rio Branco mayor Adalberto Aragão; and the entire UDR be put in prison. Branco thought it prudent to make himself scarce till things cooled down, and he flew out of Rio Branco in his plane, telling everybody he was going to Paris on previously scheduled business. In fact, he went to Mato Grosso. The mayor of Xapuri, Wanderlei Viana, who was thick with the ranchers, left for an unscheduled vacation at his beach house in Fortaleza, the capital of the northeastern state of Ceará. The *Gazeta,* which had been running headlines like "UDR IS ACCUSED OF BEING MAINSPRING OF CRIMES IN BRAZIL," included a paid supplement on its last-day-of-the-year edition celebrating all the admirable things Viana's administration had done for Xapuri, including paving more streets than any previous administration. By then the mayor had already left. Darli and Alvarino's nephew Odilon was relieved of his duties as clerk for the Civil Police and was whisked out by plane, and two of Darli's sons fled the city. Mauro Sposito was transferred under a cloud to drug duty in Cuiabá. Romeu Tuma emphasized that his departure was not a firing — that would have been a blot on the Federal Police — but a transfer. Sposito had been removed, Tuma explained on December 28, "so as not to prejudice the investigation." Sometime later, Sposito surfaced in Brasília, denying that he had warned Darli and Alvarino of the warrant out for their arrest and claiming that he had told the bishop that it wasn't the Federal Police's duty to enforce the warrant; it was the judge's job to see that the subjects were brought in.

So at the very best, Sposito had been like Pontius Pilate, washing his hands of the affair.

A few days after the murder, Custódio de Oliveira, one of the peons at the Fazenda Paraná and a member of Darli's entourage of *pistoleiros,* appeared at the union to renew his membership and was almost lynched. Pressure was building to exact the Lei de Talião, the old Hammurabic law of an eye for an eye, which was usually applied in such cases. It would not be relieved until the murder of Zezão, on January 9.

Just before midnight on December 23, Dom Moacyr received a call from a man who identified himself as Carlos Pereira da Silva, a criminal known in Acre by the nickname Goiâno. He said he was calling long-distance, but the call sounded local. Apparently he was having reservations about knocking off a man of God. "I want to tell you you've been marked for death," he told the bishop. "You won't make it through 1989. Luis Garimpeiro [the notorious drug smuggler and car thief, brother of Darli and Alvarino, believed to be a member of the State Department of Public Safety's secret death squad] and I have been contracted to kill you. But I am a car thief, not an assassin. My advice to you is, don't go to Xapuri alone."

Dom Moacyr reported the conversation to the secretary of public safety, José Carlos Castelo Branco, and was told that Goiâno was supposed to be dead, although his body had not been found. The bishop also told the press about it, joking, "I'm tall, more than a meter eighty, an easy target, fifty-two years old, and a devoted fan of the Vasco da Gama soccer team." He affirmed his commitment to land reform, saying how wrong it was that two thirds of Acre's thirty-seven million acres should be held by ten families for speculation or cattle ranching while nothing was left for those who wanted to live off the land.

Just before midnight on January 3, the phone rang at the home of Eva Evangelista de Araújo, the president of the Tribunal of Justice in Xapuri. The first female judge in Acre and the granddaughter of tappers, Evangelista was one of the few in Rio Branco's elite who sympathized with the tappers' struggle. She had promised to see that justice was done and had been making dangerously incautious statements to the press about the impunity, inoperância, and corruption in Acre. "It wasn't poor people, a single pistoleiro, who killed Chico Mendes. There are others behind this who have to be investigated. I'm convinced that there is an organized crime syndicate behind my anúncio and the bishop's."

Evangelista's anúncio had come one night when she was working late, and her eldest daughter, Gilcely, who was about to get married, answered the phone. A man's voice asked if the judge was there. Gilcely said she wasn't. "Then give her this message. Tell the judge [sarcastic emphasis] that I am being well paid for this service, and that she had better stay out of the Chico Mendes case.'' Twenty minutes later he called again with the same message. The third time he said, ''Tell your mother not to go to the Tribunal tomorrow, because when she walks up the steps, her head will roll down them, just like we did to Chico Mendes.''

Gilcely was rushed to the hospital and treated for nervous collapse, but her mother wasn't intimidated. ''I'm not afraid,'' she told the press. ''If I have to die, I'll die standing.''

Five others reported receiving death threats: Gumercindo, Júlio Barbosa (thirty-four, the new president of the union); Raimundo de Barros (Chico's first cousin, town councilman, and president of the National Council of Rubber Tappers); Júlio Nicásio, a local PT leader; and former padre Gilson Pescador. The *Jornal do Brasil* ran a photo of them with their arms around each other, promising to continue Chico's work.

The church's Pastoral Commission for the Land released a list of 350 people all over Brazil who had been threatened with death because they had supported agrarian reform. Among them were the cardinal of Fortaleza, thirty-one bishops, padres, pastoral agents, union members, and workers.

On January 27, Darci Pereira, the son of Darli Alves da Silva (''under Brazilian custom, the son does not always use his father's name,'' Marlise Simons explained in the *New York Times*), turned himself in, telling the police that he had ''hired a professional assassin to kill Chico Mendes.'' Later, Darci changed his story and said that he himself had shot and killed Mendes. Romeu Tuma didn't buy the confession. He said it was a ''smoke screen.'' The son was ''maneuvering to distract attention from his father and uncle.'' Besides, Tuma said, ''the young man apparently wanted police protection because he was scared of being lynched by the rubber tappers and others in the region.''

THE INVESTIGATION PROCEEDS

Lucélia Santos stayed in Rio Branco for a week. She took *daime* at the União Vegetal and gave José Fernando Eischenberg, the secretary-general of the Ministry of Justice, a manifesto signed by more than twenty groups demanding justice and a public investigation in the

Mendes case. They called for the firing of Mauro Sposito, accusing him of conniving with the ranchers (which Romeu Tuma, still defending his man, declared "an absurdity"); the firing of Public Safety secretary José Carlos Castelo Branco and the municipal authorities of Xapuri involved with the crime; the dismantling of the death squad; and the guarantee of the lives of the union leaders.

Lucélia also did the police's work for them, since they seemed incapable of doing it themselves. A few days after the funeral she was driving from Rio Branco to Xapuri when a Saveiro sedan passed. One of the passengers pointed his index finger at her from behind the windshield as if it were a gun and pretended to fire. "That's Oloci," her driver said, "the meanest and most dangerous of Darli's sons." She rushed to the police and told them she'd just passed Oloci, who had recently slipped their dragnet. After a chase and a gun battle in which Oloci was shot in the arm, they arrested him. Thirty policemen guarded the hospital where he was taken to have the bullet removed. Then he was moved to the *colônia penal,* the prison outside of town, and locked up with his brother Darci.

Gaston Mota was picked up at the bank in Brasiléia, where he was nervously trying to cash a telexed money order for 10.4 million cruzados — about $10,000. Detective Nilson de Oliveira suspects that the money order may have been the contract money from the UDR, but it's unclear who sent it. Lamentably, there were no grounds for holding Mota, and he was released after twenty-four hours. "We didn't have the legal instruments, the arrest warrant, to hold him," Nilson explained a few weeks later.

On his release Mota declared, "I was a friend of Chico's. In the late sixties I hired his father and sons to work at my *seringal.* No lie."

The story about Mota's coming into the Rio Branco Soccer Club with two of Mayor Aragão's bodyguards, and of the gambler Zé Arigó's predicting Chico's death, began to circulate. One of the bodyguards was tallish and white, the other short and dark — which matched the description of the assassins. But this proved to be a false lead.

Two days after the murder, Mota was seen chatting amicably with José Carlos Castelo Branco, who many people also thought was involved and ought to be removed because he had allegedly issued a gun permit to Oloci on December 5. Nilson, however, defends Castelo Branco, who hired him to serve in the Civil Police's larceny and armed robbery division. "It wasn't Castelo Branco who issued the permit," he explained, "but the chief of the Civil Police. Oloci had no record. His previous crimes had not yet been discovered. You couldn't go on what people were saying or what was printed in the *Gazeta*. The error was to give a gun permit to a son of Darli's, for whom the warrant had already arrived."

In Brasiléia, Benedito Rosas, believed to have been, with Gaston Mota, one of the masterminds of Chico's murder, sold his 105-square-mile ranch and left for Goiânia.

Also picked up and released in the days immediately following the murder were the *pistoleiro* Zezão and a brother of Darli and Alvarino's, Aleci Alves Pereira, twenty-three, a friend of Wanderlei Viana's. Viana had gotten him a job at the Ministry of Health. He was picked up in the company of the foreman of the Seringal Ecuador.

A detachment of Military Police went out to the Fazenda Paraná and was greeted with gunfire from Darci and Oloci's younger brother Darlizinho and two brothers who were part of the entourage, Edvaldo Vieira Feitosa, twenty-three, and Erivando, twenty-one. The three *pistoleiros* explained that they thought the police were the tappers coming for revenge.

Two women at the ranch were interviewed: Malena Pereira, twenty, the sister of Antônio Pereira, one of the three Mineirinhos, and Maria Gorete de Sena, twenty-seven, the wife of Antônio's brother Amadeus. Maria Gorete said Darci arrived at the ranch on the night of the murder with Antônio and declared, "The confusion in Xapuri is over. We killed Chico Mendes. Now Xapuri will be in peace." She said she had surprised Darci and Antônio various times plotting Chico's death, and she claimed to have warned them, "If he dies there will be no peace for any of us. We will live between life and death."

Detective Nilson took down the cowboy Sebastião Lourenço dos Santos's testimony that in October 1988, on the day after the discovery at the Alves ranch of the bodies of the two Bolivian brothers, he met two of the Mineirinhos, Amadeus and Antônio, who told him they had killed the brothers with Darci and Oloci. The Mineirinhos told Lourenço to say nothing or he, too, would be a dead man. Lourenço didn't know the motive.

Genésio Barbosa, fifteen, also a cowboy, was a gold mine of information. He told how the peon Raimundo Pereira had proposed to Darli's daughter Vera Lucia and how Raimundo's death was coordinated by Oloci. The body was thrown in a banana grove near the ranch and devoured by vultures.

The body of Walcir, another peon, Genésio continued, was covered with grass by Darci and Oloci and ignited. The two brothers also killed a man known only as José, who was caught stealing on the ranch. He was buried in a thicket.

According to Nilson, an unnamed witness testified that Darli, Alvarino, and Gaston contracted a man named José Campeiro to kill an inhabitant of Xapuri named Manoel Bala. Another victim of theirs was Antônio Gomes de Vasconcelos, known in Xapuri as Antônio Porco, Antônio the Pig. Porco was gunned down in his house in 1987 by contracted *pistoleiros* in circumstances similar to the murder of Chico.

Before Darci turned himself in at the police station in Xapuri, João Branco, the UDR president in Acre, called a reporter at the *Gazeta* from an undisclosed location in Mato Grosso and said that it was one of Darli's sons, Aparecido or Loci, who killed Chico. "Since the Seringal Cachoeira was expropriated the family has been like wild, penned steers, with no exit," he explained.

"Confession is the prostitute of proofs," Romeu Tuma, still dubious, said, "because it can be violated at any moment." Another official in the Federal Police echoed his skepticism: "I think Darci came in to clean the mud off his father's shoes."

But Darci's confession was rich in detail. He was taken back to Xapuri and walked the investigators through an exact reconstruction of the crime. The *Gazeta*'s full-length photograph of him flanked by the police — a handsome, well-built twenty-two-year-old, with the physique of a bodybuilder, his well-developed thighs bulging in striped pants, his arms and torso muscle-bound, his face absolutely wooden — was wired around the world. He showed them where he had stood and fired: right in front of the coconut tree, through the hanging wash.

The government was under great international pressure to show that it was handling the investigation competently. Tuma had Chico's body exhumed and examined by the forensic team, headed by Nelson Massini, that had not only identified the remains of the long-sought, elusive Angel of Death, but also had conducted autopsies of the people who had died from exposure to cesium in Goiânia.* The team's computer-aided reconstruction of the distance and angle of fire jibed with Darci's testimony. Tuma, whose initial reaction had been ''I don't believe he pulled the trigger,'' now said he thought with 90 percent certainty that Darci was the killer. He said he would send the result of the computer analysis of the dispersion of the shot to international ecological groups in the United States, to show ''the seriousness with which these investigations by the Federal Police are being taken.''

But where was the murder weapon (a twelve-gauge shotgun in most accounts, a twenty-gauge in several)? Darci said he'd thrown it in the river, but the diving team turned up nothing. The river — swollen, muddy, and fast — could have swept it away, but more probably, Darci was lying. A dozen witnesses had seen him running off with it.

His claim that he had acted completely alone was widely doubted. Darci said his motive was that Chico had been ''harassing my father'' — saying bad things about him, forcing him to hide in the forest for three months.

Here Detective Nilson made a sharp move: he offered Darci a cigarette, a Charm — the brand whose butts littered the ambush blind behind Chico's house and the same brand found at the blind from which Ivair was killed in June. Darci said he didn't smoke. Charm was the brand of Oloci and Darci's mulatto brother-in-law Antônio (a.k.a. Jerdeir, a.k.a. Francisco) Pereira, who the detective was almost sure was Darci's accomplice.

Beyond this Darci said absolutely nothing. He remained as tight-lipped as James Earl Ray. He was widely believed to be the designated fall guy, the *boi de piranha*, the steer for the piranha. Or, as Tuma had described him, a smoke screen. He had no record, and if he was convicted he'd get off in a few years.

But the mystery was why there had to be a fall guy at all, given the unlikelihood that anyone would be prosecuted. A more likely explanation was Darci's fear of being *linchado* (a word adopted into Portuguese from cowboy Westerns). In prison, Darci asked repeatedly to see his father. He had a bad cough and complained of his malaria. He said he lived alone in a shack on the ranch, didn't drink, and had been suffering for

*A man had found the highly radioactive substance glowing in a box in a dump and had fed it to his six-year-old daughter in a banana gruel.

the past five years from an ulcer. His lawyer, Antônio Rodríguez Barbosa, offered an alternative perpetrator: the Bordon Meatpacking Company. "There are minerals on the ranch that Mendes forced Bordon to abandon," Barbosa said. He called Chico Mendes the "padlock" of Amazônia.

Meanwhile, Darli and Alvarino, allegedly hiding in the forest since September, and the three Mineirinhos, were still at large. A massive, all-out manhunt, Operation Sweep, began to comb the eighteen ranches along BR-317 between Xapuri and Brasiléia. Sixty agents of the Federal Police (including a crack team with special jungle training and armed with machine guns, grenades, and tear gas), sixty Military Police, thirty Civil Police, bloodhounds, and a helicopter were converging on the scene, and the fugitives were expected to be brought in momentarily, preferably alive. They were going to have to answer a lot of questions.

There was widespread speculation that the murder of Chico Mendes was more complicated than a simple vendetta by the Alves boys. Ronaldo Caiado, the president of the UDR, held a press conference in São Paulo in which he described the murder as a "personal and family misunderstanding" with Darci Alves da Silva. The family had resorted to violence because they felt "threatened." Caiado dismissed the accusations of UDR involvement as "a ploy of the radical left, using Nazi techniques" of denouncing without proof, just as it had done in the murders of the two padres in the Bico do Papagaio. "The left needs bodies, because it doesn't have a message," he said. "What compromises Brazil is the extreme left, the lackey of international capitalism." The left, supported by "multinationals and transnationals," wanted to protect Amazônia under the veil of ecology so the region wouldn't be exploited and become the new agricultural frontier, which would make Brazil competitive in grain production. The whole uproar over the murder of Mendes, Caiado asserted, was an international game created by the left. Lucélia Santos was interested in Amazônia only "because that's where the hallucinogenic vine she's addicted to grows."

I sat on the balcony of my hotel room in Copacabana taking in all these wild developments from a stack of newspapers — the *Jornal do Brasil, O Globo,* and the *Estado de São Paulo* — which were having a field day with the story. What intrigued me, as I compared versions and underlined names, was not so much the Wild West range-war aspect of

the conflict between the ranchers and the tappers, but the global resonances of the murder.

In many ways Chico had been like Martin Luther King, Jr. (The
Jornal do Brasil was already calling him the Gandhi of the forest.) He
had been an ecologist only accidentally; in reality he was a warrior, a
troublemaker, a fighter for the rights of an oppressed minority.

I was also intrigued by how the story seemed to contain many of the
elements of classic tragedy — an inexorable denouement, even how, as
in *Hamlet* or *King Lear,* the weather had seemed to go sympathetically
out of whack in the months leading up to the murder. The nature of
tragedy, according to Aristotle, is to arouse terror and pity; when these
emotions are purified, the audience experiences catharsis. Also, the hero
must have a tragic flaw. There must be a change of condition, a passing
from fortune to misfortune. The hero can't be completely virtuous or this
passage would be odious to the spectator. Often the hero's tragic flaw is
that he is too ambitious, guilty of hubris, of aspiring to beyond what is
mortally possible; so he has to be cut down.

But the tragedy of Chico Mendes didn't really hold up to these cri-
teria. Chico had no tragic flaw, as far as I could tell. As his aunt Cecília
would tell me, it's not the bad ones who die. His murder had produced
no catharsis, only outrage and chaos. The tappers' movement would be
factionalized by the struggle for succession and the question of the
movie. Ilzamar and Mary Allegretti, Chico's real wife and his political
wife, would fall out bitterly. In other words, it was a real-life tragedy.
Chico had held everything together, uniting the disparate personalities
and egos: now they would all go at each other. The ranchers had
achieved the classic aim of political assassination — they had cut the
head off the movement. The murder had been a resounding success.
Steven Schwartzman had described it as "a disaster for the future of the
forest." But the ranchers hadn't counted on the extent of the international outrage.

A TRIP BACK IN TIME

The flight from Rio de Janeiro, some two thousand miles southeast of
Rio Branco, passed through three time zones. One could not help being
impressed by the enormity and emptiness of the Brazilian interior.

We stopped in Brasília, which André Malraux had called at its inauguration thirty years earlier "the capital of hope." Its once-intimidating modernity had already receded into vintage modern, like the Edsel. The poured-slab walls of the ministries and the rectilinear apartment blocks were already cracked and coated with the black fungus partial to concrete in the tropics.

From there we proceeded to Cuiabá, the capital of Mato Grosso, a famous ex-Nazi stronghold. I remembered the last time I'd been to Cuiabá, in 1982. The state chief of protocol, who met me at the airport, had a toothbrush mustache and had served in the SS. He kept clicking his heels. I had come to see the Pantanal do Mato Grosso, a swamp bigger than England that is home to an incredible profusion of wildlife, including millions of caimans floating in the water, monumental logjams of caimans as far as the eye could see. Poaching the caimans is a big business. Planes fly in from Bolivia and fly out with caiman skins, which are said to provide an important part of the Bolivian gross national product. No money changes hands.

At the Cuiabá airport I picked up the *Jornal do Brasil*. On page 5, the page usually devoted to the Mendes case, there was big news: Darli had turned himself in. The Federal Police had gone out to the Fazenda Paraná and started working on one of Darli's women, handsome, dark-skinned Francisca da Silva, nicknamed Chiquinha, the one who had run away to him from a neighboring ranch when she was sixteen (or twelve, according to some accounts). The police had dragged Chiquinha out onto BR-317 in only her bra and panties and threatened to turn her over to the tappers and the PT unless she told them where Darli was. They also got her in a panic that "American bombs" would be dropped on the ranch if any of them helped the fugitives. The police put out the word, which spread quickly through the ranches along the road to Brasiléia, that "the American ecologists," in another version, were going to bomb anyone harboring or feeding Darli, Alvarino, or the Mineirinhos.*

---

*This threat seems to be used quite a lot in Amazônia. In 1977 I set out with two Yanomamo Indians on a week-long trek through the forest of Roraima, in northern Brazil. The parting instructions of the *caboclo* who had arranged for them to be my guides were "Him you don't kill, or the Americans will drop bombs on you." Recalcitrant Indians like the Waimiri-Atroaris had occasionally been bombed by the Brazilian air force, but the Americans, as far as I know, have yet to bomb the Amazon. American bombs may be a metaphor for a distant dream of justice. Julio Cesar, with whom I later discussed my theory, had a different interpretation: the bombs are a metaphor for America's "phallic omnipotence."

Chiquinha finally broke down and told the police where Darli was hiding: on the Fazenda Vaca Branca, on kilometer 100 of BR-317. His seventeen-year-old son, Darlizinho, who had been in hiding with Darli, Alvarino, and the Mineirinhos, entered the forest and told them that it was useless, that they might as well come out. But only Darli returned with him. He handed over his .38 revolver with his right hand and his bullets with his left.

He was terribly emaciated, skin and bones, and was wearing only one sandal, the other having broken. Puny, with thick glasses, he didn't look at all like the ruthless killer he was supposed to be, and nothing like the sketches technicians of the Civil Police in São Paulo had worked up from old photos. The fugitives were ranchers and had no knowledge of how to live off the forest. If they had been tappers they could have stayed in there indefinitely.

Darli said, "I didn't kill Chico Mendes. I knew it was my son Darci. I turned myself in to free my family of suffering and to free the authorities of international pressure." He was taken in a Jeep to Rio Branco, and, standing unperturbed and defiant as flashbulbs popped, he posed for the photographers and was taken off to join his two sons in the *colônia penal*. Genésio Natividade, the lawyer for the Pastoral Commission for the Land, who had found out that Darli and Alvarino were wanted in Paraná, requested permission to be present at his interrogation, and the prosecutor, Francisco Matias de Sousa, granted it.

The plane took off again. North of Cuiabá, I knew, there were some very big ranches, one belonging to Coca-Cola, another to the German industrialist Prince Johannes von Thurn und Taxis. I had flown over their huge squares of bare, ferruginous earth eight years before. I knew that since then, over the course of the eighties, the big ranches and the devastation along BR-364, the road from Cuiabá to Acre, had spread like a disease, all the way up through Mato Grosso and on to the very top of Rondônia.

But it was the rainy season, and western Amazônia was totally socked in. I couldn't see the ocean of trees that begins maybe half an hour above Cuiabá, but I could sense its presence beneath the blanket of cloud: the Amazon rain forest, the object of contention, the subject of so much misunderstanding, the last primeval place on the planet. Though it is being cut back farther and farther and huge patches of it are being gouged out and incinerated, it is still the world's largest and most biologically diverse wilderness, blanketing an area two-thirds the size of the continental United States and containing perhaps a tenth of the world's species, most of them still unidentified, new trees being discovered all the time, more kinds of fish than there are in the Atlantic, the world's largest catfish, the largest cockroach, finch-eating spiders, and no fewer than 319 kinds of hummingbird.

We came down through the low clouds and landed in Rio Branco, and I caught a cab into town. It had been raining for twenty-four hours straight, the taxi driver told me as we crossed a bridge over the swollen, muddy Rio Acre, whose banks were lined with flat-roofed, double-decker riverboats. The river had been Rio Branco's lifeline to the outside world until 1969, when BR-364 was pushed west from Porto Velho, and it was still the best way to bring goods from Manaus, a thousand extravagantly meandering miles downstream. A passing truck sprayed dirty red water from a flooded rut all over our brand-new, ethanol-powered, Brazilian-made Chevette, evoking a flood of curses from the taxi driver. Then he uttered a complaint I must have heard in three dozen Brazilian cities: "Goddamn these potholes. The only thing this mayor's doing is lining his pockets."

You from here? I asked. "No," he said, and then he launched into a typical saga of modern Amazônia. "I came here seven years ago with my family from Mato Grosso, where I'd been trying to make it as a colonist, but the land was terrible. Before that I was in Itaituba prospecting gold. Before that I drove a truck on the Trans-Amazon Highway. Before that I was a peon clearing the forest for a multinational ranch in southern Pará. Before that — Piauí, that's my home state. But there's nothing there. *Clima tórrido.*" He pinched his cheeks. "You had to walk a mile just to get water."

So what do you think of this place?

"This is a no-man's-land, a complete hole. Here even the whores come — the pinnacle of unprofessionalism. There's no law, no constitution, no money, there isn't diddly-squat. But it's as good a place, I suppose, as you'll find anywhere in Brazil."

I like this guy, I decided. Your typical philosophical cabbie.

What's your name?

"Getúlio."

Rio Branco seemed a lot smaller than its most recent population es-

timate of 250,000. The main plaza was full of budding teenage school-
girls in white blouses — dark-skinned, very short, buxom, Indian-
nordestina mixes with big, lush mouths, "sensual dwarfs," as Julio
Cesar would describe them. The sort of woman whom Machado de
Assis, the Balzac of Brazil, described as "the Brazilian woman with
fleshy lips."

"Ah," Getúlio sighed, "the sweet poison of the tropics."

Off the square were the governor's palace, the Tribunal of Justice,
and a couple of other neoclassical buildings. From there the city rapidly
degenerated into a squalid sprawl of gaudily painted shacks and concrete
pillboxes. There was no little thicket of high rises, no skyline, as Cuiabá
already had. "Rio Branco hasn't started to verticalize yet," Getúlio explained. "The highest finished building is five floors. There isn't one
elevator in the whole state."

We drove past a wall scrawled with "Fed Up with Sarney, Unite the
Left." A floating population of rough frontier types was shooting
snooker and brawling in the bars, eyeing the traffic from doorways. They
all looked like killers.

I wondered how, not knowing a soul in Acre, I was going to proceed.
All I had to go on was two weeks' worth of stories on the murder in the
Rio papers. After sifting through their rumor and innuendo, several
things were clear. No one in the Civil, Military, or Federal Police could
be trusted. I'd have to deal with them eventually, but not now: on the
way out. I definitely didn't want to seem too interested in the death squad
in the Department of Public Safety. Only a few days earlier, a journalist
who had been investigating the squad in the Department of Public Safety
in Manaus had turned up dead.

It was also probably a good idea to distance myself from the environmental movement. Ronaldo Caiado had accused Chico of being a tool
of the ecologists. The ecologists were going to drop American bombs
on anyone who sheltered the Alves fugitives. I definitely didn't want to
be taken for one of them. Being American was enough of a liability.
But by now I could almost pass for a Brazilian. People hearing my
Portuguese would think, "He must come from some other part of
Brazil."

We pulled up in front of an opaque glass building, the Inácio Palace
Hotel, with air-conditioned rooms on three floors of long, smelly corridors, one of the few places in town that in my personal grading system

for Third World hostelries was above the grimness threshold. Most visitors to the capital stayed in the Inácio, if not at the slightly tonier Pinheiro Palace, run by the same management, across the street. Sooner or later everyone you were looking for showed up in the Inácio's lobby or at the Pinheiro Palace's pool, at which, as the Inácio's guest, I had swimming privileges.

I registered as a *pesquisador,* a researcher, a wonderfully vague and respected occupation that requires no further explanation in Brazil, and was taken down one of the corridors to my room, where, weary from the long day's journey, I immediately crashed.

An hour later I stepped out into the brick-wall heat of midafternoon and headed for the cathedral.

As far as I could see there were only three good guys in Rio Branco: the bishop, Dom Moacyr; Eva Evangelista, the president of the Tribunal of Justice; and Sílvio Martinelli, the editor of the *Gazeta* — all of whom had been *anunciados.*

I asked a twelve-year-old vamp cutting through a churchyard where I might find the bishop, and she broke into a run.

What's with her? I asked a woman who had seen this. She replied, "With everything that's been going on around here, she doesn't want to get involved." The woman suggested I try the rectory, which was also the headquarters of the Pastoral Commission for the Land, the CPT.

I knocked on the door but no one came. Recalling that in 1985 Padre Jósimo Tavares was shot in the back while climbing the steps of the CPT in Imperatriz, Maranhão, and that Wilson Pinheiro was shot on the steps (or the porch, in other versions) of the union hall in Brasiléia, I tried the door, but it was locked. Then I began to pound.

At last it was opened by a bearded man with long hair, dressed in white, his neck and wrists dripping with Indian beads and animal charms — Cinta Larga, the Rondonian tribe, I guessed, correctly. He looked like one of the Apostles, if not Christ himself, but turned out to be the padre of Xapuri, Luis Ceppi — definitely a New Wave priest. "Come in," he said, and explained in Portuguese with an Italian accent, "Dom Moacyr went to visit his mother in the South. He hasn't seen her since his father died, and she's very worried about him since she read of him being *anunciado* in the paper."

We sat in a meeting room, and I asked Padre Luis how a guy like him — suave, devastatingly handsome — had become a priest. Lighting up a cigar, he told me that he was now thirty-nine and had been in the church fifteen years. He had come from Milan in 1979 to practice the liberation theology of Gustavo Gutiérrez and the Boff brothers. "I started out helping the metallurgist's union in São Paulo organize strikes for better pay and working conditions. I worked closely with a *sindicalista,* a union leader, named Santo Dias, who was killed by the police."

Then, having tried to improve conditions in the urban slums of São Paulo, Padre Luis came to Amazônia to work with the peasants and the Indians, particularly to mitigate the effects of a new directive from Brasília, Projeto Calha Norte, the Special Project for the Occupation of the Frontiers. The plan of action called for four thousand kilometers of road to be built along the northern border of Amazônia, which Brazil shares with French Guiana, the last Latin American colonial nation still under French control; with indecipherable Suriname; problematic Guyana; Venezuela, greedily eyeing the mineral riches of Roraima; and guerrilla-riddled and drug-infested Colombia and Peru. The project was motivated by the same military *horror vacuui* that had inspired the Trans-Amazon Highway. The Perimetral Norte, as it was called, was begun in 1973 by President Emílio Médici, and it had two purposes: to provide a *cordon sanitaire* against exotic ideologies — contamination by the Marxist governments of Suriname and Guyana, by M-19 and Shining Path guerrillas in the jungles of Colombia and Peru, and to furnish access for aggressive Brazilian capitalism and facilitate exploitation by multinational mining interests. Only one fifth of the road, however, was completed before construction was suspended for economic and technical reasons. "Three hundred million dollars are needed to complete it," Padre Luis told me. "If they go ahead with it, it will result in the death of two hundred thousand Indians — mostly Yanomamo, Macuxi, and Tukano. The International Development Bank is considering a loan to reactivate the project — the same problem we are facing over the paving of BR-364 from Porto Velho to here."

In 1984 Padre Luis met Chico.

What was he like? I asked.

"Chico was something lamentably rare on the Brazilian political scene — a leader. How does a Lech Walesa or a Chico Mendes arise? These are creatures of events, the people who are needed, who rise to the occasion.

"By the time I met him, Chico had already broken the tappers' dependence on the *patrão seringalista* and had metamorphosed from a simple tapper to a union leader and political man, and was becoming a world leader. I lent him a book on Gandhi and King, but Chico's nonviolence arose from the somnolent 'laziness' of the tappers, who, like the Indians, are inclined to resist in a passive manner. Chico turned their passivity into an active form of resistance. They don't have the mentality for armed conflict. Last March four hyper-radicals — two Brazilians, a Bolivian, and a Peruvian named Vitor — came with violent intentions to destabilize and discredit the church's and the union's pacifism. They were just what the UDR wanted so it could have an excuse to repress the movement. But they didn't get anywhere.

"Chico wasn't a great speechmaker," Padre Luis continued. "He was just very direct and clear about what he believed in. And he was a born negotiator. He talked to everybody the same way, and listened to everybody's side, and slowly brought the different factions all together. He forged the tappers and the Indians, for instance, who had been fighting each other for years, into the Alliance of the People of the Forest. Nobody else could have done it."

I asked about the possible links between Chico's murder and the UDR and the Department of Public Safety. "Castelo Branco was seen at Darli's and he gave Oloci a gun permit. What more do you want? Darli is an actor with a mentality of complete self-righteousness. He is the owner, and everything he does is right. It's the old feudalistic attitude. He dominated his sons, and he felt that he had the right of life and death over his peons."

What about the death squad?

"Two years ago someone in the Department of Public Safety leaked to the *Gazeta* its blacklist of thirty-three people who were to be eliminated — thieves, marginals, traffickers. There was some overlap with the UDR's unpublished list of rural union leaders who had been threatened with death. All thirty-three of these people have since disappeared, although not all their bodies have been found.

"The head of the death squad was Enoch Pessoa, who headed up one team in the Civil Police's division of larceny and armed robbery. Nilson de Oliveira heads the other. Enoch was old guard. He often went to Darli's ranch. A few months ago, Enoch was fired after our Commission for the Defense of Human Rights published a photograph of one of his torture victims. The victim was hanging upside down, lashed to a pole under his knees, a type of torture known as the parrot's perch. Now there is a purge in the Military and Civil Police. Three policemen have died in the last month.''

What's the role of drugs in this story?

''Balls of *mescla* — marijuana mixed with cocaine — are smoked or eaten even by the high society of Xapuri. Many of the ranchers grow or run drugs. One of them was recently gunned down while drinking a beer in Brasiléia. The killing was not investigated.''

What about Gaston Mota?

''He was also at the Fazenda Paraná a lot. He's a key figure in the connection of Darli, the UDR, and the death squad. He's an arms and drug *contrabandista*. When a contract goes out he provides the arms and the money for the *pistoleiros*.''

Another good guy, I thought as I walked down to the main plaza. The Chico Mendes Committee was holding a demonstration in front of the library, handing out fliers on which the manifesto that Lucélia Santos had presented to the Ministry of Justice was printed. ''The assassination of Chico Mendes will not go unpunished.'' It was signed by thirty-five individuals and civil groups, including Fernando Gabeira, Fábio Feldmann, Mary Allegretti, the Commission for the Defense of Human Rights, both the Moscow and Albanian wings of the Brazilian Communist Party, the Movement of the Women of Acre, the Union of Bakers, of Workers in Industries, of Busdrivers, of Rural Workers of Sena Madureira and Plácido de Castro. The girls who were handing out the fliers were wearing T-shirts that read ''They Took Down One of the Noblest Trees of the Amazonian Union Movement. Chico Mendes, from Your Example Other Courageous Plants Will Be Born Until They Make the Whole Earth Green.''

The Tribunal of Justice was just down the road. I went up its steps and through its Greek columns and was shown by a young Military Policeman, nodding off at the door, into the office of its president, Eva Evangelista de Araújo. She was sitting at a huge desk with a Bible open on a stand and a Brazilian flag in the background. Her forearms were festooned with bracelets, and she bore a remarkable facial resemblance to the American actress Elizabeth Ashley; she had the same throaty voice. But when she got up to greet me, she was tiny. She was a gutsy, charming fireball. ''Chico was so important, he didn't even know how important he was — for Amazônia and for the world,'' she said. ''Human beings have become very egocentric since they lost their connection to nature. Chico represented harmony. He defended the last great forest reserve in the world.''

Eva's parents had come from Ceará as *soldados da borracha,* soldiers of rubber, in the drought of 1943, and she was proud of her heritage and full of love for Acre. She gave me a limited-edition book of photos of Acre in the early days, with cameos of its tamers of the wilderness.

We talked about her *anúncio.* "I don't understand the motivation of these threats,'' she said, ''unless they are because of my intervention.'' She had taken the unprecedented step of insisting that a special prosecutor and a second judge be appointed to follow the murder inquest and guarantee the ''actuation of the judicial process.'' She had toned down some of her public statements a little. ''I can't say a crime syndicate exists,'' she now said, ''but the possibility of its existence worries me. The impunity here is very great. My theory is that we are returning to the old feudal system. There have been several cases in which the ranchers have reappropriated land that was expropriated from them to give the dispossessed rural people somewhere to live, and I have complained about this publicly. Maybe this is why I received the *anúncio.''*

In a few days, she told me, ''twelve tribunal presidents are coming from all over the country to demonstrate their solidarity with me. I have four children and a loving husband, but I also have a job to do. We have to discover the authors of not only this murder, but of all the murders related to problems with the big landowners that haven't been elucidated. I believe very much in signs of God, and I think Chico died to usher in a new era of justice, to make us think about these problems and act.''

She and her distraught husband escorted me to the steps of the Tribunal, and, with nervous glances toward the street below, quickly returned inside. I didn't linger on the steps, either.

That's one brave lady, I thought. She rose to become a member of the elite, and now she's betraying it. She knows the corruption of the rich, and she's threatening to tell, and that's not playing by the rules.

By the time my taxi got to the *Gazeta,* it was pitch-dark. The paper's small upstairs offices were above an automotive-parts store. Sílvio Martinelli, the editor, forty-one, with a salt-and-pepper beard, had his feet up on his desk and was listening to an interview he had taped with Darli at the *colônia penal* that afternoon.

According to an unidentified correspondent for *O Globo,* Darli had seemed extremely nervous and had said, "I would never have authorized a son of mine, or anybody, to kill Chico Mendes. If my son confessed, you can examine him, because he can only be sick." He denied fleeing when the warrant arrived. "I wasn't at the ranch. I had gone to Brasiléia to bid for cattle."

But to Sílvio, Darli said, "I didn't kill Chico. I knew it was my son Darci. Chico Mendes was a man easy to kill. If I had wanted to kill him I would have killed him in the middle of the street."

Darli, sitting on a sofa with handcuffs removed during the interview, had revealed himself to be astute, with a very quick mind. He spoke fast, with a *mineiro* accent, dodging embarrassing questions, elaborating on his life, making frequent references to God, and often reciting country aphorisms. "I never killed anybody," he told Sílvio. "My only fault is that I like women." He admitted to being acquainted with the local directors of the UDR but said that he was not affiliated with the body.

Why did you decide to give yourself up to the police?

To clarify the whole truth. Lies always disappear when truth arrives. They say I'm a ferocious man, but it's a lie. I'm a humble person. My intention is only to work and progress.

Why did you flee in September when the warrant arrived?

I fled because I had some bills to pay. I had to sell some things to contract a lawyer to clear me of this accusation that came from Paraná.

But in this warrant, you are accused of killing someone in Paraná.

I never killed anybody. When I left there I received a document from my lawyer saying that I was free and acquitted of these false imputations.

Who told you that it had arrived?

It was my brother-in-law, Djair Gomes, who lives in Umuarama. He has a pharmacy and a ranch. He called to say that he'd read in the paper that I was going to be arrested. [Darli then confirmed that he had been waiting hidden on his ranch for the lawyer to get the charges against him dismissed.]

Do you know Mauro Sposito?

Yes, very well. I was called by him in 1980 to testify about the assassination of Wilson Pinheiro.

Did you know that Darci would kill Chico Mendes?

Now look here [pause] . . . you want me to tell you the story from the beginning? I came home one day and told my kids that since MIRAD [the new government agency in charge of agrarian reform, created from INCRA by the new constitution] expropriated the Seringal Cachoeira, I had nothing more against Chico Mendes. I say this from my heart. I bought the Seringal Cachoeira to profit from the land. When the government expropriated it, that was fine. I ended up making a profit.

But until now you haven't received a centavo for the expropriation, have you?

That's true, but the government will pay me, with interest and monetary correction for inflation.

Why did Darci kill Chico Mendes?

Look here, my friend, if I can call you that, my child Darci was always very rebellious. His mother, who stayed in Paraná, beat him a lot, and he ran away from home repeatedly. I sensed he was rebellious, but never thought it would reach the point that he would kill Chico Mendes. He often complained to me that the police of Xapuri were always bugging him, not leaving him in peace.

But Chico Mendes was not of the police.

Look here [pause] . . . if it hadn't been my son who killed Chico Mendes, his killer would be my enemy. I spoke once, twice, three times with Chico Mendes. I put my hand on his shoulder and told him I had nothing more against him, I just wanted him to stop saying things against me in the papers.

Did Darci say that he was going to kill Chico Mendes?

He did not. If he had, I'd have paid him not to do it.

Gaston Mota declared that there was a meeting in which you participated, and in it the elimination of Chico Mendes was discussed.

It wasn't like that at all. There was no meeting at all. There was no mystery at all in the killing of Chico Mendes. "You, sir, are a man easy to be dead," I said to him.

Did you realize what the death of Chico Mendes represented?

Yes, I did. That's why I'm here, to free the authorities of the international pressure it has put on them.

Do you believe in God?

I did until I was sixteen.

Until what year did you go to school?

Only forty days. What I know I learned in life.

Are you afraid?

I trust in the Lord. They said that they would drain my ponds to find bodies. They said that the police would search from planes. I'm not afraid. I could have left here alone.

To where?

To Espírito Santo, Paraná, Mato Grosso.

Where is your brother Alvarino?

As soon as the warrant arrived for him, Alvarino told me he was going to take a trip, and that's just what he did. Afterward, we were supposed to meet up, but there was a problem and I didn't see him again.

When you were hidden in the forest, weren't you scared the tappers would find you and take revenge for the death of Chico Mendes?

I was worried that they could attack me, but I wasn't scared, because I trusted in the Lord. When I saw such things against us in the paper, Chico Mendes talking against my person, I said, "My God, what do I do? I could kill this man. . . ."

Why do you talk so much about killing?

Look, if someone was saying bad things about you, putting you down all the time, things that weren't right, wouldn't you think of killing him?

Sílvio switched off the cassette player. I complimented him on the interview.

"The day after Chico Mendes's death," he said, "João Branco's wife paid me a visit here in front of the *Gazeta* and said, 'Stop bad-mouthing my husband, because you owe him.' I said I didn't understand. Then yesterday, João Branco called one of our reporters from where he is hiding in Mato Grosso and told him about a meeting of the ranchers that had taken place in 1982, in which it was decided to kill me and two other journalists. Branco said, 'Don't kill them, buy them,' and the others said, 'They won't sell. So let's buy the paper.'

"It happened that a rich rancher, Wilson Barbosa, bought the paper and we all quit, and the paper stopped. Then Barbosa called and explained, 'Look, I'm not one of that group.' So we came back and we continued the same editorial line against violence and deforestation. The only restraint is that we can't talk about meat prices. The owner has a monopoly on the meat in Acre. The meat comes from Bolivia and competes with the beef from the local ranches."

Sílvio did not say that Barbosa was a dummy owner and that in fact the real owner of the *Gazeta,* and the person who had the meat monopoly, was Flaviano Melo, now the governor of Acre.

"So the UDR didn't bury us," Sílvio continued, "but it did buy the other paper in town, *O Rio Branco.*"

Is it really true that Darli has no affiliation with the UDR? I asked.

Sílvio pressed a finger to one of his cheeks and pulled down his lower eyelid, a Brazilian gesture meaning "Open your eyes, don't be a fool."

"We know from Darli's photo album that João Branco was at his ranch for a barbecue. We know that Darli is tight with Gaston, who is linked with the big politicians and ranchers and is a former member of the Civil Police. The question is, To what point were Darli and Alvarino instruments? To what extent did the leaders of the ranchers' wing take advantage of Darli's feud with Chico, and how can this be proved?

"The Civil and Military Police don't work because they are all bought. The Department of Public Safety is a corrupt, archaic, insensitive bureaucracy. They think Chico was a Communist. So did Mauro Sposito. He had ideological problems with Chico, who he thought was an advocate of guerrilla warfare. Sposito was a paranoid militarist, and he was worried that the Shining Path was infiltrating the tappers' movement."

What was Chico like? I asked.

"I knew him in the late seventies when he was still just a semiliterate tapper. Then he started to take part in the union movement. At first he was very polemic and impulsive, a real scrapper. Then he matured. He and I founded the PT in Acre in 1980. Later we both gave up party ideology, and he dedicated himself to the struggle of the tappers to save the forest and their way of life. Chico was a rubber tapper who metamorphosed into a union leader, into a world ecologist. He was childlike. He transmitted good energy. He showed me a side of life I didn't know. He showed me the forest.''

What is this blacklist that you published?

"Someone in the police furnished me with it. Chico was on it, and so was Osmarino Amâncio, the president of the union in Brasiléia. We printed it to expose Enoch Pessoa and his death squad. A rancher can use his own *pistoleiros* or the squad, which consists of members of the Civil Police and a few Military Police, to eliminate his enemies.''

So this death squad really exists? I asked. It isn't just something the *Gazeta* invented to sell papers, as the ranchers say?

"That's not it at all,'' Sílvio said.

One of Sílvio's hard-hitting editorials predicted a domino effect, a fulminating reaction to the murder, an operation of proportions never seen before in Acre, that would expose all the "articulators of terror'' and would lead to politicians, entrepreneurs, and "untouchable figures of society.''

Isn't this work a little dangerous? I asked.

"Of course,'' Sílvio said. "This is no fiction. At any moment someone can . . . '' He put his finger to the side of his head like the barrel of a gun. "The governor has provided me with guards, but if you're any kind of a journalist you can't walk away. You live this. Either you confront, or you live like a rat in hiding.

"The other day I got a letter from a soldier in the Military Police saying there is a new blacklist and that two journalists are on it. I asked him to come and see me, but instead I got a second letter that said, 'Since you don't give importance to what I said, I'll tell you that one of the journalists is you.' ''

I stepped out of Sílvio's office into a thunderous downpour and waited for a cab, but none passed. At last a man came out of the auto-parts store and got into his pickup. He was a big, beefy man, a red-cheeked, fair-skinned European, maybe six foot four, wearing a khaki shirt and khaki pants tucked into black rubber boots. He was several heads taller than the malnourished, dark-skinned mestizos of the forest and looked like a member of a different race, like a Boer. He was a rancher, a *paulista*.

Hey, you wouldn't be going by the Inácio Palace, would you? I asked.

"Sure, I can give you a ride,'' he said. "Even though I'm one of the villains you've been hearing about, one of the ones who's destroying the forest.''

He laughed, and we rode to the hotel in silence.

AN EXCLUSIVE AT THE COLÔNIA PENAL

The big news in the next morning's *Gazeta* was that Francisca da Silva, Chiquinha, Darli's youngest concubine, had apparently committed suicide. Romeu Tuma, who had returned to Federal Police headquarters in Brasília, was dubious that it was a suicide because of the manner in which it had been done — her throat had been cut, severing the jugular, not the way most people kill themselves. It was, however, the way people on farms kill their animals, so it would have been the most natural way for someone like Chiquinha to do herself in. Chiquinha, moreover, had a history of depression, had swallowed detergent in an earlier suicide attempt, and had, just the week before, tried to kill Margarete, her main rival for Darli's affections. She was crazy about him. ''I suffered a lot to know I wasn't his only woman, but forgot everything once we were in bed,'' she had revealed in yesterday's paper. ''It was three, four times every time we were together. What a cock! It was seven matchboxes long, limp, like a burro's.''

I would be suspicious after meeting Darli about the veracity of this last statement. The *Gazeta* was selling like never before, and this prurient passage about the ''Sultan of Paraná's'' equipment smacked of embellishment. Plus it didn't seem in character for someone whose man had just been arrested for murder to rave to a reporter about his sexual prowess. Seven months later I confronted a reporter for the *Gazeta* about this passage, and he admitted that Darli's *pinto* was not unusually long, but that all of his women confirmed that he was a great lover, very tender, and that he did do it four times in a row. But the exaggerated size of his penis was the invention of the reporter, Luis Carlos.

The wildest and most rebellious of Darli's women, Chiquinha said she didn't mind his beatings. She also testified to the police that on December 21, Darli came and told her that ''Chico Mendes is going to have to die.'' She asked, ''Isn't it dangerous to kill him?'' and he said, ''There won't be the least problem. This has already happened and I wasn't arrested.''

Ilzamar and Francisco ("Chico") Alves Mendes Filho with Sandino (named after the Nicaraguan revolutionary leader), one of their two children.

Joaquim and Cecília Alves Mendes, Chico's aunt and uncle, in their home at the Seringal Cachoeira rubber estate, outside Xapuri.

Chico's younger brother Francisco de Assis, a soldier in the Military Police, who is accused of killing the *pistoleiro* José Cândido de Araújo (a.k.a. Zezão) in revenge for his brother's death.

A rubber tapper collecting latex from the latest scored incision in a *Hevea* tree.

Left: A Brazil nut tree left standing (as required by Brazilian law) in Joaquim's pasture, with his son Duda at the base for scale. Within a few years the tree will stop bearing fruit and will die. *Right:* A rubber tapper bringing in great balls, or *pranchas,* of rubber to sell at Joaquim's cooperative.

Downtown Xapuri.

The Military Police station, about a hundred yards down the street from Chico and Ilza's house.

Center: The judge of Xapuri, Adair Longhini, with the first of four prosecutors in the Chico Mendes murder case. *Right:* Detective Nilson de Oliveira of the Civil Police, who conducted the inquest of the murder.

Above left: Eva Evangelista de Araújo, the president of Acre's Tribunal of Justice at the time of the murder, who has been notified that she will die.

Above right: Sílvio Martinelli, the editor of the *Gazeta,* who also has been *anunciado.*

Left: Chico Mendes, the late president of the Xapuri chapter of the Rural Workers' Union.

Above left: Mary Allegretti, the Brazilian anthropologist who projected Chico to international fame.

Above right: Lucélia Santos, former soap opera star turned political activist, speaking out for the rubber tappers.

Left: Bishop Moacyr Grechi (also *anunciado*), who helped organize the tappers' resistance movement.

Chico and his first cousin Raimundo de Barros (*center*), at the wake of Ivair Igino, who was gunned down by *pistoleiros* in June 1988.

Alex Shoumatoff

Sergio Vale/Agenor Mariano

Above left: Antônio Macedo — the new Chico Mendes?

Above right: Gaston Mota, under investigation by the Civil Police as a suspected drug and arms smuggler and alleged to be the head of the ranchers' syndicate, implicated in the murder of Chico and many other tappers.

Right: Alvarino Alves da Silva (*far right*), who is still at large.

Sergio Vale/Agenor Mariano

Alex Shoumatoff

Oloci, Darli, and Darci Alves da Silva (*left to right*), in the *colônia penal.*

Sergio Vale/Agenor Mariano

Far left: Sérgio (a.k.a. Francisco, a.k.a. Jerdeir) Pereira, one of the three Mineirinho brothers, accused in the murder of Chico Mendes; he remains at large.

Alex Shoumatoff

Right: João Branco, former head of the UDR in Acre, alleged to have ordered the murder of Chico Mendes.

Below left: Chiquinha, one of Darli's women, who slit her own throat after dreaming he was going to kill her.

Below right: Zezão (*foreground*), shortly before he was gunned down at a bus stop outside Xapuri.

Sergio Vale/Agenor Mariano

Sergio Vale/Agenor Mariano

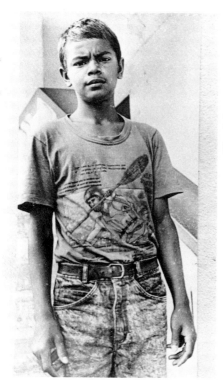

Genésio Barbosa, star witness in the case against the Alves family.

Padre Luis Ceppi at the funeral.

Ilzamar standing in the doorway where Chico was murdered.

The body of Chico Mendes.

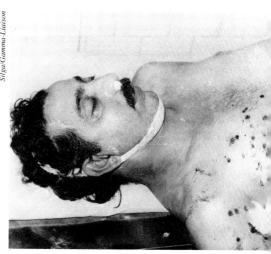

Above left: Julio Cesar, novelist and environmentalist, at the graves of Chico Mendes and Ivair Igino.

Above right: Alberto Setzer (*seated*), who analyzes satellite photos of the fires in the Amazon for the Brazilian Institute of Space Research.

Right: The burning continues.

A composite photograph of all the satellite pictures taken between August 1 and September 18, 1987, over west-central Amazônia. Published the following summer in the *New York Times,* it brought to public attention the tremendous number of fires. The central rash of glowing dots is clustered around highway BR-364 in Rondônia.

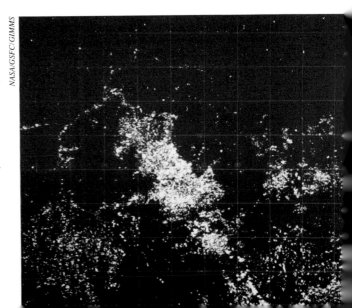

The last time she saw him was the night of December 22. He came out of the forest, made love to her four times, and returned to his hiding place.

For the last three days Chiquinha had been in a depression. The day before she killed herself she gave a Military Police soldier a box with a few jewels and said, "Take this, please. If anything happens, sell it for food for my kids." To Darli's other women she said, "If Darli goes to prison, what's going to happen to my children?"

With Chiquinha dead that left Natalina, forty-seven, Darli's titular wife, Maria Zilde, who had come with him from Paraná (he had left Darci's mother, Elpídia, there); and twenty-one-year-old Margarete, a local girl who had already given him two children and who was even more infatuated with him than Chiquinha. "My dream is for him to return so I can fall in his arms and smell him lying on my bosom," Margarete told Luis Carlos (if any of Luis Carlos's reportage is to be believed). The other women admitted that Margarete was Darli's favorite.

Margarete said it was the police who made Chiquinha kill herself. They had terrified her with threats of the tappers' revenge and of American bombs, and that night she'd had a dream in which Darli told her, "You betrayed me. For this you should die." Smuggling a kitchen knife under her dress, she had gone outside in the yard early in the morning and severed her own jugular. The police guarding the ranch found her body under the mango tree fourteen hours after Darli turned himself in. She left three children by him, two, three, and four years old.

The women lived in separate shacks on the ranch. Natalina, complaining of menopause, hated the younger and more beautiful Margarete and Chiquinha. She told Luis Carlos, "You can put down that the real wife of Darli is me. These two self-seeking bitches are his kept women."

Luis Carlos wondered how such a skinny, short, physically unattractive old woman, whose face reminded him of a coatimundi (a raccoon-like carnivore of the neotropics) could have kept Darli's interest. She confessed that part of her hold on Darli was her special aphrodisiac preparation. She called it cement, because it made you hard right away. The recipe was very complicated. The *Gazeta* revealed it in its next edition. It included the eggs of a certain tinamou called the *codorna*, and many herbs, like mint, cumin, saffron, *juca*, and *catuaba*.

Darli forbade his women to enter each other's houses even though they were less than fifty feet apart. "If one of you kills the other, either by shooting or poisoning her milk, you will also die," he told them.

After finishing the *Gazeta,* I walked up to the main square and woke up Getúlio, who was snoozing in the back of his Chevette. "Let's go to the *colônia penal,*" I said. It was ten miles from town, past the university, past the leprosarium. Acre is one of the most virulent foci of leprosy in Amazônia. I had been to the leprosarium in Manaus. There are two intermediate kinds of leprosy in the valley besides the usual tuberculoid and lepromatous ones. The lepers are segregated, although the myco-bacteria are not contagious. In Rio the lepers sell cocaine to get by.

We drove past Alto Santo, the seat of one of the five *daime* sects. According to a new book about them that I had picked up at the Inácio Palace, 120,000 Acreans have imbibed the hallucinogen.

"A friend of mine belongs to Alto Santo," Getúlio told me. "He goes twice a week. I've never taken it myself, but those who have tell me that they can read each other's thoughts and see into the hereafter. I'm all for it. If all the *pistoleiros* took *daime,* they wouldn't kill any-body."

The old Timothy Leary solution, the chemical cure, I thought. Zap the culture of violence right at the synaptic level. Slip acid to the Pen-tagon.

"*Daime* cures the ills of civilization. The cultists drink the wine of the vine to do penance for the innocents."

Why? I asked.

"Because they're getting killed right and left."

I asked him what he thought about the death of Chiquinha.

"The woman's suicide means Darli's a killer," he said. "Imagine killing yourself out of fear of being killed. Imagine how scared of him she must have been."

We fell in behind a truck laden with immense mahogany logs and passed through a zone of sawmills that were ripping the forest trees into planks. Only half a dozen species are harvested, and these only when it is practicable. The rest goes up in smoke. Besides mahogany, *cerejeira* is cut (for floors and furniture), *cumaru ferro* and *amarelão* (for floors), *imbaúba* and *guariúba* (for beams), *samaúma* (for framing), *cedro,* cedar (for furniture and finish work), *pereira,* and *angelim* (for floors and ceil-

ings). Brazil nut, a splendid hardwood, is also frequently harvested illegally. There were fifty mills in this industrial zone.

Although it was only midmorning and I'd had a good sleep, I felt
sluggish and kept woozing off. The Amazon has a soporific effect. It's
a big part of the *inoperância* problem. You need frequent fixes of nico-
tine and caffeine to keep going. So many things conspire against your
remaining on schedule and on the ball. It's a constant struggle just to
maintain consciousness, to fight off tropical entropy, torpid, rachitic,
stultified, paranoid paralysis. Eventually you simply slip into a state of
demoralized, suspicious indolence, a cynical lassitude. Surrounded by
staggering tropical rates of death and decay, eventually your own principles and resolve rot. You start making mistakes. Accidents happen.
Tasks like apprehending perpetrators, keeping them behind bars, gathering evidence, trying them and sending them up the river, become too
daunting, more than anything you think you could possibly get together.

The road became a soup of red mud, and the Chevette began to handle
like a motorboat or a collision car at a carnival, with Getúlio frantically
spinning the wheel from side to side. At last we reached the Francisco
de Oliveira Corde Penitentiary, or the *colônia penal,* as everyone called
it. It was a small building standing in about ten acres of swamp, surrounded by a concrete wall with curls of barbed wire on top. Several
Military Policemen were standing around at the gate. Security was supposed to be beefed up after an anonymous caller had threatened to free
the Alveses.

I asked for Antônio Campos, the director, and he came right out and
said there was no problem about seeing the prisoners, "so let's not waste
another minute." He led me down a covered concrete walkway over the
swamp to the prison. There were ninety-seven prisoners, he said. A
guard unlocked the door and led us to Darli's cell. And there he was, a
small, pathetic, broken old man, with thick glasses, gray sideburns and
mustache, standing behind the bars. He didn't look a bit like a vicious
killer or an indefatigable stud. But appearances can be deceiving, particularly in the case of mass murderers and psychopathic killers. I recalled how "Emperor" Jean-Bedel Bokassa, of the Central African
Republic, had seemed like such a sweet old man at his trial, hardly the
sort who would have served his dinner guests entrecotes of subjects who
had fallen into disfavor; and how completely at first Jeffrey MacDonald

had pulled the wool over Joe McGinniss's eyes. The most striking thing about Darli was that he was incredibly thin, really wasted and emaciated. He immediately recalled the AIDS victims I had seen in Africa the year before.

The cell was pretty much what you'd expect: a concrete bed with a thin mattress, a low concrete block for eating on and keeping things off the floor, a sink, moldy pinups plastered on the wall by previous tenants, a hole behind a concrete panel for relieving yourself. As the guard opened the cell door, Darli sat on his bed. He seemed genuinely depressed.

Mind if I come in? I'm sorry to hear about Chiquinha, I said.

Darli's eyes filled with tears. "I'm in great suffering," he said. "What's going to happen to our three children?"

My heart almost went out to him, until I remembered why Chiquinha had killed herself in the first place. But I played my part of the game. I came on like a friend, a truly sympathetic listener, and Darli acted like a sweet, unlettered country boy caught up in circumstances beyond his control.

He gave me the same line he had given Sílvio Martinelli the day before, and as he warmed up he became very talkative. "I don't know why my son committed this disgrace," he said. He told me how hard he had worked for everything he had, how he had taken out loans to plant soybeans, how two of his best men had been killed clearing the forest, how they were all living in isolation and only went to town once or twice a month.

I asked how old he was.

"I was born in 1936," he said, "so I guess that makes me fifty-two, or fifty-four."

I asked how many children he had, and he said about thirty.

Was João Branco ever at your house?

"Never."

Where is Alvarino?

"The last time I saw him was four months ago. He said he was going to take a trip. Maybe he did. I was alone in the forest."

But weren't you seen at the Fazenda Mineira a few days ago, asking for food with Alvarino and the Mineirinhos?

"Nothing of the sort. These papers are full of it. I respect the poor as much as the rich. I believe in God. They say we're mean, but my brother and I only live to work. If anything happened to me, Alvarino would kill himself.''

I asked if the UDR had anything to do with all this, and Darli said, ''I think in all sincerity'' — here he became incredibly sincere, even more than before, and he paused for dramatic effect, knowing that he was keeping me in suspense; this pause gave him away more than anything — ''. . . that the UDR was not involved. My son has no involvement with this organization. He did it for his own reasons. He was rebelling. He was always saying, Father, how can you let Chico Mendes say all these terrible things about you?

''They say I killed all these people, but the cemetery [on the Fazenda Paraná] doesn't exist. It's only persecution. The bodies were thrown into the pond to condemn me.''

I asked if he'd ever grown marijuana on the ranch.

''*Graças a Deus,* I've never participated in anything like that. The only fault I have, my friend, is that I like women. I believe in God, and I love the next man as much as I do myself.''

I took some pictures of Darli, then asked Campos if we could see his sons. Campos led us past a dozen cells. One of them had a color TV, a hot plate, all the comforts.

What did he do? I asked.

''He was caught on the bus from Xapuri with marijuana.''

The drug people take care of their own, I thought.

Campos said that 60 percent of the inmates were in for drug trafficking. Some were Bolivian. ''That's Vicinho,'' Campos said, pointing into another cell. ''He was in the Civil Police and did a lot of killing.'' I didn't ask if he was a member of the death squad.

Every Sunday, Campos explained, the inmates were allowed conjugal visits in the prison's ''motel.''

Darli came with us, perhaps to make sure that his sons didn't slip up and say something that would let the cat out of the bag. He shook their hands and sat with the two of them on their bed, his head down the whole time.

Oloci was twenty-two. He seemed like a friendly, regular guy. I wouldn't have pegged him at all as supposedly the most dangerous and cold-blooded member of the clan. His right arm was in a cast, healing from the bullet caught in the shootout with the police.

Darci was completely wooden and stone-faced. There was a kamikazelike intentness about him. This was obviously the designated fall guy. I managed to make him laugh by saying, You know, this whole thing is just like a *bangue-bangue,* a Hollywood Western. Even your uncle Alvarino — he looks just like Jesse James.

His father was amazed to see the boy laughing.

Darci reiterated that there was "nobody with me. I killed Chico because he was persecuting my father. I hadn't seen my father in two months. I never killed anybody else before."

And what about you? I asked Oloci.

Oloci pouted. "Lucélia says I pointed my finger at her, but that's a complete lie."

ON TO XAPURI

As I was leaving, Darli asked me sweetly, "How long are you going to be here?"

I didn't like that question at all. I told him I was headed right to the airport and flying back to Rio that very morning.

But I didn't go to the airport. I picked up my stuff at the hotel and drove to Xapuri.

It is a hundred miles southwest of Rio Branco. For the first two thirds of the way along BR-317 there is good pavement. Getúlio drove like a maniac, pushing the Chevette well over eighty, pointing out the sights. "That's Villa Acre, one of the oldest *seringais.* Now it's been subdivided into lots for weekend places. That's the home of a former *seringalista* who's now the owner of TeleAcre."

A pickup passed. "That was Mirco Soares. He owns a ranch and manages several others. He's part of the ring, one of the *articuladores,* articulators, of Chico's death. He was imprisoned and released."

We sped past the vast, empty ranches of absentee *paulistas.* Only a few token zebu steers were grazing in the desolate grassland. Clearly the clearing was not for raising cattle. It spread like a disease from the road over thousands of vacant acres, and the ranchers wanted to clear more.

(It must be said, however, that the pasture now, and even during the dry season, seven months later, when I revisited Acre, looked green and thriving. Grassland converted from rain forest does not necessarily turn to desert in five or ten years, as one often reads. The desertification is largely the result of overgrazing.)

The forest had been pushed back to or beyond the horizon. Occasionally the black, fire-eaten trunk of one of its former monarchs would still be standing like a grotesque obelisk commemorating the holocaust. These had been the emergents, the tallest trees in the forest, which rise another twenty or thirty feet above the canopy before putting out their leaves, stealing the light from the others. The writer Tim Cahill has compared them to "monstrous stalks of broccoli."

The trees in the forest have a tremendous range of consistency. Some are rock-hard and often have the epithet "iron" as part of their name. Others you can poke a fist through. When the forest is set on fire, it is a differential conflagration. The hollow-stemmed *umbaúbas* (*Cecropia palmata,* the trumpet tree or silverleaf pumpwood in English, which flourishes on already disturbed sites) roar like cannon when afire, drowning out the screams of the monkeys.

We passed a big state-owned sugarcane plantation, once 165,000 hectares of forest, sacrificed during the national push to convert to ethanol. But now oil has been discovered in Amapá, in eastern Amazônia, making the whole program uneconomical. The best thing about ethanol is that it's great for the air. Now there will be gagging fumes in the streets of Rio again.

Something small and black the size of a squirrel scurried across the road, right under the wheels, and it felt as if we had just hit a slight bump. What was that? I asked, and Getúlio said, "A *soim,* a tamarind monkey." Tamarinds are small, tremendously variable frugivorous clingers that speciate madly. Some species can be identified only by slight differences in the white around their mouth; others have long manes and exaggerated mustaches. They are also called *sagüis.* Damn! The only wild mammal I see on the whole trip and we run it over.

The Sunday afternoon I had spent at Lucélia Santos's house in Rio ended with everyone listening to a record by her sister Cristina that had just come out. Cristina was a small woman like her sister, but she had a huge, passionate, throaty voice, like that of Gal Costa or Maria Bethânia, the great stars of popular Brazilian music. One of her songs was about the *queimadas,* the fires in the Amazon. Its powerful lyrics were by the poet-journalist Aldir Blanc. The fires, Cristina sang, "are killing the seed of the soul of Brazil, and going unpunished." Blanc compared the fires with the out-of-control political and economic situation. There were two kinds of fires — forest fires, which burn animals, and inflation, which burns people. "The fires are spreading in an inflation of the red screams of *sagüis*. / In the bonfires, the vines writhe like anacondas. / Then everything turns to ash."

At a junction with a road that comes directly from Bolivia, Getúlio and I are pulled over by several Federal Policemen in snappy blue vests who are checking for contraband: scotch, electric appliances, TVs, ghetto blasters, arms, coke and grass. I explain that we are *pesquisadores,* and they wave us right through.

The pavement ends, and once again we plunge into the mud, Getúlio deftly straddling deep ruts we would never get out of. Our progress slows to five miles per hour. There is no way the reporters from *O Rio Branco* could have made it to Xapuri in an hour and a half. Big trucks laden with sacks of Brazil nuts lumber past.

Another roadblock, also manned by the Federal Police. But this one is Operation Sweep, or Varredoura: the dragnet for the fugitives. The police tell us the shortcut to Xapuri is too muddy and send us the long way around. After a couple of miles we meet another policeman in a different kind of blue uniform standing in the road — Military Police.

What's going on here? I ask Getúlio.

"This is the Fazenda Florestal, Alvarino's ranch."

It's a small spread, only five hundred acres. Alvarino hasn't been as successful as his brother. A sweet-looking old man, barefoot in the mud, with white hair and stubble, comes to the Chevette's window and introduces himself. Sebastião Alves da Silva, the eighty-six-year-old patriarch of the clan.

"I'm *mineiro,* from Minas Gerais," he says proudly. "I eat gold" (a reference to all the gold that has come out of the state of General Mines). And I say, before I can catch myself, So what do you shit?

Fortunately, Sebastião thinks that's a riot. So does the policeman. So do Alvarino's wife and teenage son, who have come down from the house. A bloody riot.

I mention to Sebastião that I saw Darli this morning.

"How's he doing?" he asks.

He's very thin and very sad over the death of Chiquinha, I tell him. Well, we'd better be going, I say. I hope everything turns out right. (A double entendre here: what I really hope is that you all get put away for good.)

Sebastião replies, "A leaf does not fall to the ground unless God wants it to."

I see where Darli gets his veneer of piety. I won't know until later that there is evidence linking Sebastião to numerous murders in Paraná back in the fifties. Today Sebastião is a fervent Baptist.

A pickup pulls up, and its driver tells us we'll never get to Xapuri this way, so we turn around and head back. The next ranch is unguarded. What's to stop the fugitives from stopping in for a beer and a bite to eat? I ask Getúlio.

"Hell, what's to stop them from dropping in at the Fazenda Florestal? The policeman is an old friend of the family."

We turn onto the shortcut and soon, after passing a deeply mired Federal Police paddywagon — part of the farcical dragnet for Alvarino and the Mineirinhos — we get stuck ourselves. Darkness falls. Insects and frogs start up a deafening samba. I push and push and the wheels spin and finally engage, and we are out and on our way again. Barefoot, midcalf in goo, all spattered with mud, I feel exhilarated.

"Come on. Quick. Get in," Getúlio says. "They could be out there."

An hour later the lights of Xapuri appear. We drive down the main street, which is lined with neat, modern houses, shiny new pickups under carports, color TVs in the living rooms — not at all what I expected, not like any other Amazon town I've seen before. This is the modern frontier.

There's money here, I say to Getúlio. What is it, drugs?

"No, it's a little more complicated," he explains. "The ranchers here also have ranches in Bolivia. They take their cattle over the border, then they go to Brasília and tell the Banco Central that they want to import some steers from Bolivia, and the bank gives them a form that allows them to buy dollars at the official rate. Once they get the dollars they sell them at the 'parallel' [i.e., black market] rate. Then they bring their cattle back over and pocket the difference. That's why there are so many nice houses on this street."

So when people say that the governor has a monopoly on meat from Bolivia, they could just as well have said that he's got the local cattle situation here in his pocket, I say.

"Exactly."

Xapuri is the sort of place — three thousand souls in town, another seventeen thousand or so in the surrounding countryside — that once you walk around it three or four times, you get the idea.

Tranqüilo, I say to Getúlio.

"*Parece,*" he says. "It seems that way."

We pull into the main plaza, which is dominated by a statue of José Plácido de Castro, who, three years after leading the tappers in the battle that won Acre's fifteen million hectares for Brazil, was shot in the back while riding through his *seringal.* The patron saint of Xapuri is Saint Sebastian. There is a statue of him stuck with arrows in a small park along the river, beside the dry-goods stores of the Syrians and the juke joints that jut out over the riverbank on pilings. It is a town of martyrs. I wonder how long it will be before there is a statue to Chico Mendes.

We get to the Hotel Veneza, a family pension run by several generations of women vaguely related to the Alves da Silvas, just before the evening deluge cuts loose. The rain acts as a curfew. Inside everyone is glued to the television, *Rocky III:* Nilson de Oliveira, who is conducting the inquest, a gaggle of Brazilian paparazzi waiting for the fugitives to be caught. They are city types from the South, completely out of their element. One is a financial reporter; everybody else in the newsroom had been off for Christmas when news of the murder came in over the wires. Another, in safari dress, is doing a thought piece on "the universe of Chico Mendes" during a lull in the action but has no intention of entering the forest. "I hear there are six different sizes of mosquito," she says. "There's no way you're getting me in there." Behind the hotel a pack of black vultures, the ubiquitous *urubus* of northern Brazil, brood in the palm trees and pace the backyard as if they, too, are on some kind of a vigil.

In the morning I went to see Adair Longhini, the judge who would be trying Darli, Darci, Oloci, and the others, if they were ever caught and indicted. I waded through the sluggish heat of the plaza, where a work crew was chipping at weeds with machetes, curbing the relentless onslaught of the green hell.

It wasn't clear which side the judge was on. Both the present judge in Brasiléia and Longhini's predecessor in Xapuri (who had married the widow of Nilão de Oliveira) were definitely with the ranchers. Judges belonged to the elite class and were thus de facto in favor of "progress." Eva Evangelista, the granddaughter of tappers, who sympathized with their struggle to save the forest, was a rare exception. But Sílvio Martinelli had said that Longhini was a good man, genuinely trying to do the best within the severe constraints of the system, and that he had shown "some independence."

Could you please ask the judge if it would be possible to have a word with him? I said to the policeman guarding the Forum. He went inside and after some time returned. "I'm sorry, but you can't see the judge if you're in shorts."

Respect is very important in Brazil. No problem, I said, I'll go back and change. But my only pair of long pants had been spattered with mud the night before when I was pushing Getúlio's Chevette, and I'd given them to the kitchen girl to be washed. By the time I got back to the hotel, they had only just been hung in the backyard, among the vultures, and were still dripping wet.

I went back and explained the situation to the policeman. Maybe I can talk to the judge through the window, I proposed. His office, I noticed, was on the back side of the Forum. The policeman went back in and didn't return for a long time.

I began to get impatient and irritable in the soporific humidity and was on the verge of making an ugly American scene — there hasn't been a trial here in twenty-three years, dozens of killers are getting off scot-free, and this guy's worried that I'm in shorts — when the guard returned and said the judge would see me.

Longhini, bearded, maybe in his late thirties, was suffering in a jacket and tie. The walls of his chambers were lined with thick, colorfully bound law books. Since his interest in justice seemed to have been (at least up to this point) purely academic, I decided to kick off the interview in an academic mode.

We were joined by the special prosecutor, Francisco Matias de Sousa, who wore aviator shades and looked like a cop, which he was, a deputy of the Civil Police in Rio Branco. Matias had no previous experience as a prosecutor and, according to Sílvio, was "doing a bad job because he's scared." Longhini explained that the prosecutor's job was to be an enforcer of the law, to hear the testimony of witnesses so they couldn't later claim that they'd been tortured, to make sure there was "neither abuse nor omission of authority.'' My impression of Matias was that his only interest in the case was to see that ''the people'' didn't get too close to what had really happened, especially to the role of the police. He told me he had interviewed Sílvio about the alleged blacklist of the alleged death squad that he had published. ''But Sílvio refused to reveal his source. We presume the head of the squad was Enoch, but there is no proof.''

I wasn't surprised to hear later that Matias was replaced a few weeks after this interview. He had been delaying the proceedings with his repeated failure to show up.

The judge and I discussed the ''modalities of homicide'' according to Brazilian law. ''The simple fact of having killed,'' Longhini explained, got you six to twenty years, but the sentence could be increased to thirty by extenuating circumstances, such as if you had killed for ''futile motives.''

The case in the Jardim Botânico in Rio that was in the paper the other day — two men were walking their dogs, the dogs started fighting, and one of the men pulled out a gun and shot the other — would that be a case of ''futile motives''? I asked.

''Exactly,'' Longhini said. ''Other extenuating circumstances are killing for money; 'perversity,' which includes *morte anunciada,* murder by poison, fire, explosion, torture, asphyxia, or ambush, or to get out of other crimes.''

So it looks like Darci is looking at at least thirty years on two counts of perversity, I said.

''Maybe,'' the judge said. ''Then there are certain 'excludants' that lower the sentence, like 'legitimate defense,' which includes killing in a state of necessity, self-defense, and 'defense of honor.' ''

In other words, I said, if a man found his wife in bed with someone else, chances are he could blow them both away with impunity.

''Exactly,'' Longhini said.

And suppose the guy is innocent, and you kill him because you just suspect that he's fooling around with your wife, I continued. Pathological jealousy, I knew, is a big killer in the interior.

''Then it goes by the type of murder,'' the judge explained. ''But often the jealous husband may go free, or only do a year or two, especially in the interior.''

But if a woman finds her husband in bed with another woman, it's a little harder to get away with killing them, isn't it? I asked.

"Precisely," Longhini said.

There was the famous case in Rio of the socialite Doca Street, who took up with another woman because her lover was fooling around. The lover killed her and got off with a legitimate defense plea. The jury accepted his lawyer's argument that Doca's lesbianism was an intolerable blow to his masculine self-esteem.

I asked Longhini if he thought there was any chance of Darci's getting off on a defense of honor plea — that he was defending his father's honor, which had been impugned by Chico's bad-mouthing — and he said, "Zero."

What about temporary insanity?"

"No, because it was obviously premeditated. If he's convicted, he'll do a minimum of twelve years with a possibility of parole after six. But because he's a primário, a first-time offender and has no previous record, he might not have to serve all of them behind bars."

Do you think he'll be convicted?

"That depends on the quality of the inquest. The prosecutor," Longhini said, indicating Matias, "has been following the inquest. Darci's confession is not fully accepted. For instance, he says he acted alone, but we know from eyewitnesses that there were two."

I asked about the possibility of a ring of ranchers under the aegis of the UDR being behind the murder.

"At this point we can neither discard nor affirm the hypothesis of a greater web of involvement."

I asked the judge if he felt in any danger.

"Most definitely," he said. "In the beginning of November, soon after we came out here from Rio Branco and I started to tackle the tremendous backlog of uninvestigated cases, my wife got a call from somebody who said, Tell your husband, if he loves his wife and children, he'd better let sleeping dogs lie. Since then I carry a gun.

"The government has to take an urgent position on the situation here," he said with a cavernous yawn. "When I came here in 'eighty-two, there wasn't a single judge in the interior. Today, all the judicial districts have judges, but there are still no prosecutors. I have inquests for more than a hundred homicides here in my desk that need a prosecutor before they can be brought to trial. The Civil Police is very destitute. Its vehicles are antique, its arms obsolete. At least they have removed Odilon as the clerk.

"I'd like to see the federal authorities give the support they're giving to the Chico Mendes case three hundred and sixty-five days a year. The other victims were human beings, too, you know.

"In my opinion, there is plenty of room in Acre for both ranching and rubber tapping. You can preserve each and develop the state. It doesn't have to be one or the other. It has to be balanced. Like justice," he said, and he held up the two pans of an imaginary scale in either hand.

Detective Nilson de Oliveira, twenty-seven, a tough, muscle-bound mulatto with five years on the force, most recently in charge of one of the robbery squads in Rio Branco, seemed motivated. He had ten days to complete his inquest and deliver it to the judge or to file for an extension. It was coming along fine, he said, and, opening his desk in the Civil Police station, he showed me the hundred pages of testimony that he'd already collected. "When I came here I found all the inquests at a standstill, here at the station, without sufficient evidence for the judge to indict. The judge just sent me back fourteen of them saying they need more work."

The case against Darci, he told me, was strong. Everything Darci had said in his confession, and when he had walked Nilson through a reconstruction of the crime, jibed with the findings of the Mengele forensic team. The shot had been fired from exactly where he said he had stood and fired it. "The weapon was determined to be a long-barreled twenty-gauge shotgun, fired from in front of the coconut tree, a distance of about fifteen feet. We spent five days diving for it. I don't believe he threw it in the river." Nilson also had the testimony of the Mineirinho Antônio's sister-in-law Maria Gorete de Sena that Antônio and Darci had returned to the Fazenda Paraná on the night of the killing and said, "The confusion in Xapuri is over. We killed Chico Mendes." "She has seen many crimes," Nilson told me.

He said he also had Darci for the murder of the colonist José Ribeiro (Oloci would later be charged with this crime). "And when the Mineirinho is found there will be more information."

Why did Darci give himself up? I asked.

"One, he had done what he wanted. Two, he knew we'd get him sooner or later."

What about Darli? I asked. How does the case against him look?

"Very possibly Darci acted on his father's orders. I have the testimony of people in Brasiléia, so I think we will get him, too."

What about the other deaths on the ranch?

"The cemetery exists, but there is no proof that the people who were assassinated were buried there. A fifteen-year-old relative of Maria Gorete's says that Darci, Oloci, and the Mineirinhos killed the two Bolivians. The peon who allegedly fished a skull out of the pond disappeared four years ago. This is possibly a journalistic story."

Why weren't these crimes elucidated before?

Nilson shrugged. "Because the police weren't secure. If an officer had fingered one of the Alveses, the next day he would have died. There are no conditions in Xapuri to guarantee the security of anyone. The police did nothing because they were afraid."

What about the wider ring? I asked.

"I think there was more than just the family involved," Nilson said. "I think there is an organization of ranchers that determines who has to die, and may be connected to the UDR, though there is no concrete proof of this. This has to be looked into very carefully. More time is needed to prove the guilt of the others, the intellectual side. I am trying to get a warrant for Gaston Mota for the murder of one of his employees whose wife he was sleeping with. Gaston was the architect and programmer of crimes for Darli."

How are you going to prove this?

"All of the nine who are in custody are saying nothing, but one man who seems to belong to the organization, Luis Assem, has a big mouth and much fear of the police. I think we will try to make a deal with him."

What about the death squad? Does it really exist?

Here Nilson drew the line. He was clearly not going to follow any trails leading to the police. That was only natural. "There is no death squad," he assured me. "It's just an invention of the *Gazeta* to sell papers. There are good police and bad police, just as there are good priests and bad priests. The majority of the thirty-three people on the alleged blacklist that the *Gazeta* published are still alive and committing crimes. Some have been killed, but not by the police. Enoch had nine

men on his squad, and nine others. These eighteen were the alleged
esquadrão. It wasn't that they were under orders from Enok. They just
did what they wanted, and Enok laughed when he saw the police committing a crime.''

Have you received any threats?

''Not yet,'' he said, ''but if one day I am killed, I did my job.'' Then
he recited one of those fatalistic expressions that Brazilians are fond of:
''Nasceu, morreu'' — ''You are born, you die.''

The amazing thing was that Chico's house — a simple shack with blue-
painted plank siding and a red-tile roof — was no more than seventy-
five yards from the Civil Police station. I opened the gate to the front
yard. A beautiful young woman appeared in the window — Ilzamar. The
lead story in that morning's *Gazeta* told how Ilza had gone the day before
to Brasiléia to have her appendix checked. The doctor, a Bolivian, had
sent away his other patients and had then tried to rape her. ''He is linked
with the big ranchers,'' she told me, spitting out the words *''grandes
fazendeiros''* with loathing.

Ilza showed me into the front room, where her brother Raimundo, a
cousin, an Indian tapper who was keeping an eye on the place, and her
two children were watching TV. On a wall unit was a display of Chico's
plane ticket to New York, his passport, his medal from the Better World
Society ''for your leadership in defending Brazilian Amazônia from deforestation and unsustainable commercial development''; the framed testament inducting him into the United Nations' Global 500 roll for
''outstanding practical achievements in the protection and improvement
of the environment''; and the key to the city of Rio de Janeiro, making
him an honorary citizen, that Lucélia Santos and Fernando Gabeira had
gotten him in November. These already moldy treasures, she explained,
were to be the beginnings of the Chico Mendes Museum.

Raimundo led me through the incredibly dense tangle between the
backyard and the river to the flattened place, now strewn with big, white,
fragrant petals from a tree above, where the killers had waited.

That evening I spoke with Raimundo de Barros, Chico's cousin, in
the union hall, a small wooden building on the plaza across whose front
a banner reading *''BASTA!* [ENOUGH!]'' had been plastered. He was a
tall, dark man, very proud and earnest, with great dignity, a man of such
wrathful righteousness and total passionate commitment that I felt a little

uneasy in his presence. "I am a tapper, a militant with my *companhei-ros*," he said, glancing nervously out the open window; he knew that he was one of the next on the hit list. "For every Chico Mendes killed, ten others will arise.

"We've been in this forest for more than a hundred and twenty years, but the government hasn't recognized our life. In the forest you take your baths in the clear creeks instead of standing under a feebly squirting showerhead. You sleep in a hammock, listening to rain hit the thatch roof. You move your bowels in open, beautiful places. You eat real food, not canned — I value these things more than the modern progress of the soap opera full of dirty dealing."

This wasn't really as much an environmental battle, I decided, as a class struggle and a war of conquest. The tappers were being displaced by the ranchers, the agents of progress, the vanguard of a "superior" culture, just as the tappers had displaced the Indians, just as we had done in the American West, as has happened again and again all over the world from time immemorial. The interesting thing was that now, in the late twentieth century, you couldn't get away with it. Wars of conquest, of imperialistic aggrandizement, of territorial expansion, were no longer possible. Armed conflict as a political strategy at the international level no longer seemed to work. Grass-roots guerrilla resistance movements were extremely effective. This had been the lesson of Vietnam and Afghanistan. You couldn't even get away with local, subimperialistic, endo-neocolonial wars of conquest like this, remote, out-of-the-way land grabs like the ranchers were trying to pull off. This was the positive side of television. The eyes of your fellow global villagers were upon you, wherever you were, keeping you honest.

The tappers' struggle bore many resemblances to the civil rights movement in the American South in the early sixties. Chico had been like James Chaney, the local black activist who was gunned down in rural Mississippi in 1964 with two educated white advisers from the outside (whose counterparts would be Schwartzman and Allegretti) by local members of the Ku Klux Klan (the counterpart of the UDR). With the complicity of the local police, to boot.

Suddenly, I realized that my work in Acre was done. I'd talked to the principals, gotten the "color," the physical setting, and the basic lines of the conflict. I felt completely drained as the full impact of the tragedy sank in. It was one of the saddest, most chilling stories I'd ever come across. Somehow this local struggle between the forces of good and evil in this obscure little town resonated far beyond Acre and even Brazil. It was as if Chico Mendes, Darli Alves, Nilson de Oliveira, and Adair Longhini had become larger-than-life figures in a morality play that was being performed for the whole world, as if Xapuri had become the center of the universe. I had the feeling that the information I had gathered, though enough for ten thousand words of investigative reportage, was only the tip of the iceberg, and that the longer I stayed in Xapuri and the more I learned, the murkier and darker the story would grow.

COVERING THE PSYCHEDELIC BASE

There was one item of business left — to take *daime* and see if it really was the "ultimate fix," as William Burroughs reported in his classic book *The Yage Letters*. People who had taken it swore it enabled them to see into the world of unseen causes. The Indians used it to divine the identity of thieves and the location of lost objects. Maybe it could help me figure out who was really behind the murder of Chico. I doubted it; I no longer had faith in chemical solutions, any more than in geographical cures. But that base had to be covered.

Late in the afternoon Getúlio dropped me off at a *daime* center, the one nearest to my hotel of the five in town — the Centro Espírita Culto de Oração, Casa de Jesus, Fonte de Luz. I was welcomed by its high priest, Manoel Araújo, a bearded old man dressed in white, with a round, white felt hat and gold chains. He told me he had sixteen children by five wives and showed me the mausoleum at the entrance of his church, blazing with mosaics of colored light bulbs, that was waiting for him. The founder of the cult, Araújo told us, Daniel Pereira de Matos, had been a disciple of Irineu Santos's and had died in 1958. "He left us more than six hundred hymns. We perform penances, praying for all humanity, for the benefit of the innocents, who don't have comprehension of the love of God."

Soon the devotees began to arrive, all in white, and, lining up at a little window to the side of the church, they were each given, from a large, ornate ceramic urn, little shot glasses of the psychedelic brew.

One was brought to me. "You will feel an irradiation, but don't worry," Araújo told me. I tossed it back.

The juice was a little bitter, but not bad. I waited, but I saw nothing: just a few paisleys and a slight brightening of the light bulbs in the church, and that was it.

THE MAKING OF THE MARTYR

I returned to my cabin in upstate New York and started writing. I'd asked Julio Cesar to follow the story for me in the Brazilian papers. Every couple of days a packet of clips would arrive from him.

The Brazilians were starting to come to grips with who Chico had been and what he had represented. Having not given him or his cause the time of day while he was alive, they were now claiming him for their own. The *Folha do São Paulo* chose him as its Man of the Year. An editorial in the *Jornal do Brasil* hailed him as the "Clark Gable of the poor" (whatever this meant), of the thirty-six million Brazilians wandering in the great empty space between the traditional and the modern worlds. "The uncontrollable machine that burns, cuts, invades, shot Chico Mendes," the editorial went. "It is a machine we are all in: Europeans, multinationals, arms factories, steel mills, banks and chemical plants. Mendes strove to stop slavery by sophisticated European business and the destruction of every type of life . . . in the name of the march of progress." It noted how *Time* magazine had chosen as its Man of the Year the degradation of the planet, and how *National Geographic* had devoted forty pages to the ecological crisis in Brazil and compared Chico's death with the massacres by right-wing death squads in El Salvador. Both exhibited the "vivid terror" in Latin America.

One Brazilian journalist told me, "Chico Mendes didn't exist until he died." The "second death" of Chico Mendes, the cannibalization of his cadaver by the media, as he put it, had begun. To Julio Cesar, Chico was the first figure of stature Brazil had produced in recent memory, and his example offered a chance for the moral rejuvenation of the country. "We produced a real hero," he said.

But the more cynical and conservative *cariocas,* or natives of Rio, like one publisher I spoke to, said, "I wouldn't pay more than a thousand dollars for a book on him. Nobody in Brazil cares about him. He was just a government agent giving free assistance to the Indians. Brazilians are already sick of hearing about him. You Americans burned down all your forests to get where you are today. If you can make an interesting story out of that loser I'll take you out to dinner.''

Some even regarded Darli as a hero and role model. The *Gazeta* ran a story about a fifty-year-old Brazil nut seller named José Domingos de Castro who had been picked up drunk and brandishing a big knife in Rio Branco. ''I'm from the same land as Darli,'' he boasted. ''I like women, too, and I'm looking for one strong enough to spend the night with me. I'll pay her well.''

Most of the stories in the Brazilian papers were about the manhunt. The Brazilian journalists stayed holed up at the Hotel Veneza, in Xapuri, for several more weeks, waiting for Alvarino and the Mineirinhos to be caught. They were an uninspired lot. They didn't see the story at all; they were baffled by the fuss. Chico Mendes wasn't a hero for the Brazilians, he was a hero for gringo consumption.

But the prospect of the fugitives being brought in was growing dimmer and dimmer. The Brazil nuts were falling, and the four men could survive in the forest for a long time, if they were in there at all. The Federal Police were getting demoralized. Five of their vehicles had been damaged during the manhunt. One man had broken his arm, and several others had infected feet or were laid out with gastrointestinal disease.

Like so many Brazilian undertakings, Operation Sweep had started out on a crest of tremendous optimism and enthusiasm. Both the Federal and Military Police had egg on their face — the first because of Superintendent Mauro Sposito's Pilate-like role in the murder, the second because of the disgraceful performance of Chico's two guards — and they wanted to redeem themselves. There was even a healthy rivalry between the two enforcement agencies.

In the beginning, the pursuers had thought they were very close. They found freshly broken branches along the trail in the forest on the Fazenda Mineira, where they were thought to be hiding, almost directly across the road from the Fazenda Paraná. One man was barefoot (Darli), another wore sandals. The three others were in sneakers. The police thought that because the fugitives had no food it would be only a matter of a day or two before they gave up. The Fazenda Mineira was surrounded. Roadblocks were set up on the road to Bolivia and escape routes to Bolivia through the back part of the ranch were cut off. On

January 7 the police announced that a helicopter was arriving, and the hunt would begin, "tomorrow." The sixty Federal Police in the elite jungle team would be going into the forest after them. Others, on horseback, disguised as cowboys, with little leather *vaqueiro* helmets, would patrol the neighboring ranches.

But the next day Darli turned himself in, not at the Fazenda Mineira, but at the Fazenda Vaca Branca, miles down the road. Sílvio Martinelli was amazed and disgusted that the police didn't go in right then and get the others, but they decided not to. Why expose yourself to attack when you had them surrounded? They're exhausted, all we have to do is wait, the police evidently figured. If one had turned himself in, the others would, too, which was a reasonable assumption.

On January 10, however, Alvarino sent out the message that he was armed; he planned to resist and would only be taken dead. It was raining a lot, so the police couldn't use their bloodhounds. But the rain must be making the fugitives even weaker, the police reasoned, diminishing their resistance. All they really had to eat was Brazil nuts. Why don't they use the tappers and the Indians to track them, I wondered, if they're really serious about bringing these people in?

The Federal Police gave the fugitives an ultimatum on January 11: if you don't come out, we're going to come in there and take you dead or alive. (How this message was delivered is unclear.) Alvarino's father, Sebastião, and his son Vantuil agreed to help the police persuade them to give up. "We'd rather have them alive because they have important information, but if they don't give up we'll go in after them with a helicopter that's coming from Cuiabá," an official said.

All the relatives at Alvarino's ranch, the Fazenda Florestal, were afraid that they would be torn apart by the tappers if they went to Xapuri. Alvarino's wife, Isolina, forty-six, and their daughter Donzila, nineteen, begged him to give up so that they could prove he had nothing to do with the assassination of Chico Mendes. Isolina swore she'd had no contact with her husband since December 22.

Meanwhile, the Fazenda Paraná was abandoned. Darli's three remaining women moved to Xapuri with their children. Military Police guards were called in, and the pigs, horses, chickens, dogs, cats, and cows, left to fend for themselves, were wandering around and reverting to the wild. In the *colônia penal*, Darli was getting more and more downcast each day. "I'm in despair. I want to die," he told the *Gazeta* on

January 13 (just as I was leaving). "I feel like beating my head against this concrete bench. Nobody comes to see me, or defends me. I'm worried about my abandoned ranch."

Darli said he doubted the police were going to catch Alvarino and the Mineirinhos. He said, "No way. The Brazil nuts are falling and the area they're supposed to be in is thirty-five hundred hectares of thick jungle. The police could hunt there for a month and they wouldn't even get close to them." He said that if he had wanted to, he could have left himself, easily slipped the dragnet, and walked to Rio Branco through the forest.

One thing wasn't mentioned in any of the accounts of the exploits of Operation Sweep: as soon as darkness fell, all the policemen went back to the barracks in Xapuri.

On January 14, the new superintendent of the Federal Police in Acre (Sposito's replacement), Ildor Reni Graebner, said that since December 23 the Federal, Military, and Civil Police had collectively spent 23 million cruzados (then around $23,000) on the manhunt, the feeding and transport of more than a hundred men, and the repair of breakdowns. Graebner admitted that the trail was growing cold and said that the Federal Police would give it five more days, then pull out. Darli's lawyer, Rubens Torres, speculated that the fugitives were probably no longer in the area of Xapuri. Alvarino, he suspected, was already in Paraná.

But José Carlos Castelo Branco, still the secretary of the State Department of Public Safety though there was mounting pressure for his resignation, told the governor that a team of Civil Police was really close to the four fugitives, that it had found new trails, and their capture could happen at any moment.

That day, too, there was an inquest by the Department of Public Safety in which Ilzamar pressed rape charges against the Bolivian doctor she claimed had attacked her, Dário Borjos Aramayos. The Brazilian consul in Cobija (the Bolivian town right across the border from Brasiléia), Paulo Salla, was doubtful that the rape had ever happened. "This is a flash in the pan," he said. Then he tried a different tack. "I've been here for four years and the cases of rape are very common. Many Brazilians rape women on the Bolivian side as well." The members of the Chico Mendes Committee insisted that the doctor was a known rapist tied to the ranchers and that he had attempted to rape Ilzamar to demoralize the family and rub its loss in. But, Salla went on, "I think nothing will come of this case. It only surfaced because of the moment. The ecologists are taking a lot of advantage of the situation. It was just a professional contact that she had with him.''

Detective Nilson says on January 16 that he thinks the fugitives are disoriented. He reveals that Alvarino and the three Mineirinhos have been spotted three days before, walking on one of the larger feeder trails in the forest toward Xapuri. The helicopter has arrived and will begin to fly over the fourteen-square-kilometer area they are known to be hiding in "tomorrow." "The problem is that now the Brazil nuts are falling from the trees," he says. "With three Brazil nuts a day and water, you can keep going indefinitely." (Visions of the desperate, emaciated fugitives smashing Brazil nut *cengos* against trees and shelling the seeds with the butts of their revolvers.)

On the seventeenth, still nothing has turned up, and the police are bickering among themselves. Romeu Tuma attacks the dead-or-alive ultimatum of the Department of Public Safety: "No one is going to shoot anybody just because he didn't give himself up by a set date. It's important that Alvarino be taken alive." But to show that there is no divergence between the two law enforcement agencies, Tuma and Castelo Branco pose together with arms draped around each other's shoulders. The helicopter is in use. Possibly the four *desesperados* have crossed into Bolivia. The government of Bolivia promises to help in their capture and to expedite any extradition orders that may be necessary. But the public is beginning to have doubts about the competence of Operation Sweep, remembering that Darci and Darli had turned themselves in and that it was only through the efforts of Lucélia Santos that Oloci was apprehended. Rumors are circulating that the ranchers in Brasiléia — the same crowd that met to plan Chico's death — have an organized structure to hide Alvarino and his companions. The manhunt and the helicopter move there.

On the eighteenth — the first sunny day in a week — the police intensify their efforts. An unidentified padre who baptized Alvarinho's children (old Padre José?) and who has been drafted into the operation says he doubts that Alvarino will give himself up. But Castelo Branco still has high hopes. After all, Alvarino isn't a superman, he says. Detective Nilson guarantees that he will turn in a "technically perfect" inquest.

Yet another brother, Dari Alves da Silva, decides on January 20 to collaborate with the police in the fugitives' capture. Alvarino's son Vantuil is still helping. Nilson says, "For some reason, I don't know why, the families of the region are oriented to give food and shelter to the fugitives" (despite the threat of American bombs), which has enabled them to hold out for almost a month. A hundred and twenty *seringueiros* are on guard to repulse the threat learned of by Gumercindo Rodrigues on the night of the eighteenth. Gumercindo had picked up the phone at the union to make a call. Evidently the lines were crossed, a frequent problem, and he overheard the following conversation between what sounded like two *pistoleiros:* "I'm in Xapuri. We got Mendes. Now there are three more to go."

January 22, status quo: tappers, ecologists, and padres are demanding the police be more efficient. Raimundo de Barros accuses the police of screwing up from the beginning. Gumercindo points out an unpardonable error: while the police were all sleeping in the barracks in Xapuri, Alvarino and the Mineirinhos appeared at the Fazenda Mineira in the night to ask for food, but the next day the police didn't track them. "Any tapper knows that at night you can only get four or five kilometers, so the police could have caught them easily." Padre Luis Ceppi says he doesn't understand why policemen trained in antiguerrilla jungle operations would have to stop when night fell. "If in one day they advanced ten kilometers following the fugitives' trail, they should spend the night at the point they have reached, so they can keep going the next day and not have to begin everything over." He adds, with irony, that if it had been an invasion of the Bolivian army instead of a simple matter of finding four fugitives, Brazil would be losing.

January 24: two armed men with hoods kidnap Fernando Lima Pontes, the twenty-two-year-old son of the director of the Civil Police in the Department of Public Safety, and force him to drive in his Brasília sedan from Rio Branco to the Fazenda Paraná, passing easily through the police barrier.

January 25: the Federal Police pull out. Sources in the Federal Police say that Governor Flaviano Melo is not interested in pursuing the case and accuse him of "impeding the process of justice." The Federal Police agents from Brasília are needed back in the capital to help enforce the government's new Summer Plan, a draconian measure to stop the runaway inflation threatening to plunge Brazil into complete paralysis, chaos and anarchy, in which the cruzado has been declared extinct and replaced with a new currency, the new cruzado (which is simply a thousand old cruzados minus the zeros) and frozen at one to the dollar.

The feud that has erupted between the Federal Police and Melo dates to several months before last November's elections, when there was a bad flood and four thousand people who lived along the Rio Branco had to be evacuated. The local scuttlebutt has it that the governor, by the simple expedient of adding a zero to the report of the disaster, declared that there were forty thousand refugees. Millions of dollars' worth of food and clothing began to pour into the state from other parts of Brazil and from abroad. But instead of distributing it to the refugees, Melo, it later came out, turned it over to his wife, Antônia, chairwoman of the incumbent party's League of Women Voters, who used it to buy votes. It had fallen on Mauro Sposito, as the state superintendent of the Federal Police, to investigate the diversion of these contributions. Now the governor is accusing Sposito of the torture of political prisoners and requesting his removal from the Federal Police by President Sarney.

On February 4 Alvarino and the Mineirinhos enter the house of some tappers, put the family to flight, devour their food, and return to the forest. Nilson sends a patrol of Military Police to the locale, but it turns up nothing. Carnaval arrives, but even as other daily activities are suspended during the four days of ritual euphoria, the Military Police keeps manning its roadblocks and checking information on the whereabouts of the fugitives. The replacement parts for Nilson's car, which broke down several weeks ago, finally arrive from Rio Branco, but there is still no sign of the thirty vehicles that the minister of justice promised to send. The detective says he hopes they will be liberated by the end of the month.

After this, the news of the fugitives petered out. On April 15, Alvarino was reported to be circulating freely in Xapuri. Nilson, asked why he didn't pick him up, complained, "I don't have a vehicle, gas, police, or a fixed prosecutor."

On June 15, Alvarino, disguised as a woman, was rumored to have appeared at the Festa de São João, an annual blowout all over rural Brazil. But it seemed unlikely that Alvarino would have chosen this ruse, unless he had shaved off his luxuriant mustache.

Already there were signs that the ranchers were just biding their time, waiting for the Federal Police to pull out. As soon as that happened, the journalists would pull out, too, and that would leave no one to protect Chico's *companheiros* or his sympathizers. On the eighteenth of January two shots were fired at the convent in Brasiléia. One of the nuns opened a window and was blinded by a flashlight. In the thicket across the street two ambush blinds just like the one behind Chico's house were discovered. Apparently they were set for Padre Luis.

Eva Evangelista was *anunciada* again on January 24.

If the phone call that Gumercindo overheard actually took place (we have only Gumercindo's word that it did, and his veracity quotient, as I would learn, wasn't the highest), the three most likely targets were he, Raimundo de Barros, and Júlio Barbosa. And if they were killed, one already sensed, their deaths wouldn't make the headlines Chico's had. They'd just be three more murders in the backlands.

Osmarino Amâncio Rodrigues, thirty-one, the most charismatic of Chico's political heirs, said that he had also been *"jurado de morte"* (yet another phrase for receiving the death threat). He asked the governor for permission to protect himself with armed *seringueiro* guards and was refused, and he denounced seven ranchers who, he said, were responsible for all the land-conflict murders in the "northern region" since 1980: Darli and Alvarino, Benedito Rosas, Crispim Reis, Joaquim Madeiros, a lawyer he identified only as Hélio, and Colonel Chicão. He also said that João Branco was involved in some crimes, as well as the judge of Brasiléia, Heitor Macedo. He said that he had gone to Macedo on December 14 and told him he had been threatened with death; the judge replied, "Be quiet, for your hour has come and your days are numbered." It was genuinely confusing that each member of the movement had a slightly different list of villains.

THE INQUISITION BLOWS THROUGH

"Seven percent of the U.S. Senate overnighted in the Amazon with me last year," Tom Lovejoy told me proudly.

This time — January 1989 — he was accompanied by Senator Tim Wirth, an environmentally hip senator from Colorado, who had been holding hearings on the greenhouse effect and was also on the board of the World Wildlife Fund and the Senate Banking, Housing, and Urban

Affairs Committee, which controls the release of funds to the Inter-American Development Bank for projects like the paving of BR-364 to Acre; his wife, Wren; Senator John Heinz of Pennsylvania and his Mozambican-born wife, Teresa, who helped with the translating; Senator Al Gore of Tennessee; Senator Richard Shelby of Alabama; Congressmen Gerry Sikorski of Minnesota and John Bryant of Texas; Ben Bradlee, executive editor of the *Washington Post,* who had had a longtime fascination with the Amazon; and Peter Benchley, the author of *Jaws,* who was working on a novel of global ecological collapse set in the Amazon.

The trip was a fact-finding mission. Its purpose was to view the devastation and study ways of generating funds to protect the region. The delegation planned to discuss with President Sarney in Brasília the possibility of converting some of Brazil's foreign debt into projects to guarantee that some of Brazilian Amazônia would be protected. The concept of "debt-for-nature swaps," as an attempt to slow tropical deforestation, was another of Lovejoy's babies, a brilliant idea, a creative solution he had originally proposed in 1984. It would make everybody happy — the conservationists would save the Amazon, and Brazil would get to pay off its debt in its own currency — except the banks, and they weren't going to get their money anyway.

The idea was first implemented in 1987 in Costa Rica, $50 million of whose debt was exchanged for special "conservation bonds" to expand and strengthen the national parks that already preserved 12 percent of the country. The World Wildlife Fund, the Missouri Botanical Garden, and the Nature Conservancy put up $1,068,750 to purchase $9 million worth of discounted debt owed to the American Express Bank, Morgan Guaranty Trust Company, and Banker's Trust. Equador, Bolivia, and the Philippines had agreed to similar swaps. The proposal for Brazil was to raise $4 billion from donors to save the Amazon rain forest, which would buy, say, $8 billion worth of discounted Brazilian debt. This would be exchanged for $8 billion in Brazilian currency, to be used to endow Brazilian environmental institutions charged with protecting the rain forest.

At first Brazil's foreign minister, Roberto Abreu Sodré, enthusiastically endorsed the idea at a meeting with the delegation at the Palácio de Alvorada, the presidential Palace of Dawn. But then President Sarney rejected the idea as foreign interference. "We're putting together a new economic package," he said, "and we don't want the debt and the environment lumped together. We don't want the Amazon to become a green Persian Gulf.'' A few days later a similar proposal by the Dutch also had cold water thrown on it.

The Brazilians, as they have been for decades (their paranoia rooted in understandable historical reasons), were very sensitive about the sovereignty question when it came to Amazônia. They resented criticism of their attempts to develop the rain forest from the First World, which had destroyed so much of its environment and was responsible for much of the world's pollution. When the delegation touched down in Porto Velho for a quick tour of Rondônia, internationally renowned for its fires, the governor called it the ''true inquisitors,'' but in an attempt to placate the Americans, he signed a decree limiting the further use of ''spray'' — chlorofluorocarbon-emitting spray cans. BR-364 was too flooded to drive on, so the delegation flew over it and took a spin on the Madeira River, with Romeu Tuma, who was in charge of security, following nervously in a second boat.

There was some confusion, which was played up by the Brazilian press, that the delegation had come to investigate the murder of Chico Mendes. One Amazonian politician complained, ''We didn't send a delegation of congressmen from Brasília to investigate the assassination of Kennedy or Luther King, so who do these people think they are?'' Senator Wirth made it clear that the trip had been planned months before and that they were not there to investigate the murder. ''But we know,'' he added, ''that this event is an illustration of the forces that exist in Brazil and have to be controlled.'' And when the delegation got to Rio Branco, they met Ilzamar and a delegation of 150 *seringueiros*. ''I admire your movement and I hope you continue,'' Senator Gore told them.

The big environmental question now facing Acre was the paving of BR-364 to Rio Branco. The International Development Bank had approved a loan for the project but had suspended it in 1988 after Brazil failed to provide plans to protect the Indian lands along it; Chico's testimony had been instrumental in the bank's change of heart. ''How do you feel about it?'' the senators asked the tappers, and Júlio Barbosa, the new president of the union in Xapuri, reiterated Chico's position. ''We are not against the paving of the road, but if the lands of the rubber tappers and the Indians are not legalized, we can say good-bye to this part of Amazônia.'' (Chico himself had told filmmaker Miranda Smith, ''We're not against the paving of the highway. We've never been against progress and development, but we're against the politics that lies behind this famous propaganda of progress and development. Despite all the money that has been loaned for the development of Acre, these projects are not benefiting the people they should be benefiting. They only benefit the half-dozen large landowners in the region.'') Senator Gore assured the tappers that no U.S. funds would be spent on the road without the rights of the forest people being protected.

The delegation met in a hot, crowded room with Governor Flaviano Melo, who dropped a bombshell. He pulled down a chart that showed BR-364 completed to Pucallpa, Peru, and continuing from there to the Pacific, where there were three arrows labeled ''timber,'' ''Brazil nuts,'' and something else that had been scratched out, pointing to Japan. ''I just got back from Japan,'' Melo told the delegation, ''and the Japanese have offered six hundred million dollars to pave and extend the road to Peru.''

The World Bank and the IDB had refused to finance this project under their new policy of not funding projects that damage rain forest. This road would provide the Japanese, who consume 40 percent of all tropical logs sold on the world market, with a back door to the untold billions of sticks of timber in Amazônia. India, Indonesia, and Malaysia had recently banned the export of their logs, and were selling only timber that had been processed in their own mills, so the Japanese were looking for new sources.

Logging, so far, is responsible for only 5 percent of the deforestation in Amazônia, and the delegation realized that if the road went through, it would be the end of western Amazônia. Senators Heinz and Wirth passed their concerns on to the National Security Council, which relayed them to President George Bush, and Bush, in Japan for Emperor Hirohito's funeral, reportedly communicated to Japan's prime minister his country's displeasure over the ecologically disastrous project. The prime minister responded that Japan had no intention of building the road to Peru and that the Brazilians hadn't even presented a proposal for the project. Someone was lying somewhere.

That the Japanese were becoming more active in funding Second and Third World development programs, that Brazil was trying to attract foreign investment to pay off its debt, and that the Brazilian finance minister had visited Tokyo in 1988 to request $300 million for project assistance are a matter of record. Both Brazil and Japan felt the Americans should keep their nose out. Japan's ties to Brazil are deep. Japanese farmers had begun immigrating to Brazil at the turn of the century, and there was a particularly large Japanese presence in the state of São Paulo. Other Japanese farmers had been growing jute and bell peppers since 1946 in the Amazon's floodplain forest at Tomeasu, a hundred miles west of Belém. The writer Alex Haley once told me that Japanese offspring of black GIs fathered during the postwar occupation were sent to Brazil, the Japanese being very concerned about maintaining their racial purity. So it was a natural and potentially powerful partnership: Japanese industrial might, capital, and advanced technology, and Brazil's tremendous untapped resources and its hunger to join the First World. As Flaviano Melo told the American delegation, "That road fits us like a glove. If Japan wants wood, we have it, and we can also think of selling our products to the rest of the world."

The road to Peru was an old dream. Lima is only a thousand kilometers, or about 600 miles, from Rio Branco, and forest products from Acre now had to travel 2,800 miles to Belém or 2,500 miles to São Paulo and its seaport, Santos. Pucallpa was the original destination of the Trans-Amazon Highway. The plan to span the continent at its broadest point, so that you could drive from Recife, on the Atlantic, all the way to Lima, was one of the earliest schemes of the generals, and at the Pan-American Congress of Highways at Caracas in 1979 there was serious talk about forging a surface connection between the ports of Lima and São Paulo — Callao and Santos — as an integral part of the Pan-American system of roads. The missing link could be completed in either of two places: through Cruzeiro do Sul, in far western Brazil, to Pucallpa, a distance of only about 250 kilometers but over some very rough terrain; or BR-317 could be continued through Xapuri, Brasiléia, and Assis Brasil to Iñapari, Peru, where Brazil, Peru, and Bolivia meet. The latter route was favored by the Peruvians because it would go through their most productive agricultural regions. But the plan was shelved as the Brazilian Miracle flamed out in a tailspin of accelerating inflation and Peru was paralyzed by even more severe social and economic cataclysms. Pucallpa is now part of an area controlled by Shining Path and M-19 terrorists that has been declared a state of emergency, so the Peruvian part of the project is not about to be completed anytime soon.

Even so it seemed strange, when this had been the plan all along, that the United States should suddenly become upset about the ecological disaster it posed now that the last leg was about to be completed. It was now full winter in the North Country, and after I had read the clips about the road, which had generated a small furor in the First World, I put another stick of birch into the wood stove and contemplated the blatant hypocrisy of the American position.

Here we are, one of the main forces behind the destruction of the Amazon through the World Bank and the IDB. We have criss-crossed our continent with tens of thousands of miles of paved road, and we stole California from Mexico so we could have our outlet to the Pacific and a western terminus for our transcontinental railroads and highways, so we could sing our anthem about America the Beautiful spreading "from sea to shining sea." Now we won't let the South Americans have their Route 66.

The Brazilians certainly smelled a rat. Was the American opposition to the road really ecologically motivated? Or was it that the United States, they wondered, didn't want Brazil to break out of its debt peonage and become competitive? The road meant a direct route to Japan's lucrative markets, not only for timber, but for minerals, grain, and beef, and direct access to Japanese advanced technology. America would be placed at a competitive disadvantage in terms of access to the world's largest remaining supply of wood, as well as to the world's largest reservoir of genetic information, whose future value cannot even be intelligently guessed.

Already the world's balance of economic power was shifting dramatically in Japan's favor. Japan's voracious appetite for the world's resources was all too apparent. Off the coast of Peru, out in the Peruvian Trench, I had watched Japanese ships sucking up anchovies by the millions through holes in their hulls, canning them on the spot, and steaming back home. Already the Japanese were stockpiling logs from the Pacific Northwest, sinking them in their lakes for future use, while leaving their own forests untouched. And — the most redolent irony of all — due to contracts we'd been locked into by rapacious timber interests in the forties, we'd been selling the Japanese magnificent Sitka spruce and hemlock at four dollars a stick from our last temperate rain forest, the seventeen-million-acre Tongass National Forest, in the cool, moist Alaskan Panhandle. According to the NBC Evening News, most of the trees are ground up into pulp for disposable diapers.

American interests would unquestionably be compromised by the completion of this road. Of the timber that is presently being used in Amazônia, 33 percent is consumed regionally, 55 percent goes to other parts of Brazil, and only 12 percent is exported. But of the twelve foreign recipients of Brazilian hardwood products, the United States tops the list. It buys the most veneer, the most plywood, the most panels and value-added wood products. It accounts for 27 percent of total Brazilian hardwood exports. Plus, substantial revenues from the Panama Canal would be lost if the road were completed.

The notion of Japan's getting its hands on the Amazon, hoovering the trees, the minerals, the nuts, the fish, the genes, and everything else, was therefore perhaps even more unbearable to the United States than the thought of the whole place burning to the ground.

But Lovejoy's concerns, and presumably those of the rest of the delegation, were ecological. An unsigned memo about the trip that I found in Lovejoy's files was a succinct analysis of everything that is going wrong in Amazônia and why it must be stopped. It warned about direct deforestation and indirect deforestation caused by increased access and population expansion, such as had destroyed Rondônia. "Rapid deterioration of the cleared lands leads to increased pressure to clear more land. The cycle is unsustainable and endless." It made the usual points about biodiversity and the atmosphere: how the forests of South America hold the majority of the continent's water supply and act as a water regulator; how they also act as the "lungs of the earth," absorbing carbon dioxide that would otherwise lead to the gradual warming of the planet. "Without the forests, the earth loses its main ally against global warming, a concern of all nations."

The memo warned that the rubber tappers and other indigenous groups along the road would be seriously affected. "Already conflicts exist between local resource users such as the rubber tappers and incoming populations. The recent murder of Brazilian environmentalist and rubber tapper Chico Mendes serves to illustrate the potential human tragedy that unplanned experience and use of natural resources can cause." It made the point that "as the local environment's ability to sustain basic human needs declines, the requirements for increased assistance would multiply."

Then it added a very important general consideration:

Just as the economies of the world are dependent on each other, so are their environments. Economic assistance must be accompanied by sound natural resource and environmental planning. The multilateral and bilateral assistance organizations now recognize this and are taking steps to safeguard against ecological disasters stemming from economic development. It is in the best interests of each nation to help preserve every other nation's ability to support itself.

But, the memo noted, "as installations such as the World Bank and U.S.A.I.D. incorporate environmentally sound finance practices, there is a great danger that their policies will be undercut when public or private funding sources, such as the Nakasone Fund, are used as lenders of last resort for unsound economic development."

A final point: the road would provide a new eastern land export route for traffickers of cocaine from Peru's Huallaga Valley, the world center of coca production, and U.S. and Latin American drug enforcement efforts could be dealt a serious blow.

FIRE

It was twenty-five below outside when I finished digesting all the material on the debate over BR-364. Winter had finally come. The smell of the smoke curling up from the chimney of the cabin, the flames dancing through the glass front doors, were so romantic, so cozy. I used to be a real devotee of the wood trip. You got hot three times: cutting the wood, splitting and stacking it, and burning it. The reversion to wood from fossil fuels was an important part of the simplification, back-to-the-land ethic of the sixties. One of the main characteristics of tribal people and posttribal peasants — who still live the way people have lived for most of human history, whose way of life I admired — is that they still burn wood. Their way of life has a special smell: the smell of smoke and sooty walls and ceilings. I felt proud when in the early seventies I became one of the wood burners of the world.

Fire was a great teacher. I learned how to position a stack of kindling so the flames from one stick would lick and catch another. I watched the flames with fascination for hours at a time. Like wind and running water, they were always changing, always the same, and they made you realize how everything, including yourself, is nothing more than a transient fusion of particles that is always breaking down and in the process of becoming something else.

But now, because of the greenhouse effect, burning wood wasn't responsible anymore. If we were going to stop global warming, one scientist warned, we were going to do no less than stop making fires — one of the oldest, most universal, and most satisfying human activities.

I recalled how the Plains Indians had used controlled burns to drive the buffalo and to keep the grassland clean and open, how periodic fires are necessary for certain forest communities, how the cones of the long-leaf pine in north-central Florida, for instance, need to be opened by fire before they can release their seeds. I reviewed the tremendous importance of fire to the Indians of the Amazon — how it was needed for the preparation of land and of food; how it represented civilization, but also an uncontrolled natural force; how many tribes told the story of fire's being stolen from Jaguar or obtained from the underworld; how in some tribes fire symbolized the fall from grace and the loss of immortality, but in others it was an agent of purification through death or was associated with the sun and the masculine reproductive force; how Jaguar originally owned fire, but now only its reflection was seen in his eyes; how when flashlights were introduced to the Kayapó Indians, they christened them "jaguar eyes"; how to the Tukano Indians the hearth represented the uterus, yellow flames symbolized the fertility of the sun, and red flames the fecundity of nature; how fire to the Tukano was an instrument of cosmic transformation, how it destroyed but also created, how their taxonomy of fire was as complex as the Eskimos' many words for different types of snow, distinguishing between yellow fire, medium yellow fire, red fire, very pale fire, fire with much light, opaque fire, fire that goes out little by little; how it was taboo to urinate on fire lest anacondas come and occupy the hearth; how the Yanomamo Indians drank the pulverized ashes of slain kin before they went off to raid each other's villages. I remembered how, paddling up the Nhamundá River in a dugout with some Kaxuyana Indians in 1984, we came upon a section of scorched riverbank that went on for miles, which they told me they had torched "just for the fun of it." I reminded myself of how dependent the Industrial Revolution and the modern world, with its millions of internal-combustion engines, was on fire, how the whole thing was, in a sense, a by-product of the need to keep warm.

And now fires — recreational fires, at least — were a no-no, one more thing to be guilty about.

BRAZIL BARKS BACK

President Sarney was livid when he learned that the United States had queered the deal with Japan. He declared the completion of BR-364 a national priority and swore that it would be built with or without foreign financing. Sarney, a bushy-mustached poet and former *grileiro* in Maranhão, had had no previous executive experience and was not supposed to be president; Tancredo Neves was, but Tancredo had died in 1985, just before he was to take office, under confused circumstances after an operation, and with him the hopes for an orderly transition to a more democratic government had also died. Sarney was in way over his head. His regime was the most corrupt in years. More than ten thousand "irregularities" were brought to the attention of or uncovered by the Ministry of Justice. One of the irregularities that, to my knowledge, was not uncovered, which I learned about on a trip to Paraguay that April, was that one of Sarney's sons had been involved with Gustavo Stroessner, the son of Paraguay's recently deposed dictator, in smuggling timber from the Mbaracarai Forest, the last large rain forest in Paraguay, over the Brazilian border.

As 1989 progressed and Brazil was increasingly subjected to the greatest international pressure it had ever experienced to stop destroying its rain forest — it had been the last country to abolish slavery, but the pressure then had been nothing like this — Sarney, who had extended his regime as far as was constitutionally permitted, became progressively belligerent. At the bicentennial celebration of the storming of France's Bastille, in July, he said, "The real French Revolution has not yet happened. It will happen only when the Third World gives a bloodbath to the seven countries that have hegemony over it."

To Sarney the international brouhaha about the fires in the Amazon was a "Trojan horse" that hid other interests (like keeping Brazil from exploiting its minerals and paying off its debt) and "uses the pure spirit of the young people." To other politicians the national honor became more important than doing right by the Amazon. The governor of Amazonas State, Amazonino Mendes, gave away five thousand chain saws to "stop poverty, so people will cut trees and become rich." But Leonel Brizola, the old Socialist war-horse running for president, proposed registering chain saws as if they were firearms.

Many Brazilians saw the uproar as a CIA conspiracy, just as in the fifties Americans saw everything that went wrong as a Communist plot. Sarney, at a military ceremony in March, told the armed forces high command that now more than ever it was their "mission to defend the Amazon," now that "Brazil is being threatened in its sovereign right to use, exploit and administer its territory. Every day brings new forms of intervention, with veiled or explicit threats aiming to force us to make decisions that are not in our interests." He charged the industrialized nations with conducting an "insidious, cruel and untruthful campaign" against Brazil, to distract attention from their own large-scale pollution, problems with acid rain, and "fantastic nuclear arsenals." Marlise Simons had a fascinating article in the March 23 *New York Times,* titled "BRAZIL, SMARTING OVER THE OUTCRY OVER THE AMAZON, CHARGES FOREIGN PLOT."

There were several other versions of the conspiracy theory besides the one that claimed Brazil was deliberately being kept a debt peon. The First World wanted to prevent Brazil from getting at its minerals either to not depress world prices or to postpone the exploitation until it could harvest them itself. A wave of xenophobia swept even the tappers. The UDR's slogan, "Amazônia Is Ours," resounded everywhere. Echoing UDR president Ronaldo Caiado, the army minister, General Leonidas Pires Gonçalves, attacked the "false ecologists" whose real objective was to internationalize Amazônia. Anti-Semitic graffiti directed at the liberal environmentalist federal deputy Fábio Feldmann — "Jewish Ecologist Go Home" — was slapped on the cathedral in Brasília. Feldmann had called for the end of tax credits for ranching, a ban on log exports, and an end to charcoal-burnihg steel plants, and he had said the real problem was the "sinister alliance of people inside Brazil who benefit from what's happening in Amazônia and who now have the ear of Sarney."

A group of conservative Brazilian senators formed a parliamentary commission to investigate the true motives behind the world's sudden heightened interest in the Amazon. Critics said Sarney was beating the nationalist drum to rally support for his weak, discredited government, that he was turning the Amazon into a big sovereignty issue, as the generals in Argentina had done with the Falklands, and was making ecologists out to be subversives and the United Nations an imperialistic colonial power. Amazonino Mendes was delighted by the controversy. It was the first time anyone had paid attention to Amazonas. In a softening of his previous defiant stance, he said that the notion that foreign powers were actually planning to take over Amazônia was absurd and that any contributions from concerned groups abroad to the state's empty coffers were welcome.

On April 6, 1989, Sarney unveiled Nossa Natureza — a comprehensive plan, pointedly labeled "*Our* Nature," to salvage what was left of the Brazilian environment — in a fanfare of publicity that cost two million dollars; meanwhile INPE complained it had no money to repair its broken computers or develop satellite images so it could analyze the data on the previous year's Amazonian fires. The plan, which was to be implemented by the military, included a five-year inventory and zoning study of the basin, the creation of several parks and reserves and of a special forest police force, a ban on the use of mercury for gold prospecting, and a suspension of tax credits and other fiscal incentives. But it was dismissed by critics as "too little, too late," "disappointingly sketchy," aimed more at calming international outrage than at doing anything substantive. The protection of Amazônia would have to wait for the next president.

"Daily we are receiving caravans of reporters, photographers, scientists, and researchers attracted by the sensationalism of the news of the devastation," Gerônimo Santana, the governor of Rondônia, complained, and the mayor of Ariquemes, one of the state's new boomtowns, suggested that the visiting Americans would have spent their time better reforesting Vietnam, which they had defoliated with napalm.

In Mexico City twenty-eight leading Latin American writers and artists, including Mario Vargas Llosa, Gabriel García Márquez, Carlos Fuentes, and Rufino Tamayo, called for an international tribunal to investigate the "ecocide and ethnocide" in the Amazon. "To invoke national security to justify crimes against nature seems to us puerile and dishonest," their statement said. "Ecocide and ethnocide cannot be excused with chauvinist, jingoist words and sentiments. We, as Latin Americans, would like to see you [the Brazilian government], with your love of national sovereignty, defend the Amazon against local and foreign predators." Vargas Llosa, who was running for president of Peru, promised that if elected he would make sure the extension of BR-364 didn't go through.

Meanwhile the Amazon Pact (the eight countries — Bolivia, Brazil, Colombia, Ecuador, Guyana, Peru, Suriname, and Venezuela — that jointly own the Amazon basin) met in Ecuador and said that "any pressure on Brazil to protect the Amazon will have to be answered by all of us. We will not accept impositions from people who are trying to boss us around."

On April 3, Ingmar Bergman, Allen Ginsberg, Günter Grass, Isabel Allende, and 121 other writers and intellectuals from forty-four countries sent a letter to President Sarney. "Don't follow the bad example of the developed countries," it urged, and contribute irrationally to the further devastation of the planet. Among the projects it beseeched him to suspend were Plano 2010 of the state power company, Eletrobrás, with its seventy-six additional projected hydroelectric dams, and the "neocolonialist corridor to the Pacific." The whole "perverse relationship" between the developed and underdeveloped countries, which exported $6 billion worth of timber while importing $10 billion in processed wood every year, should be redefined.

Brazilian-French relations deteriorated after President François Mitterrand suggested that the fate of Amazônia, which he called part of the global heritage of all mankind, be determined by an international body. A senior official at the Ministry of External Affairs said he was infuriated by France's "double standard." France has "no enchanting environmental record," he said. (Indeed, French barges had recently been caught dumping toxic waste on the coast of Guinea-Bissau, in West Africa.) The same diplomat related how at a recent international conference Brazil had tried to introduce a clause in a final resolution saying that chemical weapons were extremely harmful to the environment but was told that it was "too controversial." "So we said, all right, then let's discuss the environment. But not just the Amazon, the whole agenda, the whole industrial model we're all part of." This didn't go over well, either.

Sarney was invited to a conference at The Hague. He accepted, then backed out after being advised that his presence would represent a breach of sovereignty, since a domestic subject — the Amazon — would be discussed by other nations.

In July there was a cartoon in the *Jornal do Brasil* by Millor Fernandes. It showed a modern metropolis, a forest of skyscrapers some-where in the First World, with disembodied voices coming from various floors of the glass towers: "They can't be allowed to destroy the last forest reserve on earth!" "They're taking down a Belgium each year!" "This is going to bring the end of the world!" "They're liquidating the ozone layer!" "They're predators of nature!" "Amazônia is universal property!" "We have to establish drastic sanctions!" "These underde-veloped countries are so irresponsible with the ecology."

It all resembled a macropolitical projection of the conflict between the ranchers and the tappers. The same forces were going at each other, and the fate of the whole world rested on the outcome.

THE AMAZON AS PAWN

Brazil's paranoia about foreign intervention in Amazônia was not en-tirely unfounded, nor was its refusal to become the ecological reserve of the rest of the world all that unpardonable. Its hold over the valley had always been rather shaky. Early in the European history of Amazônia, France, Holland, and Britain had all cast longing glances at the Portu-guese colony, and Brazil was well aware that the greater share of the valley wouldn't have ended up in the national territory if Portugal hadn't persuaded Spain, which was distracted by problems with the British, to cede western Amazônia up to the mouth of the Madeira River — nearly a thousand miles of longitude — in the Treaty of Madrid, in 1750. A century and a half later Brazil had taken Acre from Bolivia by force. Many of the borders it shares with the seven other basin countries are still in dispute.

The foreign designs on Amazônia during the nineteenth century were thinly disguised. Matthew Maury, the brother-in-law of Lieutenant Lewis Herndon, who in 1849 surveyed the navigability of the Amazon with Midshipman Lardner Gibbon, became one of the valley's first American boosters. "Rice could be double-cropped and maize four-cropped in the rich soils of the valley," he reported. If the slaves in the American South were sold to planters in the Amazon, and the region's agricultural potential were realized, "the country drained by the Amazon would be capable of supporting the population of the whole world." The only problem was figuring out a way to wrest the region from the "lazy, incompetent'' Brazilians. Brazil, he wrote, ''has arrayed herself against the improvement and the progress of the age, and she has attempted by intrigue so to shape the course of events that she might lock up and seal with the seal of ignorance and superstition and savage barbarity the finest portions of the earth; and if free men were to keep their silence the very stones would cry out.'' At the very least, Maury felt, the waterways of Amazônia should be internationalized.

The renowned Harvard zoologist Louis Agassiz, who went on a collecting expedition in the valley in 1865, felt that three hundred million people could easily be accommodated there, while his wife looked forward to the time ''when the banks of the Amazons will teem with a population more vigorous than any it has yet seen — when all civilizations will share in its wealth, when the twin continents will shake hands and Americans of the North come to help the Americans of the South in developing its resources.''

The revolution that led to Acre's annexation in 1903 was undertaken after an American navy officer named Chapman Todd engaged an impoverished Spanish journalist in Pará, Luis Galvez, to translate into Spanish a secret offer to Bolivia from the U.S. government. America would defend with military assistance Bolivia's right to free river passage through the Brazilian Amazon and would pay all the costs of war between Bolivia and Brazil in return for Bolivia's handing over a third of rubber-rich Acre for an American colony. Galvez squealed to the Brazilians, whose nationalistic ire was so aroused that an expeditionary force, including twenty gunboats of adventurers provided by the governor of Manaus, steamed up the Purus and took Acre, installing Galvez briefly as emperor.*

The Amazon was the focus of all sorts of utopian visions. In the thirties, for instance, the Mexican intellectual José Vasconcelos dreamed of establishing a ''cosmic race'' of Latin American mestizos there. In the thirties and forties, the Nazis became very interested in the resources of Brazil. German scientists discovered radioactive sand on a beach in Espírito Santo and, realizing the sand's value for weapons research, smuggled boatloads of it back to the Fatherland as ballast. During the war, U-boats plied the Amazon and its tributaries, and Nazi sympathizers

---

*These examples are taken from the fascinating discussion of nineteenth-century foreign designs on the Amazon in Hecht and Cockburn, *The Fate of the Forest.*

maintained communications by means of secret radio transmitters on re-mote promontories in the valley.

In 1957, Artur César Ferreira Reis published his book *Amazônia and International Covetousness,* whose worst fears were confirmed, in the decades that followed, by the Hudson Institute's wild scheme to dam the Amazon into a great inland lake; by the United Nations Food and Agriculture Organization's 1971 study, which concluded that the Amazon, if converted to farmland, could sustain a world population of thirty-six billion people; and, most recently, by the generals' granting to Daniel K. Ludwig, carte blanche, a chunk of the valley larger than Connecticut.

No wonder the Brazilians were a little antsy about proposals, such as Mitterrand's, that the fate of Amazônia be decided by an international body.

THE LEGEND GROWS

On February 2, Nilson de Oliveira issued a warrant subpoenaing Acre's UDR president, João Branco, who had left Acre on December 26, to return and explain how *O Rio Branco* reporters had known ahead of time about the death of Chico Mendes, since their alleged hour-and-a-half drive from the capital to Xapuri was "not humanly possible"; and to explain the meaning of the statement in the paper's December 5 "Off" column about the bomb that was going to explode. Nilson was becoming even more convinced that "more people knew" about the plans to kill Chico than just the Alves da Silvas. Bolivian police picked up José Brito de Souza, an alleged *pistoleiro* of Darli's, and turned him over to the Brazilian Military Police. José Brito confessed to having bought arms in Bolivia that he sold to Darli and his two sons, including the .38 revolver fired by Oloci into the crowd of tappers protesting in front of the Brazilian Institute for Forestry Development station the previous May. After someone on the night of January 28 tried to force open a window of Ilzamar's house, she decided it would be safer if she moved to the capital.

On February 10, Darli and his two sons were taken from the *colônia penal* to Xapuri under heavy guard to testify before Judge Adair Longhini. Nilson had refused to reveal the details of the extensive security precautions, lest someone try to kill or free the suspects. While thirty Military Policemen with machine guns, rifles, and pistols surrounded the Forum, Darci retracted his confession and denied authorship of the crime. Though not represented, he seemed to have been technically instructed, since he said that he didn't recognize any of the objects recovered at the murder scene and claimed he had spent the night of the killing at his aunt Zilda's, sixty kilometers away, and that Town Councilman Luis Assem (who was included on most lists of the "ranchers' ring") and Gilson somebody-or-other, the owner of a restaurant in Brasiléia, could vouch for his whereabouts. His father continued to deny any participation in the crime.

Meanwhile, on January 25, a few days after the first month's anniversary of the murder, a requiem Mass was held for Chico at St. Peter's Church in Washington, where Robert Kennedy's body had been commended to the Almighty. Senator Robert Kasten of Wisconsin called Chico his "friend" and "ally," the man who "showed me the human face of environmental devastation." In 1987 Chico had visited the offices of Kasten, who was a senior member of the Senate's key Appropriations Subcommittee and a close friend of Secretary of State James Baker's and World Bank president Barber Conable's. One of the Amazon conservation movement's most powerful friends, Kasten was leveling his sights on the pending $500 million loan that the World Bank was planning to make to the Brazilian energy sector that would enable more devastating dams, among other things, to be built in the Amazon.

William K. Reilly, the administrator of the Environmental Protection Agency, said at the ceremony that Chico had been an "inspiration." The Brazilian ambassador to the United States, Marcílio Marques Moreira, declared that Chico's work had been "important to the whole world." Suddenly the government, which had ignored the hundreds of letters that Chico had written over the years begging for help, was claiming him as a Brazilian hero. (Barbara Bramble, the National Wildlife Federation's lobbyist against the ravaging caused by Third World development projects of the multilateral lending institutions, had gone to Ambassador Marques to express her concern that justice be done in the Mendes case and also to express solidarity in the *Bateau Mouche* tragedy. The ambassador had floored her when he said that her and her colleagues' work was directly responsible for the growing environmental awareness in Brazil and also for the flourishing of nongovernmental environmental protection groups, and he had asked her to keep it up.)

But it was Raimundo de Barros, speaking from the heart in Portuguese, with Steven Schwartzman translating, who stole the show. It was Raimundo's first trip to the United States, and he seemed completely out of his element in a checkered work shirt open at the breast, unfazed by the cold among the other, dark-suited mourners, his dignity imperturbable. His wife, Maria de Conceição, shivered at his side in a full-length coat someone had lent her. "We are so humble and poor," Raimundo said, "that I never dreamed I would be coming to this great country and talking before so many important people. I feel what Chico Mendes felt when he spoke at the IDB's annual meeting a couple of years ago. He said, 'Why do you hear us more than our own country does?'

"They will possibly kill more people, including me, but the fight of the people of the forest will not die. Chico had so much courage. I am more afraid." He mentioned the other marked men: Júlio Barbosa, Gumercindo Rodrigues, Osmarino Amâncio, Bishop Moacyr Grechi, and continued, "But we won't stop, and we invite you to form an international delegation to police and avoid new deaths." He accused the Brazilian government of encouraging killing in Amazônia and of "protecting men who have fortunes in greed." Asked if he was scared to return to Brazil after the accusations he had just made, he said, "I am not lying, and furthermore, I carry with me the certainty that, thanks to Chico, our support in Brazil and the world is much greater, and that for this our struggle will continue, no matter who is in the leadership."

Raimundo had spoken of "capitalist greed," but in his translation Schwartzman strategically omitted the word "capitalist," which seemed out of place in a gathering of congressmen from the greatest capitalist country in the world.

Two hundred and fifty people, including five senators and eight congressmen, proceeded to the steps of the Capitol, where the speeches continued. Ambassador Marques, however, did not join them. He was visibly irritated with the criticisms he had heard in the church, of the Brazilian government and of the inefficacy of its judicial system, with the insinuations that Brasília was protecting the owners of the huge ranches in the region, and with the superior moral tone of the remarks of Senator Kasten, whose nickname in the embassy was the green imperialist. Kasten had said, "The future of the tropical forest should be a cause of ours, because it is not just the tropical forest of Brazil, but ours, everybody's, and we should include it in our environmental policies." Reilly had been more respectful of Brazilian sensitivities: "Amazônia will only survive if long-term measures are enacted by Brazilian society itself, which controls the forest. What we can offer is our knowledge and collaboration."

Meanwhile, former Beatle Paul McCartney and the dying king of Brazilian country music, Luis Gonzaga, composed musical tributes to Chico. Mangueira, one of Rio's famous samba clubs, chose Chico's life as its theme for the next year's Carnaval. Higher than that on the Brazilian thermometer of immortality one cannot go.

The rain forest continued to be the hip cause of the entertainment world, and the problems of Amazônia became a hot topic in places as far away as Australia. On May 24 there was a "Don't Bungle the Jungle" concert at the Brooklyn Academy of Music, featuring Madonna, artist Kenny Scharf, the B-52s, the Del Fuegos, Bob Weir of the Grateful Dead, and a recently formed band that called itself (what else) the Jungle Brothers. To a screaming crowd Madonna proclaimed: "Every second an area of rain forest the size of a football field is disappearing. At this rate, in fifty years the entire forest may be gone — forever."

In Europe, which had been experiencing an even greater acceleration of ecological awareness, the rain forest, particularly the Amazon forest, was the rage, and Chico Mendes became an even bigger hero. A Brazilian editorialist theorized that with the political and economic situation pretty much under control in most European nations, the youth had directed its idealistic passion to a new cause: the environment. Nowhere was there a more dramatic awakening, or was Mendes a greater hero, than in Italy. Dom Moacyr flew to his ancestral homeland that spring and found that city after city had erected a monument or dedicated a park to the slain ecomartyr, or *ecocidio,* as Chico was being called in Italian, and he was swamped with appeals to appear on television. He theorized that the elevation of Chico to near sainthood in Italy had to do with the long-standing presence of Italian missionaries in Amazônia and the heavy involvement of young Italian priests in liberation theology. Later in the spring, Padre Luis Ceppi took Ilzamar to Italy for a month, which provoked rumors, but the priest swore to Julio Cesar that he took his vow of celibacy seriously.

Even in Brazil people were becoming aware of the environment and disenchanted with the government's position since the 1970s of development at any price, although, according to a poll conducted in June 1989, 81.3 percent said they received little or no information from the media about environmental questions. A majority, 53.9 percent, said they felt that development was as important as protection of the environment, while 15.4 percent gave priority to ecology even to the detriment of the creation of jobs, slightly more than those who felt that progress was more important than environmental safeguarding: 13.3 percent. To 18.9 percent, the most important environmental problem was the fires in western-central Amazônia; 17.2 percent believed it was industrial pollution.

A burgeoning grass-roots Green movement sprang up among Brazil's young. More than a thousand small environmental groups, some with no more than five members, had arisen spontaneously and were staging sit-ins at nuclear power plants and other ecohappenings, and Julio Cesar was trying to unite them.

There were new battles to be fought, and new protectors took up the banner of the fallen Chico. After a three-day trip to the Xingu Park in the fall of 1987, the British rock singer Sting had taken up Amazônia and the plight of the forest people. In July of 1988, he hooked up with Raoni, a longtime militant for the rights of his tribe, the Kayapó, and founded the Fundação Mata Virgem (Virgin Forest Foundation), whose goal was to raise $3.5 million to establish a vast nature reserve encasing the Kayapó's already Texas-sized reserve. He and Raoni went on the road to win support for the cause. They called on the Pope, on Prince Charles, on President Mitterrand. They appeared on the Phil Donahue show with Thomas Lovejoy. Raoni told how his mother, father, and four children were killed by a fever brought in by the whites. Sting called Raoni "my third parent" and absolved Brazil of guilt in the devastating fires. "I'd do the same if I found myself in the situation of the Brazilians, who are slaves of the international banking system and the multinationals," he said. "If I had to pay seventeen billion dollars a year to service a debt that will never be paid off, to survive I too would take down trees and exterminate animals and the people of the forest."

In the last week of February the first Meeting of the Indigenous People of the Xingu took place at Altamira, a city that had grown up where the Trans-Amazon Highway crosses the Xingu River. The purpose of the meeting was to protect the Karará Dam, which Electronorte was planning to have built and generating hydropower by 2000, and four other dams on the Xingu, a total of seventy-nine dams in all of Amazônia that were in the works. Sting was there, as was the singer Gordon Lightfoot. A Kayapó woman named Tuira lunged at the director of Electronorte with a machete and, screaming incomprehensible phrases that were later translated as "We don't need energy. You just want to take the land of the Indian," smacked his face and back with the flat of its blade.

The meeting was organized by Paulinho Paiakan, another Kayapó militant. The Kentucky ethnobotanist Darrell Posey had taken Paiakan and another member of his tribe, Kube-i, to Washington in February 1988 to complain to the World Bank of the destruction of the forest, the pollution of rivers, the building of dams, and the disregard for Indian rights. As a result, Posey was threatened by the Brazilian government with expulsion from Brazil and the two Indians with prosecution as aliens who had interfered with Brazilian domestic affairs. The parallel drama of their struggle was played out during the final months' denouement of Chico's tragedy. The showdown took place on October 14, when four hundred Kayapó, dressed for ceremonial battle in red and black war paint, showed up at the courthouse in Belém. The government backed down, and the charges were dropped.

Paiakan was an eloquent spokesman for Amazônia and its people. At the University of Chicago that December he made a moving plea for everyone to work together:

> The forest is one big thing; it has people, animals and plants. There is no point in saving the animals if the forest is burned down; there is no point in saving the forest if the people and the animals who live in it are killed or driven away. The groups trying to save the races of animals cannot win if the people trying to save the forest lose; the people trying to save the Indians cannot win without the support of these groups; but the groups cannot win without the help of the Indians, who know the forest and the animals and can tell what is happening to them. No one of us is strong enough to win alone; together we can be strong enough to win.

The Brazilians withdrew the request for the $500 million under pressure and negotiated a series of other loans with the World Bank that were more specifically pegged to modernizing its energy sector, at making the system more efficient, reducing the need for electricity, and introducing conservation measures that would obviate the need for the dams.

But the battle was far from over. The same forces and pressures, the same irrepressible philosophy of progress, of development at any cost, the same forces of ignorance, greed, and overpopulation, were still there and were not going to go away.

Now the Brazilian government was gearing up for Polonoroeste II, and it wangled a loan of $250 million to clean up the mess it had made of Rondônia the first time around. "But Polonoroeste Two isn't going to be any better than Polonoroeste One was," Barbara Bramble told me. "It's based on the same misconception, that pouring big money into a frontier state will somehow result in positive development. Rondônia will become a whirlwind and a magnet for more bureaucratic jobs and land speculation again. The best thing to do with Rondônia would be to leave it alone. The people there were disillusioned and were leaving. This will reverse the exodus. Polonoroeste Two will be a litmus test of whether the internal reforms within the World Bank are really working, or whether the bank will continue to aid and abet a certain mind-set in the Brazilian government that it probably inspired in the first place."

THE MOVIE

Gorillas in the Mist, the movie about the life and murder of Dian Fossey, was not a huge box office success or anywhere as good as it could have been, but it was the beginning of a genre. There was a great hunger in the industry for new ecomartyrs, and the Chico Mendes story became the hottest property in Hollywood that people could remember. Robert Redford, David Puttnam, Peter Guber and Jon Peters, Dino de Laurentiis, Cecchi-Gori and Berlus Cohi, Ted Turner, the Brazilian company J.N. Films, an Australian group, and William Shatner were all putting out feelers, and some had already begun to approach Ilzamar and the Chico Mendes Committee with offers for the movie rights to Chico's story.

Mary Allegretti and Steven Schwartzman had already pretty much decided to go with David Puttnam and Chris Menges, who wanted to do a movie about Chico and had the backing of Warner Brothers. Menges was a close associate of Adrian Cowell's and had worked with him on his documentary *The Tribe That Hides from Man.* He had gone on to direct the cinematography for *The Mission,* an epic movie about the Jesuits in eighteenth-century Paraguay. But Gilson Pescador, former padre of Xapuri and recently defeated PT candidate for mayor, strongly felt that the movie about Chico should be made by a Brazilian company. "It's our forest and our struggle and it should be told by Brazilians," he argued to Ilzamar, and she agreed with him. That would have been the way Chico would have wanted it, given his feelings about American capitalist imperialism.

My piece in *Vanity Fair* about Chico's murder hit the stands in the first week of March, and I was deluged with movie offers. After weighing them all, I decided to accept that of Robert Redford. An environmentalist of long standing, Redford had recently directed *The Milagro Beanfield War,* a similar story about an oppressed Latino minority standing up against the forces of modern progress.

Another plus was that the extraordinary movie *El Norte* had come out of Redford's Sundance Institute. There was no question that Redford, although he had no experience with the Amazon, had never even been there, could make a good movie about Chico Mendes, if he had the right people helping him.

That summer I talked with Redford, who had gone to see Ilza in Washington with Sonia Braga — a possible Ilza for the film — "to put my hat in the ring." He had asked for Ilza's backing for a big Hollywood feature film about Chico, for which he would donate to the Chico Mendes Foundation his producer's salary and his actor's salary (he wanted to play a bad guy, the ruthless American manager of a multinational project). Oliver Stone was out as director, replaced by Steven Spielberg, who would also donate his salary to the foundation. Redford also wanted to make a more documentary type of film biography of Chico to be directed by Nelson Perreira dos Santos, one of the most respected Brazilian filmmakers. Redford said that he had been planning to make a movie on the Amazon since the early eighties. A script had been written in 1982 by the late Spencer Eastman, based on Daniel Ludwig's Jarí project, but no one in Hollywood was interested. The rain forest had not yet become hot.

Redford was explaining this to Ilza with Mary Allegretti's brother translating. Schwartzman, who was also there, told him that the family was very upset by my article and didn't want it to be part of the picture, and that if Redford could see that it was cut out of the movie project, his proposal would be viewed much more favorably.

As Redford was making his pitch to Ilza, Sonia said to him, "Wait a minute, he isn't translating most of what you're saying." She asked Ilza directly, in Portuguese, why she didn't like my article. Ilza looked confused. She didn't know anything about it.

"I couldn't compute what was going on," Redford told me. "I couldn't put that together for two months, not until I found out that Schwartzman, to whom I'd given *Milagro Beanfield War* to show to the tappers, had blocked it and seen to it that it wasn't shown. When I confronted him later about this he was edgy, nervous, like a guy who is being hunted by the police. What I finally figured out was that these people were not prepared for the circus after his death. Suddenly they found power in their laps, and I think they manipulated the naiveté of the tappers."

In the months that followed there were disputes within the environmental movement regarding the film. The real problem with Redford, besides the fact that Schwartzman and Allegretti were allied with Puttnam, was that he hadn't contributed enough of his prestige and money to the Environmental Defense Fund, although he had served on its board for years, but had decided instead to work with a rival group, the Natural Resources Defense Fund.

Redford was in fact one of the most positive forces in the American environmental movement. At the Greenhouse/Glasnost Conference he put together at Sundance during the summer of 1989 he said: "We're here to overlap our professions into a larger consideration of how we can treat the planet better." Early in the seventies he and his family had been threatened with death when he opposed the construction of a coalfired power plant on the Colorado River. Now the president of the power company, which had backed down from the project, was on the board of his World Resources Institute. That was Redford's way, to win over the opposition, bring the opposing forces together and all working for the common good.

Friction also arose between the Environmental Defense Fund and the Better World Society, which had a documentary of Chico in the works, over which of them deserved the credit for creating Chico. Both groups were soliciting funds in his name. "Chico was my good friend," Barbara

Pile, the environmental program director of Ted Turner's Cable News Network told me, "and I hate to see people fighting over his bones. My friends split over it and it got too nasty, and I don't want to talk about it."

There was a public falling-out between Schwartzman and Susanna Hecht in a nasty exchange of letters in the *Nation*. The two had written several articles together about extractive reserves, and Hecht was doing her own book about Chico and the development and destruction of Amazônia with the radical journalist Alexander Cockburn. Cockburn and Hecht had published an article titled "Defending the Rain Forest and Its People" in the *Nation,* which Schwartzman and Bruce Rich, the EDF's senior attorney, criticized in a letter to the magazine. "The blanket implication that First World activists are exploiting these [local, grass-roots] movements to raise money for ends at odds with those of forest people is unfounded, and does a great disservice to their struggle for social justice," as did the coauthors' aspersion that the First World environmentalists were guilty of translating the movement's struggle "into the political syntax of First World environmentalists." (One does recall, however, how Schwartzman deleted the word "capitalist" from Raimundo de Barros's "capitalist greed," so as not to ruffle the sensibilities of those present.) Schwartzman and Rich also took exception with Cockburn and Hecht's accusation that money raised in the First World to "save the forest" was going to pay the overhead of U.S. organizations and not to "good use." The EDF duo reported that to date their organization had transferred $58,000 directly to rubber tapper organizations without overhead or processing charges and that part of this was earmarked for security for local leaders.

Replying to Schwartzman and Rich's "somewhat petulant" letter, Cockburn and Hecht explained that their article had not been intended as a "fierce assault" on the EDF but as a general statement about "the always ambiguous dialectic between First World conscience and Third World conditions." It was a characteristic of most North American environmental groups that they were coalitions, led by people steeped in the political syntax of Washington, with one ear cocked to the government, whether in the legislative or executive branch, and the other to their funders and board of trustees. They also noted how Schwartzman had dropped Raimundo's offensive words that "international capital was devastating the forest," and they criticized the fact that American labor leaders had not been invited to the receptions for visiting tapper leaders. An EDF fund-raising letter, they claimed, had "certainly exploited" Chico Mendes's murder and presented him as a kind of Albert Schweitzer figure. The uninitiated reader would not guess that Mendes was a deeply committed Socialist and founder of the Workers' Party in Acre, a man who learned his politics "at the knee" of a fugitive revolutionary.

Ilzamar told everybody who approached her in Washington about movie rights that no decision about a film would be made yet. They would all have to make their presentations at the First Encounter of the People of the Forest, in Rio Branco, a few weeks later in the spring. This was another happening crawling with media. A hundred and fifty tappers, 50 Indians, and 260 advisers and guests attended. Redford had given Spanish versions of *The Milagro Beanfield War* and *Jeremiah Johnson* to Schwartzman to show to the tappers. Puttnam still had the inside track. Mary and Ilzamar had originally offered the rights to Adrian Cowell, who wanted to do the movie with Puttnam and Chris Menges, but Cowell said that the tappers would best be served if they heard all the offers. The message, he felt, was more important than the money. Puttnam said his movie would stress the political struggle. "In a way, we felt that Chico was an environmentalist by accident, as a result of his admirable union activities," he later explained. "What he offered was an environmental solution to a political problem."

By now the offers for the rights to Chico's story were up to $1.4 million. Most of them were made through the Chico Mendes Foundation, but Peter Guber and Jon Peters, who envisioned a film like *High Noon,* were throwing piles of money at individuals, hoping to divide and conquer. Some, like Schwartzman, were worried that the sudden infusion of huge amounts of cash could undermine the fragile unity of the union and, indeed, could pull the rug out from under the tappers' way of life, which consisted largely of subsisting off the cash economy. Gumercindo was disgusted. His main concern was that the tappers retain artistic control of the movie and that it give a realistic picture of the movement. "Chico's struggle and the life-style of the rubber tappers are not for sale," he said.

Even one agent who had been in the industry for twenty-one years said he had never seen such lunacy. The other items on the conference's agenda, like the paving of BR-364, were eclipsed by the excitement over the movie. Tappers who had never seen a movie before were treated to screenings of Menges's *Mission* and *A World Apart,* to *The Color Purple, Batman, Rain Man,* and *Gorillas in the Mist,* all of which Guber and Peters had had a hand in. "I loved them all," Ilzamar would say later, "especially *Gorillas in the Mist.*" By June, nine offers between $1.2 and $1.7 million, depending on how the deal was calculated, were swirling in the wind, and the *Jornal do Brasil* reported that the offers could go up to $10 million: "Chico Mendes, who never made a cent in his life, must be chuckling in his grave." Again the decision was postponed. The Mendes Foundation created a committee to review the proposals and decide which one was best. It consisted of Mary Allegretti, Schwartzman, Gilson Pescador, and Ilza. In the case of a tie Ilza would have the *voto de minerva,* the deciding vote.

Then there was a new twist, a further complication in the story: the other widow, Eunice Feitosa, surfaced. She and her daughter by Chico, Ângela, were demanding a piece of the action. Her lawyer, João Tezza, also represented the UDR and the Mineirinhos. Allegretti suspected that Feitosa's suit was a strategy to sabotage the movie. "A lot of people don't want this picture made," she said. There was some question about whether Feitosa's brief marriage to Chico years before was valid, because of the mysteriously missing page in the notary's register and because she was unable to produce the marriage license.

On June 9, J.N. Films, the Brazilian film company that had been assiduously courting Ilza since a couple of days after the murder, announced that the foundation had chosen them to make the film. The *New York Times* ran a picture of Ilzamar, wearing a T-shirt that said "Amazônia of the Brazilians," signing the contract. Joffre Rodrigues, the head of the company, declared that it was "a binding contract, a perfect contract, so perfect that it is irreversible." Rodrigues had good leftist credentials. He had been imprisoned by the military government and had a tremendous beard, which he said he wasn't going to cut until a Socialist government came to power in Brazil. He promised that his movie would be "true to the ideas of Chico Mendes." Gilson Pescador, who had been against the internationalization of Amazônia and the film, said, "The foundation wants the film to be seen around the world, but the Hollywood proposals were badly offered and illusory. Also we thought a Brazilian film company would best show the destruction that's going on and the reality of the people of the region." The script would be by Márcio

Souza, the author of *The Emperor of the Amazon,* a picaresque novel about Luis Galvez's brief reign over Acre. The contract was for $1.76 million, of which $210,000 went to Ilza and her children, $160,000 to Eunice Feitosa and her daughter, and the rest to the tappers' cause through the foundation. A "first-rate international actor," such as Dustin Hoffman, Robert De Niro, or Al Pacino, would play the role of Chico.

So that was it. The race for the movie was over. "Now it's decided," the *Jornal do Brasil* declared chauvinistically, "and not even Robert Redford can change the decision. A Brazilian will do the film."

Or was it all over? Mary Allegretti was livid. The decision to go with Rodrigues wasn't the foundation's at all, she said. Ilza and Gilson had made it unilaterally, without consulting the others on the committee, to which Ilza countered that since she had the *voto de minerva* and had cast it, she didn't have to. Mary accused Gilson of taking money to get Ilza to make the deal with Rodrigues. She said that J.N. Films had no money, were complete deadbeats, and had no intention of fulfilling the contract; their plan was to resell the rights to a big Hollywood studio for as much as they could get (which is just what would happen). There were rumors in the Brazilian papers that Rodrigues was already talking to Redford. Allegretti said the deal was completely illegal and that she planned to sue, but Tezza, Feitosa's lawyer, maintained that the rights to Chico's image belonged exclusively to the family.

PART THREE

Doubling Back

RECONNAISSANCE

Julio Cesar kept sending me clips on the developments in Acre, because I had decided to write a book about the murder and the global, tragic ecofarce it had precipitated. There was a new phrase in the Brazilian press, the "*cabeças*." At the end of February, when they were still tight, Gumercindo, Gilson Pescador, and Júlio Nicásio had said, in a joint interview, "The Alves family is just the tail of the snake. The *cabeças* [the heads], the real mentors of the crime, are the ranchers João Branco, João Tezza, Narciso Mendes, Rubem Branquinho, and Adalberto Aragão."

These were the ones I had to meet, I realized, especially João Branco. He had been cast as the villain of the piece, the *cabeça* of the *cabeças*. Now forty-five, he had come from Mato Grosso do Sul at the beginning of the seventies and made his money as a lawyer for groups that wanted to buy land. He was a partner in the paper *O Rio Branco* and in Radio and TV Rio Branco, with Narciso Mendes, who was running for governor against Flaviano Melo. Narciso's plan, if elected, was to clear 30 percent of the state. "To export grains we'd have to clear even more — fifty percent," he said in one interview. He claimed the Amazon forest was "in decadence and needs human intervention to regenerate." In another interview he advocated cutting the whole thing down and putting nuclear power plants in its place. Forty-two years old and one of the big employers in the state, Narciso was, according to several sources, a coke head who had made his fortune in part from running drugs. There was a story about him that, when he was a state deputy, he got up stoned and danced on a table in front of the state assembly.

João Branco was no longer the head of the UDR in Acre. He had broken with Ronaldo Caiado, the organization's national president, because he felt abandoned by him when the crisis of his accusation came and Caiado said, "I have nothing to do with these *bandidos* in the Amazon." But he was still the hero of the ranchers, a brash, whiskey-swilling macho man who religiously put away a liter of whiskey a day, the best malt scotch smuggled in from Bolivia, and punctuated his re-

231

marks with an earthy, enigmatic laugh. Branco was back in Acre now, having been subpoenaed to explain the "suspect agility" of the *Rio Branco* reporters. He dismissed as "a joke" the allegations that they had been tipped off. "The only thing missing from that theory is that Chico Mendes agreed with us about when he would be killed."

Another example of Branco's wit: "I have a proposal for the international ecologists: we'll give them two and a half million square kilometers of the Amazonian lowlands, which are recognized to be infertile, in return for the foreign debt. A few years from now they will want to give it back, but we'll only accept it if they pay us double."

One Brazilian journalist said he thought he understood why Branco was laughing: he was mocking the justice system, which was doing nothing to apprehend him. Instead, he said, it was *he* who was going after the justice system. He was going to court to make sure he got to play himself in the movie.

If the police were really interested in getting the *cabeças*, Júlio Nicásio told the press, why didn't they find out who had given the Alves family their new Saveiro and Pampa sedans or checked the deposits in their bank accounts (neither of which has been done to this day)?

On February 13, Júlio César Fialho, twenty-seven, who had come from Paraná, been the editor of *O Rio Branco* for five months, and led the alleged dash to Xapuri, fled Acre, fearing for his life. He had received threatening calls, and Narciso Mendes's brother, Nildo, had burst into his room at the Inácio Palace and told him that he'd better not say any more stupid things. "My death would free the others of the accusations and they could blame it on the *seringueiros*," Fialho said in an interview in his new home in Brasília. He said that he'd started to distrust his bosses in November, when they asked him to turn over all the photos of Chico Mendes and the bishop, and ordered a complete news blackout on Chico, Dom Moacyr, deforestation, fires, and land conflicts. The previous editor had quit, refusing to engage in bought journalism. Fialho still claimed he and the others took off in the metallic-gray Gol sedan, as soon as the newspaper received the call notifying them of Chico's death, and covered the 151 kilometers in an hour and a half. Fialho's situation at the paper had begun to deteriorate when Nildo saw the photos of Chico Mendes's corpse in *Manchete* magazine with a credit line of Sigla/Gamma-Liaison instead of *O Rio Branco*. Fialho became scared when he noticed strange men lurking in the Inácio's lobby and in the long, smelly corridors. "Those people are from the *bangue-bangues*," he said, "and I am a type of archives for them." He made no direct accusation of his former bosses but found that they had every reason to want Chico Mendes dead. "They are ranchers. They have sawmills. They need wood and are thus against anyone who wants the preservation of the forest."

The only further violence against the preservationists since Chico's murder was by timber interests who belonged to the same group as the ranchers. On the evening of May 17, two unknown armed assailants in a Fiat sedan pulled over a Volkswagen Beetle. Inside were José Rente Nascimento, the coordinator of the Plan of Protection for the Environment and Indian Communities (formed to mitigate the impact of the paving of BR-364 from Porto Velho), and two others, Paulo de Sales Beninca, the regional director of IBAMA (the new federal environmental agency), and the agronomist Geraldo Callegari. The three were forced out of the car and set upon with clubs. The blows to Rente's kidney were so severe that he arrived at the hospital pissing blood. Before the assailants fled, they said, "This is a warning. Don't get mixed up in what you're not supposed to."

Later that same night, the Federal Police found the Fiat, license plate AX-0283, parked in front of a rubber-processing plant belonging to Jorge Moura, president of the Union of Timber Industries of Acre. Rente had already received a death threat at his lodgings at the Inácio Palace from the timber industry union's public relations man: "Leave the state tomorrow or die like Chico Mendes." The trouble had started when Rente, a friend of Chico's, had found forty huge boles of Brazil nut wood at Moura's sawmill and had slapped Moura with a fine of seven thousand new cruzados (a couple of thousand dollars). The fate of the wood was in the courts. Moura's wife said, "This wood only leaves here if there is blood to the level of my shins."

On February 28, Romeu Tuma made public a fifty-one-page report that included five hours of videotaped interviews and concluded — surprise — that Darci was the author of the murder. He said there was no participation by the UDR. "The UDR kills nobody," he said, and then he washed his hands of the affair. "We have the criminal. He confessed. [Darci's recantation was apparently not taken seriously.] If other guilty parties are involved, it is up to the State Police of Acre to conduct the investigation.'' Tuma was burnt out. He had already checked into the hospital the month before with ''strong emotions.''

The food scandal that had created a feud between Acre's governor and the Federal Police the previous year was also creating problems for Judge Adair Longhini, in Xapuri. The judge had seized 23.5 tons of the food that had been intended for the flood victims but had been used by the former mayor of Xapuri, Wanderlei Viana, to buy votes. Longhini had asked for police protection for himself and his family, who had received several more threats because he was proceeding with both this irregularity and the Chico Mendes case. He'd been trying to get the Mendes trial scheduled for March, April, and June, but had no luck. The only success he'd had was with his request for an air conditioner, which enabled him to block out the windows of his chambers so he wouldn't be such an easy target.

While Darli, Darci, and Oloci were giving pretrial depositions to Adair, Darli's son Darlizinho, eighteen, and his nephew Uziel Alves da Silva, twenty, passed in front of the Forum drunk, shooting pistols into the air, breaking the fences of neighboring houses, and shouting, ''Some have died in Xapuri, and there will be more.'' They were picked up at their grandfather Sebastião's house, whose lights they had shot out, and were charged with disturbing the peace. They surrendered without resistance. No arms were found. Detective Nilson de Oliveira supposed they had been hidden somewhere. He emphasized the need for security. He complained that Darli had gotten control of the people in the *colônia penal* and that witnesses, police, and judicial authorities were being intimidated. Xapuri, at this time of year, was like a caldron, virtually cut off from the world because of the impassable muddiness of the roads, reported Zuenir Ventura, a prominent journalist from Rio who arrived in town to do a series of long articles. People rarely left their verandas and spent their time running their fingers through each other's hair, looking for fleas. Little recalled the climate of tension of a few months before.

Ventura concluded that the justice system in Acre was unviable and most precarious. The witnesses were scared to death, the police had neither the equipment nor the technical means to conduct the investigation, the prosecutors were practically nonexistent. Xapuri reminded him of the town in the movie *Mississippi Burning,* except that there was no recourse to the FBI.

And yet the judge still kept hearing testimony. He heard Margarete de Goias, another of the Mineirinhos' sisters-in-law, testify that, several days before the murder, Darci had shot at targets with his shotgun. The court clerk of Xapuri, Raimundo Dias de Figueiredo, told the judge that he had heard Darli boasting in the Forum that he would kill Chico Mendes. The proceedings were held up because the car of the new prosecutor, William João Silva, broke down. At last he arrived, barefoot, his pants spattered with mud. Sueli Bettai, a lawyer observing the proceedings for the tappers, complained that the prosecutors were taking turns listening to the testimony so that none of them was getting the whole picture. The lawyers for the defense said they hoped to move the trial out of Xapuri.

The hopes for conviction rested on fifteen-year-old Genésio Barbosa, who recounted in rich detail twelve crimes that had been committed on the Fazenda Paraná. Genésio looked younger than a teenager but was psychologically a grown-up. He testified that João Branco had visited the Fazenda Paraná many times, maybe five times, along with Benedito Rosas, Gaston Mota, Enoch Pessoa, Adalberto Aragão — the whole gang. One time João Branco stayed a week, sleeping, drinking the whiskey he had brought. In November, Genésio said, he'd overheard Darli ask João Branco (they were in the house and Genésio was outside listening through the window) what he thought about his killing Chico Mendes. João Branco had said, ''If it's like the other deaths and it's no trouble, go ahead. You can kill him and if I can help, I will.''

Genésio said that he was often beaten so that he wouldn't disclose the family's secrets, like the death of Raimundo Pereira, who made the mistake of asking for the hand of Darli's daughter and was killed by Oloci, his brother Aparecido, and a cousin, Rildo. ''I rode up and found him,'' Genésio said. ''His ear, nose, and lip were cut. They put a knife to my stomach and said 'Don't tell.' ''

Genésio's version of the murder of the Bolivians was this: two strangers stopped by looking for water. One of the Mineirinhos told Genésio to get on his bicycle and bring back Darli and Oloci. The three of them jumped the two strangers, shot them, and took their ''*maconha*.'' *Maconha* is marijuana, but this marijuana was white and was in a plastic bag.

One time, Genésio said, he heard Darli say he was going to ask Chico Mendes to be the godfather of one of his grandchildren, just so he could have the opportunity to kill him. He said, "The day we kill Chico Mendes, we'll celebrate by killing a steer." And they did.

Ilzamar was worried that interest in Chico's murder was waning. Her promised widow's pension from the government had not arrived. For now her two children were not in need, but she looked at the future with apprehension. "I don't want to leave Xapuri [she had returned from Rio Branco]. I want to continue the struggle of my husband, but I have to survive." She said that the kids cried at night for their father. "He didn't stay here much, but when he did, in the evening he dedicated himself entirely to the kids and fed them and put them to sleep." The Alves family and their friends are still laughing in our faces, she said. She'd heard that Darli was comfortably ensconced in prison, living the dolce vita.

There was, however, one encouraging development: the judge decreed "preventive prison" for the Bolivian doctor, Dário Borjos Aramayos, whom Ilza accused of trying to rape her in his office in Brasiléia.

When I had talked with her, Ilza had told me that she didn't know much about Chico's early life. "When I knew him he was alone, and we never had time to talk about the past because he was so busy. I didn't know much about his work because Chico wouldn't let me go to the empates." She had portrayed the marriage as totally harmonious and full of love.

Now, however, an edge of feminist self-assertion began to creep into her interviews. It wasn't that she wasn't interested in Chico's work, she complained, but that Chico wouldn't let her participate in it. Many times he would be sitting around with his companheiros and she would have to interrupt them with mundane matters — to ask for money for food, and other domestic problems — and they would say, "Just give her a sofa and a TV so she will stop bugging you." Chico allegedly said to one of his companheiros, "I haven't had luck. Neither of my women were interested in my work." The companheiros had begun saying that Ilza never participated in the movement.

But now, five months after the murder, the new Ilza was coming into her own. In an interview with three women from Acre's small, budding feminist movement, she said, "Chico was great, a good husband, a good father. He didn't let us lack for anything, but he didn't give me space. I had to cook and take care of the kids, although I wanted to take part in the union and the women's movement. I got bad looks from his *companheiros*, as if they were jealous of the attention he gave me. When they came to the house, I was presented, 'This here's my wife,' and that was that. Then they would all leave, 'OK, see you later,' and I would be left in the kitchen.''

The movie deal solved Ilza's financial problems. She bought a new pickup, moved to a nicer, wood-frame house down the street, and opened a restaurant called Floresta. Pictures of her that periodically appeared in the glossies showed a modern, liberated woman dressed in the latest elegant fashions. By the following year she had become the most visible international spokesman of the movement. "When I saw him dead on the floor," she told *People* magazine, which sent a reporter all the way to Xapuri to do a feature on her for a January 1990 issue, ''I said to my heart, I'm going to enter the struggle. It's my answer to everybody, including the ones who killed Chico.''

"Month by month you can see her growing," said a friend. "She's stronger, more articulate, more mature. It's ironic that Chico's death was in a sense her birth.''

The question of the movie ruptured the movement, which was already divided by the struggle for succession. The more militant of the tappers had begun to feel that there shouldn't be a movie and that the whole question of the movie was distracting them from their real work of organizing against the ranchers, securing their way of life, and keeping themselves and their *companheiros* alive. So when Ilza announced the unilateral decision to do the movie with J.N. Films, which she and Gilson Pescador made without consulting the others, and then began to appear in her new pickup and smashing outfits, she naturally aroused some resentment. Schwartzman issued a statement, purporting to represent the views of "the tappers," that Ilza's decision had been entirely her own, and that they had decided for the time being that there should be no movie. How much this was motivated by the fact that he and Mary Allegretti had been cut out of any part of any movie action by Ilzamar's decision can only be speculated. Allegretti, when I talked to her in July 1989, was still very much in favor of the movie — but Puttnam's movie. She felt it should be made soon, before the global interest in the rain forest waned, and that this historic opportunity to get money and exposure for the movement shouldn't be lost.

As the T-shirt that many of Chico's sympathizers were wearing said, "They Took Down One of the Noblest Trees in the Amazonian Union Movement, But Others Will Rise to Take Its Place." It was a crowded field of saplings, none of which yet had Chico's stature. The most charismatic of the contenders, the one who gave the best interviews, was Osmarino Amâncio Rodrigues. "Chico Mendes is dead," he told the First Encounter of the People of the Forest that Easter in Rio Branco. "Things can't be as they were, and to dream that they could would be to drive us to ruin." This is as true of wilderness as it is of social movements, I thought reading this.

I had an interesting talk about this question at Redford's greenhouse conference with the biologist Daniel Botkin. "We are locked into a worldview of nature through which we filter the facts, ignoring those that contradict what we believe," he told me. "The idea that there is a constant condition of undisturbed nature that is desirable and that, after being disturbed, eventually returns to the same condition, is a product of the Divine Order idea of nature, and of our machine image of nature that has been reinforcing the Divine Order idea since the rise of science."

The Brazilians' view of nature and life is much more fluid. One of their most frequently heard expressions is *já era,* it's history. Nostalgia, the romantic yearning to go back and restore things to the way they were, Osmarino realized, was an impossible dream. The bearded, handsome thirty-three-year-old was the secretary of the Brasiléia union and, many felt, would be the next to be killed. He was born on the Seringal Beija-Flor (Hummingbird) and didn't learn to read until he was sixteen. Since 1980 he'd been a close associate of Chico's, and he had no time for soccer or women, the pastimes of his youth. He complained in an interview with Alexander Cockburn and Susanna Hecht that he wasn't allowed to carry a firearm, "but every goddamn rancher out there is armed to the teeth." The day after Chico was killed, Osmarino found an ambush blind behind his house. Five attempts on his life had already been made. Guys on horses and motorcycles, the car of Benedito Rosas, had circled his house and shot it up on various occasions. He had been struck by a stolen Mercedes truck that had proceeded to slam into a power pole, plunging Brasiléia into darkness. He complained that he had to pay for his own security — travel, lodging, meals, and bullets for four bodyguards. One of them, Sauco Lins Ribeiro, nicknamed Bacalhau (Codfish), was implicated in the murder of Zezão. Bacalhau was also caught on March 6 circling the hotel in Brasiléia where Gaston Mota was lodged. Five of the bullets in his revolver had crosses cut on top to increase the damage they would do as they tore into their victim.

In the spring of 1989 Osmarino ran for president of the Brasiléia union and lost. He alleged fraud and intimidation by the supporters of his opponent, peons of the ranchers. Some of the peons were *pistoleiros,* but they were also rural workers and thus entitled to be in the union. He warned that the conflict between the tappers and the peons could result in deaths, and he threatened to form a parallel entity, the Association of Extractivists of Brasiléia.

Osmarino explained that the political structure of Acre was more complicated than just the ranchers versus the tappers. There was the group of ex-mayor Aragão, the group of Flaviano, the group of João Branco, the group of João Tezza. What was really behind the murder was that Chico had been planning to run for governor, and if he had won, the situation in Acre would have changed completely. Chico had been summoned by General Bayma Denis, the articulator of Sarney's Nossa Natureza plan, who knew that Chico's prestige was threatening the local politicians, and offered to buy him off. Of course Chico refused. "The authorities aren't interested in getting anyone," Osmarino said. They hadn't named a prosecutor, the delivery of Detective Nilson's inquest had been delayed thirty days, the trial kept being put off.

"I had a *namorada,* a girlfriend," Osmarino said. "We had lots of fun until one day she said, 'I want to marry you but you have to give all this up.' I just laughed." Occasionally Osmarino would show up at the Casarão, Rio Branco's leftist night spot (the right hung out at the airport restaurant), whisk a girl up onto the dance floor, cut a couple of *lambadas,* and leave.

Then there was Júlio Nicásio, who had sided with Ilzamar in the movie debacle and was romantically linked with her — but then so were Gumercindo, Gilson Pescador, and Padre Luis. "They say that I was having affairs with people even before Chico was killed," Ilzamar complained. "This is a vicious lie, but I'm not going to say I'm going to be a widow all my life, either. I'm only twenty-four."

Júlio Barbosa, the new president of the Xapuri union, was reportedly indecisive and too much of a nonentity to be the next Chico. His cousin Raimundo de Barros was too earnest and not well spoken.

Then there were the Shiites like Gumercindo, the radical extremists, some of whom were in favor of armed conflict and belonged to the Albanian wing of the Brazilian Communist Party, which had been bombing banks. But Gumercindo was an outsider, so he wasn't in the running.

At the other extreme was Ronaldo Caiado, who was running for president. As he stumped through the North he did a lot of radio broadcasts. Radio is still a more effective way than TV of reaching people deep in the interior. In Mato Grosso he unveiled his new plan for Amazônia: move everybody in the urban slums there. "The four and a half million hectares of legal Amazônia can't be a horticultural park of Europe and the United States. What does Sting know about ecology? What should be done is to increase grain production, extend BR-364 so products including minerals can be sold at competitive prices. The developed countries know that by blocking the development of Amazônia they are tying up fifty percent of the Brazilian territory." Caiado branded as "calumnies" charges that the UDR was involved in the murders in the backlands. "The only thing the UDR kills is hunger. We have much more ethical responsibility than the left." He cited a recent attempt by the Workers' Party to blow up a bank in Recife, in which the device exploded in the terrorist's hand. "The members of the PT are trained in guerrilla warfare in Libya and Nicaragua. Before there is any agrarian reform there should be a moral reform of many of the people running the country."

BACK TO ACRE

The coverage of the Chico Mendes case, in Brazil and elsewhere in the world, faded away. By May, the only attention it got was the battle for the movie rights. No one kept after the police and the judicial system. The ranchers knew the media didn't work that way. Eventually the feeding frenzy would end and the uproar would be overtaken by new stories, new news. The public's television-addled attention span was growing shorter and shorter, and the news itself was becoming increasingly perishable. The media had rallied to Chico's cause and made him into a grass-roots hero, but ultimately they let it down. Or, perhaps more accurately, they picked the story up and ran with it for a while, then they put it down and moved on to other things.

A new conflict, even sexier than the one between the tappers and the ranchers, had erupted on Brazil's border with Venezuela: the invasion of the Yanomamo Indians, one of the last large isolated groups on the planet, by more than forty thousand *garimpeiros,* or gold prospectors. Some believed that there was a plan at the very highest levels of the government to use the poor, semiliterate *garimpeiros* to exterminate the Yanomamo, so that once their land had been cleared, big multinational mining companies could move in. Most of the *garimpeiros* didn't have women, so their massacres of the Yanomamo often began as rapes of the Indians' women. With many of the usual exits for Colombian cocaine shut down, a lot of it was coming in through Roraima and being traded for gold and other rare minerals. This was the new tragedy in the Amazon.

Then, late in the spring of 1989, it started to rain. The summer in the Northern Hemisphere turned out to be generally still a little warmer than usual, but nothing like the parched scorcher the year before. Thoughts turned from global warming, the greenhouse effect, the destruction of the rain forest and the end of the world, to the extraordinary political upheaval in the Second World. Nineteen eighty-eight had been a year of convulsive environmental debacle. Nineteen eighty-nine became the year the world was turned upside down politically. The year of the rain forest lasted until the student demonstrations in Beijing's Tiananmen Square in May. Then it became the year of democracy.

On July 13 I flew down to Brazil to do more research, particularly on the ranchers. For the return trip to Acre I had invited Julio Cesar to accompany me. My take on the situation there was that it could be dynamite. The word was that the police were on strike, so the place was even more lawless than usual. (This rumor from Lucélia Santos, however, was premature.) I might run up against brick walls of anti-Americanism, violence from either the extreme left or right; or Schwartzman and Allegretti, who were allied with rival movie and book projects, could have prepared an unpleasant welcome for me. All in all it seemed a good idea to have a Brazilian along. Julio Cesar, like many Brazilians from the South, had never been to the Amazon, although he had been to more than thirty countries, and he was curious to see what it was all about. Plus, he'd become very interested in the story and was thinking of writing a book himself, he told me as we drove into Rio from Galeão Airport. "But we are interested only to a point, right?" he emphasized.

"How does the song go? We're too old to rock and roll, too young to die."

Everything was copacetic in Copacabana. I spotted the Incredible Hulk on the Rua Barata Ribeiro. The *camelôs,* the sidewalk vendors, were still out there in force, hawking contraband electronics and sunglasses from Paraguay. "Only one cruzado," one of them said, holding up a pair of "Ray-Bens," "which isn't worth a thing anymore." The teenage *gatinhas,* kittens, were lying on the sand in dental floss bikinis. The shoeshine boys were slapping samba rhythms on their customers' shoes with their buffing rags.

I changed three grand into a small brick of new cruzados, bought a few boxes of Bahian cheroots, and met Julio Cesar the next morning at the airport. He was there with his suitcase containing his silk pajamas, half a dozen paperback novels, and a battery of pills, the baggage of a Rio intellectual.

North of Cuiabá, July 14, from the plane window: some haze, a grass fire near the airport, but otherwise not much burning. A clear view of the ocean of green. Over Bolivia, the Beni and Madre de Dios rivers — nothing but virgin forest. The clearing starts again as we enter Acrean airspace over Plácido de Castro, a border town the size of Xapuri. It spreads like a disease from the road to Rio Branco over hundreds of thousands of acres in which nothing is happening. "Not a cow," Julio Cesar remarks, shaking his head.

We check into the Inácio Palace, which is expanding. The whole back wall has been knocked out, which is a little nervous-making, remembering all the uninvited visitors who had been milling around when the wall was still there. Now there is absolutely no security at all.

Rio Branco has changed. It is visibly more modern since January, as Brazil is in general. Each time I go to Brazil the gap has closed a little more. It's growing by leaps and bounds, and the things I love about the country are more and more endangered. Idyllic time warps are smothered. Progress is arriving overnight, and no one is looking back.

Rio Branco's new mayor has big plans. The entire street in front of the Inácio has been torn up, and new sewer lines and water mains are being put in. There is a sign, "The Battle of Progress." It's going on before our very eyes; the workers are literally in the trenches. Across the street, next to the lobby of the Pinheiro Palace, is a new fast food,

McDonald's-type restaurant. A sign in the vacant lot next door announces the imminent erection of a shopping mall. In the Inácio's lobby, several ambitious young men are putting up an easel with a mock-up of the Villa Brinco de Ouro, an instant planned community like the ones that pop up in the palmetto scrub of South Florida. It will have its own shopping mall and, to assuage Brazilian nostalgia for the beach, a common consolation for having to live in the interior — a pool with a wave-making machine.

Up in the main plaza, a banking machine has landed like a flying saucer. The sidewalks are still lined with the ubiquitous vendors. Some of them have opened attaché cases on the pavement that contain little vials of oil of the overhunted and rapidly disappearing Amazonian manatee, which has alleged aphrodisiac properties. Others are selling *churrasquinhas* (little sticks of roasted meat), pantyhose, *pastéis* (baked meat pastries), bric-a-brac. The *camelôs* are proliferating all over Brazil in the failing economy. Inflation is running at 37 percent a month.

Twenty Jaminaua Indians have camped under the bridge over the Rio Acre and are going from door to door begging used clothes. They are refugees of an earlier, saner time, overridden, like the tappers, by the will of Brazil, which would brook no interference. "This force," Julio Cesar says, indicating the open trenches and the "Battle of Progress" sign, "this is what killed Chico."

We go to one newsstand after another, but there isn't a map of Acre left for sale in the whole capital. They've all been cleaned out by the invasion of the press. But the new issue of *Corpo a Corpo* magazine has arrived from Rio, with Robert Redford on the cover. Inside is an interview with him explaining how he has been wanting for years to make a movie about the Amazon rain forest.

The city has returned to normal. There is more concern about the outcome of the Copa América — a South American warm-up tournament for the coming year's World Cup — than about seeing justice done in the murder of Chico Mendes. All the excitement over Chico has always been a foreign trip anyway. The average Brazilian is far more interested in the Cup being Brazilian than in Amazônia being Brazilian. If instead of trading the debt for the protection of Amazônia you could have delivered the World Cup, you would definitely have had a deal.

Now that the Mendes affair has died down, the business of selling papers has reverted to the usual formulas, sex and crime. The pages of the *Gazeta* and *O Rio Branco* are filled with the usual stabbings and four-color spreads of local teenage beauties thrusting their buttocks at the camera (in Brazil *bundas* are more lusted after than breasts). Wanton Miss Pantherinha is wearing a jaguar-spotted bikini that disappears in the crevices of her obligingly proffered tush. She is "only seventeen," the caption reads, "and the sort of fulminating beauty capable of provoking another revolution in our land."

Mephistopheles, *O Rio Branco*'s social columnist, relays the usual local gossip and rosters of last night's parties. There is a picture of him over his byline looking positively Mephistophelean in a pencil mustache and pointed Jack Nicholson eyebrows. He announces the arrival in town of Rogéria, an old transvestite who has been reduced to traveling around the interior, telling jokes, dancing, singing, and doing impersonations.

But it is the *Gazeta* that comes up with the most amazing stuff in the days that follow. One item describes a "Paraguayan panty-sniffer with a strange mania: he loves to smell women's panties, preferably dirty." The pervert is denounced by Lucirena Alves da Silva (a member of the clan?) at the Third Federal Police station. But not only soiled lingerie is found at his digs. There are photos and strands of hair, apparently for *macumba* rituals, to attract the women's love.

Headline, July 26: "AIDS HAS ARRIVED. AIDS CREATES PANIC IN THE CAPITAL." The model and student Ruric Mendonça has come down with the withering syndrome. The *Gazeta* neglects to reveal that Ruric is the lover of a blond masseuse all the husbands in Rio Branco's elite have been getting it on with. The high incidence of syphilis and gonorrhea in the capital (reported in a previous item) will accelerate the spread of the disease by providing "portals of entry."

Item, July 29: The Mad Tit-Sucker. Last night at ten o'clock he accosts a woman walking home from work and makes her take off her blouse. After sucking the trembling woman's tits, he shows no further interest in her and flees into the night.

O Rio Branco has an ecology page, which is more than can be said for the *Gazeta*. It reports an alarming proliferation of houseflies in the capital of late. There are no fewer than 85,000 species of these insects, *O Rio Branco* informs its readers, and they can transmit typhoid, intestinal infections, miiasis and other skin problems, and can contaminate food left out in the kitchen or displayed by sidewalk vendors. On another day the paper reveals that there are 200 species of scorpion in South

America, and that Acre possesses one of the biggest. Called the *lacrau* (*Padinus imperador*), it grows to eighteen centimeters. "Scientists have discovered that the scorpion is immune to nuclear bombs." So there's no way they can be intimidated into turning in the fugitives.

The clearing season is over, and the burning season has begun. In the last thirty days, the *Gazeta* reports, there were five fatal chain-saw accidents. During last year's clearing season more than fifty peons were killed by falling trees and *macacos*, dead branches.

It is amazing how the *Gazeta* keeps coming up with an incredible murder almost every day in this small city. July 20: Last night, right in front of the judicial Forum, a guy washing his car unwittingly splashed the shoes of another guy passing by, César Bode, who started beating him up.

Two Military Policemen nearby didn't like César's brutality and tried to grab him. César's brother Cacá had been killed after a short life of crime, and he was looking for revenge, so he wasn't scared of the cops. Breaking free of them, he ran down the street. The police gave chase. One of them fired and dropped César near the broadcast tower of Radio Diffusora Acreana. The other administered the *tiro de misericórdia*, putting the agonized victim out of his misery with a point-blank shot to the head.

TeleAcre, the local TV station, promises the *decongestionamento* of the telephone lines in the capital "next month." Fat chance.

But there is nothing in the *Gazeta* about Chico, the tappers' struggle, the land conflict. Where is Sílvio's brave line against the ranchers and the UDR? Something has happened.

WHERE HAVE ALL THE HEROES GONE?

We took a cab to the *Gazeta,* and as we drove through the streets of the capital I saw clearly for the first time that there were two different races in Acre; one short, dark, malnourished, poor, weak, the mestizo offspring of native Acrean Indians and northeastern *flagelados;* the other tall, white, well fed, well dressed, European, rich, ruthless, and racist. Acre was basically a two-tiered feudal society, the exploiters and the exploited, the oppressors and the oppressed, the good guys and the bad guys. The battle lines were drawn on the T-shirts the short, buxom teenage girls were wearing. Some of them said "Chico Mendes, World Hero for the Ecological Cause." Others said "The Conquest of Acre" and showed a modern city rising out of the jungle.

We found Sílvio in his office.

I hear the police are on strike, I said.

"Not yet, but they're planning to be in a couple of weeks."

What's happening with the hunt for the fugitives?

"Nothing," Sílvio said. "Detective Nilson pays periodic visits to the Fazenda Florestal, but he's no longer actively looking for them. The Indians and tappers offered to help set a trap for them, but he refused. One thing has been clarified. The Mineirinho who was Darci's accomplice was not Antônio, Jerdeir, or Francisco, but Sérgio Pereira."

We talked about the political structure of Acre. "Flaviano represents the traditional politics," Sílvio explained. "His father was a state deputy and mayor of Rio Branco, and he has a certain conflict with the ranchers. The danger is that there will be a 'Rondonization' of Acre if the ranchers take power. Flaviano and the new mayor, Jorge Kalume, who are old political enemies, have united against them. If their candidate, Narciso Mendes, gets to be governor, he has promised to clear thirty percent of the forest and Acre will explode.

"There have been no further assassinations," he went on. "But that's because the press was on the ranchers' cases. It's calm now, but the violence will return. The ranchers are just waiting for the waters to settle to start a new wave of killing. Osmarino is living in a very dangerous situation, and it will be no surprise if he is eliminated."

Is the death squad still functioning?

"No," he said. "Castelo Branco, who let the squad function, has been replaced. One of the squad's members, Sear Jasub, was just sentenced to four years for the homicide of various marginals. He's in the *colônia penal* with Darli. One of his victims, the mechanic Wilson dos Santos Clara, was found last October seventeenth without his head or hands in a shallow pit in the subdivision of Ipê. The other inmates in the *colônia penal* tried to strangle Sear. He cut throats, disfigured people."

Is there any connection with the *daime* cults and the tappers' movement? I asked.

"No, the *culto do daime* has nothing to do with the struggle, except that it is in favor of it, because the destruction of the forest would be the destruction of their religion. The *daimistas* are very apolitical. Most of them are poor people who don't have access to society and live in the slums and sterile projects on the peripheries of Rio Branco.''

I sensed that Sílvio was holding something back, and, knowing who his boss was, I thought it unwise to ask him why Flaviano had, in my opinion, lost the chance to win a national victory over the ranchers and political prestige for himself by vigorously prosecuting the murderers of Chico. If he could have shown that justice worked in Acre, he would have been hailed as a national hero and would have restored credibility in himself, which was badly tarnished by the food scandal. He also would have effected a badly needed moral rejuvenation of the image of Brazil, which — who knows — maybe he could even have ridden to the presidency. But for some reason he was dragging his feet in the investigation. Why?

A few days later Julio Cesar and I ran into one of the *Gazeta*'s star reporters, Flamínio Araripe, at the poolside bar of the Pinheiro Palace. A handsome young man of thirty-six, who bore a remarkable resemblance to the actor Sam Waterston, Flamínio had written some of the most hard-hitting stories about the struggle, but he told us that he had just quit the paper and was moving to Ceará. The *Gazeta*'s coverage of the tappers and Chico's murder had been stopped by order of the governor, he said. ''Sílvio is making money and has sold his soul. The situation is completely rotten. Even Sílvio has been coopted by the system. Flaviano has a ranch in Aragão's name. He's selling the land set aside for colonization projects to the big *fazendeiros* [just as Eva Evangelista had told me]. He's into all kinds of illicit enrichment, like dealing with the Japanese for the road. There's a plan to detimber all the forest from Rio Branco to Sena Madureira.''

Flamínio said that he had come to Acre in 1983 from São Paulo. ''I am a participant of the União Vegetal, a *daimista*.'' This surprised me. He seemed such a clean-cut, hardworking guy that I had pegged him as a Brazilian yuppie. Then I realized I was projecting the sixties American drug culture onto the *daime* cult, when it was something quite different.

''In 1985 a group of journalists, including me, went to talk to Flaviano, who was then the mayor, about starting a newspaper,'' he told me. ''Being mayor, he could put his hands on funds. The ownership of a paper augments your prestige and projection and it's a way to get money from the government, so Flaviano agreed to finance the paper.

"The death of Chico was the best thing that ever happened to the *Gazeta,*" Flamínio said. "Circulation jumped from seven thousand to twelve thousand the day Zezão was killed. As long as the paper was selling, there was no problem printing criticism of the governor by the Chico Mendes Committee. But some of the ranchers linked to the murder explained to Flaviano that the tappers were going to vote for the PT and not for him. If you're politically astute you'll know whom to side with.

"The coverage didn't stop all at once. It trickled out. The ranchers used the governor's fear of not being reelected to stick it to the tappers. He realized his real, common interests lay with the elite."

So that explained the sad gagging of the once-proud and independent *Gazeta,* the pinups of fifteen-year-old *pantherinhas.*

"A few months ago Flaviano made a pact with the ranchers and the other rural entrepreneurs," Flamínio went on. "Sílvio was there, and it was after that meeting that the coverage cooled down. Antônio Moraes, a big rural entrepreneur in Mato Grosso, said he had six million to put into Acre. He had already invested five, but if the press continued the way it was behaving, making the ranchers out to be villains, he said he would undo everything and pull out.

"But by then the snowball was already rolling. The governor had to reposition his conservationist's defense of natural resources. As of this year, IBAMA now requires an impact statement for any deforestation greater than fifty hectares. The rural entrepreneurs were up in arms over this, and they used Flaviano as a political ally to *dar um jeitinho,* to find a way around these deforestation restrictions. A new racket — turning out impact statements, or RIMAs, as they are called, to satisfy appearances — came into being."

What's happening in Xapuri? I asked.

"There's no clearing going on there at all. The tappers won't allow it. But the struggle has already been decided in favor of the ranchers. This media-mobilized environmentalism is all ballet. Pictures of places with only trees are beautiful. They sell papers, but the ranchers will win because they have the power. There are only three things that could stop the ranchers. One, stiff legislation. Two, the organization of the tappers. Three, the network of international support. But the problem is that one, the legislation is not obeyed; two, the organization of the tappers is in shambles; and three, the international network is not proving efficacious. It's consuming itself in trendiness.

"Whoever knows the reality of Acre knows that this governor is finished, *dançado*. He has danced his last dance. The real struggle is not between the tappers and the ranchers, but for control of the state government. It's the government that makes money circulate here. Ninety percent of Acre's income is from federal subsidies that flow through the state government. Extractivism produces only six percent. The rest is ranching and agriculture. So the important thing is getting the votes. That's why Flaviano's wife, the *governadora,* was buying votes with the food and clothing that came in for the flood victims."

So you're leaving because you're disgusted with the whole situation? I asked.

"No. Actually I'm leaving for climatic reasons. I have terrible asthma. This oppressively humid environment affects me not only physically but psychosomatically. Some days I don't have energy to do a thing. I don't know how I ever managed to write so many stories."

A few days later there was an advertisement in the *Gazeta:* "Flamínio is leaving. He's selling his house, his straw hat, his *eletrodomésticos* [household appliances] and his '79 Chevette."

You know, this place is getting to look more and more like the movie *Chinatown,* I said to Julio Cesar as we drove out to Eva Evangelista's for dinner.

"It's all the same network," Julio Cesar said. "Even political enemies have cousins married to each other's brothers-in-law. It was Acre who killed Chico Mendes, a silent consensus of the whole society. He clashed with the model of development. His prestige was growing too fast. He was like Spartacus, the leader of the slaves in Rome. After Spartacus was killed, the revolt factionalized, just like what's happening here."

Eva had suffered a severe reversal since I'd last seen her. Her trajectory, in fact, seemed much closer to the classic tragic pattern than Chico's. She was still a judge but was no longer president of the Tribunal (though this was simply because her term had ended), and she was now totally ostracized by the Rio Branco elite, whom she had betrayed. She was "frozen out by everyone because she threw dirt on the image of Acre," Sílvio had told me. She had alienated the ranchers by blowing the whistle on their attempts to reappropriate the 1.3 million hectares near Plácido de Castro that MIRAD (the agency directing agrarian reform) had expropriated for a colonization project, and of course because of her outspoken zeal in the Chico Mendes business as well. Moreover, she had alienated the governor by prosecuting his wife over the food scandal, and as a result Flaviano had cut off funds to the Tribunal of Justice. Eva's popularity there, which she had bought by getting better salaries and other perks for her colleagues, had collapsed. Hers was a classic case of hubris. Eva had overstepped the bounds imposed by society, broken its rules, and now she was paying for it.

As one rancher put it with sardonic glee, she had "shrunk back into her insignificance."

Her husband, Menandro, an agronomist, showed us into the large, ostentatious house, with a top-of-the-line Opel sedan in the garage. There were no police guards protecting her anymore, because she was no longer a threat. She was finished, *dançada,* like the governor. A completely different woman than the spunky, ebullient fireball I had interviewed seven months earlier rose to greet us in the living room — pale, etiolated, forlorn, crazed by isolation like a victim of cabin fever.

The decor was real hokey. The cushioned banquettes along the walls, where dozens of guests at her lively *festas* had sat, were now vacant. There was an illustrated Bible on the stand and a bust of Christ in a niche. "I hardly ever leave the house anymore," she said. "We have no social life. Our children go to the *colégio* and come right home again. Our friends have all dropped us." She seemed to regret now that she had opened her mouth and ruined a beautiful career. Menandro brought a tray of sumptuous hors d'oeuvres and Glenfiddich scotch from Bolivia into the huge, empty living room.

I asked if she had ever gotten to the bottom of her *anúncio.*

"Luis Garimpeiro, Darli's kid brother, was suspected of the *anúncio* of me and the bishop. I had him brought up before me. Luis cried and said, 'I'm not a *pistoleiro.* I'm just a small farmer.' He looked *muito tranqüilo,* like an addict. He has since been busted for drug dealing in Rondônia."

"It doesn't look like she's going to be our entrée into Rio Branco society," Julio Cesar said as we drove back to the hotel.

We went to the Military Police headquarters in the main plaza and asked to see Genésio Barbosa, the prosecution's star witness, and were told that he had been transferred to Rio de Janeiro for his own safety. We drove out to the *colônia penal* to talk to Darli but this time had no luck. It was Sunday, and we couldn't reach Antônio Campos, the director, whose permission we needed, at his home because his phone was on the blink.

AT LAST A HERO

IBAMA, the new federal agency charged with protecting the Amazon rain forest and indeed the entire Brazilian environment, was on strike. Its forest protection enforcement agents were risking their life for 272 cruzados a month (maybe $130), Paulo Beninca, the institute's regional director, told me. Beninca had been beaten up in May along with José Rente Nascimento, but not as badly. The night before, somebody had fired shots at Beninca's house even though it was being guarded. He had been working in Amazônia since 1983 and had come to Rio Branco only four months before.

"The problem of enforcing the deforestation restrictions is like marijuana control," he said. "We have to fight the cultural tradition of burning, internal corruption, insurmountable logistical problems, and the proverbial lack of funds." I asked him how much of the state had been cleared. He said that as of 1987, the most recent year for which LAND-SAT data had been analyzed, the total was 813,256.96 hectares, or 5.33 percent of the state. Ten thousand three hundred hectares had been authorized for deforestation in 1988, and 13,900 this year. Any fire more than 50 hectares required a RIMA, but these bigger fires were not in IBAMA's jurisdiction. "We're only responsible for fires less than fifty hectares. The bigger ones are handled by IMAC, the State Institute of the Environment."

Aha, I thought, so there's the *jeitinho,* the way around the deforestation restrictions that Flamínio had been talking about. And IMAC, I take it, being a state institution and the state seeing itself as engaged in a battle of progress, is less than conscientious, I said to Beninca.

"*Certo.* You got it. None of the RIMAs that I've seen reach the required technical level. The tappers could be challenging the RIMAs, but they aren't."

Beninca told us that there were twelve enforcement agents in Acre, but that since the sixteenth of June everyone had been on strike. I asked if there had been many fires this year, and he said no. "INPE just telexed us the coordinates of two small grass fires. Apart from them there have been maybe half a dozen that we know of. But the season is still young. It peaks around Independence Day [the seventh of September]."

With us was an agent of IBAMA's judicial division who was investigating internal corruption, looking for evidence of bribes by ranchers and timber interests. He was just starting and had nothing to report yet. "But with the agents' salaries, how can they be expected to be clean?" he said.

So the structure is there to stop deforestation, I said. It's also there to burn away to your heart's content.

"*Certo,*" Beninca said. "We've just received word of a fire in the municipality of Feijó, but we don't have any way of getting there. We don't have a plane, and Brasília won't even give us the money to book passage on the air taxi. You wouldn't want to lend me a hundred cruzados so I can go and do my job?

"I find the deforestation a disrespect of the traditions of the state, a total discharacterization," Beninca continued. "It wouldn't be happening if there hadn't been an invasion of capital from the South. You have to ask yourself who is benefiting from the cattle ranching. Fifty percent of the people in Acre live from extractivism, forty percent from the state bureaucracy. Only one percent benefit from ranching, because it doesn't provide jobs."

How much of Xapuri has been cleared? I asked.

"Fourteen point three percent as of 1987," Beninca said.

Not as much as Chico had claimed.

"Guys like this make me optimistic," Julio Cesar said on the way back to the Inácio. "They give me the feeling that Brazil is not a lost cause."

TO XAPURI

Julio Cesar and I were coming to the conclusion that there were three sets of killers, three levels to the question of who killed Chico Mendes: one, Darci and his father; two, the ring of ranchers; three, a larger, silent consensus of Acrean society. And at the bottom of everything was the struggle for the governorship between Flaviano Melo and Narciso Mendes.

We caught a ride to Xapuri with Padre Luis, who had returned a fortnight ago from three months in Italy. With him was Chiquinho, the elflike younger brother of Júlio Barbosa. *Ipê* trees were in blazing yellow flower along the road. They were a harbinger of spring, like cherry trees in the temperate zone, but for the last couple of years, because of the unusual heat, they had been flowering a month or so early.

I asked about the state of the movement, and Padre Luis said that two *empates* had been carried out this year but no more were scheduled for the moment. The next big battle was going to be a colonization project on five *seringais* that had been disappropriated; eight hundred families of tappers were going to have to find another place to live.

Everybody was sitting in front of the TV at the Hotel Veneza, just as I had left them. This time they were watching the play-offs with Venezuela in the Copa América, which Brazil was winning. A cautious wave of optimism was sweeping the country. It looked like Brazil was putting together a good team for the World Cup.

The Veneza had done well from Chico's murder and was adding several more rooms. Among the glazed-over spectators of the soccer match sunk in the row of armchairs before the TV was the new prosecutor, the fourth since efforts to bring the murderers to justice began; a sultry, acne-scarred teenage niece of Darli's; Nilson de Oliveira; and a representative of J.N. Films whose job was to keep people from getting to Ilzamar lest she change her mind, and to cater to her and her relatives' every whim, flying them to Rio Branco at the slightest ache of their teeth. Tomorrow was the last day for the defendants' lawyers to appeal Judge Longhini's decision to submit the case to a jury trial. "The climate is one of condemnation," Detective Nilson told us.

Before the J.N. rep could stop us, we went to pay our respects to Ilza, who was living in a new house several houses down the Rua Doutor Batista de Moraes from the one Chico had bought her.

We talked about everything that she had been through. She hadn't enjoyed her trip to Washington in March. "It was so cold," she said. She had a new house, a new truck, a nice TV, a house girl. Chico's aunt Cecília said that she was looking down on people a bit. One morning as I walked down the Rua Doutor Batista de Moraes, I found her leaning against Júlio Nicásio's big, shiny black motorcycle. She was wearing black slacks and a black blouse and had a black leather pocketbook over her shoulder; she looked right out of a Calvin Klein ad. But who could blame her? She was playing the role that any Brazilian woman in her place would have, making sure that she received all the compensation she was entitled to for having her husband taken away from her. It was inevitable, too, that her neighbors would be envious, but more than envy I felt a wave of compassion for her isolation. She had been invited to step through the picture tube. She had been tapped by the *telenovela* and her life would never be the same.

A few days later we stopped by again and sat with her brother Raimundo listening to a beautiful tribute that the Acrean country singer Tião Natureza had written to Chico. It was called "King Chico."

> "This forest that kills this unhappy people
> One day has to make a King Chico, a happy tapper.
>
> [Several bars of weeping electric guitar]
>
> From Xapuri the whole world cries.
> It echoed, it echoed, it echoed."

"It's beautiful, but it's a form of exploiting his image," Ilza said. "Today somebody offered to sell me two T-shirts from São Paulo with his image. His trademark is registered. I'm thinking of taking action.

"Steve [Schwartzman] has seventy thousand dollars that I know of, that he's refusing to send because he's upset with my decision," she went on.

"I don't want the body of my husband transformed into dollars."

THE MOVIE II

Ilza had signed with J.N. Films because, she told us, Chico was Brazilian, so she thought the movie should be Brazilian. Joffre Rodrigues, the long-bearded director of the firm, had been jailed for years for guerrilla activities. The company had a good leftist image, but Julio Cesar, who said he knew its members well, described them as "bar Socialists."

They had hired Nelson Perreira dos Santos, he told me, for a movie they were doing about the *jogo do bicho*, the illegal numbers game that is incredibly important in the sociopolitical structure of Brazil. "Rodrigues planned to have the *bicheiros*, who are black, played by white actors. 'Brazilians are racists. They won't go to a movie about blacks,' he explained to dos Santos. Dos Santos said he wouldn't do the movie unless the *bicheiros* were played by black actors, and he pulled out.''

I asked Ilza why she didn't want Nelson Perreira dos Santos.

"He came here and tried to talk me into going with him and Redford," she told me. "He said he wanted to do a film about Amazônia, and I said, You don't need my permission for that, but if it's going to be about Chico that's another question. The next day he told the *Gazeta* that he was going to do a movie on Chico. He blew it.''

Rodrigues's representative, Adalberto Calabrese, said that they were going to make the movie in spite of the opposition from the tappers, and that they were going to make it in Xapuri (another bone of contention). They were going to build a movie theater, which the town didn't have, and all its proceeds would go to the movement. He said they were looking for a coproducer. Puttnam, he said, didn't want to do it without the tappers' cooperation; it was too messy. But Peter Guber and Jon Peters were willing, and they were already deep in advance negotiations, Calabrese said. He'd love to do it with Robert Redford, but Redford wasn't going to go in with the company that had snookered up the rights over his man, nor would he touch the project unless it had the blessing of the tappers. Neither would Spielberg, who was extremely sensitive about criticism.

Mary Allegretti had already accused Redford of being an opportunist who had "parachuted" into the situation. Calabrese showed me a contract in which Guber offered Schwartzman and Allegretti $100,000 apiece, but only if they got the rights for him. "But if we go in with Guber, they don't get anything," Calabrese explained. "Since they aren't getting anything, Schwartzman's noble decision not to make the movie and Mary's calling us sleazes all make sense.''

But it looks like Allegretti was right, I thought. These J.N. guys don't have the money to make the movie on their own. Their plan from the beginning was to snap up the rights and turn them over to the highest Hollywood bidder. So it wasn't going to be a Brazilian production after all. I wondered if Ilza realized that she'd been taken.

On September 13, back in upstate New York, I picked up the *New York Times* and read an announcement that Guber and Peters, Hollywood's hottest duo, had acquired the movie rights to the Chico Mendes story from "his widow and other heirs," and from Gilson Pescador, the secretary of the Chico Mendes Foundation, for nearly a million dollars. "We've been down this road before," Peters said, referring to the frantic maneuvering to make *Gorillas in the Mist.* He claimed he'd had "someone in Brazil working on it every day for eight months," that they'd leased airplanes to fly the family to meetings in Rio, flown in VCRs and videocassettes of their movies. "This has been a full-court press," Guber told the *Los Angeles Times,* making it sound as if he had beaten out the other contenders in a fair and square, all-American competition. There was no mention of the role of J.N. Films, of the fact that Guber-Peters had simply bought the rights from the Brazilian company. Citing his movies *Gorillas in the Mist, The Color Purple, Midnight Express,* and *Missing* — the Costa-Gavras film about the radicalization of an American father, Jack Lemmon, looking for his *desaparecido* son in South America — Peters said, "We have a real history of doing films with political, emotional and ultimately dramatic content and effect." Then Peters said something that may well prove prophetic:

"In a lot of cases people acquire the rights and never make the movie."

Thomas Belford, the executive director of the Better World Society, part of the Ted Turner empire, said that Turner might still go ahead with his made-for-TV movie. The Guber-Peters project, he said, "does not include what we consider to be the bona fide representatives of the movement. If there is a way to bring them in we'll go forward." He added that he'd be delighted to work with Redford, too.

Schwartzman, meanwhile, announced that Pescador had been removed from the foundation, which had split with Ilzamar over the issue, and that the movie project had been scrapped because "many foundation members felt that a film would impede the continuation of Mr. Mendes's work."

The day after this release, the *Hollywood Reporter* printed a cease-and-desist letter that J.N. Films had sent to Alan Schwartz, who claimed to represent the Chico Mendes Foundation and the members of its deliberative council. "Unless you cease and desist from challenging the integrity of a contract solidly entered into . . . our only recourse will be to hold you personally liable." The letter also challenged Schwartz's claim to represent the foundation.

Schwartz responded by calling the letter "libelous and absurd. It's all part of their attempt to mislead people into thinking they have the movie rights from the foundation.'' Guber and Peters "beat out nobody,'' he said. "They didn't get the rights from the parties that have the rights. The basic facts of who Chico Mendes was and what happened to him are in the public domain. But the story of the foundation and the rights to the foundation's story belong to the foundation, and not to Ilzamar Mendes, who was speaking for herself when she made the deal.''

Guber told the press, "We have all the rights we need and we're making the picture,'' and he added, "This is the last comment Jon and I will make on a Brazilian political controversy. It is neither befitting the subject nor in our creative self-interest to engage in these types of polemics.

"The movie we make will bring honor to all those involved in Chico Mendes's cause, and profits to the foundation, raising the consciousness of the world to Mendes's life and work, and equally important, it will entertain the audience powerfully.''

After that, as the fall progressed, I heard nothing more from Brazil about the movie fracas. The only news was three small items in the *Jornal do Brasil* that Julio Cesar told me about. One reported that a preproduction crew of Guber and Peters's had come to Xapuri and been met by an *empate* by the tappers. Another said that Ilza was suing the governor of Acre for not providing Chico with adequate protection. The third item reported that Ilza had had a heart attack and had been rushed to São Paulo, where an artery was removed from her leg for an emergency bypass surgery. But she seemed to have been fully recovered by the time the reporter from *People* magazine came down and interviewed her in December. The article made no mention of her heart attack, or of her rift with Schwartzman, Allegretti, and the tappers.

In fact, while Guber and Peters were celebrating their acquisition of the Mendes rights, they were deep in negotiations with Sony, which had bought Columbia Pictures and was trying to hire the pair away from Warner Brothers for the unheard-of sum of three quarters of a billion dollars. The Japanese were buying American blue-chip properties like Rockefeller Center right and left. The global numerology that ranked the United States as the cream of the First World would have to be revamped.

A few weeks later Sony, Columbia, and Guber-Peters announced their deal. Warner Brothers promptly sued the defecting duo. A settlement was reached. The properties that they had acquired or put into development while at Warner's — *Batman II* and *III*, Tom Wolfe's *Bonfire of the Vanities,* and the Mendes story — would stay there.

"What usually happens in cases like this is that the project languishes," a Hollywood agent said. "If Guber and Peters try to wrest their project from Warner Brothers, it's going to cost them big money, and so they are inevitably stymied." The Chico Mendes movie project may suffer the same fate as the musical *Evita,* which, since its debut in London in 1978, has been on the verge of being made by four studios, seven directors, and at least thirteen actresses, and still there is no movie.

But there may be a movie yet. The latest word was that Warner Brothers had turned the rights over to David Puttnam, whose script for a more political film, Puttnam told me in March 1990, would be ready in "six or seven weeks." The movie, he said, would portray the history of the *seringueiro* movement, and Chico as the last of a series of leaders, taken up almost by accident by the international environmental movement. Like the movie tragedies of the forties, the film would depict the inexorability of the two groups' being drawn into conflict by forces beyond their control. Puttnam, who would be working closely with his friend Adrian Cowell, was more acceptable to the tappers, who still refused to touch the $500,000 J.N. Films had offered for their cooperation. But the problem was that the *seringueiro* council refused to consider working with a project that J.N. Films, which did an end run around it, had anything to do with. "How do I take advantage of the rights at Warner Brothers without confirming the *seringueiros'* worst fears?" Puttnam asked. "That's the circle I haven't yet been able to square."

It would be very sad if there were no movie, because there ought to be one, especially after all that everybody was put through, the Hollywood reps descending on Xapuri, raising people's hopes of stardom and more money than they'd ever seen in their life. But that's Hollywood. "I don't know which is worse," Julio Cesar said, "to be attacked by an army of *pistoleiros* or told by Hollywood that you're going to be in the movies."

BACK TO THE FOREST

One morning we had breakfast at the Hotel Veneza with Antônio Modesto da Silveira, a human rights lawyer and a prominent member of the
Moscow branch of the Brazilian Communist Party. Compassionate, educated, he projected gentle wisdom, the special Brazilian sweetness.

Modesto didn't agree with our theory that Chico Mendes had been
killed with the silent consensus of Acrean society. To prove his point he
asked two carpenters, who were building the new rooms at the hotel,
what they thought of Chico. "He was a really great guy," one said.
"He defended the worker and nature. He stood up for people like us,
but he crossed the *pistoleiros* and look what happened."

"See?" Modesto said.

But these guys are former tappers, I pointed out.

"The liberal property owners feel Chico was fighting for good, too.
So it wasn't the will of the majority, but only of the elite," Modesto
said.

We talked about the ruthlessness of Brazil's savage capitalism, and
how the society was definitely due for a purge, which it seemed to stand
a chance of getting soon because Lula, the Workers' Party presidential
candidate, was gaining daily in the polls.

But the problem is, I said, that land reform and class revolutions are
only temporary rectifications of social imbalance. They can never be a
permanent solution, because people are only human wherever they are
on the social ladder. If you turn the tables and let the oppressed run
things, they would be doing the same thing. So what's the point of
revolution? So you level the society. Start at zero, with a tabula rasa.
You can clear-cut, but you can't completely eradicate the root system.
There will always be new sprouts. Some will inevitably have more talent
and initiative, and will be more ambitious and greedy than others. So
you can't keep them all down at the same low level indefinitely. After
fifty years or less an upper class of party bosses develops that's just as
venal as the one in any capitalist society, the people get sick of repressive
totalitarianism and want something new. After a couple of generations
the situation becomes intolerable and the youth break free. Look what's
happening in China. (The even more cataclysmic events in Eastern Europe were still a few months off.)

The *seringueiro* movement, I continued, is against the predominant social current, against the march of progress. It's antimodern, anti–Western consumerism, back to sustainable, precapitalist subsistence. It's a sort of retrorevolution, like Iran's. And these kinds of revolutions are even harder to institutionalize. There's the continual threat of ideological contamination. You'd have to destroy all the TVs in Acre if you were going to get everybody happily working their three *estradas* in the forest for the rest of their life.

Look how quickly the Indians' culture is destroyed, I pointed out. A plane flies over and they think it must be a god. The shotgun blows away the whole technology of the bow and arrow. I've traveled a lot in the backcountry of the Third World, and the only people I've ever met who've been able to resist the seductive advances of the modern world are the pygmies of equatorial Africa. You give them a T-shirt, they'll wear it for a day or two and then you'll find it lying in the dirt at the edge of the village. They're one of the few peoples who've been able to see through the agricultural revolution. Why spend your day digging in the hot sun from dawn to dusk when you could be roaming in the forest, gathering honey, hunting for mushrooms and little antelopes? The only thing they've ever accepted from the outside was *bangi*, marijuana, which the Arab slavers introduced them to.

"But we have to simplify and cut down consumption," Modesto said gently. "The ideal would be if man could live without using nature. But since this is not possible, the next best thing is to destroy as little of it as we can, and that is why we must all look very carefully at the tappers' model."

The problem for the tappers, I said, is that even if they win the battle with the ranchers, even if not another tree or acre is cleared, the tide of progress will inevitably sweep many of them out of that way of life. Their tightly circumscribed existence isn't for everybody. Given the opportunity, most of them, I suspect, would bolt. It's only human nature. As with the Indians, you can't keep them in a bell jar.

If you gave people the chance to have a perfect society without oppression or discrimination, could they accept it? Saints must die. The impossibility of being totally good is built into the human condition, whatever the stage of culture, and that's why we have to periodically come up with martyrs like Chico to propitiate the gods, so we can keep on with our two-faced, prevaricating ways, and be both good and evil at the same time.

"But the Indians had a perfect society," Modesto argued. "Land had no value. There was no private property to hoard and fight over. There was no oppression because everybody was equal, until the roads came in and their life was destroyed by the avalanche of progress."

What if there were an Indian village that had obtained shotguns by raids on the *caboclos* years ago, but apart from that was still completely traditional? I asked. (I had spent a month, in fact, in such a village in 1976 — Mekranoti, a Kayapó community that had had shotguns since 1930, twenty-five years before their first friendly contact with Brazilian society.) And what if one of the Indians, who saw how the shotguns were wiping out the game and their culture, so that the younger generation had lost the art of making bows and arrows and hunting with them, rose up among them and said, "We must get rid of these terrible devices"? What would the others do? Especially the ones with the most women, which they obtained by raiding other villages with their superior force of arms. They would probably kill him, no?

"Yes, I suppose they would," Modesto admitted.

Not sure about what kind of welcome I would get, I had not checked in with the union. Instead I asked Chiquinho, Júlio's brother, who was a member of the union's executive board and with whom I had a good rapport, if he would take us out to the Seringal Cachoeira. He lined up a pickup. Lots of people piled in back, including Modesto, who was going to visit another *seringal*. We drove on to Joaquim and Cecília's spread at the Colocação Fazendinha.

"We are fighting the whole society," Chiquinho said. "Already the battle has been lost in Rondônia. It's just an immense *fazenda*."

Duda, one of Joaquim and Cecília's sons still living at home, joined us for lunch. His young woman — very *buchuda*, about to have a baby — was in the kitchen doing most of the work, like the new woman in the man's clan the world over. She and Duda had been living together since March, but they hadn't gotten around to getting married. Such formalities aren't important in the tappers' culture. It is common for the young man and woman to elope: the expression is *virar jabuti*, to turn tortoise. Later the young man goes to his bride's father and explains

.that he didn't have the courage to ask for her hand. Usually all is forgiven.

After lunch Julio Cesar and I go with Duda into the forest. I take a picture of him standing at the foot of one of the immense Brazil nut trees that has been left standing in the pasture. (Back home, when I developed the film, I measured the tree. In the picture it was four inches tall, Duda only an eighth of an inch. If he is five and a half feet tall, that makes the height of the tree 176 feet.)

It is against the law to cut Brazil nut trees, but it happens a great deal because the wood is high-grade. Leaving the Brazil nut trees as is seems a nice gesture, but within a couple of years they stop bearing fruit and die. You may as well cut them and not let them go to waste. It's not just the radical change in their microclimate, in the light and moisture, when the forest around them is eradicated, that does them in. To reproduce they require a series of intricately coevolved interactions, involving a large network of forest organisms, which has only recently been discovered. As the botanist Ghillean T. Prance, one of the investigators, reports in a collection of scientific papers called *Tropical Rain Forests and the World Atmosphere,*

> The flowers need to be cross-pollinated with pollen from another tree in order to set fruit. The flowers are of an extremely complex structure, with the androecium extended laterally into a hood that covers the ring of fertile stamens around its base. Nectar is secreted in the hood and the pollinator must lift the hood to obtain access to the nectar. The flowers are visited by large bees, mainly of the subfamily Euglossineae, but also carpenter ants (Xylocopa). These bees land on the hood and enter the crack between the hood and its base. While they forage for nectar in the hood, their backs rub against the fertile stamens of the ring and they become heavily dusted with pollen, which they carry from flower to flower. The brazil-nut flowers for about a one month period in November and supplies good sustenance for the bees during that time. Our phenological studies . . . have shown that the pollinators of the brazil-nut also visit a whole series of other species. Many of these species reach flowering peaks at slightly different times from the brazil-nut and thus help to feed the pollinators over a longer period. The

brazil-nut will therefore not produce its fruit without the bees, nor without its related species to provide bee food at other times.

"The male Euglossine bees," Prance continues,

are also dependent on some of the epiphytic orchids in the forest because they visit these and gather their fragrances. They pack the scents in their hind legs and fly off to form a lek, a group that attracts the females for mating to take place. Therefore, if the orchids are not present in the forest, the brazil-nut will also not produce. . . .

In addition, the brazil-nut falls to the forest floor where the outer shells are eaten by agoutis. The agoutis bury the seeds and forget some of their caches, thereby causing dispersal of the seeds. The survival of the brazil-nuts is therefore dependent on this large rodent of the forest floor as well.

Prance goes on to list several of the hundreds of other cases of interactive coevolution that have been discovered in the rain forest. The forest, it would appear, is like a house of cards: flick one and the whole thing collapses. Or a suspension bridge: chop one strand and the entire cable unravels.

As soon as I step over the barbed wire fence and enter the forest I can feel an intensity in the half-light — the strands of all these invisible interrelationships. What's that? I ask Duda, noticing a camouflaged scaffold in a tree. "A hiding place for shooting *paca*" (as the Brazilians call agoutis). A *tocaia,* then? I ask, using the word for the type of ambush blind used to kill Duda's cousin Chico. Duda looks at me as if I had made a joke in poor taste. Clearly the word doesn't apply to killing animals.

I wonder: a jaguar kills a *paca*. A man kills a *paca*. A man kills a man. At what point does it become murder?

This is Julio Cesar's first time in the Amazon rain forest. I hope that he isn't going to be let down. Much of it has a drab sameness: to the untrained eye, one tree looks much like the next. The leaves are all long and broad and do not broadcast their identity. This is the most effective and the most common survival strategy, the best camouflage — to blend in with the others, to cleave to the norm. Just as in human society, conformity is the safest way to get through life. To stand out, to be too conspicuous, too charismatic, too good, is to ask for trouble. You end up getting your head cut off, like Chico.

But this is one of the most spectacular stands of virgin rain forest I've ever seen. "It's like a great cathedral," Julio Cesar says. Trees of tremendous girth, supported by huge, flaring buttresses, rise a hundred feet before putting out their first branches, from which thick, taut lianas twist to the ground. Beside a towering tonka bean tree, we find the first rubber tree on the trail, with the small halved *cengo* of a Brazil nut tree jammed at the vee, instead of a tin can or cup. These cuts were made by Chico Mendes, Duda tells us proudly. Chico once tapped ninety days straight, two hundred trees a day. Already the legend is growing.

I notice that the latex in the *cengo* is hard and full of debris that has fallen from the canopy. It hasn't been collected in days. It seems as if the *seringal* has been getting so many visitors since Chico was killed that Duda and his brothers don't have time to tap rubber anymore. It's probably more profitable, too, to take the visitors around. I already have the sense that we are getting the tour, that the *seringueiros* here are passing into the replica stage, as I call it. How vulnerable these last subsistence cultures are. A visitor from the modern world comes for a visit and is so swept away by the beauty of the forest, by the purity of the people, that he gives the guide who takes him around for an hour a generous present — let's say twenty dollars. That's more than the tapper gets for two days' backbreaking work. The visitor means well, but the tapper has been derailed. (I heard later that the tappers had begun to charge admission to Chico's home in the forest.)

Duda peels a strip of *cernambi* from one of Chico's cuts and stretches it taut between two saplings — a fifteen-foot rubber band, which he twangs like the string of a washtub bass. He explains how a new *estrada* is cut in virgin forest: "Two of you go out. When you find the first rubber tree, one of you stays with it, and the other keeps going. When he finds the next tree he whacks it with a machete and the other cuts toward the sound."

The piercing whistle of a screaming *pia* comes from somewhere not far away. Backwoods Amazonians call the bird *daí-a-pior,* from here to worse, after the sound of its call, which the anthropologist David Price has rendered well, as *wheetweeo.*

Duda shows us another latex-yielding tree, a smaller "second cousin" of the *seringal* that he calls the *cautchu.* "Deer come to eat the fruit of this *gogozinho* [a liana]. This tree yields the pomade used for Ben-Gay. You chew the leaves of this 'jaguar ears' plant for heartburn. This *pluma* stops bleeding.''

A flock of raucous parrots passes overhead.

Duda strips some bark off a tree and passes it to me. ''This,'' he says, ''is quinine.'' Foolishly I chomp on the bark, scalding the inside of my mouth with its excoriating bitterness. Until the development of sulfa drugs, quinine, from the bark of the cinchona tree, was for centuries the only treatment for malaria. There was a cinchona boom in the Amazon that the people who went through the later rubber boom could have learned from, but they didn't. It all began in 1638, when the countess of Chinchón, the wife of the viceroy of Peru, was cured of malaria by a tea brewed from the bark of a forest tree, which was later named for her. The Jesuits took the bark to Europe, and soon it was in great demand all over the world. The supply seemed inexhaustible, but eventually the trees were wiped out of a large part of their range, and that was that. The last stands were jealously guarded. A few seeds were smuggled to Kew Gardens, to become the basis of great cinchona plantations in Java and India.

Duda flakes off the reddish bark of a different tree and says, ''*Canela.* Have a smell.'' We inhale the ambrosial aroma of fresh cinnamon: what an olfactory hit! Julio Cesar is transported. ''Can you imagine destroying all this for one or two cows?'' he says.

La Canela was the other fabulous kingdom, besides El Dorado, and rumors of it lured the ill-fated expedition of Gonzalo Pizarro down into the unknown territory east of Ecuador in 1541 and led to the European discovery of the Amazon Valley.

Duda now has a joke for us: a guy is lying on the forest floor, staring up at the canopy. ''God did everything wrong,'' he thinks. ''How come that big tree has such small fruits, while that little creeping vine sprouts big pumpkins?'' At that moment a small nut falls from above and hits him on the head. ''I get it,'' he thinks. ''God made everything right after all.''

We hit the edge of the clearing, which is choked with barbed shrubs in the pea family aptly called *esper' ai,* hold it right there. One barb catches my earlobe, another my shirt. I try to continue, but the barbs won't let go, and they start to tear my skin and clothing. Duda has to come back and extricate me.

"They're proud of the forest," Julio Cesar says as we come back into the clearing. "This is what they have to show. The forest is the one thing that distinguishes them from other peasants. But it's nice to have this open area, too, to be able to see your borders, to have the feeling, This is my land. Here in this pasture a human standing is the highest thing. In there he is a very small thing. People need to create a space that is comprehensible to them. The forest is not comprehensible."

We cross the soccer field behind the school — a conversion of rain forest you'd have a lot of trouble getting Brazilians upset about. Duda tells us that he and his brothers have the best team in the *subúrbio*.

I remember one of my favorites among the efforts made to bring home the fact of the destruction, a sentence in a newsletter called *Guaraná*, put out by Brazilian expatriates in New York City: "This week, last week, and every week, 113,000 soccer fields are being cleared."

VISIONS OF THE FOREST

I'd brought a guitar, a beautiful classical Di Giorgio I'd bought in Co-pacabana. It had a black jacaranda fret board. Julio Cesar opened one of the bottles of *cachaça,* the raw Brazilian rum, that we'd brought as a house present and mixed up some *caipirinhas* with crushed lemon and sugar (similar to margaritas). And soon we were singing *carimbós* (dance music from Pará), sambas, and *baião.* "We haven't had any live entertainment here in a long time," Joaquim said, "just the radio and the *guaribas*" (the howler monkeys, whose cascading roars erupting in the hours before dawn are the most chilling, unearthly sound in the forest). For supper we had a *paca* that Toto, one of Duda's brothers, had shot. It was a beautiful animal, the size of a duiker, the diminutive forest antelope of Africa. Its brown pelt was striated like a watermelon, with lines of white spots; its meat was superb.

After the *seresta,* the sing-along, Duda slung some hammocks for us in the schoolhouse, and we crashed. As the night progressed, it cooled down drastically. A *friagem,* a cold snap, had descended. Julio Cesar woke up with a bad cold. As is de rigueur among Latin American urban intellectuals, he smoked like a chimney, and though he was a strapping young man of thirty-three, he had a neurasthenic outlook, a heightened sense of his own decay. To protect himself from the degenerative assault of nature, he took a daily battery of pills, which, he now complained, I'd made him leave in his suitcase in Xapuri. This was more nature in the raw than he'd ever been exposed to: he stayed in his hammock till afternoon.

The others had left early for the forest, so I went off alone, in shorts and flip-flops, pen and notebook in a Ziploc bag, down the trail that led to the clear, sparkling creek behind Joaquim and Cecília's house. A pile of clothes on the bank was swarming with day-flying Urania moths — among the world's most spectacular insects, iridescent green with black bars and swallowtails. They were probing for sweat minerals in the wet fabric.

The path, a small track known as a *picada* or *pic,* went up through a stand of forty-foot-tall wild bananas. Wandering among the tattered sheaves of gigantic leaves, I felt like a mouse lost in a field of tall grass. After half an hour the *pic* teed into a major thoroughfare, connecting the *seringais,* that the tappers took when they came in from the forest with their *pranchas* of rubber loaded on burros. I kept taking rights, doubling back. After an hour I reached a rude shrine along the trail — a wooden cross with old, now worthless cruzeiro notes (bills from two currencies before) pinned to it, covered by a rotting roof. "A tapper fell off his mule and died here," Joaquim told me when I got back. I sat down beside it and pondered, once again, why the Amazon rain forest had suddenly become such a big deal in the First World. Why the sudden concern, the incredible indignation about the murder of Chico Mendes?

It wasn't just the climate linkage, the media bandwagon effect, the panicky projection of our own anguish, or the ecovogue. The Amazon was the source, the holiest natural sanctuary on the planet, and the man who had been guarding it had been killed.

This vision of Amazônia as the source, the mother, the womb, has been there from the beginning. Most of the Indian tribes have legends about an ancient matriarchy: vaginal imagery abounds in their myths and animal stories. But the forest is not an entirely safe womb: the toothed vagina is one of the recurrent myth motifs.

The idea of Mother Amazon also gained currency among nineteenth-century anthropologists, such as João Barbosa Rodriguez. A fascinating character — explorer, botanist, Indian pacifier, first director of the Jardim Botânico in Rio — Barbosa Rodriguez was convinced, partly by the enthnographic evidence, partly by mystical intuition, that all the Indian cultures of South America emanated from Amazônia. His theory was rejected by the more scientific anthropologists who followed him, but recently evidence has turned up to suggest that it isn't that farfetched, that the human presence in the valley is much earlier and more elaborate than previously suspected. The archaeologist Anna Roosevelt, who has been excavating the jungle-smothered ruins of lost civilizations in the Lower Amazon, at Santarém and on Marajó Island, has come up with ceramic dates of six to seven thousand years before the present — older than anywhere else in the Americas and as old as anything on the planet.

The biologists have even better reasons for thinking of Amazônia as the source: more than one tenth of all the species on earth — the greatest concentration of biological diversity — are found in the valley. Many of the life-forms in the New World radiated out of the Amazon Valley and find their fullest, most complex expression there.

There is also the concomitant idea that the forest is something that must not be disturbed. To the Gavião Indians of Rondônia, the trees guarantee the peace of the water beings during the dry season. If there is no shade for them, these beings disturb each other and men, too. Man is completely dependent on the equilibrium between the tree beings and the water beings.

And this belief that trees are beings, that they talk to each other, is not so farfetched either. Scientists have recently discovered that trees warn each other with subtle chemical signals of the approach of insect predators. I have always felt an intensity in forests, a connection with the other forms of life, as if there were invisible strands between us. This sense of kinship is, of course, much more developed among preindustrial people. To the half-evangelized Tikuna of the Solimões River, the animals in the forest are ancestors, reincarnated relatives. "If you're good, you go to heaven. But if you're bad, you go into the forest and become an animal," a member of the tribe told me. Each Yanomamo Indian believes that he has a *rishi,* an alter ego, that has taken the form of a hawk, a jaguar, a butterfly, or some other animal, and is living an existence parallel to his own.

The forest is a half-lit dreamworld, the realm of the irrational, the unconscious. Its hallucinatory quality impressed even the rigorously scientific Henry Walter Bates. Here is his description of running into a boa constrictor in his nineteenth-century classic, *The Naturalist on the River Amazons:* "On seeing me the reptile suddenly turned, and glided at an accelerated rate down the path. . . . The rapidly moving and shining body looked like a stream of brown liquid flowing over the thick bed of fallen leaves.''

The first time I asked Joaquim if he had had any experiences with the beings in the forest, he dismissed them as superstitions; but on the third morning, when I returned to the subject, he said, ''I was born and raised, I grew my teeth in this forest, and I can tell you, it is full of strange things.

''There's the *onça pé de boi* [a particularly aggressive jaguar]. It only travels in pairs, and waits for the man it has treed in shifts.

''There's Mapinguarí, a giant who wears armor of turtle shells and can only be shot through the navel. He exists in the valley of the Purus, but nobody's seen him here.

''There's the Mãe da Água, the Mother of the Waters, who changes from a snake to a woman and steals children.

''There's the *jabutiaçu* [a possibly enchanted giant tortoise]. He weighs thirty kilos. He can make any kind of deal with a big ball of rubber [i.e., he weighs as much].

''There's Honorato Cobra Grande, the Great Snake. He was origi- nally human, but his mother got tired of giving him milk, and threw him into the water with his brother Caninana, and they became snakes. He killed his brother, overturned boats, and was a despicable character. But one day a man disenchanted Honorato by dripping mother's milk on him. He became a man and remembered nothing.''

What about the Caboclinho da Mata, the Little Man of the Forest? I asked.

''I've never seen him, but he exists,'' Joaquim said. ''My brother Chico, Chico's father, met him when he was fifteen years old. He was walking alone in the forest. The Caboclinho was yea high [he put out his hand two and a half feet above the floor], and he had hair to the ground. When he saw my brother he bolted immediately.

''Another time my brother and I were in the middle of the forest when we smelled tobacco. Who could be smoking? we wondered. Then we saw a deer and shot at it. It fell but didn't die. It had four ears and antlers like this [he pointed both index fingers up]. I think it was the horse of the Caboclinho.''

So little is known about this forest, I thought. If the Brazilians could only wait a couple of years: they are sitting on a gold mine, on the greatest repository of germ plasm and genetic information on earth, on maybe a third of the world's species, and they're spending less on genetic research annually than the average American drug company spends developing a single new product. Meanwhile, they're giving away billions of dollars in incentives that subsidize the clearing and burning. This shortsightedness isn't only stupid. It's criminal.

I thought of what has already come out of the forest: quinine for malaria, and curare, the muscle relaxant vital in modern surgery. The Indians were using it as an arrow poison. Capoten, the medicine for hypertension recently developed from the study of viper venom, works on the angiotension system and permanently lowers blood pressure. Squibb is making millions from it. Pilocarpine, from the leaves of the *jaborandi* tree, used in the treatment of glaucoma. The Amazon has the world monopoly. The leaves are harvested by men dangled from helicopters hovering over the canopy. It's a $25 million-a-year business for Vegetex, a subsidiary of Merck.

Who knows what miraculous compounds lurk in the minds of the Indians, in the bark of some tree? (One tribe, the Chacabo, was found to use 82 percent of the species in a sample hectare of rain forest, 95 percent of the 619 individual trees. Another, the Tirió, has 300 medicinal plants in its forest pharmacopoeia.) Seventy percent of the 3,000 plants identified by the U.S. National Cancer Institute as having anticancer properties are rain forest species, Catherine Caufield writes in her book, *In the Rainforest*. Two thousand rain forest plants have anticancer properties, a newsletter from Cultural Survival reported. Others are used to treat lymphotic leukemia, Hodgkin's disease, and amoebic dysentery. In all, more than 7,000 pharmaceuticals, 25 percent of all the drugs sold in pharmacies, contain rain forest ingredients. Yet fewer than 1 percent of the tropical species have been analyzed.

As for AIDS: Francis Black, a virologist at Yale, told me a few years ago that he drew blood from some howler monkeys stranded on islands of forest created by the back-flooding of the Tucuruí Dam, in 1984, and found evidence of retroviruses closely related to HIV-1, the cause of AIDS, but these were not pathogenic. He also drew blood in sixty remote Indian villages in Amazônia and found similar retroviruses in the women who butchered the monkeys that the men brought back from their hunting trips and who were thus exposed to the monkeys' blood. The implications of Black's discovery are very intriguing: retroviruses must have been with primates for a very long time, since even before the evolution of humans and the splitting of the continents. The news of Black's discovery was distorted by the typically defensive Brazilian press: "U.S. SCIENTIST ACCUSES BRAZIL OF BEING SOURCE OF AIDS."

Maybe there's an undiscovered slime mold deep in the forest that will prolong human life, or double human intellectual capacity, or prove to be the key to world domination. Any of this is within the realm of possibility.

Whenever I read something new about the Amazon I clip and file it. Here are some tidbits: Every time you take a step in the Amazon rain forest you tread on about fifteen hundred species of animals and plants, of which only 30 percent are known to science. Most of these are insects. One tree was found to host forty-three species of ants. Some insect species require only a few square meters to maintain a genetically viable population. The jaguar, one of the species most critically affected by deforestation, needs up to five hundred thousand hectares. The rates of extinction from human conversion of the rain forest are proceeding five hundred times faster than the natural rhythm of evolution of new species.

Estimates of the number of different forms of life in the Amazon range from a few million to thirty million. But maybe the forest is infinitely richer and more complex than anyone suspects. A recent article in the Science Times section of the *New York Times* had this amazing lead: "Sea water and natural fresh water contain up to ten million times as many viruses as has been previously thought, scientists reported last week." Who knows what's in the Amazon? The state of our actual knowledge is still very primitive, not really that much further along than that of the seekers of El Dorado. The numbers that are thrown out with such an air of scientific authority are actually only the language of modern myth.

I got up and started walking again, taking a right each time there was a choice, and after an hour, just as I was starting to get nervous, the path I was on came out at the creek again. Dropping my shorts and hanging them on a branch, I slipped into one of the creek's delicious pools and lay there, watching small fish nibble my toes.

That evening Duda invited us — Julio Cesar was feeling better — to go hunting for *paca*. *Paca* was the main source of protein around here. Deer were scarce, and you ran into *iraras* (weasels), tinamous, howler and capuchin monkeys, only if you were lucky. "Sometimes we kill forty *paca* in a month," Duda told me.

And the Caboclinho doesn't get on your case? I asked. "No," he laughed.

To hunt *paca*, you hide near a tree whose fruit they like, and wait for them to come and feed. You build a platform or sling your hammock in a nearby tree a few hours before it gets dark, and when you hear them feeding you freeze them in the beam of your flashlight, line one up, and pull the trigger.

Duda stationed us in an alcove formed by two flaring prop roots and told us not to move or make a sound. We sat there for two hours, with our backs against the immense buttresses, known as *sapopembas*, listening to the teeming silence, occasionally broken by the scream of a *pia*, a nut tearing through leaves, or the whir of a bat.

As we furtively passed a cupped cigarette back and fourth, I remembered how, when I was a kid, I used to go into the woods of northern Westchester County and smoke cigarettes with my neighbor Davie Holderness. My brand was Philip Morris. The place where we usually went to smoke was a big dead maple tree that had split in half in the woods behind my house. One of the halves had fallen over and was suspended ten feet from the ground by its branches. We would sit on it and light up, then swing, like Tarzan, to the ground on the saplings that had grown up around it. I spent a lot of time in the woods as a kid. It was the place where I went to be free.

It grew dark enough to make out a faint glow — the bioluminescence of some decaying wood — at our feet. The insects and tree frogs began to emit a dense field of rhythmic sound, a deafening samba, and every once in a while there was a crazy bird call that sounded just like a *cuíca*, an instrument in the samba band that adds capricious, hysterical punctuation to the steady, intoxicating beat of the drums and bean canisters. I have often wondered whether Brazilian samba, to me the most euphoric, infectious music in the world, was originally inspired by the night sounds of the rain forest. As far as I know, the connection has never been investigated.

This pet theory of mine expanded in the darkness. Brazilians, I thought, have adopted inappropriate American models: the nineteenth-century Manifest Destiny conquer-the-wilderness model, which is no longer a good idea anywhere; the *Dallas* model of the big *fazenda,* beautiful women, and money to burn, which only the most ruthless of them will ever have. But in fact the best model for Brazil as it actually is, is the forest itself. The country is verging on complete anarchy: the only law, literally, is the law of the jungle. The economic system, to the extent that there is one, is "savage capitalism," with real estate owned by the person with the quickest draw or the biggest army of *pistoleiros*.

Brazilians aren't up-front like Americans, or the way Americans like to think they are. There's a very different cultural attitude toward deceit and lying, an admiration of what is known as the *jogo da cintura*, the game of the waist, of artful dodging, disguising your true intentions. One of the great cultural heroes was a soccer player, a contemporary of Pelé's named Garrincha. His footwork was so mesmerizing — he did such a dazzling samba around the ball — that he could outfake an opponent without ever even touching it.

In my research into the murder of Chico Mendes and its context, I kept running into the term "smoke screen." Darci Alves confessed to the murder as a "smoke screen" to protect the real killers. Brazilian diplomats are throwing up the "smoke screen" of national sovereignty in complicated negotiations over canceling some of the foreign debt in return for assurance that the Amazon will be protected. Maybe the Bush administration's sudden environmental concern about the extension and paving of BR-364, and about the Amazon in general, is a "smoke screen" for other concerns, having to do with the resurgence of the Japanese.

And then there are all these *fantasmas*, phantoms. Corporations in the South of Brazil create phantom companies in the Amazon to get a 25 percent break on their income tax. Politicians in the interior regularly win elections with the help of phantom voters — people they truck in and bribe with a free meal to register under the name of those who have died since the last election, the old "dead souls" ruse. And once they get into office, they put all their friends and relatives on the payroll. Half of these are *fantasmas* who don't even bother to show up for work.

The society is permeated with illusion. Brazil is the mecca for face-lifts. It does the most expert dubbing of foreign films. And, most important, it has the best carnival, and this four-day spree — in which everyone dresses up and acts out his or her fantasy of being someone else, usually someone better off — is the most anticipated event of the year, the key to the culture.

Where did this fascination with illusion and dissembling come from? I think that, like many other elements of Latin American culture, it's an Arabic trait that was acquired by the Portuguese during their eight-hundred-year domination by the Moors. Another cultural element is the jive that the enslaved Brazilian blacks, like their brothers in North America, developed to get back at their masters. But there's also a great deal of deception and *jogo da cintura* in the rain forest.

The forest itself seems a riotous, dead-serious carnival in which everyone wears a mask. Camouflage and crypsis — keeping a low profile — are favorite survival strategies. Moths simulate leaves, snakes look like vines, hawkmoths pose as hummingbirds, orchids alter themselves to look like the sex organs of female bees, butterflies perform all kinds of mimicry.

Among the most common forms of butterfly are lazily flapping, elongate, two-tone types, usually brown and yellow or red and blue. Some are heliconians — a foul-smelling and unpalatable group avoided by birds because of the toxic alkaloids they absorb as caterpillars from their food plant, the passionflower vine. But others are Dismorphia, a completely different family. They are perfectly palatable but in flight are indistinguishable from the heliconians and are therefore also left alone by birds. Pierids eat plants in the pea family and are also perfectly palatable, while ithomids are unpalatable because they eat Solanaceae — another toxic plant family. The true identity of the butterflies of this type can be ascertained only by careful examination of the disposition of their veins and genitalia. Forms that are not sufficiently deceptive to fool their predators are eliminated by natural selection.

The actual heliconians and the passionflower vines that their caterpillars feed on are locked in an elaborate coevolutionary dance of deception. The plants have acquired chemical defenses — alkaloids and saponins — to discourage the caterpillars, which do extensive damage to the vines. But the caterpillars have learned to absorb the toxins without harm, so the vines have developed a devious assortment of mechanical defenses as well. To encourage the caterpillars to eat their own eggs, the plant has evolved an egg mimic: a supernumerary yellow flower bud on its meristem tendril. It has also developed modified hooked leaf hairs, known as trichomes, which are capable of puncturing the caterpillars' abdominal cuticle, causing death. As another ploy, it has also acquired deciduous stipules that resemble small tendrils; the caterpillars lay their eggs on them, and they fall off the plant before the eggs hatch. Near the places where the caterpillars are likely to lay, the plants also have extrafloral nectaries that secrete sugar attractive to ants and other egg predators. The coiling tendrils fasten onto other plants, providing access. Other tendrils may crush the eggs or larvae as they are hatching.

The caterpillars react with a number of counterstrategies. Their well-developed vision makes it difficult for even the most inconspicuous vine to escape detection, and they distinguish real from false eggs by probing with their antennae and proboscis and tapping with their forelegs. They also use their organs to determine plants unsuitable for laying their eggs on — plants that aren't big enough to feed a brood of larvae, that are diseased or infested with egg predators like ants, spiders, and other caterpillars of their own species. When they do lay, they choose the tendril tips, which are out of reach of ants. To avoid being slit open by the trichomes, the caterpillars walk gingerly on specially evolved silken pads. And, finally, the caterpillars use the toxins that the vines evolved in self-defense to defend themselves against their own predators. As already mentioned, birds find the butterflies they turn into unpalatable and avoid them for this reason.

But the duplicity in the rain forest is nothing compared to what is found in human society. Blackmail, kickbacks, the *anúncio,* the contract hit, the dozens of reasons for lying (which is simply deceit in words), the ten thousand "irregularities" found in the government of President José Sarney: such *raffinements* are found only in our species. Human deviousness — not just in Brazil, of course — is limited only by the imagination. Man imitates nature but does nature one better.

Then there are the many sociobiological patterns that humans are into, too, like "interference mutualism." Two monkeys will form a temporary alliance to prevent a third from gaining access to the fertile females or the fruit of a certain tree. This is just what the governor of Acre did after Chico's murder. He formed a temporary alliance with the tappers to discredit the ranchers and their candidate in the next elections. Later he was convinced that this alliance was politically unwise, and he abandoned the tappers.

The hard-core sociobiologist believes that virtually all animal and plant behavior can be explained in terms of genetic self-interest. Humans are more complicated, but the bonds of kinship — of shared genes — are still very strong, especially in traditional societies like those of Amazônia. The anthropologist Napoleon Chagnon once watched a fight that started between two Yanomamo men. The sequence of other men in the village who grabbed their clubs and joined the melee, he told me a few years ago, broke down neatly according to the coefficient of kinship — first the brothers of the antagonists, then their uncles, then their first cousins, et cetera. The revenge murder of Zezão by Francisco de Assis falls into this pattern, as does the revenge killing of the rancher Nilão de Oliveira after the murder of Chico's predecessor, Wilson Pinheiro, in 1980. The fact that the judge of Xapuri refused to do anything about Pinheiro's murder is easily explained, elementary, once you know the overriding kinship lines: he married de Oliveira's widow.

The *pistoleiros,* in this scheme, are the low-level predators. That is how they make their living. The journalists and the movie reps snapping up the rights to everything in sight are opportunistic feeders, exhibiting classic feeding-frenzy behavior. The anthropologists and environmentalists who promoted Chico and his cause before he died act proprietary, controlling access to the tappers and to information about Mendes. But a few of the scientists, like Lovejoy and the equally remarkable botanist Ghillean Prance, are men of vision. Among the forest trees, they are the emergents.

A final analogy: the more species multiply, the more specialized they become. In the Amazon, the most diversified terrestrial biome on the planet, specialization reaches its peak. At least sixty-eight species of plants and animals, for instance, restrict themselves to the pools of water trapped in bromeliads. Many species have no apparent ecological difference from one another. They seem to share the same niche — a phenomenon that has been called niche partitioning. You find the same thing among humans. There are five subsects of the *daime* cult, each claiming to be the true lineage of Irineu Santos. At least four books on the tragedy of Chico Mendes are in the works. The recent democratic opening in Brazil has spawned a chaotic *pluripartidarismo,* a tremendous number of small, bickering leftist groups.

The struggle for succession among the tappers is reminiscent of a different pattern in the forest. A majestic tree in the forest crashes to the ground. In the flood of sunlight, the sudden opening created by its absence, there is ferocious competition and a frenzied spurt of growth among the saplings that have been waiting beneath the tree for such an opportunity.

But in the end only one of the saplings can take its place, and none of them that I've met possesses the stature to become the next Chico Mendes.

I remembered, as Julio Cesar passed me his cupped cigarette for another drag, how I had taken my two sons to the toppled maple tree where Davie Holderness and I had gone to smoke twenty-five years before. But the tree was gone. It had rotted almost completely away. In its place was a linear heap of wet red matter, more like dirt than wood, that crumbled in my fingers. The saplings were young trees now, too thick to bend under a boy's weight. But the struggle for succession was still going on.

A RUN-IN WITH THE SHIITES

I watched through the slats of Joaquim and Cecília's house as a Volkswagen Beetle arrived, and Gumercindo, who had grown a beard since Chico's murder, got out. With him were Júlio Barbosa, who had a revolver in a belt holster, and two German agronomists who were helping them get cooperatives for the tappers going. Julio Cesar was sacked out in his hammock in the schoolhouse.

Uh-oh, I thought. Could be trouble.

Gumercindo came into the kitchen and, finding me there, said, "So you're the one who sold the rights of Chico's story to Robert Redford."

I didn't realize the full strength of this in Portuguese. Julio Cesar later explained that it had the same impact as if he had accused me of feeding Chico's body to vultures, or as if I were Judas, who had sold Christ for thirty pieces of silver. The words "Robert Redford" were uttered with supreme disgust and contempt, as if Redford were the arch-capitalist gringo devil incarnate.

Yes, I said, I am. Is it something I should be ashamed of?

Then he called me a *picareta,* a word that, fortunately, I didn't know. It means "slimeball," "sleaze." It's a very bad word, fighting words for any red-blooded Brazilian.

I'm sorry, but I don't know that word, I said. What does it mean?

Gumercindo looked a little nonplussed.

"A *picareta* is . . . a *picareta.*"

Hey, Julio Cesar, you'd better get over here, I yelled over to the schoolhouse.

Half-awake, he stumbled down through the grass, and, sensing that a bad scene was brewing, he said, "Well, what do we have here, PT radicals?" which didn't help one bit.

"No," said Júlio Barbosa, who had more couth than his *companheiro*. "It's just that we're tired of all these people coming through here."

Gumercindo, cooling down a little, asked, "Why didn't you send us your article?"

I said, Because I thought Schwartzman would have. Doesn't he send you everything that comes out about the movement in the North American press? I just gave Ilza a copy. I'm sure she'll let you borrow it.

"Good," he said.

The two of them continued with their German guests, whom they were taking on a tour of the rain forest. Júlio Barbosa exchanged sharp words with Chiquinho for bringing us here without his permission, and they had a little sibling tiff. "I'm a member of the board, too," Chiquinho argued, "and I don't need your permission for anything."

"Okay, but don't take them to the Colocação Pote Seco" — Chico's birthplace, several hours deeper into the forest, which we had planned to visit that afternoon.

After they had left, Chiquinho apologized and said, "I'm sorry, but I won't be able to take you there after all."

I don't get it, I said to Julio Cesar: Redford's work is so antisystem, and he's such a clearly dedicated environmentalist.

"But he's also a glamorous, handsome guy," Julio Cesar explained, "and such an American icon that the Shiites can't react to him simply. The word 'Redford' is like waving a red flag in their face. The PT's line is, if you drink a Coke and buy a Ford you're a victim of ideology. They think that American capitalists are accomplices of the ranchers, and it's useless to try to convince them otherwise, because they don't want to be convinced. Even if they don't believe the party line, they have to pretend they do to maintain their leftist credibility."

"Don't pay attention to Gumercindo," Cecília said. "He's getting to be too much."

When we got back to Xapuri the next day, we discovered that Gumercindo had been going around telling everybody that I had come to start filming Redford's movie and that he had beaten the shit out of me.

"Let's face it," Julio Cesar said, "we're ideological lepers."

"*Já vai? 'Tá cedo.*" — "Already leaving? So soon?" Cecília said with typical Brazilian graciousness the next day when the pickup came to get us.

Spectacular people, I said to Julio Cesar after we had hugged and said good-bye.

"Yes," he agreed. "You can see why Chico was so special."

But the energy of Chico was no longer in the movement. It had been replaced by that of contentious hotheads like Gumercindo.

"If I were you I'd just forget about it," Julio Cesar said. "Steer clear of them and get on with your business. I'll find out what's happening at the union."

We drove on to Brasiléia, the seat of the second level of Chico's murderers, the ranchers' ring, sometimes called the articulators. We had lunch at a *churrascaria,* a restaurant where the waiters keep bringing you all kinds of barbecued meat — half a dozen cuts of beef, sausages, chicken hearts, on long skewers — until you can't eat any more. The driver told us that the two young men at the next table were *pistoleiros* who worked for Gaston Mota. Chiquinho told us about a Communist group he'd heard about called Libelu (for *liberdade,* liberty, and *luta,* struggle) that sent beautiful girls from Rio and São Paulo to seduce people into the movement.

We went to Osmarino Amâncio's house, a simple shack in one of the *bairros populares,* working-class neighborhoods. A guy who was working on a car told us that Osmarino was in Amazonas and that he'd just gotten word he had been in an accident but was all right.

Is Gaston around?

"I haven't seen him. When Osmarino's around, they're here. When he isn't, you don't see them. I did see Benedito Rosas and Tilinho [Darli's nephew, who was Rosas's partner], though, a couple of days ago."

So Benedito Rosas hadn't absconded to Goiás.

One of the purposes of our going to Brasiléia was to talk to Gaston Mota. Chiquinho had said that there was no problem with that, but I now realized that he was just trying to be helpful and polite. He didn't want to say no — a source of confusion for centuries of foreigners in Amazônia. When it became clear that I was really serious about looking up Gaston Mota, he said, "*É meio perigoso*. It's a little dangerous." The driver came right out and said, "You can go, but I'm not taking you there."

"You can't ask them to do that," Julio Cesar said. "You can't ask them to take you to their enemy."

But that's what we came here for, I said. Look. You let me out and wait for me in the plaza and I'll go find him. I'll go to the police station. They'll know where he is. I'll be perfectly frank with him and tell him that I want to get his side, the ranchers' side of the story.

That was my way, the gringo way. Barge right in. It usually worked.

"Look. I'm not going, either," Julio Cesar said. "I'm not messing with a bees' nest."

I began to get cold feet myself. Maybe you're right, I said at last. Maybe the best way to do this is through an introduction. Let's just make this an afternoon of tourism. Let's go over to Cobija and see what it's like in Bolivia.

"Good idea," Julio Cesar said. "When the driver said he wouldn't go, an alarm went off in my head. A good horse stops at the edge of the abyss, even if you don't know it's there, and refuses to go on."

It was an open border into Bolivia: there were no guards. The people along the road on the other side of the bridge were much more Indian in appearance. The frontier was like a cultural ecotone. The main square was colorful, antique, arcaded, more in the crumbling Spanish colonial mode, like Mexico. It was like a movie set, the caricature of a South American hole — Cobija, the notorious border town. Many of the stores were completely devoted to scotch. Bottles of the best brands, Chivas, Glenfiddich, trucked up from Chile, stood in glass windows and display cases. A painted, dolled-up sensual dwarf in a tight blouse and skirt with platform shoes sashayed across the square for our benefit as we sat licking mango ice cream cones. A guy came up and offered to buy the pickup. Indian money changers had set up on the sidewalk, ready to convert cruzados into Bolivian pesos with pocket calculators. Other stores sold jeans, electronics, handguns — .38 and .22 caliber pistols that were very expensive because they were "cold," untraceable. These were the sort of weapons that were used to kill tappers across the border, along with pistols stolen from the Brazilian army and from private homes. In my personal rating system, this place was definitely BGT, "below the grimness threshold," several notches down from Xapuri. "The difference is that Xapuri is a small part of something. This is a small part of nothing," said Julio Cesar.

Back in Xapuri, I had a good long talk with Chico's brother Zuza in his fenced, guarded compound. He told me that Euclides Távora's widow, Dona Neuza, was still alive and lived on a farm outside of town with another man, and that he'd be glad to take me there tomorrow. But when I arrived at the appointed time the next morning, Zuza said Dona Neuza had gone to Rio Branco, and he didn't know when she was coming back. This seemed suspect. It was unlikely that he would have already gone out there to set up the interview and come back; it wasn't the Brazilian way. It was more likely that Adalberto Calabrese had gotten to him, reminded him that J.N. Films owned his exclusive cooperation, and told him not to help me. Later that morning Adalberto chartered a plane to fly Zuza to the dentist in Rio Branco. He offered us a ride. Thanks, we said, but we're still having a great time in Xapuri and are not quite ready to leave. So our access was being blocked from several directions.

At the Civil Police station Detective Nilson explained where the case stood now. Each witness had to testify three times: first to the investigator (Nilson), again to the judge in front of the prosecutor to show that his original testimony wasn't coerced, and the third time before the jury. "I turned in my inquest to the judge on the twenty-third of January," he explained. "The second round of testimony has been completed, and the judge has decided that there is strong enough evidence for a jury trial."

What about Darci's retraction of his confession? I asked.

"That," he said, "changes nothing. We have the forensic findings, the reconstruction of the crime, the testimony of three neighbors, and of Genésio when he came back to the ranch — all of which point to him as the killer. Plus, there's a new bit of evidence: hair on a raincoat found at the *tocaia,* the ambush blind, matches Darci's."

What about Darli? I asked.

"We have another witness, a peon named Alício Oliveira Dias, who says that four days before the murder, Darli came out of the woods to the house and told Darci to set up the *tocaia.*"

So the *tocaia* wasn't manned for twenty days, then?

"It doesn't look that way," Nilson said. "Initially, Darci refused, but Darli said, I'm not asking you, I'm ordering you. It looks like you're not a man. So Darci chose Sérgio and Oloci to wait with him."

Where is Alício now? I said.

"He's under guard at a ranch at kilometer seventy-one on the road from Brasiléia to Assis Brasil."

What if one of the witnesses is killed before the trial? I asked.

"His early testimony will be valid because, since he is dead, he won't be able to claim that it was forced."

And Genésio is staying safely in Rio until the trial?

"Right. He was paid to stay at the Hotel Veneza to see what was happening. When we said we were going to charge him with informing for Darli he said, I'll tell everything."

What happened when you subpoenaed João Branco to explain the *anúncio* about the bomb in *O Rio Branco*?

"He denied any involvement. He said it referred to a tip that the paper had received that two hundred kilos of cocaine would be coming in through Cruzeiro do Sul. But nothing like that happened."

What about the new cars the Alveses are supposed to be tooling around in?

"There are none that I know of. If they had received money they would be foolish to buy new cars now."

What about the others?

Nilson took a stack of apricot folders out of his desk drawer. "We're investigating Gaston Mota as one of the masterminds and for murdering one of his workers, Antônio Gomes de Vasconcelos Neto, in 1987. We suspect him of drug and arms traffic, but whenever we bring somebody in to testify about that, he clams up."

Thumbing the bindings of the folders, he said, "These are the inquests of Benedito Rosas, Gentil Alves da Silva [Tilinho], José Brandão Assem [a councilman in Brasiléia], Luis Brandão Assem, José 'Josinho' de Brito, a.k.a. 'Bemvindo,' Antônio Guilherminho de Jesus [Antônio 'Piceno'], and Edimar Ferreira Galvão ['Querido']. Genésio and Alício have testified that these people held monthly or weekly meetings to inform João Branco of the plans to assassinate Chico and problems about clearing and property."

These are the ones who formed the so-called ranchers' ring, or ranchers' syndicate of crime, as it is sometimes called?

"Correct."

What about the biggies in Rio Branco, the so-called *cabeças?* Do you think you'll get to them?

"We are investigating links to Wanderlei Viana and Adalberto Aragão. So far we have nothing against Rubem Branquinho and Narciso Mendes except that they had friendships with the suspects. But a journalist at Radio Rio Branco and a real estate developer told us that Branquinho and Mendes were at the meetings where Chico's death was discussed, and their testimony confirms that of Genésio and Alício, so I think I'll get to the *cabeças,*" he said, smacking the folders. "If I do, I'll get ten. If I don't, I'll get five."

Have you received any threats?

"Only indirectly. People have told me, for instance, that two men are coming to Xapuri to kill me. But until now there hasn't been any attempt."

What about Odilon, Darli and Alvarino's nephew?

"He's been transferred to Rio Branco and is under investigation."

We saw Francisco de Assis the other day, I told Nilson. "I have to investigate him, but he's still my friend," he said. "It's very hard for me."

He showed me a grisly snapshot of bearded Zezão's naked, bullet-riddled body lying on the ground with a white towel over the loins. He looked like a thief who had just been taken down from the cross.

As I walked up to the Forum the blond traveling salesman of Dutch ancestry and his mulatto partner, Negão, with whom we'd stayed up the night before drinking and tapping out sambas in a store across the street from the Veneza, waved from their truck. Samba blared into the street from megadecibel speakers over the cab.

The windows of Judge Longhini's office were still blacked out. Luxuriating in its air-conditioned coolness, I lit up one of my Bahian cheroots, and as I drew its pungent smoke into my mouth I remembered the wonderful description of a loving couple in Nikolay Gogol's *Dead Souls:* "And all at once, for no apparent reason, he would put down his book and she her knitting, if she happened to have it at hand, and they would implant upon each other's lips a kiss so prolonged and languishing that a small cigar could easily have been smoked while it lasted." I offered the judge a cheroot from my box. He accepted and proffered one of his scrumptious candied, roasted Brazil nuts. As in our previous encounter, he yawned a lot between florid Latinate polysyllables, and I myself had more than the usual difficulty keeping up an incisive battery of questions. The whole feeling of our exchange amid walls of colorful law books was provincial nineteenth century, prerevolutionary, right out of Gogol.

"I mandated the three, Darli, Darci, and Serginho, for jury trial. Yesterday, lawyers for the accused entered a *recurso em sentido estrito,* which is like an appeal, to overturn my mandate. I was convinced of their guilt. The defense has other convictions. They, logically, as defenders, have to take the opposite position, and this is a way of gaining time. The Tribunal in Rio Branco is in recess this month. When it reconvenes it will either sustain or overrule the defense's maneuver. I took a quick look at their appeal, and my impression is that they will certainly uphold my decision."

I asked again about how the trial would be affected by the assassination of the star witnesses, and the judge allowed as how "if Genésio or Alício is killed this will impede their being heard. But they have already testified before me in the presence of their prosecutor and their lawyers, and that testimony will be admissible.

"The Tribunal will also have to decide whether the jury trial, for reasons of security and partiality, should take place here. So far, the trial will be in Xapuri. I don't know how long the Tribunal will take to rule on these matters, maybe fifteen or thirty days, but we are definitely on the last leg. If everything goes right the trial could begin as early as August. Chico's will be the first case to have been processed so quickly. I have around fifty murders to try, going back ten, twelve years, ten to fifteen of which have occurred recently."

How is the jury selected?

"Twenty-one candidates are chosen by lot from a pool of a hundred and eighty, and then reduced again by lot to seven. These seven must survive examination by both the defense and the prosecution."

What about the ranchers' ring?

"If Detective Nilson can prove the ranchers' ring, we can indict it. But he needs to be really smart to discover the people involved. For proof he needs documents, testimony. So far I have nothing in my hands that compromises any but the three defendants, nothing concrete. The commentary of the press is inadmissible hearsay and innuendo."

Have there been any more threats?

"In the beginning there were problems. My family received anonymous calls. 'Watch out. You and your three kids could die.' But we are being completely impartial, and thanks to our conduct, respect is coming. As an example of our impartiality we have charged Wanderlei and two councilmen with electoral fraud in the matter of twenty-four to twenty-five tons of diverted flood relief. If we were scared or submissive to executive power we wouldn't have touched this business.''

I said that I, too, was concerned about being impartial and was worried that the image of the ranchers that I had been getting and transmitting without question might have been distorted. It's very important, I said, for me to get their side of the story. You wouldn't happen to know a decent, reasonable, nonviolent rancher that I could talk to? I asked the judge.

"Yes," he said, and he gave me the name of a friend of his in Rio Branco, Assuero Doca Veronez.

I asked how he felt about the ranchers, what he thought about the future of Acre.

He replied, "This is a poor, miserable state. It has no industry or source of work. This is unjust. I think that providing incentives for cattle ranching is the most practical way of getting something going here. Rubber prices have slumped, and the whole tappers' culture wouldn't be able to exist if it weren't subsidized by government taxes on cheaper and better-quality rubber from Asia. Fifteen years ago you had to stand in line for meat here. Today Acre has the best meat in Brazil.''

The judge was impartial but conservative. He wanted what the majority, or perhaps only the elite, wanted. There is no such thing as absolute justice, I reflected; justice is only the expression of the will of society or, as Modesto da Silveira had argued, of those in control of society. The judge socialized with the ranchers. At the end of the day he went home and watched *Dallas*.

After I got back to the States there was very little further news about the trial. The *Gazeta* reported on October 22 that an anonymous note was slipped under Detective Nilson's door at the Veneza. It told about a conspiracy of the ranchers to kill Chico Mendes, how they had put up 20 million cruzados — around $30,000 — to eliminate him. A court strike was hampering the case. Nilson was finding it difficult to indict new suspects because of the lethargic pace of court proceedings. Key witnesses like the *vaqueiro* Alício had disappeared, split for other states, or turned up dead, like Zezão and Military Policeman R. Freito, whose description matched that of one of Aragão's bodyguards with whom Gaston Mota entered the Rio Branco Soccer Club four days before the murder. Gaston himself continued to evade the arm of the law. Supported by "important godfathers," he had been named highway superintendent of Rio Branco by Mayor Jorge Kalume, a former partner of his in a *seringal* in Xapuri. The lawyers of the defendants said that the longer they were able to put off the trial, the more international pressure would wane and the better their chances would be for acquittal. Darli had been leaving the *colônia penal* twice a week and spending the night with one of his three remaining common-law wives. His lawyer claimed that he had an ulcer, and indeed, he was becoming even more dangerously emaciated than he had been when I had seen him in January.

The following February — February 1990, after thirteen months in prison — Darli and his two sons escaped, as everyone had said they would. Somebody simply let them walk out the gate. But Darli was so weak that he had to be supported with his arms over either son's shoulders as the three of them made their getaway. And an hour and a half later the police picked them up and took them back to jail.

There was still no word about the trial. The appeal by the defendants' lawyer, Rubens Lopes Torres, offered a fantastic alternative to the prosecution's case. He maintained that the murder of Chico Mendes was a plot between agents of the CIA and a group of tappers in Xapuri. What their motive could have been he didn't go into, except that both wanted the forest to remain as is for different reasons. Torres didn't conceal that his objective was to buy time so that the trial would be postponed until the following year. He was also counting on "a certain tradition," according to which it is difficult to prove, in the Brazilian justice system, the coauthorship of a crime.

Next on my list was a certain Dr. Diane (I hadn't yet been able to learn her last name). She had rushed on her bicycle to attend Chico after he was shot. But she turned out to have left town because Xapuri, she said, was "turning into a *bangue-bangue*." She had three children and was worried about the "growing militancy of the local radicals" and the wrath of the *multidão*, the masses. "Chico Mendes held everything together," she said.

Ilzamar's brother Raimundo Gadelha drove us out to the cemetery in her black Ford Pampa LX pickup, racing through town, scattering people, dogs, and chickens right and left. In Brazil the man behind the wheel has the right-of-way. If the pedestrian is too old or slow, *já era,* he's history.

Raimundo disputed the forensic findings. He said he thought that Darci had fired from much closer, because the wash that Ilza had hung out was impossible to see through to shoot, because the house was full of gunpowder smoke, and because the wad from the shell made a big hole in the towel and entered Chico's body.

The cemetery had a low wall around it, and the smoke from a nearby brushfire scented the air as we paid our respects to Chico's remains. In the sarcophagus beside him lay his *companheiro* Ivair Igino, born 1962, killed June 18, 1988. Chico's own sarcophagus had not yet been finished. It was a simple, concrete box with a black wooden cross on it that said, "Here lie the mortal remains of F. Alves Mendes Filho." Several bricks with plastic flowers in their holes had been placed on it. Raimundo said the grave was going to get a first-class tile job "next week."

Julio Cesar was very moved, and he asked me to take a picture of him at the grave, which I did. He looked grimmer than I had ever seen him. Then we changed places and he took one of me, then one of me and Raimundo.

Again the tragedy hit home, the fact that overshadowed everything — this gentle man's needless death. I recalled the reaction to Chico's murder, quoted in the *Los Angeles Times,* of a public relations man in a firm that specialized in emotive language. Describing it as "the dark, brutal killing of an old-fashioned hero," he said, "You can feel it. You can smell it. You can see it in your mind, and it fills you with sorrow and dread."

And even guilt. Chico had been in the way of the American way of life.

Ilzamar took Julio Cesar to talk with Júlio Nicásio, twenty-three, the local PT leader. He seemed embittered. He told Julio Cesar that the PT had won several times in Xapuri. The judge had told him informally that they had gotten more votes, but because of election fraud — the opposition's stuffing the ballot box with the names of people who had died since the last election — the winners hadn't been allowed to take office.

"The extractivist model in its present mode is death," Júlio Nicásio said. "Our rubber is of the worst quality, and we can sell it only because of the pressures of international groups that want to save the forest. The tappers lace it with clay or pebbles or bits of wood, to make it heavier. Because of the deforestation, the rivers are drying at their sources and are getting lower and lower and becoming unnavigable.

"The contribution Chico made after his death is incalculable. It's three times more than if he had lived. For all of us it was very clear that he couldn't live long, because he would have been the next governor of Acre. The nineteenth of January was to have been the public launching of his candidacy. Lula for president, Chico for governor, and the assassins knew he would have won."

That night, as we ate dinner before the Veneza's TV, the news showed the American hostage Lieutenant Colonel William Higgins, hung by real Shiites.

Julio Cesar had made friends with the granddaughter of a merchant named Rui Sodré, who had been a friend of Euclides Távora's, and they had a date that night. As we walked through the streets to the Sodrés' house we could not help but observe how youthful the population of Xapuri was, like the population of Amazônia and of Brazil in general. This explained the comparative youth of most of Acre's leaders, how the governor and all of the *cabeças* were barely in their forties. Most of the major players in the tappers' movement were still only in their twenties. It explained the shift in the general taste in music, why Xapuri's discotheque, with its derivative, soft-rock *ye-ye,* was more popular with the television-nurtured younger generation than the traditional *forró* juke joint on the river.

Strolling in the pleasant evening coolness, we passed Xapuri's extremely modest mansion district. It consisted of a single white wedding-cake-like structure and a second large home in construction on the adjacent lot. The wedding cake, we were told, belonged to a *marajá,* a "maharajah," someone who sucks money from the government. We passed several Holy Roller evangelical churches, whose congregations were raising joyous hymns to the Lord through the open windows. We were beginning to get an idea of the spectrum of leisure activity in Xapuri: dominoes, snooker, getting drunk, disco, *forró,* television, praying, *politicando,* making kids, walking around and seeing what was happening. Of these, television won hands down. The Sodrés were completely mesmerized by a new *telenovela* that had just started to air.

Julio Cesar was good-looking, well dressed, and his eyes could melt a woman at fifty paces. But most important, *he was from Rio,* as his date's mother explained to the other visitors in the living room. A toddler named Sheldon, his mouth plugged with a pacifier, was rolling around on the floor.

The new *novela* was set in Rio in 1929, just after the crash of the American stock market had destroyed the Brazilian coffee trade. A ruined plantation owner had killed himself, leaving his wife and two handsome daughters destitute, and the three women had come to the city. One had fallen for a handsome *malandro,* a good-for-nothing pimp. You were sucked right in by the great music and the *novela*'s period *boêmia.* One of its subplots was the Lieutenants' Movement, led by Luis Carlos Prestes, the mentor of Euclides Távora and thus Chico's political grandfather.

Julio Cesar told me that he came from a prominent old family that had owned a lucrative notary public's office, in Rio, and it was around this time, after Getúlio Vargas seized the presidency, that it was impounded and the family was ruined. His beautiful mother had become a professor of American literature, passing on her love of letters to Julio Cesar before dying in her forties of cancer. His younger brother was a surgeon, though only twenty-three.

Everyone in the Sodrés' living room was so absorbed by the *novela* that hardly a word was exchanged. It reminded me of the sixties, when everyone sat around stoned, listening to the Rolling Stones. At last the show ended, and we all went off to a shindig in another part of town. We passed a Roth Dog stand (how ''hot dog'' has to be spelled in Portuguese to approximate its pronunciation in English) and came to a crowd in the street, consisting largely of teenage girls in white school blouses. In a small bar with loudspeakers blaring over the scene, couples were doing the fantastic, erotic new dance that was sweeping Amazônia, the rest of Brazil, and, with the speed with which hot new things travel around the world these days, had even reached Europe that summer, later becoming the rage in New York. It was called the *lambada,* or whiplash. The music is nothing special — lively three-chord tropical polka, slightly acclerated *forró* — but the moves of the dance were something else. The man inserted one leg between his partner's, as in the *maxixe* or tango, and the pressed couple writhed and wriggled and shimmied and shook. I grabbed a tall cinnamon schoolgirl who had just finished her night classes, and she, squeezing my thigh with hers until I could feel her wetness, gave me a taste of what it would be like to do it with her. Most of the pairs were girls dancing together, short tight skirts riding high above their knees, unmated teens locked in an unabashed, perfectly synchronized courtship display. It was incredibly sensual, and yet very innocent.

Julio Cesar ditched his date for an even more beautiful girl. I surveyed the hundreds of teenagers milling around the bar and thought how hundreds of thousands of other adolescents must be dancing the *lambada* tonight, all across the country, and how their half-formed aspirations were the unfathomable, unreadable future of Brazil, possibly glorious, possibly tragic.

We ran into the new prosecutor, Eliseu Buchmeier de Oliveira. He told us that the knockout at the next table was Darli's kid sister. The guy next to her, he said, came from Rio Branco and opened the first record shop in town. He seduced her, and Darli gave her two choices, marriage or death. "They will marry next week."

The lyrics of the *lambadas* were explicit: "My sex and my talent for the Brazilian people." Couples were making out passionately in the darkness. At the end of each tune, the dancers, after their intense session of intimacy, would separate without a word, like shy prom partners, the girls returning to one side of the crowd, the boys slinking into the shadows with shriveling hard-ons.

"The women here ripen quickly," Eliseu told us. "They are most desirable between fourteen and sixteen. By thirty nobody wants them. Xapuri is extremely liberal sexually. A lot of the gay hairdressers in Rio are from here."

Maybe that's the only solution for Acre's problems, I said to Julio Cesar: let time take care of them. In another generation the children of the ranchers and the tappers will have intermarried, and there will be no more conflict.

"Yes," he said, "but can Acre afford to wait that long? That's the question."

BACK TO THE CAPITAL

Eager to leave Xapuri before we were subjected to any more serious attacks, we caught a ride to Rio Branco with Eliseu. Julio Cesar, in his search for real Brazilian heroes, might have found another. Short and physically unprepossessing, but smart and principled, Eliseu was thirty-six and came from a poor family in Rio Grande do Sul — his maternal grandmother had been German — and had worked his way up through study and good scores on the highly competitive examinations for government positions. On the seat beside him was a loaded .38 revolver — "my own protection," he said. "But I've only been here a few days. They don't know me yet."

On the backseat sat a cardboard box containing the thousand-some pages that the Chico Mendes case had generated so far. "If anything happens to that," he said, "that's the end of the case."

Eliseu had just transferred from the state prosecutor's office in Cruzeiro do Sul to become the only prosecutor in any of the fourteen interior judicial districts, the fourth man to hold the post in the last seven months. "The Brazilian only remembers to cover himself when it's raining," he said. "If there had been a judge and a prosecutor here on a regular basis, none of these killings would have happened. The violence here is typical frontier violence. Often the aggressor is inebriated, to give himself courage."

Eliseu's taxonomy of homicide according to Brazilian law was slightly different from Judge Longhini's. There were two basic types, he explained, *culposo* and *doloso,* manslaughter and premeditated murder. I asked how easy it was for a jealous husband who killed a man who was fooling around with his wife to get off on a self-defense plea. Eliseu said, "That depends on the cultural level of the society where the case is being heard. It's quite easy in rural societies, less easy in big cities, but not impossible."

What about if you knock off someone you thought was fooling around with your wife but was completely innocent? I asked.

"Well, then your plea would be putative self-defense. You had reason to think that you were threatened. That could be an extenuating circumstance. You'd still do time, but how much would depend on how good a reason your lawyer convinced the jury you had. In general, all acts of unilateral violence are punishable. If someone insults you, you can't legally react with violence. It can only be returned in kind — in words, in other words — or what are known as the *equivalentes dos antepassados.*"

Julio Cesar told us about a famous murder in Niterói, the city across the bay from Rio de Janeiro where he lived. "For six months every day this guy kept coming into a bar and saying to the waiter, 'Hey, *cabeça chata* [flat head, a disparaging term for a *nordestino*], bring me a toothpick. *O Seu, paraibano safado,* you worthless lowlife from the state of Paraíba, where's my napkin? Step on it.' Finally the waiter couldn't stand it anymore. He brought everything the guy asked for, then he pulled a gun and blew him away.

"The lawyer for the defense began his opening remarks: 'O most illustrious, most meritorious, most excellent Judge Antônio de Pádua de Oliveira,' and then he addressed each of the jurors by his full name, preceded by three or four effusive honorific epithets, 'O most worthy, most eminent, most renowned Eleunida Carda Pereira Lima do Nascimento' — one by one, until finally the exasperated judge interrupted him and said, '*Como é?* How about it? Are you going to get to the arguments or not?'

"So the lawyer said, 'Imagine if an educated person like you gets impatient after only five minutes of slight irritation, how would a beast like my client feel after six months of extreme provocation?' and the defendant was acquitted."

Eliseu said, "For property and sentimental reasons people will do anything. Law is central because it is involved in the most sensitive aspects of the human being."

We stopped for refreshment at a little roadside watering place where, the bartender told us, there had been a cowardly murder the previous Sunday. A different bartender and a *cachaçado,* a patron drunk on *cachaça,* had gotten into an argument. The patron placed his gun on the bar, and when he wasn't looking a friend of the bartender's removed the bullets. Then the bartender produced a gun and said, "You're armed, well, use it," and the patron picked up his gun, aimed at the bartender, and squeezed the trigger. Then the bartender fired his gun and killed the guy.

We drove on and were treated to the sight of a greater yellow-headed vulture, larger and more majestic than the dime-a-dozen *urubus,* rising up from a road kill. A new species for my life list.

"In the *seringueiro* movement there are idealists and opportunists," Eliseu said. "This is natural." And he told us that two days before the murder of Chico Mendes, his roommate in Cruzeiro do Sul, a veterinary doctor from Paraná who was tied to the ranchers, got off the phone with someone in Rio Branco and told him that before Christmas a bomb was going to drop. "Each rancher is chipping in."

"Did you ever read *Bury My Heart at Wounded Knee?*" he asked. "There's a beautiful speech that one of the Sioux chiefs makes about the meaning of the forest."

We passed an abandoned agricultural colony that had been started by the previous administration. "At the end they were all growing marijuana," Eliseu said. Then the Playboy Motel, where the Rio Branco elite went for illicit trysts. "The presidential suite has rotating walls," he told us. "On each wall there is a beautiful scene — snow peaks, waterfalls."

As we waited in the car while Eliseu delivered the Chico Mendes case to the adjunct of the Tribunal, Julio Cesar's suggestible metaphorical imagination started working, and he said, "You know how we should be thinking about this whole situation? You have to open the hood and look at the engine, the machine, and understand how each piece works. Some parts are clean, some are dirty. Some make noise, others don't make a sound. But each has its special purpose, its own agenda, and all work for the engine. Maybe we should suspend our preconceptions about who is a good guy and who is a bad guy until we understand the system better."

THE END OF THE ROAD

The Inácio Palace Hotel's restaurant, with its air-conditioning and pink tablecloths, seemed now like a swank, midtown restaurant. We ordered *suburim,* the succulent leopard-spotted catfish of Amazônia and, crossing our fingers that it wasn't contaminated with mercury, discussed our plan of action.

The best idea seemed to split up. Julio Cesar was still somewhat under the weather, as much from culture shock and a psychosomatic reaction to too much outdoors as from illness, and I, having come all the way to the Amazon, wanted to get deeper into the forest, to go to the end of the road, to Cruzeiro do Sul, about four hundred miles to the northwest, and see what I could find out about the plans to pave and extend BR-364 from there. I also was interested in visiting some of the Indians of the Upper Juruá Valley. The Katukina and the Campa still take *daime* (which they have their own names for); the Poyanawa had been broken of the practice a long time ago by missionaries. I wanted to try to find a guy named Antônio Macedo, who sounded as if he could be the next Chico Mendes. No one I'd met in Xapuri seemed to have the stuff. The tappers in Xapuri, despite the continuing danger to their leaders, were comparatively well off. They were organized. They had thrown off the yoke of the *patrão seringalista,* unlike their counterparts on the Upper Juruá, who are still in inextricable hock to their bosses. This Macedo apparently had a boat and was running goods to the tappers and selling them at fair prices, undercutting the grotesquely inflated monopoly of the *seringalistas.* He was also helping the Indians demarcate their land and fighting for their rights. He was, in fact, more of an *indigenista,* a champion of the Indians, than he was of the tappers. He was doing the work, not fighting for the leadership of the movement or sitting around and arguing about movie rights.

While I was up there checking things out, we decided, Julio Cesar would stay in Rio Branco and try to charm his way into the elite. We went over the names of a couple of dozen people, including Assuero Doca Veronez, Judge Longhini's friend, who might be able to provide entrée.

I had learned about Macedo from an article he'd written for the *Gazeta,* relating how he had founded an agro-extractive organization for three hundred *seringueiros* on the Rio Tejo, way up the Upper Juruá, through which they could sell their rubber themselves. He had introduced *empates,* but there most of the tappers were still paying rent and were still in hopeless hock to the *seringalista.*

I went over to CIMI, the church's organization for the Indians, and asked a lay missionary girl, What's the story on this Macedo guy?

"He's the new troublemaker who's doing the work of Chico," she said, "and his life isn't worth . . ." She blew out an imaginary candle.

Where can I find him?

"At the *Gazeta* or *O Rio Branco.*"

The latter seemed odd, considering the paper's politics, but after trying Sílvio first, who said he hadn't seen Macedo in a while, I called *O Rio Branco* and asked where I could find Antônio Macedo.

A suspicious voice said, "Who wants to know?"

I explained that I was a writer from New York doing a book on the "development of Acre."

"Hold on," the voice said. "He's in a meeting."

The director of the paper came on and tried to find out as much as possible about me. I could hear his mind working. Alex, from New York, writing on the "development of Acre," wants to talk to the "*indigenista.*" He said, "No, we don't have any *indigenista* here. We have a guy named Antônio Macedo who works setting type. You can find your Macedo at the *Gazeta,*" and he gave me the *Gazeta*'s number.

Damn. That was pretty tricky, I thought: lie about Macedo in order to find out everything he can about me. If he'd seen my *Vanity Fair* piece and put two and two together, I could be in trouble. At least he'll think I'm out to lunch.

Leaving Julio Cesar in the world of lies and dirty dealing, nursing his cold in his silk pajamas, I took a cab to the airport. If I'm not back in a week, I said (it was Saturday), call out the National Guard.

I waited for three hours, among tearful reunions and departures, for the air-taxi flight to fall into place. There was an article in the *Gazeta* about two fires lifting huge clouds of smoke in Xapuri that had been picked up by the NOAA satellite. Their coordinates had been telexed to Paulo Beninca of IBAMA's Rio Branco headquarters, who located them on the property of one Eliezer Teixeira. They were *capoeira,* grass fires, rather than fires of felled, dried slash.

I thought about Julio Cesar's metaphor of the machine, how some parts are clean, some are dirty, some make noise, others go about their business undetected. Some don't do what they're supposed to do. Some misfire out of *preguiça* (sloth), cooptation — because they've been bought. Some play multiple roles, are chameleons, opportunistic double or triple agents. Nor are the roles fixed. Shifting temporary coalitions between parts are constantly forming and coming apart.

But above all it must be seen that neither this machine nor any of the parts of which it is the sum is in perfect working order. This is not a Cadillac, but a beat-up tropical jalopy ready to throw a rod. There is no truth, no justice, no money, no stable anything in this system. No rock, mon, I thought, recalling the Jimmy Cliff song: "You gonna run to de rock for rescue, but there will be no rock." This was a war zone, a nightmare of complete instability. The key concepts for understanding this machine are *inoperância, jeitinho, jogo da cintura.*

A little box on the *Gazeta*'s front page said that twenty years ago to this day, Neil Armstrong and Edwin Aldrin stepped out of Apollo 11 onto the moon. Many older Acreans still don't believe that this landing ever took place, because of their extreme religiosity and because at that time there was no television in the state. Some of the young are willing to accept that it happened, but the majority of Acreans believe that if anyone ought to step on the moon, it should be Saint George.

As we lift off in the six-seat Piper, the clouds are as scarce as the cattle in the cleared land below. There are only half a dozen wisps in the whole sky. The only signs of fire are a few furtive whiskey-colored plumes of smoke in the distance. The expected conflagration has not materialized. At least Chico Mendes didn't die for nothing. The murder seems to have bought the forest some time. By this time last year thousands of square miles in the valley were on fire. Smoke blanketed much of it; the Paraguayans complained about the sooty pall that drifted over from the east. The airports of Porto Velho and Rio Branco were shut for a month.

But now the ranchers' hands are tied. The world is watching them. The European and American press have flocked to the Amazon and are just waiting for someone to strike a match. This is the year of the rain forest. Twenty-three thousand miles above, the satellites are hovering. One of them, LANDSAT, can zero in on a patch of the forest the size of a tennis court. The ranchers are crying foul; when the North Americans were taming their frontier and rising to greatness a hundred years ago, they didn't have the twentieth century spying on them.

Before long we have left the desolation around Rio Branco and are following highway BR-364, a thin red accent in an ocean of green, heading straight to the vanishing point. It was extended in the late seventies from Rio Branco to the other cities along Acre's backbone: Sena Madureira, Feijó, Tarauacá, and Cruzeiro do Sul. But unpaved and at the mercy of torrential rains, it has since become little more than an overgrown track. We can see at each of the numerous creeks and rivers it crosses an oil-drum raft on which vehicles must be driven and poled to the opposite bank. Except for the years when the highway is open for a month — and this doesn't look like it's going to be one of them — the only way to get to these four forgotten cities is by river, which takes weeks, or by air taxi, which costs several times more than most of their inhabitants make in a month. So it isn't surprising that almost everybody in Acre is dying for the road to be paved and continued to Pucallpa,

Peru, only a few hundred kilometers from Cruzeiro do Sul. Even the rubber tappers are in favor of it, as long as their rights to the forest it cuts through are respected (which, if the past is any indication, they won't be).

The only encouraging part of this sad, sordid, and complicated story, I realize as we fly for hours over the sea of trees frothing out to the horizon in every direction, is that most of Acre's forest is still there. "*Mata virgem, por enquanto,*" the pilot beside me yells over the engine's drone. "Virgin forest, for now."

The trees eventually fill an area greater than the United States west of the Mississippi, equivalent to fifteen Frances (or is it thirteen?). But one of the Frances is already gone.

As I look down at them I recall what the naturalist and engineer Euclides da Cunha, arriving in Acre in 1904 with a joint Brazilian-Peruvian expedition to reconnoiter the Upper Purus River, wrote of the great endless forest: "Man, there, is still an impertinent intrusion. He came without being awaited or wanted, when nature was still furnishing her vast luxurious living room. And he found an opulent disorder." To him it seemed "the last chapter of Genesis, still being written."

Acre hasn't had a good rain in weeks, and the green ocean below is drab and dusty. Many of the tallest trees, the emergents, have shed their leaves and are skeletal gray. Here and there *ipês* are in flower. The *ipê* is in the begonia family, and the color of its large, showy flowers varies from tree to tree. Most of the ones below are yellow, but I saw a few blazing scarlet outside of Xapuri a few days ago. To the south, in Mato Grosso, the *ipês* are mostly lavender. I wonder why.

Most of the trees we're flying over, I realize, still don't have names. The botanist Ghillean Prance surveyed a hectare of the Amazon forest outside Manaus and found in it 183 different species of trees whose trunks were too big around to enclose with his hands. On every hectare one or two of the trees may be new to science.

And so it is with the other forms of life. New fish are turning up all the time in the ichthyologists' nets. The entomologists especially have their work cut out: millions of species await identification. In Acre alone, one of Amazônia's smaller states, there are some twenty Indian villages, belonging to five separate linguistic groups, which no modern person has entered. One is just a hundred miles from Xapuri.

We have hopped from Sena Madureira to Feijó to Tarauacá. For a long time the only break in the canopy has been the occasional small clearing of a *colocação,* where a family of tappers, still undisturbed in the depths of the forest, has its huts and gardens.

The pilot points down to a *maloca,* the communal great house of the Katukina Indians. BR-364 was run right through the Katukina's homeland. They are in transition: they still do their dances and drink *daime,* which puts them in touch with the deities of the forest. The women are betrothed before birth and begin sexual relations with their husbands at the age of six, Eliseu Buchmeier, the prosecutor, told me. Their vaginas are rubbed with stinging nettles so they will swell to adequate size. But already the men hunt with shotguns; the only bows they make are for sale in the airports of the big cities in the South. The Katukina have entered what might be called the early replica stage. The bows are still good bows.

Incredibly convoluted tributaries of the Juruá meander through the trees below. I can make out the outlines of cast-off loops that have eutrophicated back into terra firma and been recolonized by trees. They look like — I jot down several possibilities in my notebook — lozenges, eyebrows, fingernail parings.

That so much of Acre's forest remains can be directly attributed to the efforts of Chico Mendes. How much more he would have saved if he'd been allowed to live is a question that's maybe too painful to think about.

At last the Juruá itself appears, with dark, naked bodies waving excitedly from its sandbars, then a small conurbation — Cruzeiro do Sul. There's a big fire off to the right. No, it's an ashen curtain of rain sifting down from the underbelly of cumulus congestus, a local cloud blessing.

We landed. I got out with the two passengers who had boarded at the last stop. One was a ruthless- and cunning-looking man in his fifties, Darli's type, wearing jeans, cowboy boots, and a straw cowboy hat — a local big shot, clearly a bad guy. The other was his thug, a burly flunky who carried his briefcase, laughed at his jokes, and agreed with everything he said.

The big shot's car wasn't there. He tried the phone, but it was out of order, and he sat at the airport bar fuming and drinking Bare, a delicious local soft drink brewed from the beans of the native *guaraná* tree, which contain twice the caffeine in coffee beans.

There was no alternative except for the *capo* and his thug and me to split a cab into town. Thirty bucks for five miles — frontier prices. The road was fresh tarmac. There were no holes, an achievement of the previous mayor, the taxi man told me. The asphalt came up on barges from Manaus, a month downriver.

What about the road to Rio Branco? I asked. When is that going to be paved?

"*Asfalto,*" the big shot said. "I've been hearing that word in the mouth of the *políticos* since I was a kid."

We reached the city. It had lots of little hills dotted with colorfully painted shacks, like a primitive.

What do you do around here? I asked my companion.

"Oh, nothing much," he said, winking to his flunky. "A little *seringal,* a little business.*"

The thug understood that he was meant to laugh, and he did.

We drove through a *chuva do sol,* a rain falling in sunlight, a beautiful, Magritte-like phenomenon more common in the tropics, and at last pulled in to the squalid main square. Taking leave of my companions, I walked up the stairs to the lobby of the Plínio, which Eliseu had said was the only hotel in town that wasn't BGT. The girls, he said, would be waiting at the Bar do Bigode next door.

I flagged a cab and said, Take me to the Rural Workers' Union. The cabbie's name was Antônio. We talked about the road. "If they pave it, it will be all over for this Amazonian forest," Antônio said. And yet he was in favor of it. "They won't even open the road this year because the rains have been so bad. Last year Flaviano and a busload of *políticos* came here promising *asfalto,* but up to now nothing has happened," he said, with disappointment in his voice. I remembered the metaphorical importance of roads in Brazil, how they represent tangible accomplishment. If the roads have holes, the mayor is doing nothing, but if they are given a fresh coat of asphalt, the mayor is performing, not putting the public funds into his pocket. And once the roads are in, everything follows. The modern world rushes in, local customs, ecosystems, and immune systems break down in short order.

Antônio told me that the last mayor, who had paved the road to the airport, had been a good one, "but the present political situation is one of friction between the mayor and the deputy mayor. When the mayor is traveling the deputy mayor undoes what he has done."

How's the road to Boqueirão da Esperança? I asked, referring to the village on the Peruvian border that is separated from Pucallpa by a hundred miles or so of barely explored wilderness.

"It's just a footpath," Antônio said.

Antônio had grown up in the *seringal,* and he regarded Chico's murder as a horrible tragedy. "The population was upset by his death because he was poor [which supports Modesto da Silveira's reading of its impact]. I think that this *machismo,* this enthusiasm of the *seringalista,* is going to end."

Antônio limped badly because one of his legs was shriveled. "I was putting out a fire when I was seventeen," he explained. "It started to rain and I caught a fever. The fever did something to my bones and made me a cripple."

He knew Antônio Macedo well and had this to say: "I think Macedo, with his will to help the people, is in trouble. One time, while he was taking goods in his boat to the tappers, he was arrested. Another time, one of the big *empresários* in town punched him in the face."

Where's he taking the goods? I asked.

"To the tappers on the Amônia, the Tejo, the Dourado, the Arara, the Pajé, and the Gamelhão rivers.

"When my father died, I came to the city," Antônio went on. "My brothers are still at the Seringal São João, on the Arara River, nine days by boat from here.

"Thank God it's still calm around here. There's less violence than there is in Xapuri. The *fazendeiros* have bought the land, but they haven't started clearing it yet."

A woman in the shack behind the little union hall told us that Macedo was with the Poyanawa, in the municipality of Manso Lima. I remembered that the director of CIMI in Rio Branco had said you could drive right into their village. "The Poyanawa are completely destructured," he had told me. "There are a hundred and sixty of them at most, and they are very mixed. Every one has a little *cachaça* bar in his house."

(Later, when I got home, I looked them up in the *Handbook of South American Indians,* but they aren't listed under that name. They seem to be Katukinan, rather than Panoan or Arauacan.)

I asked Antônio if he could take me to them, and he said, "*Vamos.*" Not long after leaving the little city of Manso Lima, we crossed a rickety bridge of logs and boards laid this way and that over a dark, tannin-steeped creek that flowed out of a swampy grove of *buriti* palms. Then we passed through a natural wet prairie, and after that the soil became pure white sand that was capable only of sustaining a lower, more xeric type of forest, rich in orchids and bromeliads, known as *caatinga* — an unusual vegetation type in Amazônia.

Finally we came to a sign that said "FUNAI (the National Indian Foundation) — Prohibited to Strangers." We opened the gate and drove up onto an open, grassy ridge with *caboclo*-style huts up on pilings strung out along it. Antônio drove up to one of them and, limping up to the door, clapped his hands to announce our arrival. An old woman appeared in the window and directed us to the hut where Macedo was staying.

We found him in the kitchen mixing *caipirinhas*. He was a young-looking thirty-seven-year-old, with curly, dirty-blond hair, a fleshy, sensual mouth, and blue eyes behind round, metal-rimmed glasses. He thought that one of his grandfathers, a *gaúcho* from Rio Grande do Sul, might have been Italian. Sitting at the table with him were three *mameluca* (Indian-with-mestizo) beauties — very short, buxom, with straight black hair, a slightly different racial type, several clicks more Indian than the girls in Xapuri. Many of the Poyanawa, Macedo told me, look like the local *caboclos,* but their sense of themselves is still distinct. I offered a cheroot to an old man squatting in the corner, and he accepted it eagerly.

Macedo said that he was born on the Colocação Bagaceira, on the Seringal Cumaru, between Tarauacá and Feijó. There and on subsequent *seringais* he came into close contact with the local Caxinauá Indians, sharing with them the life of debt peons, learning their language. "I've been taking *daime* since the age of thirteen," he said. "I take it to acquire astral knowledge, to ask things from this higher force that people call God. It is a door to self-awareness. When I am tired, it restores me. When I am sick, it cures me. It won't permit errors."

Macedo's talk was not that of a rude backwoods tapper. He is completely modern and worldly, I thought. The Indians are eating out of his hand. They look at him adoringly. This is obviously not the first time he has told the story of his life. He understands that my presence represents an important PR opportunity and has slipped deftly into the interview mode.

"One day two *patrões* came to get the rent from my father," he went on. "I was only thirteen and was not allowed to talk in front of elders, but I intervened and said, 'My father works here. He does everything himself, and his only help is me. The land is of God. Why do you want to demand rent?' One of the *patrões* pushed me away and said, 'Shut up, I'm talking to your father.' After that I put it into my head to fight for the rights of the people of the forest.

"I studied and became the only person in my family who could read, and then I gave lessons to my six sisters. My father sold a cow to get me a book called *Brazilian Pages,* which told the story of the discovery and colonial occupation of Brazil and its division into hereditary *capitanias.* When I was fourteen and fifteen I worked as a stevedore carrying rubber to boats and earning money to buy more books. When I was eighteen I was recruited by the army. At that time I understood nothing about the evil of the military. I had ruined teeth. The army pulled them out and gave me false teeth." He took them out and showed me. "I was trained in Cruzeiro do Sul as a mechanic of heavy machinery.

"In 1979 FUNAI arrived in Acre, and I started to work at the post they had established for the Apuriná. I quickly realized that instead of being an organ to help the Indians guarantee their rights, it monopolized their rights. But the state director was a good guy. He saw that I wanted to help the Indians and trained me to be an *indigenista.* From 1976 to 1980 I started the first Indian cooperative. The colonels who ran FUNAI said, You're putting things in the heads of Indians, not helping them develop. In 1977, a reserve for a hundred-some Apuriná Indians — five kilometers by forty — was demarcated. But there was no anthropological study of the territory that they had been occupying from time immemorial, which was much larger. The fishing and hunting grounds, the cemetery, and the Brazil nut trees were all out of the area. I asked for these to be annexed, and that started a big fight. The Military and Federal Police and the *jagunços* [gunmen of the ranchers] came in. In 1980 I went to Brasília with nine Indians to plead for the rights of the Apuriná and was fired for insubordination.

"But then the Indians of many nations — Xavante, Kayapó, Xaminaua, Borora, Craú, Mauxineri, Apuriná, Caxinaua, Bakairí — proposed a total change of FUNAI, to get rid of the colonels and put in themselves and competent *indigenistas* of their choice. I joined in the protest. I helped break the windows of the Ministry of the Interior. Then

I returned to Acre and worked without salary or affiliation, eating sweet manioc with the Indians and continuing the struggle.

"In 1981, the Federal Police picked me up in Rio Branco. I was held for five days with no rights. My request to make a phone call was denied, and I was threatened with torture. After I was released I walked through the forest for a meeting with Raimundo de Barros in Xapuri. It was one of the first meetings to set up cooperatives for the rubber tappers. I was so persecuted by the police that I couldn't go by way of the road. To them I was a Communist, a species of conspirator against the country.

"The first time I met Chico was in 1981. He didn't strike me at the time as very expressive. He had been councilman but had been expelled because he wouldn't go along with the bad deeds of the municipal chamber. Not until 1985 did we get to know each other. At congresses in Rio Branco we sat down and talked for hours about how we could realize our hope of bettering the level of life of the workers. We talked about the Alliance of the People of the Forest. Both the Indians and the tappers have the same life. Both are suffering from the *patrões*.

"I found him brilliant. Although he was not schooled, he knew how to hear you. He had human sensibility on a large scale. He knew how to give you a light and how to ask for one. He had many *jôgos da cintura,* artful dodges. Chico was going to take *daime* with me and talk about liberating the tappers on the Tejo, but then he was killed. Now the thing is not as I knew it.

"During the eighties I began the dangerous work of organizing the tappers on the Upper Juruá," Macedo continued. "Once a *seringalista* was about to attack me with scissors, but an Apurinã policeman who was with me shot him in the arm. I was beaten up by Orlei Cameli, one of the biggest *empresários* in Cruzeiro do Sul, who is into timber, rubber, gold, land speculation, and cocaine. I heard from a guy in the rubber bosses' union that there was an agreement among the *seringalistas,* politicians, and *traficantes,* the drug traffickers. Everybody had chipped in fifty thousand cruzados, and *pistoleiros* from the South were being flown in to get me. The big *empresários'* fortunes all come from drug traffic. The drugs come over the border by boat. All the rivers of the Upper Juruá are born in Peru."

Osmarino Amâncio would say in an interview by Alexander Cockburn and Susanna Hecht for the *Nation:* "No doubt Macedo — who organizes people not to pay rent — is going to die."

There were twenty thousand tappers in the Juruá Valley, Macedo told me, and only eighty *seringalistas*. So why can't the tappers get political control? I asked.

"Because the politicians are on the side of the *seringalistas*," Macedo said. "Being on the side of the tappers doesn't pay because many of the tappers don't have identity cards, let alone voter registration cards."

Macedo explained his grand scheme for the tappers on the Tejo River: a one-million-hectare extractive reserve to be surrounded by four Indian reserves that are already in place. The land, he figured, would cost a million dollars. "A million for a million," he said. "What do you think? That's not such a bad deal. The land now belongs to an Arab group from São Paulo. If we got it we could stop the *traficantes*."

Milton Nascimento, the great Brazilian singer, who had gotten interested in Macedo's work, was coming in two weeks to go up the Tejo with him.

As the old guy puffing on my cheroot and I talked, I began to piece together the history of his ravaged people. "In 1913, Colonel Manso Lima came and converted us. My mother gave me my name, Camilo. I have no Indian name."

Do you know any words in Poyanawa?

"Only the names of the animals. Guys like you — whites — we call *cariú*."

I wondered if that was a corruption of Tupi-Guarani, the lingua franca that all Indians in the Amazon spoke until it was replaced by Portuguese. The Tupi-Guarani word for "white" is *cararuá*.

"When two people meet, my people say *Chauwiki*, I have already come," Camilo went on. "The other says *Mautá*, Come on in. When he is leaving, the *cariú* says *Até logo*, See you later. We say *Cha kai ke*, I am already going, and the other says, You can go."

Two parrots in a cage hung from the ceiling. What language do they speak? I asked.

"Portuguese," Camilo said.

It didn't come out until later that until 1983 the entire tribe lived in debt peonage, owing their souls to a rubber boss. It was Macedo who came and freed them from their sad situation, turning the *seringal* into an Indian reserve. That was why to the Poyanawa he was like a king, and their gratitude to him was unending.

The sky went green between the rose clouds, and there was a beautiful sunset. Macedo took me to the church, where a service was in progress. The ridge resounded with the passionate strains of women belting out hymns. The chief, the *cacique,* whose name was Mário, backed them up. He played good country-western church guitar. It was a long service, in lieu of a Saturday night party. The congregation went through dozens of hymns. I did a guest performance of "How Great Thou Art." The pastor, beaming with the goodness inside him, filled with the *alegria* of the Holy Spirit like a black preacher, gave a sermon about the first murder. "We must arm ourselves not with guns and machetes but with the word of God. Walk in the light with Him." He preached about the untrustworthiness of "material friends" and related how years ago his best drinking buddy had stabbed him seven times.

After that we went to the schoolhouse. The girls all had on party dresses and lipstick and disco bags. The little desks were moved against the walls, and as *lambadas* gushed from a ghetto blaster two girls would start shyly two-stepping and a boy would cut in. The *lambadas* of the clinging couples were far more inhibited than the ones in Xapuri. After each number the girls would break away and flee to one side of the room.

"One time I came here and I found a Shining Path guy teaching martial arts to the young men," Macedo told me. "They'd been recruiting the Indians on the frontier, killing their parents if they objected."

We walked in the bright light of a full moon. Somewhere in the darkness a *bacurau* called — one of the strange, primitive members of the crepuscular and nocturnal nighthawk-nightjar group, known as bullbats in the American South, of which twenty-seven species are identified in Rodolphe Meyer de Schauensee's *Birds of South America.*

This *pião* bush (the bellyache nettle-spurge, *Jatropha gossypifolia*), Macedo told me, is *pra tirar panema:* you rub the juice of its leaves on you to get rid of bad luck in hunting.

In the morning we went to pay our respects to the chief's father, Mompa, a very old man who had trouble holding his neck up, one of the last of the tribe who still had an Indian name. He was squatting on the floor against the slat wall, his face etched with bars of sunlight. I gently squeezed his liver-spotted hand. "Mompa is the last who knows and cares," Macedo told me. "They have already lost their crafts. In another generation, or two at most, they will have been completely absorbed into the national society."

"Have you come alone?" Mompa asked me.

Yes, to learn, I said.

"What will you give me?" he asked. I took out the box of cheroots from my bag.

"No," he said, "I'm not interested."

"He's just pulling your leg," Macedo said. "Go ahead and ask him some questions."

What was it like before the *cariú* came? I asked.

"We lived on the Igarapé Sete do Setembro, the Paraná do Moura, also known as the Paraná de Viuva, the Igarapé Bom Jardim, and the Rio Môa."

How did the nation begin?

"A *capemba de paxiubão*, the frond of a big *paxiúba* palm tree, fell to the ground. Rain fell on it and submerged it in a little pool with leaves of *caxinguba*, and it was mixed in the water with *rau* [a medicinal plant whose leaves are used to treat headache], and from the mixture in this pool there arose after a time the people of the Upper Juruá: the Poyanawa, the Katukina, the Caxinaua, the Arara, the Red People. The chiefs of these people started to sing to the force that created them for the lands to be made high."

Why? I interrupted. To avoid flood?

"Yes. Colonel Manso Lima dragged us out of the forest in chains in 1913," Mompa continued. This would have been at the climax of the rubber boom. "In 1940 the captives of the colonel tried to go back to their old abandoned village and found that the land had risen greatly. They couldn't get to the place. There was too much bamboo. Thorns impeded them. The place was called Tekomachi."

Do you have any stories about old floods? I asked. I was very interested in this. At one point — there is debate about when exactly; some argue as recently as several thousand years ago, within human memory, in other words — much of the valley was flooded by a vast inland sea. All the tribes have a flood myth, similar to the biblical one, in which humankind is purged of its wicked ways and all but the few good people are drowned. Often the race is reconstructed from clay statues into which life is breathed. (In another myth motif, women used to run the show, until the deluge, after which the men became dominant.) The main point of divergence among the myths is in what beasts survived. If the projections of global warming are right, industrial society will be similarly purged, punished for the arrogance of thinking that it could conquer nature — how can you conquer what surrounds and in the deepest sense also constitutes your being? — and the Amazon Valley will be flooded once again. Particularly devastating floods strike the Amazon once or twice a century.

"No, I know of no such stories," Mompa said, but his wife, Francisca, whose Indian name was Parouri, a tiny woman whose eyes gleamed in their deep wrinkled sockets, had been listening in the kitchen, and she said, "Baloney, he just doesn't remember. He told me about old floods many times."

His memory refreshed, Mompa launched into his story. "Once there was a reunion of all the Indians. The rivers were so low their feet sank in the sand. An old lady was poking holes in the sand as she crossed the riverbed. She hit a mound of sand that was covered with butterflies and disturbed a beast, and he came out, wanting to kill. His name was Paracunua. He was like a big lizard except that he had two saws in front. He sang, 'I want to *rolar gente,* to fall on people.' Some of the Indians withdrew to one bank, and the others withdrew to the other. They tried to build a bridge to get back together, but the beast kept knocking it down. Thus the nations separated.

"Then the river rose and a big flood scattered the people even farther. It didn't kill them but it stranded them. They were afraid of the flood and moved to high lands."

I asked if he knew any stories about women who lived without men, i.e., Amazons — another common motif.

Mompa said no, but when a woman married a man who turned out to be lazy, her father would take her away and give her to someone else. Marriages were decided before birth. As in the Katukinan custom, at the age of six the girl already started living with her husband. The husband raised her. He hunted and fished for her to please her father. She slept on his breast.

"How old were they when they started to have relations?" Macedo asked.

"Already at the age of six. The husband had the right to all her sisters, too, if they let him.

"To balance all the young girls who were going to old men, the old women went to young men. A man could have many wives, so that when one was pregnant, he could get another so the tribe would multiply more rapidly. The *tuxaua*, the chief, had eight. He would lay them on the ground and take them all at once. At that time there was no *cachaça*, only the vine. The people drank the wine of the vine for health, to have force. They sang and danced for three or four days in a row, without stopping.''

Mompa said he never took the vine and didn't remember its name. Macedo told me that the Caxinaua still take it and tell the following story about how they got into it. One day a handsome young man who was hunting for meat was kidnapped by the *cobra grande,* the mythical huge snake, who took him to a beautiful house in the river. The snake became a beautiful woman, and they lived happily together for several years. But one day a small fish came and said to the man, Your people miss you terribly and want you to come home. They want me to take you back to them. The *cobra grande* allowed him to go on condition that he tell nobody about his experience. But he told his family, as a result of which he died. And from his tomb grew the vine. Everybody made tea from the vine and drank it to incorporate he who had died. Thus it started. ''The Campa Indians on the Rio Amônia call it *camarambi*,'' Macedo said. ''They sing with their hands outstretched to the sky. With the vine you can see a tree talking to you, telling you it needs air. The vine is an affirmation of everything that exists.''

In the evening Antônio came back for me in his taxi, and I gave Macedo and the three Poyanawa girls a lift into Cruzeiro do Sul. They all lived in a house on one of the little hilltops. The place was like a sixties crash pad for Indians and tappers, except that the refrigerator was empty and there was no periodic check from somebody's parents to keep the scene going. In lieu of chairs or sofas, there were hammocks. An Indian woman who had just had a baby was asleep in one. One tapper, who stood on the porch for hours, gazing silently at the city, told me that he had felt a fever coming on and had come from six days up the river to get it treated; if he had waited and it got worse, it would be too late. Everybody looked up to Macedo. He was their only champion.

As I went around talking to various segments of Cruzeiro do Sul society about Macedo and about BR-364, it was the same thing all over again. The same lines between classes and philosophies were clearly drawn, and Macedo was the local Chico. Everybody knew Macedo. His niche in the system was defined. He was a part of the ecology.

The manager of the local office of Varig-Cruzeiro Airlines, whose twice-weekly flights from Manaus stopped in Cruzeiro do Sul on their way to Rio Branco, was sweating and trembling through a malaria attack. "Kubitschek promised the road thirty years ago. All the conditions were there for its completion, until the ecologists kicked up a fuss.

"Look at him — an ecologist." Macedo had just walked in to book a flight to Rio Branco for a meeting of the National Council of Rubber Tappers.

Is he good or bad? I asked.

"He's living, like you. The rubber tapper is already superseded. The tendency here is that rubber is at an end because the communications media have brought civilization to the *seringueiros*. The *seringueiros* only put up with their life when they didn't know what the rest of the world was like. This is logical. The army recruits from the *seringueiros,* and once they are in the army, they don't come back."

The church here was represented by conservative Germans. There would be no overturning of the social pyramid here. I walked up the knoll surmounted by their comfortable compound and was shown into the office of Bishop Luis (Ludwig) Herbst. "Not another story on Chico Mendes," he said, clasping his hands in prayer and looking up to heaven. He spoke Portuguese with a heavy German accent.

"Our mission is long-term spreading of the Gospel. We're not for fast change. We want change to come based on the principles of evangelism, not on violence or Marxist ideology. People are stirring up the tappers, and I don't know if it will help them. As long as they lived from what they grew and raised, and from the riches of the forest, it was a human life. But now there's terrible inflation. The rubber prices are fixed, while the price of goods keeps going up for the poor guys.

"Macedo? He's an agitator. I have a suspicion that he's using the tappers to realize his own political ambition. I've been here a few years — since 'fifty-two — long enough to know what Brazilians have in the back of their mind.

"The road? I think 364 will bring good, but not only good. You know, where there is light, there is shadow. There will undoubtedly be an invasion as there was in Rondônia. Speculators — our senator and who knows who else — have already bought the land along it from here to Peru. The land itself is nothing. You would think that this virgin forest that has been here for millennia would have built up a crust, but it hasn't. After the second planting nothing comes."

The office of Orlei Cameli, the *empresário* who had beaten up Macedo, was on the second floor of an expensive new building. He was a big, beefy, sullen man of Lebanese descent, dripping with gold chains, chain-smoking Marlboros, frequently pounding his fist on his conference table. "Our business has stopped because we're prohibited from working here by you American ecologists. We had a thriving lumber company that we're going to have to close down because of IBAMA. Fifty percent of the municipality was declared a national park on the nineteenth of June.

"My brother and I were born and raised here, but we've been condemned to live in misery because here there is nothing but misery. We give seven hundred jobs. We have a rubber factory, but rubber is dying. The maximum rubber yield in the municipality is three thousand tons, but this year there will only be twelve hundred tons because of the creation of extractive reserves, which don't work. The reserves are turned over to marginals, *corruptos,* thieves. The biggest thief is Antônio Macedo. He left FUNAI because he was stealing the money of the Indians.

"We were tappers who got where we are today by hard work. I'm totally in favor of capitalism and private enterprise. The proof of this is the misery of the Socialist countries. Countries only develop because of initiative. In the United States you work and have your rights, which is not the case here. The bureaucracy is so developed, you give up. If you buy a *seringal* of twenty thousand hectares, only two thousand are documented. To get title to the rest you have to fight the bureaucracy.

"We're trying to figure out a way to liquidate our holdings and leave. We're laying off our workers. I'm not going to wait any longer. We're not in favor of devastation but of decent zoning that will preserve the development of the state. Many sectors of the state are not productive. They should be the parks. Here we have almost two thousand children a year dying of malaria, hepatitis, dysentery. That's not right. You should see the way the *ribeirinhos,* the people along the rivers, are living. It pisses me off when these people cry out for human rights, and kids are dying and there's no education. Everybody who is born has the right to have a dignified life. These are human rights."

I asked him what he thought about the story in that day's paper about an Italian group's offer to buy the 24,000 square kilometers of forest on the Rio Tejo, where 1,500 families of tappers lived, and turn it into an extractive reserve. The idea was for each of the 32,000 members of the Italian Order of Biologists to kick in 30,000 lira (about $25).

"The Italians want to buy the most fertile area identified by RADAM. The lands of the Tejo belong to an Arab group in São Paulo, Santana Agropastoral Empreendimentos. Macedo is trying to shake down the government and the Inter-American Development Bank for money for extractive reserves. He is living off this. He never did anything in his life except for this. It's the same type of thing the PT, the Moscow branch of the Brazilian Communist Party, and the Pastoral Commission for the Land are into, just like Chico Mendes. It's they who sponsored the death of Chico Mendes and are living off it and fighting over the money it is bringing in. They don't even respect the memory of the poor guy.''

A friend dropped in with a present — a plastic bag full of river turtle eggs (which it is against the law to dig up) — and placed them on the table.

"I have three ranches totaling twenty-three thousand hectares, eleven thousand head of cattle, a road-building and landscaping company, but most of the land was just expropriated for the park, thirteen thousand hectares. I was paid with a document called a *letra da dívida agrária*, a letter of agrarian debt, which I may as well take and rip up. If I tried to sell it, I wouldn't be able to get twenty percent of its face value.

"Only fifteen thousand hectares of the land is pasture, the rest is forest. I was planning to clear half of it over the next ten years. But now I'm going to kill my cattle and split.''

What do you think of the UDR?

"I would like it here. Who produces the grain and the food? It is an entity that has good and bad. This bit that they are assassins is shit.

"If the international community is really worried about saving the Amazon they should send each family two or three thousand dollars a year, and we won't touch a leaf or raise a head of cattle. But see that it really reaches us and doesn't end up in the hands of this Macedo. I already hit him. He came here to ridicule me. In my own office. He's a *maconheiro*, he only lives drugged. If somebody came to your house or place of work to provoke and demoralize you, what would you do?

"There are lots of funny things in this region. There's an American woman on the Rio Amônia who runs around naked and only wants to have sexual relations with Indians [Macedo later said he must have meant Tania, a nineteen-year-old English girl who was letting her hair down]. They say Macedo took a boat full of French and Americans up the river. They stopped at the house of some *ribeirinhos*. Everybody stripped and went swimming nude in the river. Imagine the lack of respect!

"I will be an ecologist, too, but only in Rio, drinking champagne and eating caviar. And from there I will say how to save Amazônia."

An hour later I was sitting in the mayor's office being harangued by a big, loud councilwoman named Maria Nazaré — "We are living here abandoned. You go into the forest and you'll see things that will break your heart. Why do we want these reserves when we are already a reserve? I don't accept any of these impositions from abroad" — when in came Senator Aloysio Bezerra, the main defender of BR-364 and champion of pan-Amazonian friendship, with an attaché-case-bearing entourage. The congress in Brasília was in recess, and Bezerra had come back for a quick sweep of his constituency. Everyone went around the room giving each other the ritual hug and hearty backslaps. The senator asked me to join him for lunch, and I fell in with the entourage.

Everywhere he went, petitioners were waiting for him. An old lady in front of the Plínio had a simple request: money. Mothers would push their nubile daughters at him and he would whisper in their ears, "See me later." I have no idea what the mothers were after.

Over lunch — bouillabaisse of *tucunaré,* another of Amazônia's piscatory delights — Bezerra told me about his remarkable rise to the national political arena from humble tapping origins. Born in Manso Lima, he was the first son of a tapper to reach the federal congress, he told me. "Mother taught me in the house. I studied with the German padres. I was the best student. Then again in *ginásio* [secondary school] in Cruzeiro do Sul I was the best student. I won a scholarship to a *ginásio* in Rio."

All this was interrupted as he chewed carefully, sorting through mouthfuls of *tucunaré* with his tongue, easing bones out through his lips into his fingers and placing them on the edge of his bowl. This man loved to talk, especially about himself: self-esteem was not a problem. He was a classic demagogue. "He's just a puffed-up windbag," Antônio the taxi man would tell me, "he promises but never delivers." His best line at lunch that day — "Peru is starving with its nose in the butter" — surprised even him. He laughed. A good one.

"Upon graduation from the University of Brasília in 1969 with degrees in law, business administration, and macroeconomics, I went on to the Sorbonne to study international law and relations. Then I studied the United Nations to learn its structure. In 'seventy-eight I came to Acre. The PMDB was then the opposition party." Clodovis Boff mentions a rally in front of the governor's palace at which Chico Mendes and Aloysio Bezerra were among the speakers. So he was once a liberal.

"Already in 'sixty-nine, before I went to Paris, I had a plan for South American integration. But it was there, in discussions at the Centro de Altos Estudos Latino Americanos, that my plan of integration matured. BR-364 was completed to Cruzeiro do Sul in 1974 as part of PIN [the National Integration Program]. I was the author of the idea to continue it. Fernando Belaúnde Terry, the president of Peru, dreamed of a Carretera Marginal de la Selva, a marginal highway of the jungle, that would be a catalyst of occupation of the Peruvian Amazon. But to this day only a few sections have been completed.

"In 1983 I participated in the Macro-Regional Frontier Project of Integration with Peru and Bolivia. I came from Paris with an integrationist vision perfectly defined from a technical point of view. The second meeting in 1984 broke all barriers of communication," he continued, smacking his lips and sluicing out another bone. "I took many trips to Peru.

"Last year the governor and President Sarney and I met to discuss the completion of the road." Bezerra did not mention that Sarney reportedly gave him a radio station in return for his endorsing Sarney's reelection. "The conclusions of our viability study are scheduled for release on the twentieth of July. The road will be here in three to five years, I can assure you," he said. And then he used a common Brazilian expression, "*Vai ter que dar certo*" (It has to be a sure thing).

"The road is not how it appears to many ecologists, as bad ecology. It will be the first road with the protection of agro-ecological zoning in the world, I think. It will be a penetration harmonious with nature. Techniques of tiered agriculture that mimic the forest will be implanted, and the cattle ranching will be limited to the needs of the local population. The wood will be exploited sustainably. In one five-thousand-hectare lot near here the value of commercial timber, not counting mahogany and cherry trees, was recently calculated at fourteen million dollars. The invasion will have to obey rigorous agro-ecological zoning."

He punctuated the rap with a swallow of beer poured by one of his half-asleep yes-men.

"The road could develop Peru and relieve it of terrorism, and strengthen democracy. Otherwise, the Shining Path could become like Pol Pot. Bush should study it more closely from this angle. The fewer the roads, the more guerrillas like it."

He was starting to get bored, sated. He got up and went over to two pretty girls waiting outside the restaurant. He told them, "I'll be with you in a moment," came back energized, and continued. "Bush should realize that the integration of Amazônia is going to take place whether he likes it or not, and it would be better if it didn't happen under an anti-American banner. The Japanese government has not abandoned the project. It could be financed by private Japanese companies tied to the government. We'd like to see the IDB get involved. Bush's opposition to the road unified all the sectors that are in favor of it. I have the approval of the senate to complete the road independent of external resources, if necessary. All it would take for a paved road from Rio Branco to Pucallpa is three hundred and twenty million dollars."

In Don Stap's new book, *A Parrot Without a Name: The Search for the Last Unknown Birds on Earth,* he describes the wilderness between Pucallpa and the Brazilian border as "one of the largest unexplored areas on earth, approximately 300,000 square miles of wilderness — an area three times larger than Wyoming. No one, except a few local people, has been to these mountains," an anomalous, isolated cluster of low-rising peaks, known as the Cordillera Divisor, which rise along the border. It was in these mountains that the American ornithologist John O'Neill discovered, in 1963, a new bird, the orange-throated tanager, defying the conventional wisdom that there were no more new bird species to be found. Who knows what other unknown animals are in there? Macedo had been telling me about a hot springs that gushed out of one of the mountains, and was only three days by boat. This was the area that Bezerra was so keen on putting the road through.

The senator continued to sell himself as a concerned environmentalist. "The *seringueiro* is the greatest ecologist of all because he's been living in Amazônia for more than a century and hasn't destroyed more than one percent. But now he's living in misery. Extractivism does not provide a dignified life. I've been pushing for the cultivation of *dendê* [the African oil palm], which is four times more productive than soy."

He was making political capital off his early relationship with Chico. "Chico and I worked together in three elections. We had the same political line. He was an honest and dignified man, and a fighter. The ecology of Chico was not that of the university. It was not idealistic or intellectual, it was realistic. The *seringueiro* lives from the forest, so logically, obviously, he can't take it down.

"Above all, he was a union leader. I requested a homage to him in the senate. I am distributing to the schoolchildren of Acre fifty thousand notebooks with a photo of him and his wife and kids on the cover."

What do you think of Macedo?

"Macedo has Indian protectionist ideas that are out of touch with the rest of society," he said, but when the two of them met at the airport the following day, they greeted each other like old friends, embracing and slapping each other's back.

I asked if he had any personal interest in the completion of the road. His answer was well phrased. "I have no personal interest, near the road or anywhere in the country. My line of business is political actuation. There is not one hectare *in my name.*"

This reminded me of a wonderful answer by the new president of Paraguay, General Andrés Rodríguez, who built up a personal fortune in the early seventies through his friendship with Auguste Ricord, the heroin kingpin of the French Connection: "You can be sure that at no moment will it be possible to demonstrate that I had any connection to these things."

Antônio drove me out to the huge *fazenda* of the previous mayor, João Soares de Figuereido, known to everybody as Toto. He had sold the city the land for the airport and paved the road for it. We were almost hit by a weaving car, whose driver Antônio identified as José, the director of the funeral home. "He's drunk again. He's already rolled three cars."

We passed beneath the huge bole of a former forest monarch, held up by two others, from which a sign was hanging: "Don't Envy Me, Because I'm Not Rich. I Just Work Hard." Toto had arrived in Acre in 1968 as an agronomist, and it was rumored that his spectacular rise was fueled by the smuggling of Peruvian coke. His driveway passed through several miles of rolling pasture in which sleek black water buffalo, imported from Africa, were grazing. "They used to attack strange cars," Antônio, who had worked for Toto a couple of years earlier, told me.

He described him and his wife, Maria das Vitorias, as good people. "They do what they say they'll do. They deliver." Macedo had said Toto was "a great guy face-to-face, but in practice another story."

At last we came to a huge mansion on a bluff overlooking a sweeping bend of the river Môa. It was totally *Dallas*. Maria das Vitorias greeted us and took us out for *cafèzinhos* on the veranda by the pool, where there were enough wicker chairs and baroque banquettes to seat hundreds of guests. Across the river the forest was still untouched, and you could see clear to Peru. "Others have three times what we do," Maria das Vitorias assured me.

She launched into the usual harangue. "You think it's right that we pay the onus of not being able to develop, so Americans can breathe our oxygen?" She said that she had known Chico "well. He was an idealistic man and he was used. The wife is letting herself be exploited. But here there are not these problems. The people are very serene. Everybody is *louco* for the road, including the *seringueiros*. But I don't think we will see it for at least ten years. No country is going to give us the road, to be the good father for Brazil, for nothing."

Late afternoon fell on the splendid *fazenda*. A flock of white ducks trundled down the bluff to the pond used for Toto's private hydroelectric turbine. The buffalo started moving down to the river.

"Toto came with nothing," his wife told me, "and he paved the road. Nothing new has been done here since. The present mayor doesn't even know how to talk."

MEANWHILE, BACK AT THE POOL

I would have loved to go up the Juruá for a couple of weeks or months, visit the Campa on the Rio Amônia, the tappers on the Tejo, poke around in the Cordillera Divisor, but time was of the essence, so I flew back to Rio Branco on Tuesday.

I found Julio Cesar fully recovered, in shades and a skimpy striped bathing suit, immersed in one of his paperback novels and soaking up the rays beside the Pinheiro Palace's pool. *Tudo bem?* I said. What's happening?

"*Tudo bom,*" he said. "I wasn't expecting you back so soon."

There's this whole new level of ranchers that I wasn't aware of, I
reported. It's only the low-level *pistoleiros* who pattern themselves after
bangue-bangue bad men. The really big *fazendeiros* are on a complete
Dallas trip. What did you come up with?

"I've got good news," he said. "I had a long talk on the phone with
this Assuero guy, and he's anxious to meet both of us for dinner — at
the airport restaurant, with João Branco.

"Assuero is not a liberal, he's right in with the top echelon of the
ranchers. He says the tappers have done a complete number on João
Branco. He swears Branco had nothing to do with Chico's murder, that
he's just this good-hearted life of the party who wouldn't hurt a fly.

"A lot of stuff goes down right here at the pool. I picked up a number
of intriguing subplots," he said. "There's this former padre who lives
in Rome and is high in the Italian Freemasons and seems to be involved
in Bolivian cocaine. The hotels are full of Japanese."

Indeed, the poolside fauna was quite interesting. There was a young
Japanese man in one chaise longue who was as inscrutable as a fish. I
had a momentary fantasy that there was webbing between his toes. Two
big, beefy white guys with crew cuts, obviously Americans, were reading paperback novels at opposite ends of the pool and pretending not to
know each other. One got up and walked by the other, who gave a slight
twitch of recognition.

God, I said to Julio Cesar, how embarrassing. They're so obvious.
They've got to be U.S. operatives of some sort — CIA or, more
likely, DEA.

"It does look like something's about to go down," Julio Cesar said.
"I heard one of them talking on the phone in English in the lobby. 'We
can't do anything until he gets here.' "

That evening we returned to the pool bar at cocktail hour. There was
a natural history workshop at the university, and a number of old friends
of mine who were devoting their lives to small, carefully defined fragments of the Amazon's hugely complex biology were there — the botanist Doug Dailey of the New York Botanical Garden, the British
primatologist Anthony Rylands, who had married a Brazilian woman
since I'd last seen him and become a professor of zoology at the University of Minas Gerais. "There are more marmosets there than in Amazônia," he explained. "And more infrastructure for raising a family."

He was a delightful, turned-on fellow, well on his way to being completely Brazilianized. "If I'd stayed in England," he told me, "I'd be watching some flycatcher twitching its tail."

The ménage also included a brilliant but arrogant ornithologist whom I had nicknamed the insufferable birder. Not one of my favorite people, he was the sort of fellow one occasionally runs into in my line of work, who says things like, "How can I put this in terms easy enough for you to understand?" In fact, he was the type specimen for a monograph on the field biology of the field biologist that I planned to write someday describing a new subspecies, *Academico biologus var. insufferabilis.*

The two crew-cut operatives were also there, trying to fit in but sticking out like sore thumbs. I asked one what he was doing in Acre. "Oh, we're paleontologists," he said. "We've been coming here for a couple of years. There are some amazing things in Acre — shark's teeth in the deltaic soil on the hills." He said that he and his partner had been cruising the rivers and plucking fossils out of slumped banks. Even I could see that this was not very scientific.

I asked him what he thought of the work of Hilgard O'Reilly Sternberg. He confessed, a bit nervously, that he had never heard of him. Sternberg is the dean of Amazonian geographers, and his work on the hydrodynamics of the Amazon system is state of the art. It was impossible that any paleontologist working in the valley would not have known who he was.

How about the controversial theories of Anna Roosevelt?

Again my interlocutor drew a blank.

She's been finding some really old pottery around Santarém, I said.

"Where's that?" he asked.

Give me a break, I thought. Santarém is only the third-largest city in Brazilian Amazônia.

Well, how about Dr. John Lawn? I asked. The two "paleontologists" exchanged a quick look. Their cover was blown. Lawn was the head of the Drug Enforcement Agency, and an old school buddy of mine.

I definitely did not want to be seen associating with these guys. The Brazilians might think *I* was CIA or something. The role of the CIA in Amazônia is one of the modern myth motifs. The Summer Institute of Linguistics, an American Bible Belt missionary group, was thrown out of the country on suspicion of being a CIA front. Daniel Ludwig was supposed to be training a CIA army on his Connecticut-sized spread on the Jarí. Of course, the Latin American paranoia about the CIA is not completely unjustified. A botanist friend of mine, who has since died of AIDS, once told me that his graduate work on *Erythroxylon,* the genus to which the coca plant belongs, was supported by an outfit in Iquitos, Peru, called the Amazon Drug Company. He later learned that he and one other botanist were being used as the legitimate front for a CIA operation in the jungle that was training an army to go up against Che Guevara.

The theory of CIA involvement in the murder of Chico Mendes has several versions. The "Japanese version," which I heard from one of the ranchers, is that "the CIA fomented it. They took him to the United States and gave him medals so he came back with a leadership that he had never had. From then on Toyota trucks and Belgian arms started pouring into the movement. The CIA didn't pull the trigger, but they fomented the climate for his murder. Their motive was to save the forest so the Japanese wouldn't get it."

Another, less sophisticated theory, which might be called the debt-for-nature theory: Chico was a *mafioso* of the CIA whose goal was to get the debt paid with the resources of the forest. The military, according to this source, was worried that Chico was a CIA agent, because he was getting Ford Foundation money. But Mauro Sposito was worried that he was a Communist for the same reason.

DANCING WITH THE RANCHERS

The farmer and the cowman should be friends,
Oh, the farmer and the cowman should be friends,
One man likes to push a plough,
The other likes to chase a cow,
But that's no reason why they cain't be friends.

Territory folks should stick together,
Territory folks should all be pals.
Cowboys dance with the farmers' daughters,
Farmers dance with the ranchers' gals.
                                    — *Oklahoma!*

It was my turn to be bushed. The quick trip to Cruzeiro do Sul had been too intense. It had left me debilitated and neurasthenic. All I wanted to do was stay in my air-conditioned room at the Inácio watching the new *novela, Kananga do Japão,* to withdraw into that far more appealing world. I recognized that part of the problem was cultural. After a month or so in the tropics my organism, even after all these years, starts rejecting its strange surroundings. There is a systems overload that just has to be worked through. But there was also something physical going on. The next day I began to have violent, terrible-smelling diarrhea every half an hour or so. I was really laid out. I started myself on a round of tetracycline and went to a pharmacy and bought Cebion, effervescent Alka Seltzer–like vitamin C tablets, and a box of ampules of a yellow liquid called Necroliver, which activates the stressed liver. Maybe it was all the *caipirinhas* I'd drunk with Macedo on Saturday night, followed by the *caititu,* the delicious but strong ribs of wild white-collared peccary we'd had, or maybe it was something that went up my nose when we went swimming in the Igarapé that afternoon.

In the middle of *Kananga,* an announcement came over the TV: "Sister Samara has just arrived in our city. She reads the fortune of whatever person, gets rid of the vice of drunkenness, and the evil eye that doesn't let your business prosper." Then the fried fawn commercial, part of a new government campaign to discourage forest fires, came on. It showed a newborn fawn, only a couple of days old, sniffing around and gamboling on long, gangly legs in a beautiful green forest. In the next frame, the charred body of the young fawn lay in the black, smoldering wreckage of the gutted woodland.

By the next morning I was OK.

Julio Cesar came in to see how I was doing and to report a second long telephone conversation with Assuero Veronez. He was thirty-eight, literally a *paulista,* from a family of ranchers in São Paulo, and was one of the owners of the only meat-packing plant in the state. He was also a veterinarian and a staunch supporter of the UDR. He had previously been responsible for rural credit at the Banco do Brasil, which was how Judge Longhini knew him.

" 'There is a habit of depicting Acre as a vision of *muito conflito,* ' " Julio Cesar quoted Assuero as saying, reading from his notes on the conversation. " 'But that's not the way I see it. The politics of the rural property owners has always been one of accord. They bought the *se-*

ringais and called in the tappers to discuss how much they thought they should be indemnified for having to leave their land. In many cases each family was given the deed to fifty hectares. Chico Mendes participated in many of these transfers. One proprietor near Xapuri made out more than two hundred such deeds, all of which Chico participated in. But then the church entered the situation and complicated and radicalized it, and wouldn't permit the tappers to agree to these settlements. There was a case near Xapuri where a proprietor proposed five hundred hectares and a house for each family, plus a school and a health post, and the church wouldn't allow it.' "

This sounds to me like a cowboy story, I said to Julio Cesar.

" 'Chico Mendes was an idol fabricated by the church and the German Green Party,' " the interview continued. " 'For us he was never a problem. He was an excellent negotiator and go-between, and we weren't into violence and radicalization. Chico died because he was induced to pick a fight with Darli Alves, who everybody knew was a violent man. All this involvement of the UDR is a political orchestration. Darli is not a member of the organization. We created it here to defend our class, which had no representation. After Chico was murdered, his *companheiros* thought, Now we have a very valuable corpse and let's transform him into a martyr. There's no use looking for the involvement of the UDR, because it doesn't exist. Not one shred of evidence points to it. For us the death of Chico was a bad business. We already knew the repercussions that it would bring, that it would make things worse for us.

" 'After Chico's death, the UDR became stigmatized. Many members denied that they belonged to the organization, but I never did. João Branco became the symbol of the enemy, and he had to leave the state for fear of his life. But he had nothing to do with it.' "

"So then I asked him," Julio Cesar told me — he was beginning to get into being a reporter — "what Chico's death had changed for them.

" 'We thought it would make things worse, that we wouldn't be able to clear any more forest. But now we're beginning to feel that we'll benefit a lot from it. We're learning that we can do less harm to the environment and make more profit. The consciousness of the rational exploitation of the forest is rising now, but we still don't have the technology to make it work. Nobody should burn a mahogany tree, but it happens because there's no way to profitably harvest it. There's no market for it because there are no sawmills because there's no electric energy.

" 'I don't think there is a better area in the world for cattle than Acre. You leave Acre and go down to São Paulo and all you see is dead, bone-dry pasture. While here the pasture is green year-round. Only Acre keeps producing fat cattle throughout the year. But we don't have any way to get the meat out of here, because there's no road.

" 'Today we have a cold-storage slaughterhouse, and last year we shipped twelve thousand head to Rondônia. Cattle raising is always the pioneering activity that opens regions, because all you have to do is clear and burn and throw around some grass seeds from a plane. It's the cheapest way to do an economic activity in a recently tamed area. In time, grain producers come and push the cattle raisers farther out on the frontier. Once the trunks have been removed, it's easy for mechanized agriculture to move in. But today growing things is still antieconomic in our state.' "

Julio Cesar asked him about BR-364.

" 'The road to Peru is fundamental, and it will be completed without doubt. It's a question of national honor. It will permit the export of grains, primarily from central-eastern Brazil, to Asian markets, and will open the backbone of Acre, with all its isolated municipalities.

" 'Look at São Paulo. It was all forest, now it's all production. And this doesn't make it an ecological disaster. Disaster for Acre is *miséria*. Amazônia is sixty percent of Brazil, of which thirty-six percent is flood-plain. Acre, which is twelve percent of Amazônia, has the greatest percentage of fertile land. No one fights for an ugly woman or for bad land. By law, only fifty percent of it can be cleared. In fact, less than that, because half of the state is protected state land, so maybe only twenty-five percent is developable. What are we supposed to do? Leave it all as a sanctuary? Brazil can't afford the luxury of leaving Amazônia un-touched. We are not such a rich country.

" 'We are living through a passionate, almost hysterical phase, but this whole thing will become clear in time, including the murder of Chico. I know the whole Alves family. They came to me for bank loans. I know Gaston and Rubem Branquinho. João Branco is a personal friend of mine. He's an exceptional guy. He wouldn't hurt a fly. He has two ranches out of town and has never been to Darli's ranch. The campaign against him is political assassination. He's a partner of Narciso Mendes's. They're trying to get him so they can get Narciso. That's why the *Gazeta* is touting him as a *cabeça*.' ''

Well done, Julio Cesar, I said.

THE AIRPORT RESTAURANT

That evening at about ten o'clock, Assuero picked us up at the Inácio. He seemed to be a perfectly decent, presentable, civilized guy, the sort of a guy you'd have no qualms about including in your Thursday golf group. He wore glasses and appeared to be sensitive, a man with a conscience — "How do you think I feel, knowing that this meal is a *salário mínimo?*" he said that night — not a crude, redneck macho boor. The problem, his moral dilemma, was that he had fallen in with the wrong crowd. He was culturally a killer.

With him was his wife, Marisa, a throaty-voiced, vivacious vixen with smoking black eyes, a fiery, funny, sensuous Brazilian beauty chicly done out in bracelets and beads that looked suspiciously like ivory. They were a very attractive couple, always joking and laughing. Except for the language difference, they would have fit right in with many people I knew back home. I learned later that they were, in fact, first cousins. She was the daughter of Benedito Tavares de Couto, the legendary rancher who burned the church in Dourados, Mato Grosso do Sul, and pioneered the destruction of Acre.

We drove out to the airport, which was deserted. It was a little creepy, this restaurant in the middle of nowhere, a perfect place for conspiracy, for Chico to have been sentenced to death.

We parked, and Assuero led us to an unobtrusive door, which he opened. Inside, a party was in progress. A couple of dozen men were sitting at the table with their beautiful, elegant wives, who looked like they had stepped right out of a *novela,* out of the pages of *Town and Country* or its Brazilian counterpart, *Casa da Fazenda.* They were all sitting there carving up thick, juicy steaks, drinking the best malt scotch, and screaming with delight at each other's jokes.

"Good meat, good women," Julio Cesar muttered. "The wives have to be good fuckers to compete with all the others."

We sat with Neto, Assuero and Marisa's blond, redneck, impeccably

Aryan cousin, who was a lawyer for the UDR. "Shake the hand that pulled the trigger," he said, and everyone erupted in laughter. There was nothing sensitive about him. He was one of the defenders of the idea that Darli should be released. "We're a small class," he said, "the noble elite of *fazendeiros*. We are the real heroes, the new pioneers, not Chico Mendes." Then he took a big slug of scotch and shouted so the whole room could hear, "We're gonna make a big one. I don't need to say the date, because the satellite will tell. We'll throw up so much smoke the satellite won't be able to see what's going on."

"What's the maintenance day of the satellite?" a *paulista* at one of the other tables asked. "That's when we oughta do it."

Neto's wife was the classic bored suburban matron. She dabbled in *daime* and herbal medicine. Marisa was warming up to the spirit of the soirée. "You killed your Indians, and ours aren't even beautiful," she told me. "They're squat and fat and half-naked. We used to live across the street from FUNAI, and I would watch the *piranhas*, the little Indian whores, sitting there delousing each other."

"Chico was their Sitting Bull," Assuero said. "In the agony of their decadence they created a crystalline leader. We all killed him in our mind, but it was really the PT who killed Chico Mendes. They forced him to go after Darli. They got him all these awards. They set him up."

The door opened and everyone looked up to see who it was. A man walked in, a real man, a man's man, who walked tall and looked you in the eye. Facially, he resembled a tough Conway Twitty, but his demeanor was more like James Coburn's. The entrance was like that of the lead man in a *bangue-bangue* bursting into the saloon. A wave of heightened deferential anticipation swept over the room. He sat at our table and, gripping my hand firmly, said in a low, deep voice, like a braying bull, "Branco." The waiter quickly brought him his customary liter of scotch, a glass, and a bucket of ice.

After the usual pleasantries had been exchanged we got down to business. Branco — the word means "white" in Portuguese and was the perfect name, I suddenly realized, for the leader of the big, beefy white guys from the South — told a different version of events from the ones we'd been hearing. "Six months before Chico was killed, I said, We are not idiots, to give these guys a martyr. Chico was a tremendous innocent. He was well intentioned and he did a great job for the tappers, transforming them into property owners.

"At the bottom of everything is the battle between Flaviano and Narciso," he said, which we had heard from several people and had been coming to believe ourselves. "I betrayed Flaviano in the last mayoral election," he explained. "At the last moment I withdrew my support of his candidate, so he took revenge on me by implicating me in the murder through the *Gazeta*. The death of Chico was gasoline on the fire."

He mused, "It was the greenhouse effect that brought notoriety to Chico.

"There are people worried about our commercial advance. Brazil is becoming the second-biggest producer of orange juice, soybeans, and tropical wood. If we started to mine the minerals in Amazônia we would quickly pay off our debt. If we got the right technology, we could decimate the entire world paper market. So these people killed Chico to keep us down."

The women at the next table were talking too much, disturbing Branco's train of thought, not giving the proper respect. In a sudden, violent motion, frightening in its authority, he slammed his fist on the table, and the women clammed up. That was a revealing moment, I said to Julio Cesar later. He's definitely not this lovable character who wouldn't hurt a fly, as Assuero described him.

"We're suffering from this festival of disinformation," he went on. "There's a lot of disinvestment. Investors are pulling out of the state. My daughter comes home from school and says, 'Papa, is it true that you put the forest to fire and that we're all going to die because of what you're doing?' Do you think I want to leave my ranch a desert for my daughter or for a bunch of miserable wretches to invade?

"We have only one point in our favor: the truth."

Silence. Approval. Branco has the floor.

"In your constitution, people are innocent until they're proven guilty, but I have to prove that I am innocent.

"The environmental movement is a wave, and when the wave draws back, the sand is uncovered."

What a phrasemaker, I thought.

"You Americans, I believe, have a saying that a woman under twenty-one is protected by law, and over seventy-five, by nature. Two thirds of Amazônia is protected by nature, and two great Americans, Ford and Ludwig, fell on their faces trying to get something going here."

I asked about his relationship with Darli.

"I saw Darli once, in my office," he said.

But what about all the testimony that puts you at the ranch? I asked.

"I never go to my own ranch, which is only fourteen kilometers from here, so why do you think I'd want to spend the weekend all the way at Darli's?"

So why did Genésio say you were there?

"Because somebody put words in his mouth to sell papers. I can't sue him, because he's a minor, or the *Jornal do Brasil*'s reporter [Zuenir Ventura], because he was supposedly reproducing an interview."

What about Darli's photo album?

"Where is this album? I'd give ten thousand dollars to see it."

The hot car?

"New cars these days cool down in fifteen minutes."

The international bomb?

"One of our reporters investigating a political matter, the transfer of federal money to the state, that was badly spent and not accounted for."

But that would have been a national, not an international bomb, pal.

The waiter brought another platter of thick steaks.

"Do you know why Xapuri is the heart of the violence in Acre?" he asked. "Because the church and the PT are most powerful there. We have one of the most progressive bishops here in Acre. But the most violent place in all Brazil is the Bico do Papagaio, and who's the bishop there? Dom Pedro Casaldáliga, a Jesuit who throws one class against the other."

Back in my room in the Inácio, I poured nightcaps for Julio Cesar and me from the *frigobar*. What if Branco was telling the truth? I asked. What if his involvement in the murder was pure fabrication, disinformation?

But I had a gut feeling that Branco was in it to his eyeballs. Maybe it wasn't constitutional, but he didn't succeed in convincing me of his innocence. I kept thinking about that violent moment when he slammed his fist on the table.

Julio Cesar told me about the new state of Tocantins, which had been created by the new constitution from the upper half of Goiás. "The Xingu Park [the most important Indian reserve] is there. The new capital is called Pasargada, after a poem about an imaginary paradise with that name, by Manuel Bandeira. It's going to be a huge city with two wings, like Brasília. Everything is being brought in by plane. The governor is

UDR, and the UDR has total control of the state, i.e., there's no law but their law. It has the largest fluvial island on earth, the Ilha do Bananal. Already the Indians and the small farmers on it are being kicked out by big *fazendeiros*.

"That's something, isn't it? Split a state so you can have your own area of influence, your own filet mignon."

The next morning I got the lowdown on the Brazilian rubber industry from Adonai Santos, the last superintendent of SUDEVEA, the Superintendency for the Development of Rubber, which was subsumed into IBAMA. Malaysian rubber is two and a half times cheaper than Brazilian, and the Brazilian rubber industry wouldn't survive without the import tax imposed on it since the war. Synthetic rubber has replaced much of the historic market for latex, but there are still certain needs for which natural rubber is irreplaceable: airplane tires, surgical instruments, condoms. Even with the government subsidies, 75 percent of Brazil's rubber comes from Malaysia, because the price a tapper gets from rubber, now about fifty cents a kilo, is hardly worth the effort, and a huge rural exodus has resulted.

"There's a lot of fantasy over the death of Chico," Santos told me. "A lot of *seringais* are uninhabited that many tappers would go back to if the price of rubber were half-decent. Many people are living on the death of Chico Mendes.

"I got the price of a kilo of rubber up to twelve hundred old cruzados, but the government put an end to SUDEVEA because of the influence of people who want to buy rubber directly from Malaysia and not pay the tax, the multinationals, like Pirelli, Goodyear, and Firestone.

"And this is going to put an end to the tapper.

"The politics is to end with rubber in Brazil. Already the production in Acre is falling. This year it's already down by fifty-four thousand tons."

TO THE SANCTUM SANCTORUM

That afternoon Assuero, in jeans and cowboy boots and hat, picked us up in his new four-by-four Chevy pickup, and as we sped down unpaved, heavily rutted BR-364 toward Porto Velho, kicking up dust, I almost forgot that we were in the Amazon and not Texas. Assuero had even been to Texas. He'd gone there to buy a quarter horse.

The first stop was the *frigorífico*. He was really proud of the modern, new slaughterhouse, and as we approached it his attitude became almost one of reverence. He insisted that we witness and understand every part of the operation, how beautifully efficient, what a masterpiece of modern technology this was.

After a while a truck full of humped white zebus pulled up. The cattle were coaxed with electric prods from the back of the truck into a narrow corral, and, single file, one by one, too dumb to know what was in store for them, they allowed themselves to be prodded on into the building. As soon as the lead steer was inside, a metal gate came down behind it and a man in a white apron knocked it on the head between its horns with a sledgehammer. POW. Sometimes he had to do it twice, and there was a second terrible thud. Then a trough opened at the bottom of a pen and the animal, not dead but out cold, its eyes open, all its vital functions still working — it was important for the heart to continue pumping so the blood would drain fast — was dumped out on a bloody slab. Another man in a white apron fastened one of its back legs to a pulley, and it was hoisted upside down into the air and sent down the production line. A cut was made from between the legs up to the chin by another worker, and several gallons of blood gushed out. The horns were sawed off to be made into buttons and combs. Then another man expertly stripped the hide with a curved-back skinning knife and, peeling it down over its legs, shoved it into a chute, where it would be salted and sold for shoe leather. One man severed the forefeet and another the head. The feet would be sold in the market for a type of food known as *mocotó*. The heart, liver, and lungs were destined for tripe or sausage. The bones would be ground into chicken and pig feed.

Assuero was as proud of his slaughterhouse as the tappers had been of their forest. "All this stuff goes to the owners of the *frigorífico*," he explained. "The *fazendeiro* profits only on the carcass." He took us downstairs to a room where several dark-skinned women in blood-spattered white uniforms, the native *acreanas*, the other race, were washing stomach walls. I couldn't help marveling at the geometry of the walls, how they were webbed with raised diamonds, like honeycombs. I imagined that after some time working in this place your attitude toward death

would change. You would become inured to killing. If the chance arose
to moonlight at slitting the throats of humans instead of livestock, you
might have little trouble making the transition.

"This is a five- or six-million-dollar investment," Assuero said, "and
if we don't keep expanding, it will go under. It's just barely hanging in
there. There are five hundred thousand head of cattle in Acre. Two
hundred thousand are cows, and they produce a hundred fifty thousand
calves a year. These calves will need seventy-five thousand hectares of
new pasture a year. The herd is growing by a hundred thousand head a
year, and so it needs a minimum of fifty thousand new hectares of pasture. If the pasture is good, you can graze one and a half to two head
per hectare and get nine hundred kilos of meat, which sells for five
hundred cruzados — these days about two hundred bucks. So you can
get back your investment in your first year."

But look at all the pasture that isn't being used, I said. Why do you
need more? Why don't you use what you've already cleared?

Assuero's answer was that it was "resting."

I took a last look at the steers being prodded along the narrow corral
into the knockout pen. It was as efficient as Auschwitz. For a moment I
imagined it wasn't zebus, but meek tappers and idealistic young ecologists going to be sacrificed in the Temple of Progress.

Assuero then took us to the showcase ranch of Alemão, the German.
This Alemão wasn't even German, he told us. He was a blond Aryan
Brazilian from the South who looked German, like Assuero's cousin
Neto.

There were actually, lo and behold, a couple of hundred cattle on the
ranch. Assuero claimed that as long as you grazed no more than two per
hectare and rotated them to new pasture every thirty days, the grass held
up indefinitely.

From there we proceeded to a cattle auction that was being held by
the UDR. Again I had trouble believing this was the Amazon. The men
were all dressed in Western duds. The women had on designer jeans and
shades and lizard-skin cowboy boots. The whiskey and the beef shish
kebobs were free. Everybody sat in the bleachers as the next lot of breed-
ing animals to go on the block was released into a circular pen below.
The UDR took 10 percent from the proceeds for the use of its facility
and to pay the auctioneer and miniskirted cowgirls who walked around

taking the bids. It was as if they were aping a whole life-style, like the Japanese who go out on the golf course in lime-green pants, white shoes, and alligator shirts.

We ran into João Branco again, and he sat beside us and continued his apologia. "We are not devastating, we are creating. This is the only visible activity. This bit of picking little fruits in the forest for ice cream for the United States [one of the new markets for Amazonian forest products that is being developed] is poetry."

I said that this whole scene could have been somewhere in Montana. "A rancher is a rancher," Branco said. "It's in the blood. You'll find the same culture in Australia. One of the big mistakes of the Brazilian government is to give the land to people without vocation for it. They just turn around and sell it. The conflict only arrives when the land is good and the government's policy is lousy. There is no reason for it in Acre. There is plenty of land and few people. If the militancy of the church were controlled and the government came up with a comprehensive plan for what to do, there shouldn't be any trouble here at all."

A drunken cowboy several rows below looked up at me hard and said, "Better write well of us or we'll burn down the whole thing."

LEAVING

I was ready to go home and start writing, but the planes out of Rio Branco were all booked for "fifteen days." According to one explanation, which I wasn't sure I believed, all the lovers of the blond masseuse, freaked out by her boyfriend Ruric Mendonça's coming down with AIDS, were rushing down to Rio to be tested. The prospect of being stuck here was not appealing. There had to be a *jeitinho*, some little way, to arrange our departure. We approached a small-time hustler Julio Cesar had met at the Pinheiro's pool bar who called himself Baiano, the guy from Bahia. He said he had just gotten a friend on the plane right away and not to worry. Wanting to show us that he had pull, he assured us almost threateningly, *"You will fly tomorrow and we'll drive you to the airport."*

His take on the murder was that "Chico died from the absence of answerability, like the kid who was shot right in front of the Forum the

other day. He was an enemy of progress. Acre is not structurally prepared for progress, but time will take care of that.

"If a judge gets in the way of the Mafia in your country, what happens? Chico died because of his mouth. The murder got rid of two birds
with one stone, Chico and Darli."

Of BR-364 he said, "It would open a competition with the United
States. As I understand it, the senators who passed through here complaining about it were from grain-producing states."

In the lobby of the Pinheiro Palace I collared the American chargé in
Brasília, James Ferrer, Jr., a cool professional who was filling in until
the new ambassador arrived. He was on his way back to the capital after
a meeting with the acting governor (unfortunately for us, Flaviano, for
whom we had a lot of questions, was out of town) that probably had
something to do with the two crew-cut operatives down at the pool.

"We recognize a tremendous Brazilian movement forward," he said,
unleashing a seamless stream of double-talk that made Aloysio Bezerra
seem like a third-degree stutterer. "We all understand that the process
is going forward, and there's not much anyone, especially we, can do
about it. Our concern is that it take place in a way that will be a good,
balanced treatment of the ecology and be sustainable, not two or three
years of fast growth that leave you worse off.

"The Pacific aspect of the road was not talked about much before
this year, and it's secondary because the Peruvians have a long way to
go. The project was approved some time ago. Possibly the IDB, if the
environmental conditions for the paving of the road to Rio Branco are
met, may be willing to finance it. The bank is very liquid now, and we'd
rather have it involved than private Japanese companies, over which
there would be no control. But a good, solid ecological program has to
be part of the package.

"The hundred-, hundred-and-fifty-mile stretch to Pucallpa that hasn't
been built is going to be very difficult. There are mountains in there.
And given the situation in Peru, it's going to be even harder. Peru will
first have to come to terms with the international financing institutions."
(President Alan Garcia had angrily suspended payments on the foreign
debt some time before.)

The chargé claimed that Bush and the Japanese prime minister did
not discuss BR-364 at Hirohito's funeral. They had discussed ecology
in general, and before the funeral the Japanese had issued a statement

that the road was not under consideration. He said that no American timber company was seriously looking at the Amazon, nor was the Japanese hunger for tropical hardwoods a worry. "The stuff here is very expensive because of the distances involved.

"This American concern about Amazônia and the rain forest in general may not be real. But what is real is that Americans feel it's a real problem. We need more research."

The typical bureaucratic do-nothing approach, I thought. This was how Bush's policy was shaping up after all his environmentalist campaign rhetoric. Stall on the greenhouse effect. Don't meddle in other countries' internal problems, whether human rights or ecological. It was the classic Kissinger approach to international relations — deal with Noriega as long as he was more valuable than the damage he was doing in other areas.

I said, You know, your operatives down at the pool should really get their cover down a little better. After a couple of questions it was obvious they weren't paleontologists.

Ferrer didn't flinch. He just nodded slightly.

Gotcha. Information received.

We continued to see a lot of Assuero and Marisa. It wasn't just that they wanted to show us a good time and thus make us like them and gain sympathy for their class; we were a welcome change from night after night in the airport restaurant. The *paulistas* were a small group. There were only 130 of them, and they were hated by most of the people in Acre. "From twelve to two you only find dogs and *paulistas* in the street," Assuero complained. "The only solution is artificial insemination." He and Marisa weren't such bad people, despite her flashes of racism. They had come here to the "asshole of the world," to the new frontier, with the best intentions. Hey, let's do a ranch in the Amazon. How romantic. What a challenge and adventure. But, as the Randy Travis song goes, "I hear tell the road to hell is paved with good intentions."

On the national day of Peru, they took us to a *vin d'honneur* at the Peruvian consulate to raise a glass to the country. It was incredibly hot and sticky in the crowded little room, and everybody was dripping and fanning himself like mad. I talked to the consul about the road. Like the Brazilians, he saw it very differently from the American chargé, as a new trade route from El Dorado to Cathay that would break both countries out of the American stranglehold on their economies. The consul said, however, that Peru would prefer it if Brazil extended BR-317 — the road through Xapuri — rather than 364 from Cruzeiro do Sul. But he said that, frankly, it was probably going to be a while before either road went anywhere.

I chatted with a tall, beautiful *acreana* who could have been Ilzamar's twin but was a little more sophisticated, and from there we proceeded to the third Nobel Ball — the social event of the year, Marisa assured us. Miss Bum Bum, the girl who had been voted to have the best buns in Rio that year, was there, and the house band from Carinhoso, a famous nightclub in Ipanema, provided the music. Everyone who was anyone in Acre was there. We said hello to Judge Longhini, shook hands with Narciso Mendes, a smooth, crafty-looking little guy in a pencil mustache. I talked to an architect who was the son of a German. As far as he knew there were no ex-Nazis in Acre. The closest one he knew of had been Klaus Barbie, who had had a ranch in Mato Grosso. It was too bad. I'd looked hard but found no evidence of ex-Nazi involvement in the murder of Chico Mendes. Former Nazis in Acre were, as Julio Cesar put it, a *suvaco de cobra,* a snake's armpit.

I danced with the foxy director of TeleAcre. "With Chico's death, maybe the tables are turned, and it is the ranchers who are in extinction," she said. "This is a closed, provincial society. Everyone knows what happened, but the press and the judge are scared to follow clear leads to certain prominent figures in the high society of the capital, lest they meet the same fate as Chico. A friend of mine who broadcast the news for the radio station was too outspoken and he had to leave, in fear of his life."

In the end it was João Branco who got me on the plane to Rio Branco. A seat or two was always saved for the UDR. Julio Cesar had to stay another day. During that time he was asked how much he wanted to write a favorable book and was offered to be sent to the congress in Brasília as the ranchers' political representative. He was definitely not interested. Assuero saw me off. "Let us know when you finish the book, and we'll kill another one for you," he said, joking, of course.

I'll be the first to get there, I said. Forty-five minutes from America.

Neto said, "Please, use some Vaseline [i.e., when you ream us], will you? And you'd better make it good, or we know where to find you." Even João Branco showed up to say good-bye.

THE JAPANESE SIDE OF THE STORY

I stopped in Brasília and met with an American diplomat, who backed up Ferrer's claim that Bush "didn't, to the best of our knowledge," talk to the Japanese prime minister about BR-364 and that the Japanese never received a project proposal, nor had the IDB. The whole thing was a misunderstanding perpetrated at a press conference by a source that remained vague.

Toyoharu Fukuda, the first secretary of the Japanese embassy, who dealt with environmental and agricultural matters, promptly honored my request for a meeting. He spoke no English and very little Portuguese and had a pretty young woman to translate for him, which emphasized the almost extraterrestrial remoteness of his culture. I felt very much like an inferior earthling as he read the answers to my questions from long columns of calligraphy. By the time you learn all those characters you have a greater intellectual capacity and a much more refined framework of perception than people in other societies. The Japanese, as the cab driver who had taken me to the embassy had observed, are very clever. They are also among the most nervous diplomats, terrified of giving offense.

Fukuda confirmed the American story: that Japan had received no solicitation from Acre, and even if it had, because of the environmental impact it wouldn't have considered the project; it was all a baseless rumor spread by the press. "We consulted private Japanese companies to see if any of them had been approached, and they hadn't, and we are a little sick of the whole business," the young woman translated.

"This came from a misunderstanding. Flaviano Melo was in Japan, and there he emphasized the importance of the road for Acre, and maybe when he got back, for political reasons, he said he had signed a contract with Japan."

The interview began to take on the quality of a game against a highly intelligent opponent.

Is Japan the largest importer of tropical wood? I asked.

"I don't have the statistics, but I think so," Fukuda said. "Japanese culture traditionally uses a lot of wood — for houses, utensils, et cetera. Most of our imports are from Indonesia. Hardly anything comes from Amazônia because the distance is so great."

But wouldn't the road change things?

Fukuda smiled. "According to the information I have, there is not much interest in Amazonian wood, because of the environmental problems that harvesting it would bring. Plus, the woods themselves are few that could interest the Japanese industrial and consumer markets."

Cedar?

"Yes."

Mahogany?

"Yes. The information we have is that most of the *árvores nobres,* the big, valuable trees, have already been extracted."

Bull, I thought. Then I asked, The wood here can be imported as logs, can't it? (One of the problems with Indonesian timber, besides the fact that the supply is giving out, is that the Indonesian government no longer allows the export of logs, but only of boards sawed in the country's own mills, which makes the wood less desirable to Japan.)

"Yes."

What are Japan's environmental reservations about logging in Amazônia?

"The Amazon forest," Fukuda finally said, "is the biggest in the world, and if it is cut it will radically alter the state of the sun. And the correction of this alteration will be very difficult. The Japanese government thinks that at this time the technology for this does not exist. And since Amazônia is the patrimony of humanity it would be a big responsibility to run such a risk. Japan has had pollution problems, and its people have respect and concern for preserving the environment. There is a traditional respect in our culture for the cycles of nature. This is why, for instance, Japanese immigrants have become such successful farmers in Brazil."

I asked if he had any traditional Japanese thoughts on the importance of trees and water that he could pass on. Fukuda was stumped.

"The Japanese are generally an agricultural people," he said at last, "who believe that there are divine presences in all nature, including trees and water, and have a certain reverence for them. Naturally, many urban children, who do not have contact with nature, have lost a bit of this."

But Japan is also a small area, with many people, that needs to be supplied from the outside. And maybe the people who are doing this don't have the traditional respect for nature, either, I said.

Fukuda smiled. Good shot.

The problem of whale hunting, for instance, I pushed.

"The fact that the Japanese hunt whales doesn't mean that they have a small interest in nature," Fukuda said. "Whale hunting is a traditional activity. Most of the forms of Japanese food are found in the sea."

Then he looked pointedly at his watch. It was all so polite.

We bowed.

THE SATELLITES

From there I flew south to the urban jungle of São Paulo. On the plane I read Ignácio de Loyola Brandão's novel *And Still the Earth*, set in São Paulo in the not-too-distant future. The hero crawls under wrecked cars, past the Region of Plastic Garbage, to a scorched toxic wasteland on the outskirts of the city, until at last he comes to the place where, he has heard, the last stand of trees and the last wild animals, whose existence is forbidden, are supposed to be. But he is too late. They have been destroyed by people from the pauper encampments.

Driving for miles through a vast forest of dingy white high rises, I checked in at last to the futuristic Maksud Hotel, centuries ahead of the world of Acre, and rose in a glass elevator up to the fifteenth floor of its giant courtyard, which was dripping with plants.

I didn't reach the apartment of Fábio Feldmann, the Brazilian environmental congressman, until eleven-thirty that night. We stayed up late, talking. Feldmann was only thirty-four and a bachelor. By his calculation there were no more than two thousand environmental activists in Brazil, who belonged to some eight hundred different groups.

In a recent interview in the Brazilian *Playboy*, Feldmann had seemed to suggest that there was a deliberate plan to make a martyr out of Chico. "The PT couldn't give a damn about ecology," he explained, "but the Shiites perceived that the environmental question would open a lot of doors. There was an extremely efficient strategy to give him international visibility, but Darli doesn't read the *New York Times*. That was the error in their thinking. It would only have cost a hundred dollars a month to keep Chico alive, but the union didn't have the money to provide him with security. The people who projected him did. That is the big ethical objection I have: they projected him, but didn't protect him.

"And now that he's dead, there's even less money in the union, and the movement has stopped for now. Now everybody was his friend.

Chico had a bigger vision than the PT. He was accused of revisionism and retrogression, but now everybody — the PT, the PV — wants to adopt him.

"He was a gentle man, the owner of an enormous sensibility. I first met him three years ago. We were not intimate friends. I was not a protagonist. I had a parabolic role. All environmental questions passed through me. Who created him was Adrian Cowell. Mary Allegretti was created by Adrian, too. He also projected José Lutzenberger [another prominent Brazilian environmentalist, who has since been named head of IBAMA]. He was the one who came up with the strategy of visibility and got him all the prizes. Adrian is the key. He discovered him. He was the environmental kingmaker."

In the morning, the television announced that Luis Gonzaga, the greatest culture hero of the *nordestinos,* was dead, and I myself felt like I was dying. Whatever gastric distress I'd been having had returned. It was apparently sensitive to alcohol and had been reactivated by the whiskies I'd drunk with Feldmann. But I had to go out to INPE, the Brazilian space agency in São José dos Campos, a couple of hours out of the city. Laid out in the backseat of a cab, I was driven through the high rise forest and into a pastoral-industrial-multinational-corporate-headquarter countryside. It could have been New Jersey. We passed the glass buildings of Kodak, Phillips, Johnson and Johnson. At the entrance to the thoroughly First World facility of INPE I was issued a security badge, and I proceeded to my appointment with Paulo Roberto Martini, the chief of technical orientation.

The question of how much of the Amazon is gone was a tremendous political controversy. INPE had calculated in a report released that April that 5.12 percent of legal Amazônia had suffered a loss of "dense, humid forest" (i.e., the real rain forest, not the "transitional forest" between the *cerrado,* or savanna of central Brazil, and the rain forest proper, which covers much of the southern fringes of the area). This figure was challenged by environmental leaders like Feldmann, who, admitting that he was acting on no more than a gut feeling, accused INPE of giving it a "makeup job" under orders from President Sarney to keep it low. Feldmann argued that the real figure was probably closer to the 12 percent published in January in Dennis J. Mahar's "Government Policies and Deforestation in Brazil's Amazon Region," a study by the World Bank in cooperation with the World Wildlife Fund and the Conservation

Foundation. This figure was blasted by Sarney as a "vicious slander," part of the "international conspiracy to portray us as ecological villains." The World Bank backed off it, claiming that it had never been intended as anything more than a projection based on the amount cleared up to 1987. But Mahar's table showed 12 percent in the "percentage cleared by 1988" column. There was nothing about it being a projection.

It seemed curious how everybody looking at the same pictures and using the same data could come up with such different numbers. Philip Fearnside, an ecologist at INPA, the National Institute for Amazonian Research in Manaus, who is generally conceded to have made the most thorough and meticulous examination of the problem, pointed out the confusion between the burning of forest and the burning of pasture, and he revised Mahar's figure down from 12 to 8 percent. Adding old fires in Pará and Maranhão going back to the last century brought it up again, to 9 percent.

INPE, its scientific credibility under fire, produced a second report, in which it revised its figure up to 7 percent. This figure was acceptable to Feldmann. But George Woodwell told me that INPE was internally riven, that there was tremendous backbiting and confusion in the agency among colleagues who could not agree on the deforestation rates. "The more they open their mouths, the deeper in the mud they get," he said. "The numbers are all rubber. The estimates range from five to twelve percent of legal Amazônia, and there's no basis for choosing, although the true figure is probably on the high end."

Part of the problem, I realized as I compared Mahar's numbers and those in INPE's second report, was that there wasn't agreement even on the size of legal Amazônia, or of the seven states and territories and parts of two others that make it up.

Martini took me into a staging room whose walls were papered with multicolored images from LANDSAT 5, the more accurate of the two satellites that monitor what is going on in Amazônia. He said that all of Amazônia fit on a mosaic of 234 images, each of which took in thirty-four thousand square kilometers. "A new set is produced every sixteen days, but because of the cloud cover we can only get one complete mosaic once a year." The images were so detailed, he told me, that you could zero in on an area the size of a tennis court, and they were being used not only to monitor the ongoing process of deforestation and conversion into various types of land use, but also to map mercury poisoning and residual turbidity from mining activity in the river system. We looked at a blowup of the area around Rio Branco. The *fazendas* along routes 364 and 317 appeared as pink squares, and after ten kilometers on either side of the roads they gave way to the dark green of the still-unattacked rain forest. Martini showed me the illegal airstrips of the prospectors in the Yanomamo reserves in Roraima. Their number had nearly doubled in the last six months, from thirty-six in December to sixty-six in March.

What can be done about this? I asked.

"That's another department, on the ground," he said. "But my impression is that IBAMA could cease to function and it would probably make no difference."

We talked about the confusion over how much of the rain forest was gone, and Martini explained that you can have fires without deforestation, deforestation without fires, or deforestation followed by fire. "That's why it's so complicated."

When I asked what he felt when he looked at these pictures of devastation, he said, "We must work with our minds, not with our hearts."

I then went over to the building where Alberto Setzer did the fire depicting, the day-to-day vigilance with images from NOAA-9, whose results are telexed to IBAMA's regional agents, like Paulo Beninca in Rio Branco.

Unlike Martini, Setzer was emotionally involved. "It's something we have to stop," he told me. "It's a crime against our planet, a crime against the resources of Brazil."

Beside him was a sensitive-looking, gray-bearded man with Indian bracelets on his wrist who was looking intently at an image on the multispectral analyzer of a place in Rondônia that he later explained he'd visited the year before. I realized after a while that he could be only one person: Adrian Cowell. We had talked while I was researching my *Vanity Fair* piece, and he had sounded very simpatico. I had the highest admiration for the powerful documentaries about Amazônia that he had produced over the years, and I wasn't about to confront him with Feldmann's charges that he had fabricated Chico as a martyr. Besides, I wasn't convinced that Chico probably wouldn't have been killed anyway, whether he had been projected or not.

We talked about the movie mess.

"We who knew Chico are concerned not only that he come out well but that there be some faint resemblance to him," he said. "I suspect that the more money that is put into the movie about Chico, the less real it will be."

A SAMPLER OF FIGURATIVE FIRES, COLOSSAL CONFLAGRATIONS, AND DIZZYING RATES OF DISAPPEARANCE

Huge fires are one of the modern myth motifs in Amazônia, like the surreptitious activities of the CIA. Perhaps the most famous one was the conflagration on the Volkswagen A.G. Ranch, in Pará, in 1976, which I erroneously reported in my book *The Rivers Amazon* to be "bigger than Belgium." The diligent fact checkers at *Vanity Fair* discovered that my source had been exaggerating, and the fire was downgraded in my piece to "bigger than Rhode Island." When the London *Times* excerpted the piece several months later, the size of the fire was translated for British readers into "bigger than Gloucestershire."

Belgium, however, for some reason remains one of the most popular standards of comparison in the literature. Both *Time* magazine and Reuters reported that the fires in Amazônia in 1988 were collectively "larger than Belgium." The *New York Times* maintained that the area was "larger than Switzerland," while the *Baltimore Sun* said it was "twice the size of Virginia." According to the BBC, "an area the size of Great Britain" went up in smoke.

In 1987, the big year, there were 5,000, 6,000, 7,000, or 8,000 fires in a single day. A total of 175,000 fires, each bigger than one square kilometer, were set over the entire burning season, and the area destroyed was the size of Maine, Uruguay, or South Dakota. "What state shall we say is burned?" Fábio Feldmann asked in *Playboy*. "An Alagoas, or a whole Paraná? Or how about Rio Grande do Sul?"

The estimates for the total amount of rain forest destroyed globally also vary dramatically. The World Wildlife Fund says 54 acres per minute, an area the size of New York State each year. The Rain Forest

Action Network goes a lot higher: 100 acres a minute, or an area the size of Michigan — two New York states — each year. The World Resources Institute says 74,000 acres a day, or roughly one Pennsylvania a year. The Smithsonian Institution: 100,000 square miles a year, or nearly half of California a year. The New York Rain Forest Alliance: 50 to 100 acres a minute, or a Central Park every sixteen minutes. Earth Island Institute: 100 acres a minute, or a football field every second. The Office of Technological Assessments (which does studies for Congress): 7 million hectares a year, or two Delawares. The National Academy of Sciences: 6 percent of the remaining forests per year.

Two other categories in which there is even wilder divergence are the estimates of the number of species in the Amazon and in all the world's rain forests (because most of them haven't even been identified yet), and of the rate at which they are becoming extinct. One reads, for instance, that two dozen species a day are disappearing around the world, and at the present rates of destruction more than half the world's species will be wiped out, more than a million in the Amazon alone (which has 10 million or 30 million species).

There is no more consensus on how much the burning is contributing to the greenhouse effect. The estimates for the contribution of the fires in the Amazon to the annual accumulation of atmospheric carbon dioxide range from 5 to 25 percent. Setzer's figure of 17 percent is accepted by many Western scientists. Like the number for how much of the Amazon is gone, the number tends to rise proportionately to the distance from the equator of its source. These controversies are very much like the Vietnam or Afghanistan casualty figures, or the number of cases of AIDS in the countries of equatorial Africa.

In July of 1989, Marlise Simons broke another extraordinary story in the *Times,* which should make the picture even more confusing. A team of West German scientists discovered alarming amounts of acid rain and ozone over the rain forest of central Africa, which they attributed to the annual burning of thousands of square miles of grassland by African farmers. The burning of the African savannas, they reported, generated three times more atmospheric carbon dioxide than all the fires in South America. (But grasslands, Thomas Lovejoy points out, regrow, so in the end there is not a major *net* CO_2 increment.)

THE LUKEWARMING ABOUT THE GREENHOUSE EFFECT

The confusion spreads out like an uncontrolled fire, calling into question the validity of the greenhouse effect itself. In the summer of 1989 the rains came with a pent-up vengeance. The woods around my cabin, especially the spruces, stressed by several years of drought, seemed to rejoice. It was a disastrous summer for my brother-in-law, a house painter. In the Amazon there was massive flooding on the Rio Negro, and floods drove 62,310 *flagelados* from the Northeast. The TV and papers ran shots of *nordestinos* poling down usually dusty streets in dugouts.

Due to the wettest "dry season" in a decade and vigilance by IBAMA and the national and international press, only 13,000 square miles of the Amazon forest — the combined size of New Jersey and Connecticut — had been destroyed as of September 17. This was way down from 1988 (50,000 square miles) and 1987, the peak year (80,000 square miles). Alberto Setzer explained to James Brooke of the *New York Times* that five consecutive days without rain were needed before slash was dry enough to burn. Yet it had hardly rained at all during the three weeks I was in Acre. Day after day there had been beautiful conditions for burning, but hardly a fire. So the reason Amazônia got off light that year wasn't only the rain, but fear on the part of the ranchers.

When I got back to the States in August and went out to Utah for Robert Redford's global warming conference, there was actually frost one morning, which was a little embarrassing. Before all the publicity about the greenhouse effect came out, scientists were saying that we were at the tail end of an interglacial era and that it had been much hotter five to ten thousand years ago. But then one recalled "the year without a summer," 1816, when there was a killing frost every month of the year in New England and ice lingered in the bays of Lake Champlain through the summer, and the famous blizzard of 'eighty-eight, when the snow drifted to eighteen feet in Westchester County. And even the old-fashioned winters of my childhood, in the fifties, now seemed to be a thing of the past. So I was still very much in the global warming camp, as were most scientists. When I confronted Lovejoy about the frost in Utah, he said, "Don't confuse the weather with the climate." As the climate expert Stephen Schneider explained, the dice were loaded for hot. It didn't mean that they'd come up with a scorcher every time.

That fall there were further confirmations that the climate was still seriously out of whack, in keeping with the greenhouse scenario. Hurricane Hugo, with sustained winds of 135 miles per hour, leveled the gracious architecture of Charleston, South Carolina, and the following month, just as Game 3 of the World Series was about to begin, the worst earthquake since 1906 shattered San Francisco.

But then December turned out to be the coldest on record, and the first real old-fashioned winter in years seemed to be shaping up. Evening grosbeaks and white-winged crossbills drifted down from Canada in great numbers. They come down only when there's a hard winter with a scarcity of conifer cones to the north. I sent a Christmas card to Lovejoy of a flock of grosbeaks at my feeder at twenty-five below, facetiously captioned "Evening grosbeaks pigging out in a weird feedback loop of the greenhouse effect."

If Chico had been killed in December 1989 instead of December 1988, I reflected, the murder would have caused nowhere near the stir.

A small school of skeptics still argued that the hot summers of the eighties had been within the parameters of normal climate fluctuation, like the drought of the thirties, or that the heat was produced not by the greenhouse effect but by a fluctuating atmospheric pattern in the Pacific known as El Niño. I met a proponent of the latter theory at INPE, a meteorologist named Luis Carlos Molion. Molion took part in the discovery, in July of 1975, that 50 percent of the rain that falls in the Amazon never reaches the sea and that, as a corollary, 50 percent of the rainfall in Amazônia is from internal sources. This discovery has become the basis for one of the most important arguments for preserving the forest: the effect its removal would have on rainfall patterns in South America and on the continent's already advancing desertification.

I asked Molion about Hadley's Cell, a circulation pattern that disperses airstreams from the equator and would seem to be the mechanism by which carbon dioxide releases from the fires are whisked up to North America, having a disproportionate effect on our climate.

Molion explained that there was another pattern of circulation called the Walker Cell — in fact, three separate Walker cells — which causes high-level winds to disperse from the three equatorial continents: South America, Africa, and the maritime continent of Indonesia. "These cells are a heat source for the atmosphere. Hot, humid air ascends from them, condenses into clouds releasing rainfall and enormous amounts of heat. As the vapor reliquefies, part of this heat is lost to outer space by infrared radiation, and part of it is transported to the poles by Hadley cells. So is the carbon dioxide. So in the long run, cutting down the Amazon forest will not raise world temperatures, it will decrease them by reducing its power as a heat source. You guys will be colder.''

Molion confirmed that immense clouds of smoke from the fires in Amazônia, containing millions of tons of carbon, were rising twelve thousand meters above the stratosphere and into the thermosphere, the highest level of the atmosphere, whose temperature is controlled by solar wind, and were being dispersed from there by Hadley's Cell to North America. But ''there is no proof of CO_2 warming,'' he claimed. ''It is bullshit, a bunch of wise guys who want to take money from the government. Six to seven thousand years ago the temperature of the globe was two to three degrees higher than it is today, but the atmospheric CO_2 levels were twenty-five percent lower than at present. We know this from paleoclimatic data obtained from old bubbles in Antarctic ice and air trapped for millennia in Egyptian tombs. So whatever the mechanism was that caused that heating, it wasn't CO_2.

''Cutting down the forest, of course, will enhance the greenhouse effect. But if half of the Amazon forest remains, as it must by law, that will be sufficient to absorb twenty-five percent of the fossil fuel the world is burning.* Every human being is responsible for releasing one metric ton of carbon equivalent — CO_2 or CH_4 — per year. So why don't we start with ourselves?''

In this vein I recalled an interesting fact put out by the World Resources Institute: ''The average American car, driven ten thousand miles, will release approximately its own weight, between one and two tons, of carbon into the atmosphere.'' The average American family has two cars, each of which is easily driven ten thousand miles per year. Could we be persuaded to give up one of them, any more than the tropical peasant can be persuaded to refrain from slashing and burning his little patch of equatorial forest? I doubt it would be any easier than getting Americans to give up their God-given right to own guns.

Another interesting fact: the average tree absorbs twenty-three pounds

*Lovejoy says this is not true and dismissed the paleoclimatic data as ''lags in the system.''

of carbon per year. So that means each of us ought to be planting around a hundred trees to offset the deleterious effects of our existence.

Lovejoy had described to me a fascinating phenomenon that he had once witnessed from the air: a wall of rain moving westward across the rain forest toward the Andes, and in its wake plumes of evapotranspiration already rising into the air, forming a secondary wave of condensation. I asked Molion about this, and he explained that low-level prevailing trade winds from the Atlantic can form rain and dissipate within one to three hours.

He described how the atmospheric pressures over Indonesia and the west coast of South America are always opposite to each other. "When one is high, the other is low, and vice versa. This seesawing is known as the Southern Oscillation. El Niño is an oceanic atmospheric phenomenon characterized by the presence of abnormally warm water in the eastern equatorial Pacific, which feeds back into the atmosphere and changes the Walker component in such a way that produces drought in the Amazon and northeastern Brazil, and wetter-than-normal conditions in the Northern Hemisphere.

"Why did you have your droughts?" he asked. "It was caused by the anti–El Niño, the presence of cold water in the eastern equatorial Pacific. The drought of 1988, in which the Mississippi basin experienced one of the driest years in history, was not caused by the greenhouse effect, but by the anti–El Niño, also known as La Niña. What causes the Southern Oscillation is not known. Keeling [George Woodwell's colleague, who pioneered the measurement of atmospheric carbon dioxide from the top of Mauna Loa] thinks it's affected by the amount of snow cover on the Tibetan plateau. But there is a new study that shows a striking correlation between seismic events on the ocean floor — strain released by earthquakes along the east Pacific rise, from the Gulf of California to Easter Island — and recurrences of El Niño every five to seven years."

Some people began to feel in 1989 that they were being forced into a sort of emperor's new clothes situation vis-à-vis the greenhouse effect. Typical of the "Hey, wait a minute, I don't buy this" point of view was former Washington State governor Dixy Lee Ray. So the temperature rises four and a half degrees over the next fifty years, Ray argued. It'll be like moving from Alaska to Palm Springs. What's so bad about that? So a number of cities are flooded. Venice and Holland have been coping with this sort of thing for centuries. "Why do so many people believe in the dire forecasts? Perhaps the historian Hans Morgenthau was right when he wrote in 1946, 'The intellectual and moral history of mankind is the story of insecurity, of the anticipation of impending doom, of metaphysical anxieties.' " She also cited the editor of the British journal *Nature*, John Maddox, who observed that "these days there also seems to be an underlying cataclysmic sense among people. Scientists don't seem to be immune to this."

Stephen Schneider, one of the most eloquent exponents of the greenhouse scenario, explained the need for the scientists like him to come up with dire predictions:

> On the one hand, as scientists we are ethically bound to the scientific method, in effect promising to tell the truth, the whole truth, and nothing but — which means that we must include all the doubts, the caveats, the *if*'s, *and*'s, and *but*'s. On the other hand, we are not just scientists but human beings as well, and, like most people, we'd like to see the world a better place, which in this context translates into our working to reduce the risk of potentially disastrous climate change. To do that we need to get some broad-based support to capture the public imagination. That of course entails getting loads of media coverage. So we have to offer up scary scenarios, simplified dramatic statements, and make little mention of any doubts we might have. This "double ethical bind" we frequently find ourselves in cannot be solved by any formula. Each of us has to decide what the right balance is between being effective and being honest.

No one was a greater master of the arresting statement than Lovejoy. I recalled my initial skepticism at his prediction in 1976 that a million tropical forest species would become extinct before they were even discovered. Now I realized that to quibble with the arithmetic is to miss the point. The question is, Should this be happening? Should we condone senseless destruction for short-term greed in Amazônia or anywhere? What side are we on?

On the subject of the rain forest, Lovejoy refuses to water down his words. "The most critical issue of our time, indeed of *all* human history," he wrote a few years ago, "is the unprecedented biological destruction involved in the massive and accelerating loss of tropical forests." Nowadays, he says, "I would add climate change."

As far as the greenhouse effect, he told me, "Every time someone comes up with a reservation, evidence that it isn't going to be a problem, there is more evidence that it will. Who wants to get on an airplane that has a forty percent chance of not getting there?"

THE LEGACY OF CHICO MENDES

By Labor Day, 1989, the stack of notebooks I had filled since the beginning of the year had all been indexed, and I started what a writer friend of mine calls "the vomit draft," scribbling furiously on yellow legal pads. When I finished the draft 714 pages later, it was December 22, a year to the day since Chico's murder. I hunted in the papers and flipped the channels of my TV in vain for some mention of him, some update. But there was nothing. No one was interested that the trial had been postponed again and that the prospects of the murderers' being brought to justice were growing dimmer and dimmer.

That day it was bitter cold — twenty below — in much of the Northeast, and 129 cities across America logged in with record low temperatures. The thought of the murder of that gentle, special man filled me with an even deeper sadness than it usually did, because no one remembered. On that frigid day, it and the teeming tropical world to which it belonged seemed very remote. It seemed like just another act of violence in another country with a lot of problems. There were other claims on our attention. Thousands of Romanians were being slaughtered in the last gasp of the Ceausescu dictatorship. The year "when the environment spoke back," as Bush called it, had segued into the year of democracy, as a series of political upheavals took place, not seen since 1968 with all its rebellions, and worthy of comparison with the collapse of colonialism and perhaps even with the *annus mirabilis* of 1848. Television played a vital role in the incredible, spontaneous domino effect, as one Eastern bloc totalitarian regime after another toppled. *Dallas,* the world's most eagerly watched television program, was being beamed to fifty million people by a different set of satellites from the ones monitoring the fires in Amazônia, hurtling along in geosynchronous orbit 22,000 miles up, at nearly 7,000 miles per hour.

I called Julio Cesar, and he said that in Brazil the anniversary of the murder passed virtually unnoticed. Mangueira for some reason had dropped Chico as its theme for Carnaval and was doing the "baroque churches of Ouro Preto" instead. "I read there was a big commemoration of Chico in Australia," he told me. "Thousands of rubber trees were planted. It seems they remember him more in Australia than in Brazil. Here his name only crops up when his image is being politically exploited, when the Communist Party or the PT calls itself the party of Chico Mendes."

Brazil that fall was preoccupied with its own exercise in democracy, its first presidential election since 1961. A Carnaval atmosphere swept the country as the elections approached. The streets were filled with the klaxons of cars flying the blue banner of Fernando Collor de Mello or the red banner of Lula, with processions of mothers pushing banner-draped baby carriages under banner-draped balconies. The majority of the population, which was under twenty-five and had known nothing but the military regime, had never seen anything like it.

In many ways the campaign between the two young presidential contenders was a projection into the national arena of the struggle between the ranchers and the tappers, of the same clash of classes and social philosophies. Collor was the candidate of the ranchers, Lula the candidate of the tappers. Bearded, fiery Lula was, in fact, an old *companheiro* of Chico's. He had been arrested after the revenge death of Nilão de Oliveira, and he had spoken at the funerals of both Wilson Pinheiro and Chico. In 1952, at the age of eight, he had fled the Northeast as a *flagelado* and gone to São Paulo. There, with only a fourth-grade education, he became a metalworker. Then he became involved in the union movement, led strikes, was jailed by the military, and founded the Workers' Party, in 1978.

Charismatic, handsome, patrician, Collor was a forty-year-old child of privilege. His father, also a politician, had shot a rival in the senate of Alagoas, the state where Collor eventually became governor (a fact that was carefully suppressed in the campaign). He had been, in his youth, the karate champion of the federal district, and he was tight with the military.

Lula offered a socialist state that would serve the long-neglected needs of the people. The privatization of state companies would be stopped. Land reform — Chico's dream — would be enacted. Payments of the debt incurred by the corrupt military without consulting the people, with collusion of the elite and multinationals, would be suspended.

While Lula offered to make Brazil the leader of the Third World, Collor offered the American *Dallas* model of capitalistic free enterprise and the old dream that Brazil would finally arrive in the First World and take its place in the hegemony of the *grandes,* becoming the eighth superpower. The country was as seriously divided between the left and the right as Spain had been on the eve of its civil war. Everything Chico stood for hung in the balance.

There were threats that if Collor won, the people in the slums would pour down on the cities; that if Lula won, hundreds of thousands of *empresários* would leave the country. But Brazil was not as violent a country as the Hispanic nations of Latin America. A conciliatory tradition underlay Brazilian politics, of which Chico was a beautiful example and which a Brazilian diplomat once explained to me by pointing out that the Portuguese, in their bullfights, do not kill the bull. Brazil had managed to get through the dicey transitions in its history — independence, abolition of its monarchy and of slavery — with little or no bloodshed, and I was confident that it could get through this election in a way that everyone would be proud of.

With TV sets in three fourths of Brazilian households and only half of the eighty-two million voters having finished primary school, television played an extremely important role in the race. Two weeks before the election, Sílvio Santos, the immensely popular host of a ten-hour marathon variety show with games, raffles, samba bands, and scantily clad women that had aired every Sunday for years, joined the race and immediately knocked Collor out of first place. I recalled de Gaulle's famous remark about Brazil: "This is not a serious country."

The son of Greek immigrants, Santos had started selling knickknacks on the streets of Niterói at the age of fourteen. Now, at fifty-eight, he owned the second most profitable TV network after Rêde Globo, which supported Collor. He said that he was running because he wanted "to return to the people a little of what they have given me."

Both Collor and Lula cried foul and appealed to the Electoral Tribunal on the grounds that Santos's candidacy was illegal because he was the owner of a medium of mass communication — the same grounds on which the newspaper baron William Randolph Hearst's candidacy against Teddy Roosevelt was rejected. The Tribunal ruled in their favor, and Santos withdrew from the race.

On November 19, the runoff between the remaining candidates took place. Collor won handily, and Lula, the furthest to the left of the top five vote getters, edged out Leonel Brizola, who had been waiting for twenty-five years for a chance to run for the presidency.

The liberation theology wing of the church was firmly behind Lula. Its priests described Collor to their congregations as "the new representative of the old ruling classes." When you are voting, stop and think: are you a boss or a worker? The Vatican resilenced Leonardo Boff after he said publicly that Collor "plans to maintain the hegemony of the ruling class." But the bull did not go into effect until January, after the elections, so Boff was able to continue his vociferous support of Lula.

I called Julio Cesar for an update, and he said that the outcome of the election was impossible to call. Lula was gaining daily in the polls. The gap was closing. He was within striking distance. With his common-man appeal, he scored a stunning victory in the first television debate with Collor, in which he confronted Collor with the three thousand *fantasmas* he had hired in his last week as mayor of Maceió, the capital of Alagoas. Collor, part of whose platform was his promise to root out corruption in the government ("We have a corrupted, degenerate capitalism. We have to reduce the participation of the state in the economy"), to boot out the *marajás,* the high government officials living like Indian princes off the public dole, was completely speechless.

Lula was strongest in the big cities, and there were huge rallies for him. All the great names of Brazilian popular music — Chico Buarque, Caetano Veloso, Gilberto Gil — got together and composed a catchy jingle for his coalition, the Popular Brazil Front.

Collor, meanwhile, portrayed Lula as a radical advocating class struggle and armed violence.

Lula's people worked up an effective TV commercial: a bloodstained butcher is interviewed. He says he cannot afford meat. One of his customers, a rich, vapid housewife, tells the camera that she feeds her dog meat three times a day. Then Lula comes on. "My adversary says let the cake grow and then we will distribute it. Well, since the 1960s the cake has grown and grown and the workers have ended up sucking their thumbs."

Collor dug up a woman (whom Lula's people later revealed had been paid twenty thousand dollars) who said that Lula knocked her up in 1974.

Lula countered by appearing with his arm around his illegitimate but beloved daughter Lurian.

A float came down along Ipanema beach. In it Lula, the bearded frog (bitter Brizola had said, "Wouldn't it be amusing to watch Brazil's ruling class swallow this frog?"), was being kissed by a beautiful princess — Lucélia Santos. A guy dressed up as Uncle Sam butted in on a samba line of supporters in bathing suits and bearded frog hats and demanded payment of the debt.

A few rocks were thrown at cars that dared to display Collor stickers, and some of the people in the street shouted up to the rich looking down from their apartments on Rio's Avenida Vieira Souto, "Fat cats, fat cats. Now you're going to have to work." In the closing days of the campaign Lula was asked if his plans for Brazil weren't out of step with the developments in Eastern Europe. He made a good comeback: "We are going to knock down our own Berlin wall, a wall of hunger, prostitution, illiteracy, and poor health."

But in the second TV debate Collor was in top form, and Lula, who seemed exhausted and unable to think clearly, came off badly. This was very Brazilian. I had often seen Brazilians close to victory in competitive situations unable to pull it together when it really counted, succumbing at the final hour — the national inferiority complex.

So Collor won. The people chose *Dallas*. What that means for the Amazon is still too early to tell. Collor's people had run some appealing ecological commercials, in one of which a naked man, with his hands held rigidly to his sides, was toppled like a tree, dramatizing the human effects of deforestation. On a quick tour of the First World before taking office, Collor assured the people who expressed their concern about the destruction of the rain forest at every stop that he was open to debt-for-nature swaps and was really going to do something about the problem. But many suspected that his rhetoric would prove no less empty than Bush's and that he had no intention of allowing environmental problems to slow down the march of progress.

What that means locally is that the chances of Darci's and Darli's ever coming to trial and of the tappers' definitively securing their life in the forest are even slimmer. Collor's representative in Acre is none other than Narciso Mendes.

So there will be no change, I said to Julio Cesar, no purge after all.

Plus ça change. There's been no real change in Brazil since the monarchy.

"Doesn't look like it," he said. "If you look under the rug, all societies are rotten."

The union is still in acephalous, factionalized confusion. No lucid new leader of Chico's stature has emerged. The problems remain: lumber companies, multinational corporations, and landless peasants, not only in Brazil but all over the world's tropics, continue to exert tremendous pressure on the last shrinking stands of tropical rain forest and to indirectly threaten the climate of the globe. "For centuries there has been moral outrage about disparities in standards of living," said Alan During, a staffer at the Worldwatch Institute. "Today we find poverty not just a moral issue, because we now have a situation where poor people endanger the well-being of the better-off."

The gap between the rich and the poor continues to grow in Latin America, as everywhere, and the two classes have become separate, wary societies — which was not the case when I first came to Brazil, fourteen years ago. The richest 20 percent enjoy a life-style little different from that of Americans or Japanese, while the remaining 60 to 80 percent live below or just above the poverty line in a state of misery and deprivation, little different from that of sub-Saharan Africans or the people of Bangladesh. The rich invest their money abroad, or sink it into domestic tax havens like phantom projects in the Amazon, and dodge taxes that could help the situation. There have been food riots in Venezuela, Argentina, and, most recently, Brazil, and widespread malnutrition is producing a generation of stunted, mentally deficient, dark-skinned have-nots who will only make Collor's dream of bringing Brazil into the First World that much harder to realize. With the economy crippled not only by an external debt of $120 billion but an internal debt of $180 billion, and inflation running at the last tally at 48 percent, there is no money for big projects, and the existing infrastructure is crumbling. More blackouts and energy rationing are predicted for the nineties. In the last five years the failure rate for an attempted phone call has risen from 7 to 27 percent, and the congestion and *inoperância* of the telephone systems are expected to get worse.

The World Bank is "really trying" to clean up the damage it did to Rondônia, according to Lovejoy. Others are less sanguine and predict more of the same, another Polonoroeste. The Yanomamo are being raped, massacred, and exposed to the deadly diseases of civilization. Rumors about the completion of BR-364 are cranking up again.

In April of 1989, the Brazilian government announced the suspension of tax reliefs, subsidies, and other incentives for cattle ranching in "dense forest areas." Since it had pumped $1.5 billion into Amazonian development schemes in two decades, these measures were apparently only symbolic. That year SUDAM continued to distribute $70 million in tax incentives to private companies. John Barham of the *Financial Times* wrote: "Years of free-flowing public money have created a coalition of business, political, and even criminal interests that vigorously oppose change." Six hundred and forty million dollars in the form of a 25 percent corporate tax cut was granted to the São Paulo soybean king, Olacir de Moraes, for his $2.5 billion project, a thousand-mile railroad from Mato Grosso, on the southern fringes of Amazônia, to the South of Brazil. And grants have also been allocated for twenty-one highly controversial pig iron and manganese plants in southern Pará. But in 1990, the new administration revoked all incentives.

Land in the Amazon, which is lightly taxed, remains a popular tax shelter for corporations and wealthy individuals. Clearing by farmers big and small, who show "productive use" to raise loans or to turn over the property for a quick profit, continues.

The best hope for saving Amazônia, besides the debt-for-nature swap, is still the extractive reserve. This will be Chico's lasting monument. Since January 1990, four big reserves collectively the size of Massachusetts have been established and ten more are in the works. One reserve, run by the *daimistas* at Céu de Mapiá, three days downriver from Rio Branco, is already in operation with the help of a large grant from the United Nations Environmental Programme. Others are being planned, including the Seringal Cachoeira, and four in Rondônia that are being funded by the World Bank. Aid for various agroforestry projects is pouring in from all kinds of sources, ranging from the Japanese, to the International Tropical Timber Organization, to the British Overseas Development Agency, to Kiwanis Club International, that stalwart of the American heartland.

Jason Clay, the executive director of Cultural Survival, is introducing the First World consumer market to some three hundred rain forest products: nuts, fruits, oils, fibers, essences, flours, pigments, and crafts from twenty-five countries. Working with the new cooperatives in Xapuri and elsewhere, he has lined up $1.2 million of orders of Brazil nuts and cashews for a Brazil nut–cashew brittle called Rainforest Crunch that the Ben & Jerry's ice cream company is bringing out.

The economic possibilities of such oils as *copaíba, andiroba, babaçu,* and *piqui,* and of drinks like *guaraná* and *copoaçu,* look very promising. As far as I know, no one is looking into the exquisitely tasty, blue, grapelike, wintergreen-flavored berries of the *pouruma* tree. Soon Americans may be using condoms made of Amazonian latex; and the tappers will become soldiers again, in a new war — the one against AIDS.

There are two basic approaches to saving the Amazon: you can try to buy a chunk of the rain forest and maintain it in perpetuity, or you can support the local people who are living sustainably and harmoniously there. Cultural Survival has opted for the second approach, but for it to work, Clay told me, the local people must gain control of the entire marketing process, all the way to the buyers in the First World, so they aren't ripped off by middlemen. As Lovejoy said, "There's a social landscape these things have to fit into as well as an ecological and physical one."

Chico's model of the extractive reserve has spawned a new concept in conservation, a new type of park especially well adapted to the needs of the Third World, which includes the local people and refutes the old criticism that the animals are being protected just so a handful of elite First Worlders can come and study them.

At the forefront of the application of this concept is the tropical biologist Daniel Janzen, who has worked for many years in Costa Rica. Janzen has articulated one of the most moving analogies in his plea to stop the destruction of the rain forests: "It is as if the nations of the world had decided to burn their libraries without even looking to see what was in them." He has recently begun to advocate, controversially, that "national parks . . . be instruments of social change. They should become models of how we should live with nature."

Other countries are not as enlightened as Costa Rica, with its extensive park system. Guatemala, for instance, has lost 40 percent of its forest cover and 50 percent of its annual rainfall. The last two-hundred-foot virgin mahogany trees are being logged from its Petén rain forest. There is another product in the forest that could be harvested sustainably without destroying this spectacular wilderness: *xate,* the chamaedorea palm, an evergreen, fernlike palm that is used in North American and

European flower arrangements and that grows there in abundance. But somebody like Chico Mendes is needed to organize local resistance against the loggers and develop an alternative *xate* economy. The Guatemalan author Victor Perera writes, "While the assassination last year of Chico Mendes . . . focused international attention on the massive deforestation of the Brazilian Amazon, no such event has called the world's attention to a comparable ecological calamity in Guatemala and [right over the border in] Chiapas, Mexico."

It is unfortunate that in much of the stuff written about Chico, his martyrdom is perceived as his main achievement, that, as John Barham wrote, "Mr. Mendes achieved more in death than during his years as an obscure agitator," because the rain forests of the world and the people of the rain forests need more leaders like him — alive, not dead.

LAST DAYS IN BRAZIL

After my visit to INPE, I flew to Rio and gave myself a few days of R and R in Copacabana to prepare for reentry into the temperate zone. Julio Cesar called me at my hotel when he got back. As he described how the flight south had been, he sounded strangely chauvinistic for a young ecologist. "When I saw the big clearings, the squares of tilled farmland in Mato Grosso after flying for hours over empty nothingness, I found myself cheering, in spite of myself, as a Brazilian," he confessed.

"I've flown over Vermont, Illinois, Michigan, and it's all farms. And what do we have? Half our country is in geopolitical limbo. You didn't have Greenpeace when you were conquering your frontier. And you didn't have Chico Mendes. You had General Custer. So how can you put us on trial?

"We want to put our own satellites into orbit. We made a deal with France for rocket technology but the U.S. fucked it up, just as it fucked up the deal we had with the Japanese for the road. We don't want to depend on anyone or be their market. We want to be a big power. The national will is to get there, and whatever the social cost, even if it means burning the forest, we will. That's why the ranchers will win, because they are the national will. We don't want to be the backyard of anyone anymore. When my mother was a kid even the butter came from the

Netherlands. You have all these hundreds of species of hummingbirds, and you're miserable. You can't buy a car or dignity with hummingbirds, so what's the point?

"No people will give up building their own nation."

God, I said to Julio Cesar, you've missed the whole point of the exercise. The problem for Brazil is that the people are going to have to realize that it's no longer ecologically possible to become like the United States,* to accommodate everybody into the modern consumerist dream, to invite them into the television, and burning down the whole forest won't get them there. It will only make things a lot worse. Does it make sense to destroy the Amazon so João Branco can put one head of cattle per acre there?

Julio Cesar backed down. "Okay, maybe we'll never get to be like America. But at least we could become like Italy in a couple of generations. Brazil just wants to be a decent country. A country where half the people by the age of twenty have lost their teeth — this is not a decent country.

"And you can't expect us to leave the Amazon as a garden, a sanctuary."

But at least until you have better knowledge of what it is, don't you think it would be best to move slowly?

Across the Avenida Nossa Senhora de Copacabana, below my window, a vision of loveliness broke out of the crowd of shoppers, tourists, urchins, prostitutes, and transvestites poring over the tables of the *camelôs*. A tall, lush, honey-skinned beauty with high breasts straining in a T-shirt as she dashed across the street, she was the Girl from Ipanema. I could just make out, before she disappeared back into the crowd, the four words that were printed across her T-shirt. They posed what had become by now an unanswerable philosophical question, which few people cared about anymore, if they ever had: "WHO KILLED CHICO MENDES?" It was undoubtedly an unauthorized use of the name.

---

*To the extent that it ever was; the ecologies of the two countries are completely different.

Epilogue

In the latest episode of the ongoing *novela* that is Brazil groping for its niche in the modern world, President-elect Collor, on his grand tour of the superpowers, is told in no uncertain terms by everyone he meets, "If you want to be accepted as one of us, clean up your act in the Amazon." Prince Charles, especially, lays it on the line about the genocide of the Yanomamo. Collor promises to do something about it and invites the "Green Prince" to take a trip to the Amazon with him in early November.

Collor is sworn in on March 15, and he immediately enacts a series of sweeping changes on the economic and ecological fronts. With inflation running at 80 percent a month, he freezes for eighteen months all bank accounts with balances of more than $1,200 — a total of more than $100 billion — and declares the new cruzado extinct. The currency goes back to cruzeiros. These radical stabilization measures, socking it primarily to the middle class and the rich, seem more in character with someone like Lula than a free-market capitalist born to wealth. The arts, which depend on government subsidies (corporate tax incentives like the ones destroying the Amazon), are paralyzed. The newly renovated opera house in Manaus, which had booked Placido Domingo, cancels its season. Multinationals like Ford, General Motors, Johnson and Johnson, Citicorp, and Quaker Oats post alarming losses, and the highly specialized and very tricky secondary Brazilian debt market slumps as zero inflation produces a recession. Restaurateurs overcharging for their beers are hauled off to prison for "crimes against the people's economy," and — on the positive side — thousands of prospectors leave Roraima because the agents have no cash to buy their gold dust. The 10 percent of Brazilians with more than $1,200 in the bank begin to call Collor's package *catastroika* and to accuse him of betraying his class.

Collor's choice for special secretary of the environment is equally shocking: José Lutzenberger, a dedicated, slightly eccentric conservationist and an old friend of Chico's; Adrian Cowell was instrumental in the international promotion of both their careers. Lutz, as his admirers call him, flies up to Roraima and is appalled by the chaotic situation he finds there, with 45,000 prospectors overrunning the villages and the forest home of the neolithic Yanomamo, who have by now been reduced to fewer than 10,000. At Lutz's suggestion Collor orders that the hundred-some clandestine landing strips of the prospectors be dynamited. None other than Romeo Tuma, the burly arm of the Brazilian law, who has been retained as the head of the Federal Police, is put in charge of the operation. One hopes it will be more successful than Operation Sweep.

The world applauds these steps, but the situation in Roraima may not be salvageable. The prospectors, who are themselves victims, rejects of the Brazilian Miracle, and have nothing to lose, will only build new strips. "How can we be expected to stand with our arms folded before a mountain of gold?" as the governor of Roraima, Rubens Villar, puts it. But the inside information is that Collor is really serious about saving the Amazon. He is far more impressed with Lutz's proposal for Amâzonia — light management of no more than 80 percent of the valley — than with the military's old recipe: fill it up with people before others get in there. Lovejoy's take is that "it looks like the ice jam is beginning to break. A moment of real hope may be here. We'll just have to see."

The debate over the greenhouse effect continues and is reflected by confusing headlines in the *New York Times:* March 30 — "NO GLOBAL WARMING SPOTTED"; April 16 — "TEAM OF SCIENTISTS SEES SUBSTANTIAL WARMING OF EARTH." The Bush people are still stalling; "We need more study," they keep saying. Tempers — as well as temperatures — are rising, although the rain this spring has been excessive, and as I look out my window on this dank May 22 morning, the mountains in the distance, none of them more than a mile high, are dusted with snow. The effect seems to be taking a break again.

The road to the Pacific and the lucrative markets of the East has a new champion: Alberto Fujimori, a Peruvian of Japanese descent, who recently displaced the novelist Mario Vargas Llosa as the front-runner in Peru's upcoming presidential race.

The news from Acre remains grim. Detective Nilson, who had been really trying to get to the bottom of the murder and to nail the *cabeças,* is taken off the case and replaced with a puppet. Ilzamar goes to Rio Branco to demand his reinstatement and on her return to Xapuri is beaten up in the street by Darli's youngest son, Darlizinho, and a bunch of his friends. The *Jornal do Brasil* announces that the trial of Darli, Darci, and Oloci will finally take place, in June. It will be a jury trial, and a big media event, with international observers, and the *cabeças* will be brought to justice, not only the Alves da Silvas. (I am skeptical when I read this: the powers that be in Acre aren't about to let a full public investigation of the murder of Chico Mendes be conducted any more than the powers that be in Washington are going to allow the clear leads to the White House in the Iran-contra affair to be followed. Indeed, the story turns out to be only a rumor: to date no trial has been scheduled.)

As usual, it's impossible to figure out what, if anything, is happening with the movie. Peter Guber has been telling people that he is going to make it, but David Puttnam says that's not true, that Guber has been helping him mend fences with J.N. Films and the tappers' movement (but why would Guber help Puttnam?).

Meanwhile a new *telenovela, Pantanal,* has replaced *Kananga do Japão* and is attracting viewers in record numbers. The first ecological soap opera to air in Brazil, it's set in the Pantanal do Mato Grosso and has breathtaking footage of the great swamp's wildlife; the protagonists are young environmental activists battling the poachers of the caimans. "It's amazing how ecology has become prime-time in Brazil when just a few years ago nobody had even heard the word," Julio Cesar writes. "Maybe it's the Indian in us reasserting itself.

"By the way, you don't really think I really meant those prodevelopment, antiecologist remarks at the end there, do you? They were just an exercise in sophism. Sometimes I take the persona of a Nazi, a racist, a Rastafarian, or a Jehovah's Witness, to provoke debate. This doesn't mean I'm one of them."

Which brings us back to the caveat raised at the outset: how can you believe anybody?

Acknowledgments

This book, if nothing else, stands as something of an athletic feat. The vomit draft was handwritten on 714 sheets of legal notepaper in three and a half months. In the next seven weeks I dictated the draft to the writer and editor Chris Shaw, who typed it into a word processor and made a lot of useful suggestions. The printed draft came to 709 pages and was sent in weekly installments to Pat Mulcahy, my editor in New York, who made invaluable recommendations about resequencing and pruning the narrative. Numerous vital details were attended to by her assistant, Christine Archibald. The final, meticulous copyediting was performed by Deborah Jacobs, in Boston. Julio Cesar Monteiro Martins followed the story in the Brazilian papers, offered brilliant insights into Brazilian society, accompanied me on my second trip to Acre, and reviewed the text. Thomas E. Lovejoy also reviewed the text. At his suggestion I had already begun research for a book on the effect of the fires in the Amazon on global warming, so much of the background was already in place. My agent, Deborah Karl, called nearly every day to see how it was going. My fiancée, now my wife, Rosette Rwigamba, took care of material-plane distractions. All these people really put out for this book. It is a collaborative effort.

Sources

The most important written sources were daily articles in the *Jornal do Brasil* and the *New York Times*. Extensive bibliographies on the Amazon are provided in Shoumatoff (1986) and in Hecht and Cockburn, *The Fate of the Forest*. The following books and articles were particularly useful:

"Amazônia: Onde está a verdade?" *Veja,* July 5, 1989.

Bates, Henry Walter. *The Naturalist on the River Amazons*. New York: Penguin, 1988.

Bierhorst, John. *The Mythology of South America*. New York: William Morrow, 1988.

Boff, Clodovis. *Deus e o homem no inferno verde* (God and man in the green hell). Petrópolis, Brazil: Editora Vozes, 1980.

Brandão, Ignácio de Loyola. *And Still the Earth*. Translated by Ellen Watson. New York: Avon, 1985.

"Brasil, Anistia Internacional documento." London: September 1988.

"Brazil: Who Pays for Development?" *Cultural Survival Quarterly,* vol. 13, no. 1, 1989.

Burroughs, William S., and Allen Ginsberg. *The Yage Letters*. San Francisco: City Lights Books, 1988.

Caufield, Catherine. *In the Rainforest: Report from a Strange, Beautiful, Imperiled World*. Chicago: University of Chicago Press, 1984.

da Cunha, Euclides. *Um paraíso perdido*. Rio de Janeiro: José Olympio Editora, 1986.

Eiten, George. *Classificação da vegetação do Brasil*. Brasília: CNPq, 1983.

Fearnside, Philip M. *Human Carrying Capacity of the Brazilian Rainforest*. New York: Columbia University Press, 1986.

Froes, Vera, *Santo Daime, Cultura Amazônica; história do povo juramidam.* Manaus: SUFRAMA, 1986.

Furneaux, Robin. *The Amazon.* London: Hamish Hamilton, 1971.

Hecht, Susanna, and Alexander Cockburn. "Defending the Rain Forest and Its People." *Nation,* May 22, 1989; also letter to *Nation,* September 18, 1989.

———. *The Fate of the Forest.* London: Verso, 1989.

Hecht, Susanna, and Schwartzman, Steven. "The Good, the Bad, and the Ugly: Amazonian Extraction, Colonist Agriculture, and Livestock in Comparative Perspective." Draft, September 1988.

Hemming, John. *Red Gold: The Conquest of the Brazilian Indians.* Cambridge: Harvard University Press, 1978.

———. *Amazon Frontier: The Defeat of the Brazilian Indians.* Cambridge: Harvard University Press, 1987.

Herring, Hubert. *A History of Latin America.* New York: Alfred A. Knopf, 1968.

Hill, Alfred F. *Economic Botany.* New York: McGraw-Hill, 1937.

"Hydroelectric Dams." *Cultural Survival Quarterly,* vol. 12, no. 2, 1988.

Joly, Aylthon Brandão. *Botânica.* São Paulo: Companhia Editora Nacional, 1976.

Kalstone, David. *Becoming a Poet.* New York: Farrar, Straus and Giroux, 1987.

Kelly, Brian, and Mark London. *Amazon.* New York: Holt, Rinehart, and Winston, 1983.

Kleinpenning, J.M.G. *An Evaluation of the Brazilian Policy for the Integration of the Amazon Basin (1964–1975).* Nijmegen, Holland: Vakroep Sociale Geografie van de Ontwikkelinsgslanden, Geografisch en Planologisch Instituut Publikatie 9, 1979.

Lambert, Craig. "Global Spin." *Harvard Magazine,* January–February 1990.

Lovejoy, Thomas E. "The Transamazonica: Highway to Extinction?" *Frontiers,* Academy of Natural Science of Philadelphia, Spring 1973.

Mahar, Dennis J. "Government Policies and Deforestation in Brazil's Amazon Region." A World Bank publication in cooperation with the World Wildlife Fund and the Conservation Foundation. Washington, D.C., January 1989.

Maybury-Lewis, David, Jason W. Clay, et al. "In the Path of POLONO-ROESTE." Cultural Survival Occasional Paper 6, October 1981.

McKibben, Bill. *The End of Nature.* New York: Random House, 1989.

Melo, Hélio. *História da Amazônia.* Brasília: Senado Federal, 1986.

———. *O caucho, a seringueira e seus mistérios.* Rio Branco: Fundação de Desenvolvimento de Recursos Humanos da Cultura e do Esporto, 1986.

Mendes, Francisco Alves, Filho. *"O testamento do homen da floresta: Chico*

Mendes por êle mesmo." Interviews with Cândido Grzybowski. Rio de Janeiro: FASE, 1989.

Meyer de Schauensee, Rodolphe. *A Guide to the Birds of South America.* Wynnewood, Penn.: Livingston Publishing Co., 1970.

"Multilateral Banks and Indigenous Peoples." *Cultural Survival Quarterly,* vol. 10, no. 1, 1986.

Myers, Norman. *The Primary Source.* New York: W. W. Norton, 1984.

Prance, Ghillean T. "The Origin and Evolution of the Amazon Flora." *Interciencia,* vol. 3, no. 4, 1978.

————, ed. *Tropical Rain Forests and the World Atmosphere.* Boulder, Colo.: Westview Press, 1986.

Price, David. *Before the Bulldozer.* Washington, D.C.: Seven Locks Press, 1989.

Reichel-Dolmatoff, Geraldo. *Amazonian Cosmos.* Chicago: University of Chicago Press, 1971.

Roe, Peter G. *The Cosmic Zygote.* New Brunswick, N.J.: Rutgers University Press, 1982.

Schneider, Stephen H. *Global Warming.* San Francisco: Sierra Club Books, 1989.

Schwartzman, Steven. "Extractive Reserves: The Rubber Tappers' Strategy for Sustainable Use of the Amazon Rain Forest." Draft 1989.

Schwartzman, Steven, and Allegretti, Maria Helena. "Extractive Production in the Amazon and the Rubber Tappers' Movement." Washington, D.C.: Environmental Defense Fund, May 28, 1987.

Shoumatoff, Alex. *African Madness.* New York: Alfred A. Knopf, 1988.

————. *In Southern Light: Trekking Through Zaire and the Amazon.* New York: Simon and Schuster, 1986.

————. "Murder in the Rain Forest." *Vanity Fair,* March 1989.

————. *The Rivers Amazon.* San Francisco: Sierra Club Books, 1986.

Smith, Nigel J. H. *Rainforest Corridors.* Berkeley: University of California Press, 1982.

"The Social Impact of Development on Ethnic Minorities," Cultural Survival Grant #AID/otr G.1683, March 15, 1980.

Stap, Don. *A Parrot Without a Name: The Search for the Last Unknown Birds on Earth.* New York: Alfred A. Knopf, 1990.

Stewart, Julian H., ed. *Handbook of South American Indians.* 7 vols. Washington, D.C.: Bureau of American Ethnology Bulletin 143, 1944–49.

Taussig, Michael. *Shamanism, Colonialism, and the Wild Man.* Chicago: University of Chicago Press, 1987.

Taylor, James L. *A Portuguese-English Dictionary.* Stanford, Calif.: Stanford University Press, 1958.

Van Domelen, Julie. "Power to Spare: The World Bank and Energy Conservation." A joint publication of the World Bank and the Conservation Foundation. Washington, D.C., 1988.

Zweig, Stefan. *Brazil: Land of the Future*. Translated by Andrew St. James. New York: Viking Press, 1941.

Index